AF476987

CHINESE
PAINTING TECHNIQUES
for Exquisite Watercolours

Lian Quan Zhen

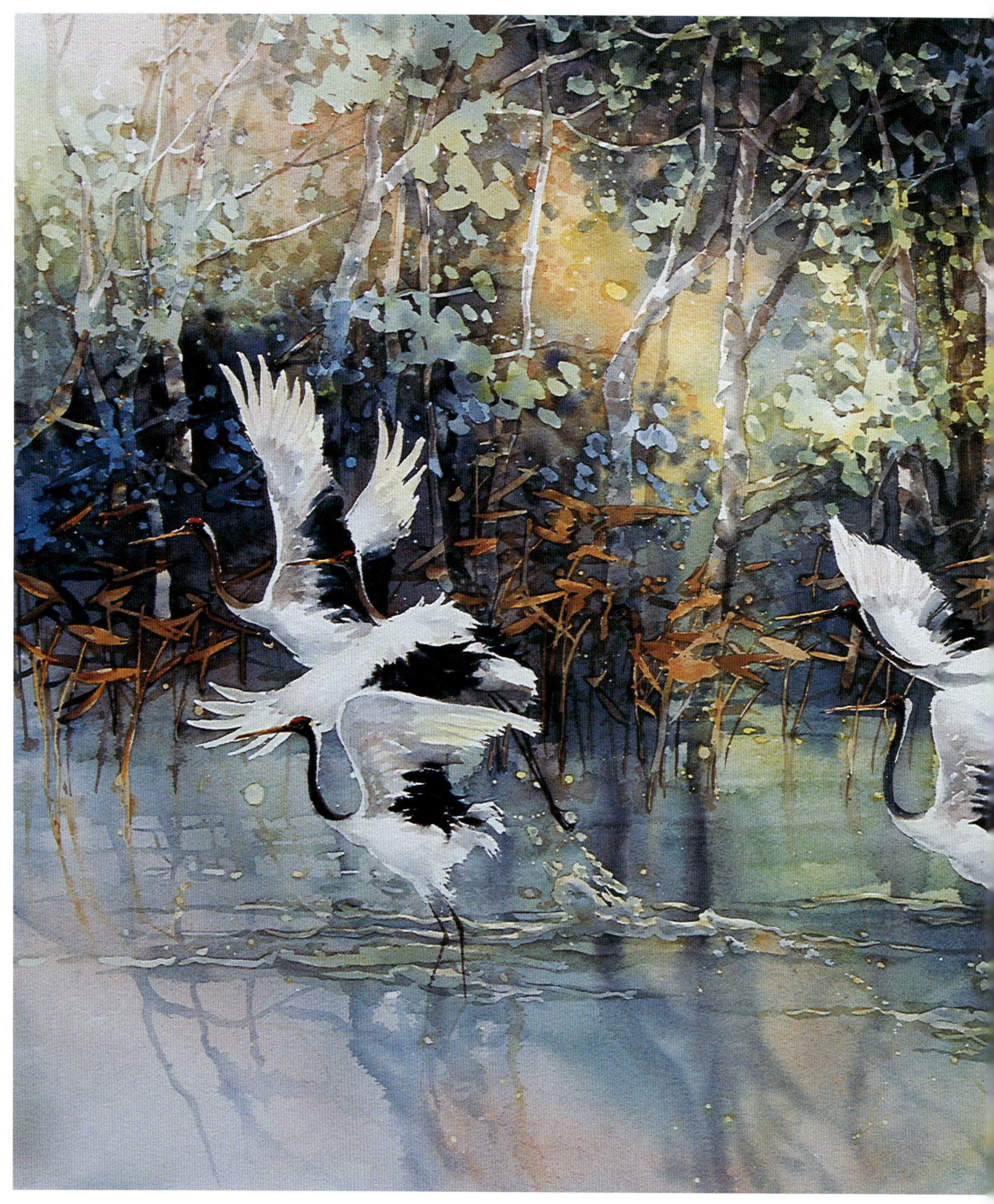

HARMONY
74 x 53cm (29 x 21in)

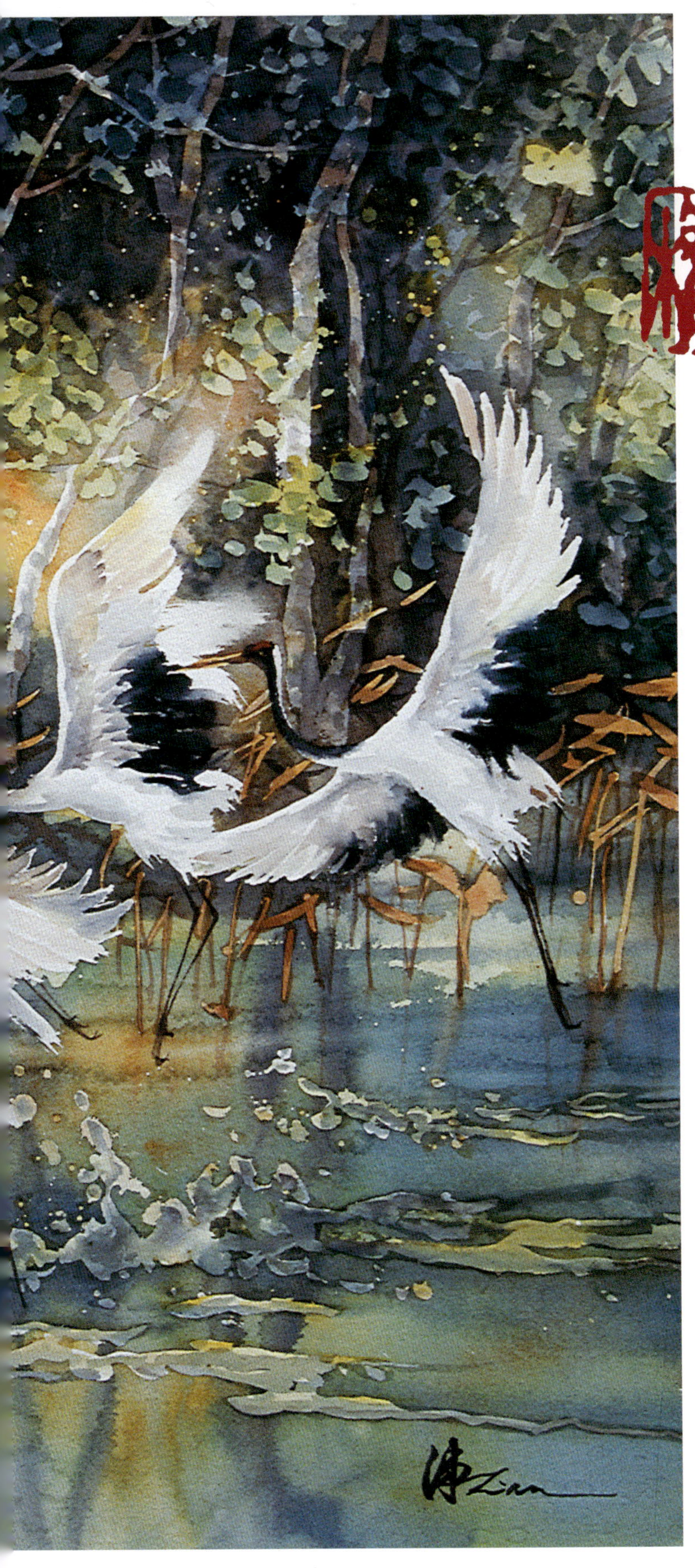

Lian Quan Zhen

CHINESE
PAINTING TECHNIQUES
for Exquisite Watercolours

David & Charles

About the Author

Lian Quan Zhen was a physician in Canton Province, China. He started sketching and painting when he was ten. He is a self-taught artist who learned Chinese painting techniques in his native country. After emigrating to the United States, he focused on watercolour painting in addition to Chinese art. In 1992, he received a Bachelor of Arts Degree from the University of California, Berkeley, and in 1996, a Master of Architecture Degree from the Massachusetts Institute of Technology (MIT).

Throughout the past decade, he has held one-man shows in California, Louisiana, Massachusetts and Hong Kong. MIT Museum has collected 14 of his paintings. His paintings are also found in corporate and international private collections. In 1997 and 1998 he received the International Animal in Arts Competition awards. He has been featured in *Watercolors '94*, Spring Issue, *Collectors* (Hong Kong) and *Splash 4*, published by North Light Books.

Lian teaches watercolour outdoor sketching at the University of California at Berkeley. He conducts workshops nationwide and on-site sketching in China. He has been an invited juror for art shows. For information on his paintings and workshops, see his Web page (www.zhenstudio.com), send an E-mail to lianzhen@yahoo.com or write to Zhen Studio, P.O. Box 1060, Pinole, CA 94564.

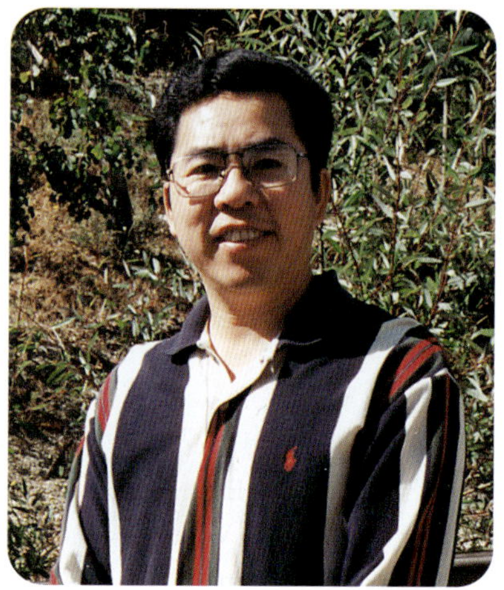

A DAVID & CHARLES BOOK

First published in the UK in 2000
First published in the USA in 2000 by North Light Books, Cincinnati, Ohio

A catalogue record for this book is available from the British Library.

ISBN 0 7153 1159 X

Printed in China
for David & Charles
Brunel House   Newton Abbot   Devon

Editors: Amy J. Wolgemuth and Michael Berger
Cover and Interior Designer: Amber Traven
Production Coordinator: Kristen D. Heller

Acknowledgments

Many thanks go to Shirley, my wife, who worked overtime and six days a week to support our family during the time I studied; to Amery, my daughter, who was quiet in the nights when I was painting and studying during her baby and toddler years. She also contributed her art to this book.

My thanks also go to the following: Mr Chang, my high school teacher in China, risked his political life to unlock the door of the art materials storeroom for me so that I could learn painting during the Cultural Revolution. I regret he could not live to see this book. Professor Sim Van de Ryn has greatly influenced my art in a positive way. My teacher and friend Karin Payson gave me confidence through her encouragement. Professor Ellen T. Harris, Liz Connors and Susan Cohen promoted my art career. Professor Vernon Ingram and Beth Ingram allowed me to exhibit my paintings in their home.

Ray Fugatt and Michelle Fugatt, thank you for introducing and promoting my paintings in Louisiana. Grace Clark, Marjorie Haggin, Nancy Thompson, Sue Clanton, Irene Pearson and Imogene Dewey, your hard work has made many of my workshops possible. Carole Hilton and Paddy J. Johnston, thank you for taking your valuable time to proofread my manuscripts.

I also thank Rachel Wolf for her recognition of my paintings and for making this book possible through North Light Books, and Amy Wolgemuth and Michael Berger, my editors, who patiently edited my Chinese version of English writing.

Finally, I thank numerous collectors who love and own my paintings, and all my friends and students who have helped me in different ways to finish this book, my dream come true.

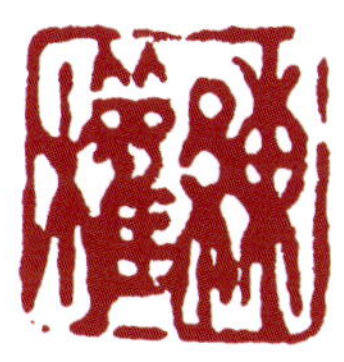 *To the memory of my mum, who taught me to be a good*

man. To my wife, Shirley and my daughter, Amery, who both love and

support me from their hearts.

1 CHINESE PAINTING BASICS

- The Six Laws
- Three Categories of Chinese Paintings
- Three Styles of Painting
- Materials
- Using Your Materials
- Brushstrokes
- Stretching Your Paintings

2 CHINESE PAINTING COMPOSITION & BASIC PAINTING TECHNIQUES

- Composition Methods
- Detail-Style Painting Techniques
- Spontaneous-Style Painting Techniques

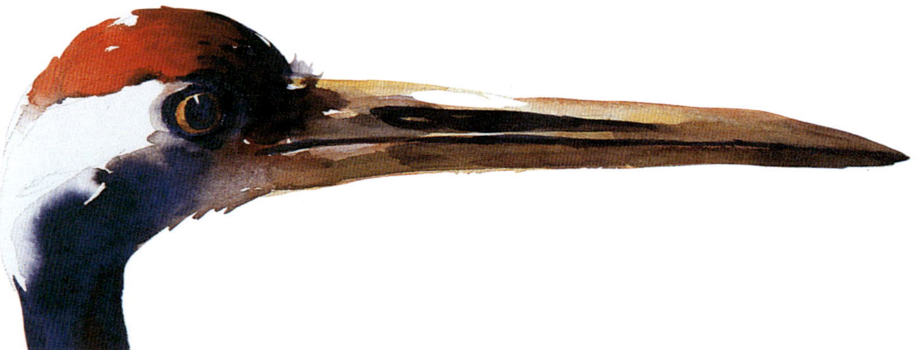

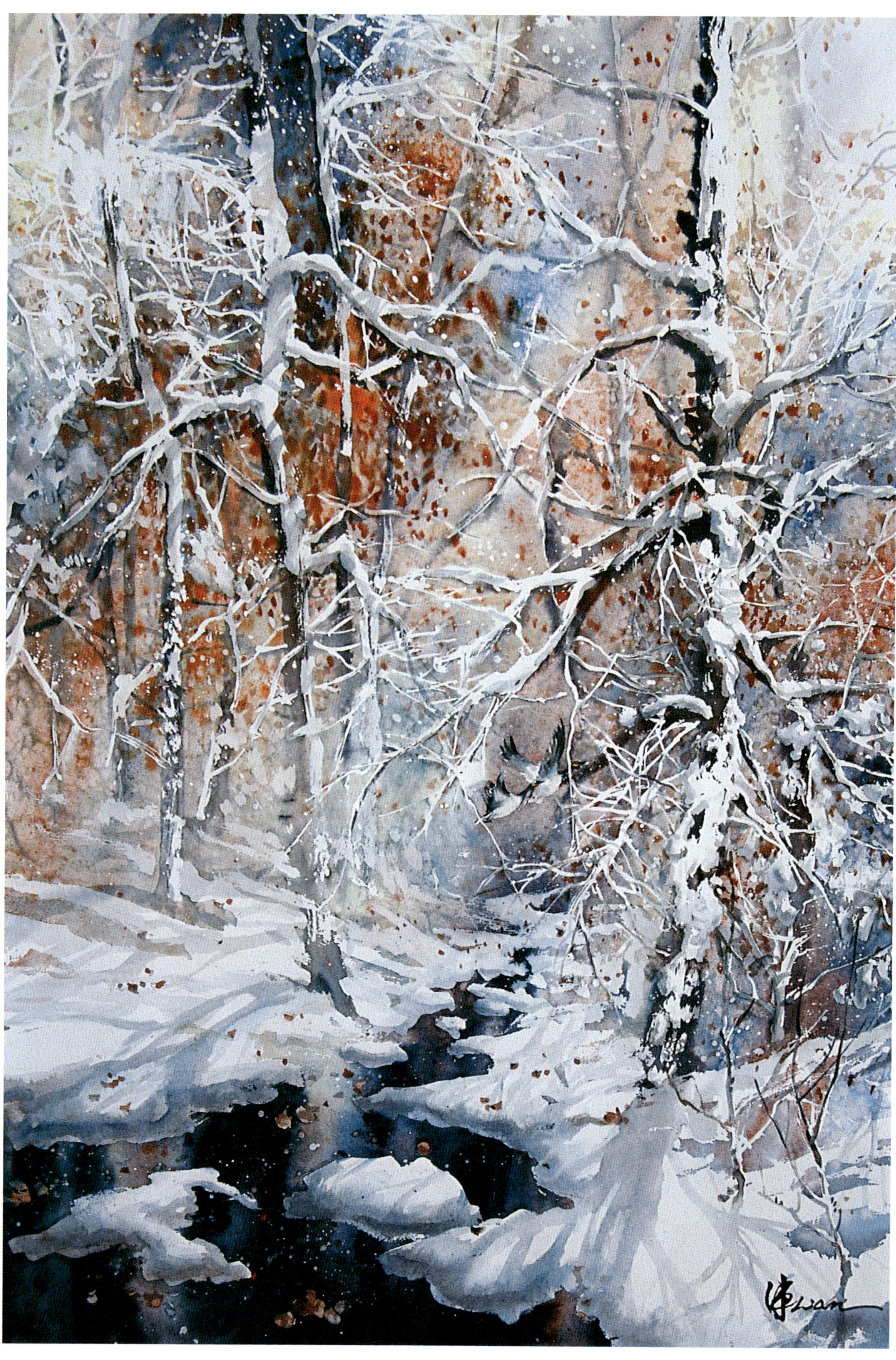

Lian Zhen is a rare and wonderful talent. Trained as a physician in China, he has always had a love for classic painting and calligraphy and the natural world. I came to know Lian as a student in my architectural classes at the University of California, Berkeley, and later in my outdoor watercolour sketching class where I encouraged him to discover his own style; he in turn introduced me to the classic tradition in Chinese painting, which he shares with you in this book.

His book is his gift to you, a sharing of his knowledge, passion and skill in an ancient tradition, interpreted through his unique vision. Lian is a compassionate and enthusiastic teacher. This book is his gift to us. Enjoy it and learn from Lian's art.

Sim Van de Ryn
Professor Emeritus, University of California, Berkeley

SNOW
53 x 74cm(21 x 29in)

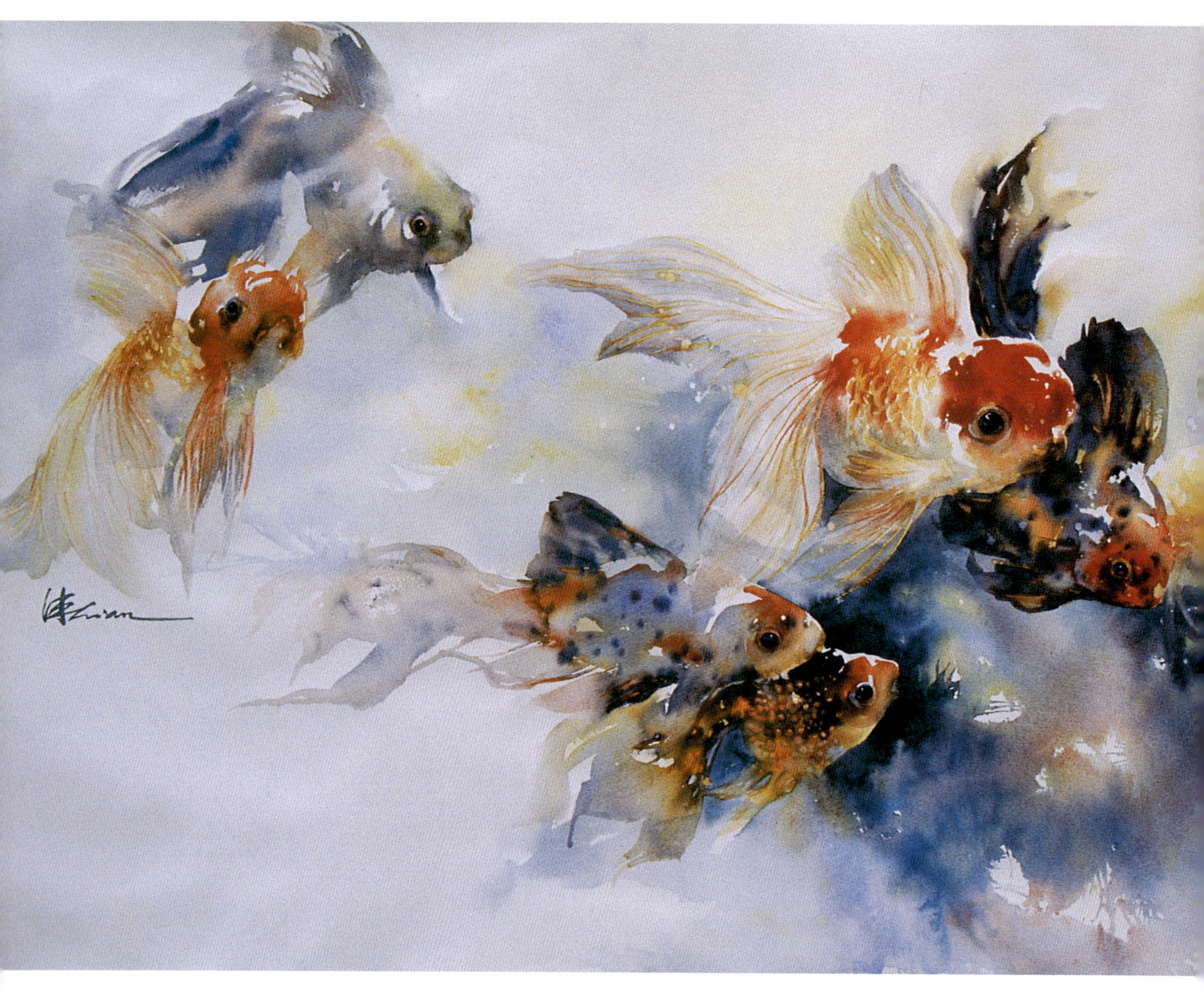

GOLDFISH
74 x 102cm (29 x 40in)
Watercolour on Arches 300gsm (140lb)
cold-pressed watercolour paper
Colour pouring and blending

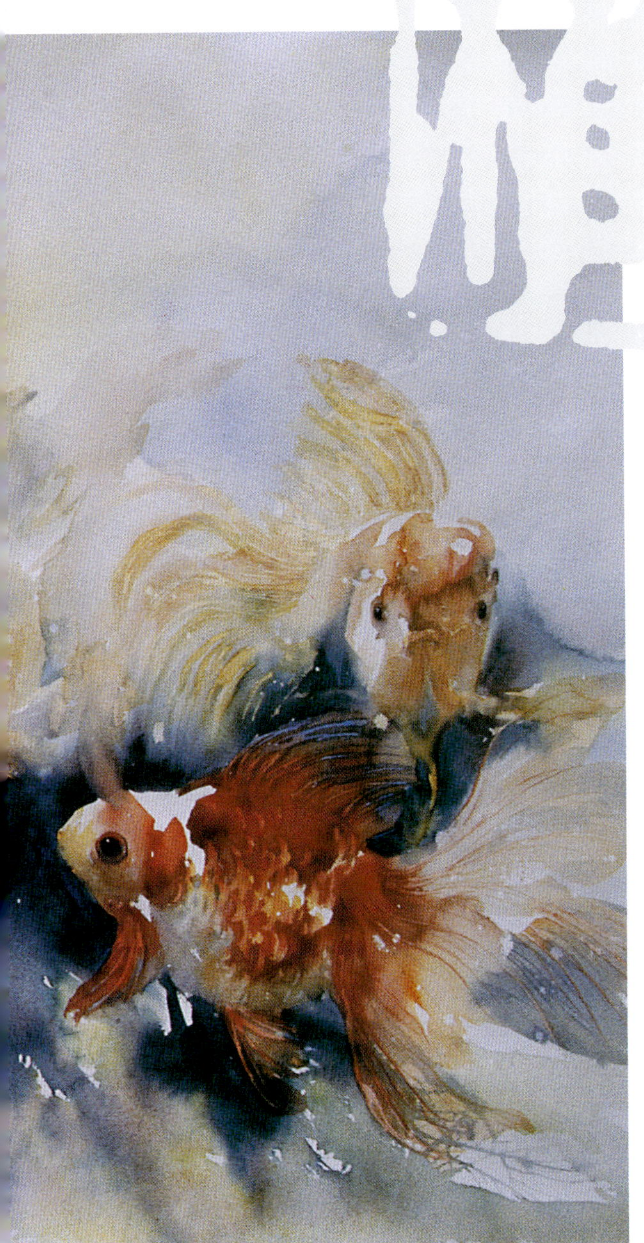

CHINESE PAINTING
BASICS

1 What is a Chinese painting? A Chinese painting is mainly line art painted with a Chinese brush, ink and colours on rice paper or silk. Often, the painting is in linear perspective. On the painting, there is Chinese calligraphy that inscribes the name of the painting, a poem and the artist's signature, along with a red chop. (A 'chop' is similar to a rubber stamp that contains the artist's name or a phrase.)

Traditionally, Chinese artists define objects with lines rather than surfaces. They mainly use ink to paint. The idea of simplicity from both Taoism and Buddhism deeply influences artists who consider other pigments as secondary media that serve the purpose of perfecting the ink.

THE SIX LAWS

During the Eastern Tsin dynasty (AD 317–420), Hsieh Ho, an artist and the first art critic in Chinese history, established the Six Laws of Painting. First, *vitality resonates from a painting*. This means that a painting should carry lively forces that touch viewers.

Use bone manner brushstrokes, or brushstrokes that are confident, strong and elastic. They should resemble bones in content – not necessarily uniform, but strong in texture.

Capture the forms of nature's objects. In other words, sketch nature with the intent to capture its forms and spirits.

Apply colours according to each object's category. When painting a group of trees, there is no need to differentiate each tree's colour. Paint all of them using one colour, such as green or yellow.

Properly place the objects. A great painting always has a well-organized composition.

Transfer masters' techniques. Learn from the masters by copying and analyzing their artwork. As a result, you will learn a variety of techniques and theories with which you can develop your own.

The first law is most significant. It seeks to blend the artist's spirit with the rhythmic vitality of nature. A great painting should not only demonstrate outstanding technique, but should also express harmony and vitality. When painting a bird, it does not matter how much detail your painting has, nor what technique and media are used. It is essential to capture the *essence* of the bird: its texture, activity and sound – its life. The bird should be able to communicate with its viewers.

Chinese artists are encouraged to learn from nature. If you paint landscapes, for example, then practise sketching as many magnificent landscapes as you can. Likewise, if you paint fish, then observe fish as often as possible.

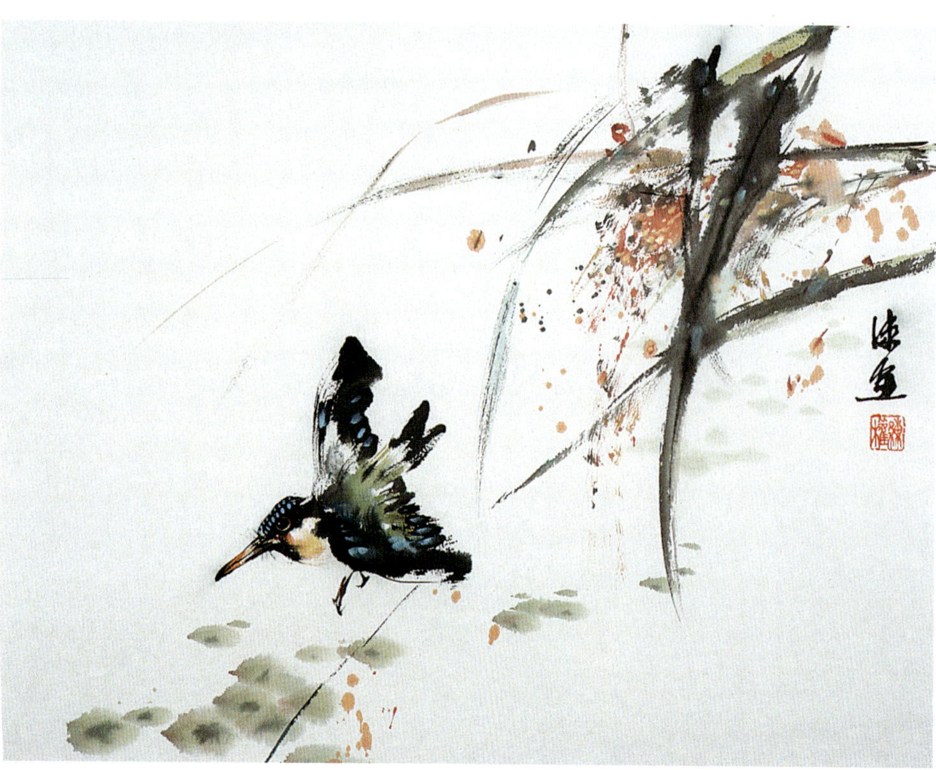

Using the Six Laws
This painting further explains the Six Laws. It depicts the moment just before the kingfisher catches a fish. It is a vivid painting that captures harmony in nature (first law). The minimal brushstrokes are sure and forceful (second law). The bird is lively and energetic, and is derived, rather than copied, from nature (third law). The colours on the water plants are uniform, according to category (fourth law). The objects are arranged on a diagonal line from bottom left to upper right to further emphasize the motions. The white area in the kingfisher's direction of flight allows viewers to use their imagination (fifth law). Finally, the painting techniques are influenced by the Lingnan School (sixth law).
FISHING
46 x 56cm (18 x 22in)
Chinese ink and colours
on Korean paper
Spontaneous style

THREE CATEGORIES OF CHINESE PAINTINGS

Figures

Figure paintings focus on people, although other objects, such as rocks, trees and flowers, also appear. The golden age of figure painting occurred during the Sui and T'iang dynasties (AD 589–906). Artists used a variety of beautiful brushstroke styles with descriptive names to emphasize textures and the movement of clothes, and to capture the essence of the figures. For instance, iron wire strokes were uniform, strong and threadlike. Moving cloud and flowing water strokes were fluent, long and thin with soft turning angles. Bramble brushstrokes were thick, large, broken and abbreviated. Typically, only one brushstroke style was used to paint the figures in a painting.

Landscapes

Landscape paintings are dominated by mountains, clouds, rocks, trees, bridges, houses, waterfalls, rivers and boats. People are small in these paintings. Landscape painting reached its prime during both the Five Dynasties period and the Northern Sung dynasty (AD 906–1127).

Floral/Bird

Floral/bird paintings include flowers, rocks, creeks, grass, insects, birds, fish and other small objects. Similar to landscapes, these paintings gained popularity during the Five Dynasties (AD 906–960) and flourished in both the Northern and Southern Sung dynasties (AD 960–1279).

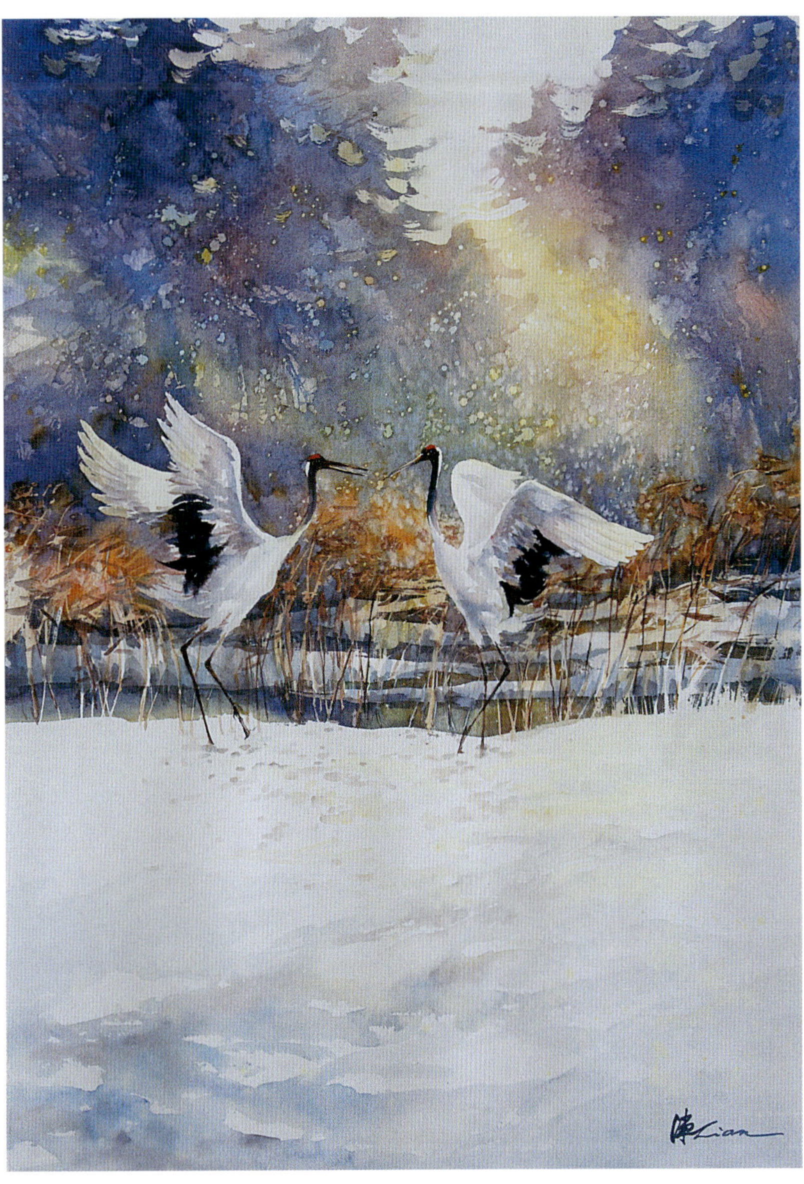

LOVE DANCING
97 x 69cm (38 x 27in)
Watercolour on Arches 300gsm (140lb)
cold-pressed watercolour paper
Colour pouring and blending

THREE STYLES OF PAINTING

Detail Style

Detail-style paintings show a lot of small details. For example, in bird and fish paintings, feathers and scales are clearly depicted. Artists handle their brushes carefully and slowly, and the brushstrokes are smaller and more uniform than in other styles of painting. In addition to ink, vivid and intense colours are also used. Artists use surfaces that do not absorb water, such as alum rice paper and alum silk.

Detail style is the basic training for Chinese painting students. It teaches them to manipulate their brushes to acquire proper strokes, to observe and analyze details and to use colours.

Spontaneous Style

Also known as scholar style, this type of painting is strongly influenced by Chinese calligraphy and poetry. It has remained the dominant style since its full development during the Sung dynasties. According to scholar-style painting theory, poetry, calligraphy and painting (the *three perfections*) are inseparable. A great artist should master them all.

Spontaneous-style artists reinterpret rather than copy nature. They manipulate brushstrokes in an abbreviated manner. As a result, spontaneous-style paintings can be semi-abstract and may use metaphors to depict the essence and spirit of objects without emphasis on details. Breaking a mountain into segments in a landscape, for instance, is a traditional metaphor for losing one's homeland. Bamboo symbolizes honour

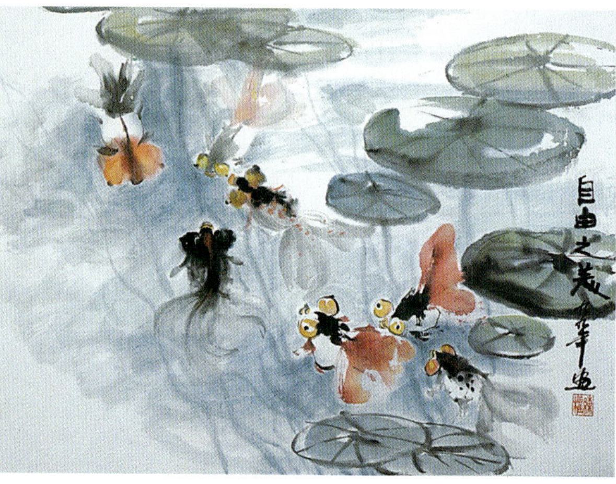

Spontaneous-Style Painting

This spontaneous-style painting shows no small details. The brushstrokes are not uniform as in the detail-style painting, and the variety of strokes suggests texture and movement. Notice how the tails and fins of the goldfish are defined by wide brushstrokes rather than outlines.

BEAUTY OF FREEDOM
43 x 61cm (17 x 24in)
Chinese ink and colours on double-layer raw Shuan paper
Spontaneous style

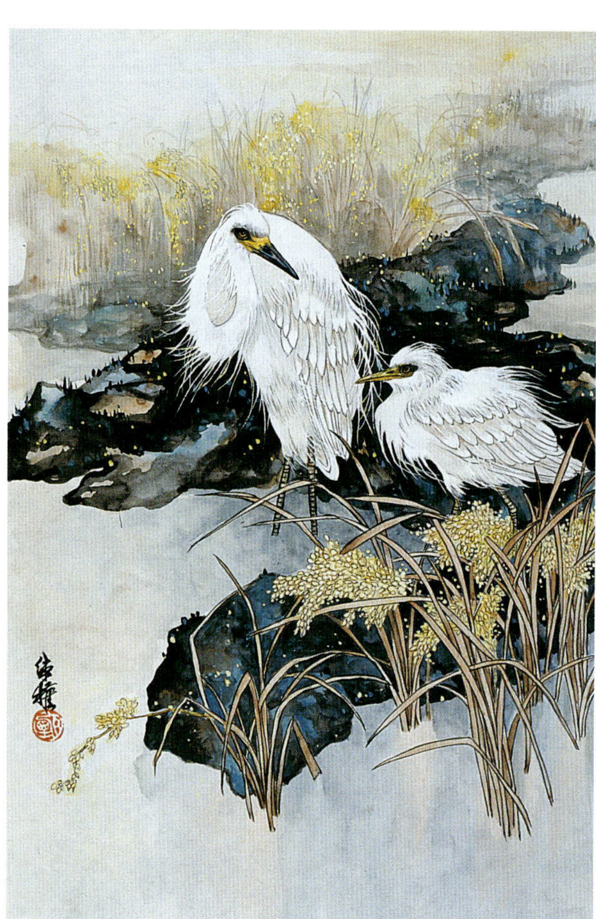

Detail-Style Painting

This typical detail-style painting depicts small details, such as the egrets' feathers and individual rice grains. The objects are painted with outlines and then filled in with colours.

TWO EGRETS
43 x 28cm (17 x 11in)
Chinese ink and colours on mature Shuan paper
Detail style

and dignity, while palm flowers are symbolic of encouragement and nobility. Orchids connote high morality. If an artist gives you an orchid painting as a gift, most likely the artist considers the relationship between you and him as pure and strong.

The ink-pouring technique, created by a famous drunken artist called Wong Mo during the T'iang dynasty (AD 618–906), could be considered the extreme of the spontaneous style. Before Wong Mo would begin to paint, he would first drink a lot of wine. Then he would start pouring ink on silk, laughing and chanting all the while, smearing his hands and feet across the silk while he danced. When the images revealed themselves, he adjusted and transformed them into mountains, bridges, trees, houses, rocks and figures. Unfortunately, none of his paintings survive today. I have tried Wong Mo's technique and must admit it's a lot of fun; however, I did not drink while I was painting.

Half-Detail, Half-Spontaneous Style

Obviously, this style is a combination of the detail and spontaneous styles. Some artists like to paint floral-bird paintings in this style. The paintings are not exactly equally half of each style. In most cases, the focus objects are in detail style and the others are in spontaneous style.

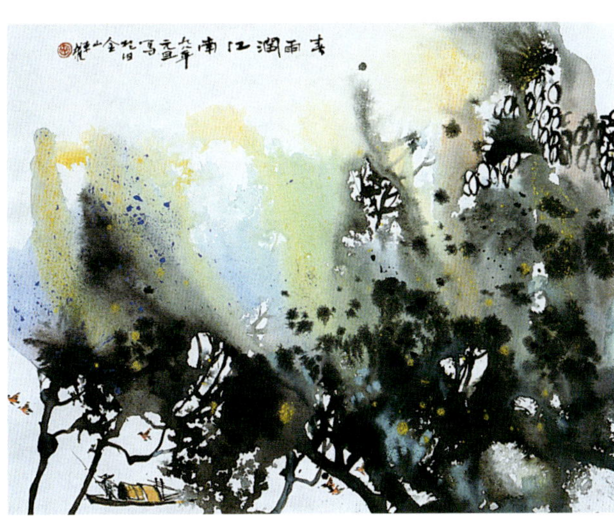

Having Fun With Ink Pouring
I knew I wanted to paint a scene with trees. However, I did not have a composition in mind. I started by wetting the upper and middle portions of the paper with a water sprayer. I then poured ultramarine blue, pure cadmium yellow light and cadmium red deep on the upper part of the paper. Next, I poured Chinese ink along the bottom of the colours and left the colours and the ink to blend for about half a minute. Then I tilted the paper so the colours and ink would flow towards the bottom to create the branches and trunks. I further defined the trees with a medium brush and added a few birds, a boat and a boatman.
SPRING RAIN
25 x 36cm (10 x 14in)
Chinese ink and colour on Academie sketch paper
Spontaneous style

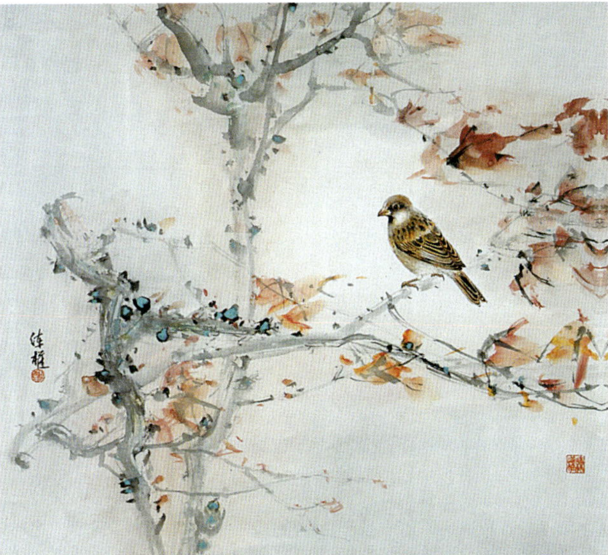

Half-Detail, Half-Spontaneous Style
Notice in this painting how the sparrow is in detail style while the tree and background are in spontaneous style.
SPARROW
71 x 71cm (28 x 28in)
Chinese ink and colours on mature Shuan paper
Half-detail, half-spontaneous style

MATERIALS

Getting the right materials is a good start to learning Chinese painting. Rice paper, bamboo brushes, ink sticks and ink stones are the traditional materials. They are also the materials used for writing and calligraphy. The Chinese refer to them as the 'four treasures of a scholarly library'. You may have noticed that colours are not listed as one of the basic materials. Chinese artists consider ink as a colour because they dilute the ink with water to create a number of tones. Chinese artists are judged by how well they manipulate different tones of ink. This is not difficult to understand if you have made pencil sketches. The more tones you have on your sketch, the more depth your art will possess.

Most of these materials are available in Chinese bookshops and art galleries in Chinatowns all over the world. I bought all my materials in Chinatown in San Francisco. In addition, some major art supply stores carry basic Chinese painting materials such as rice papers, brushes, ink sticks and ink stones.

Rice Paper

The rice paper I used for most of the Chinese painting demonstrations in this book is called 'Shuan paper', produced in Jing County, Anhui Province. There are two kinds of Shuan papers: raw and mature. Raw paper is untreated, soft and very absorbent, and is used mainly for spontaneous-style paintings. It comes in either a single, highly absorbent layer, or a double, gently absorbent layer. Start painting on the double-layer Shuan paper when you paint in spontaneous style, as the paper is easier to control than the single-layer paper.

Mature Shuan paper is made by applying alum to both sides of the raw Shuan paper. It is also soft, but not absorbent, making it great for detail style and half-detail, half-spontaneous style.

Korean and Other Papers

Korean paper can also be used for spontaneous-style paintings. It is similar to the raw Shuan paper in absorbency. However, it is more resistant to tearing and blends ink and colours differently. I also paint on Western art papers, such as Arches 300gsm (140lb) watercolour paper and Academie sketch paper. I'm not concerned whether those paintings are considered Chinese paintings or not. To paint is to create, and creation usually begins without names.

Brushes

Chinese brushes are made with animal fur tips and bamboo handles. There are three groups of brushes: soft, medium and hard. Soft brushes are made of soft furs, such as goat. The hard brushes are made from furs such as wolf and horse. A brush made of both soft and hard furs is considered of medium texture. Artists tend to use their favourite kinds of brushes. As a new student, the rule of thumb is to use soft brushes for painting soft-textured objects, such as flowers, and for colouring. Use hard brushes for painting rough-textured objects, such as rocks and tree trunks, and for detailing. It is handy to have all three kinds of brushes in sizes from small to large. Unlike watercolour brushes that have a numbering system, Chinese brushes are simply defined as small, medium or large. You can refer to the numbers on Japanese Sumi brushes for comparison. A small Chinese brush is the same size as a Sumi No. 4 brush. A medium brush is

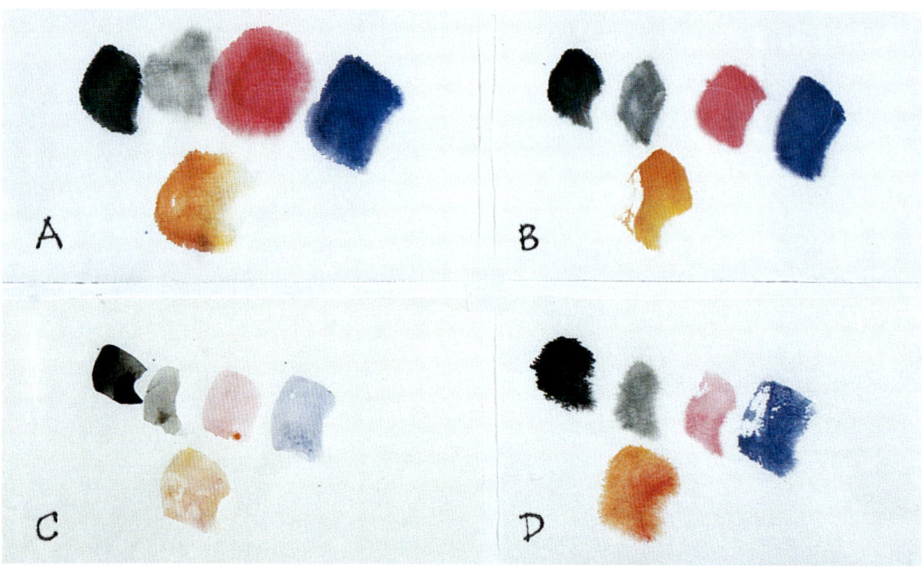

Different Papers Give Different Results
Notice how the colours respond differently on these four types of paper.
A. Raw Shuan paper (single layer)
B. Raw Shuan paper (double layer)
C. Mature Shuan paper
D. Korean paper

similar to a Sumi No. 6, and a large brush is equal to or larger than a Sumi No. 12. Before you use a new brush, soak the brush tip in clean, cold water for half an hour. The water will remove the glues that adhere the fur together. This creates an 'open brush'.

Ink and Ink Stone

For hundreds of years, Chinese artists ground ink sticks with clear water on ink stones to get ink for painting, calligraphy and writing. The ink sticks for painting are made of rosin soot from burning oil, and are called 'old-smoke ink sticks'. Ink stones are made of natural rock. They are not only tools for making ink but also collectible sculptures. The best ink stones are called 'Twan ink stones', quarried in Twan County, Canton Province. If there are circular spots with light earth colour on an ink stone ('eyes'), the rock is a good age and carries the best textures for producing higher-quality ink. This kind of ink stone costs much more than regular ink stones. As a beginner, you need only a regular ink stone.

It sounds complicated to produce ink before you start painting. Actually, during the time you are grinding the ink stick, you are calm and able to compose your painting. It is a meditation period before painting. In recent years, bottled ink has become available. Many artists use it because it is of good quality and is easy to carry while travelling. I used bottled ink for the Chinese paintings and demonstrations in this book. Its brand name is China Ink, made in Shanghai.

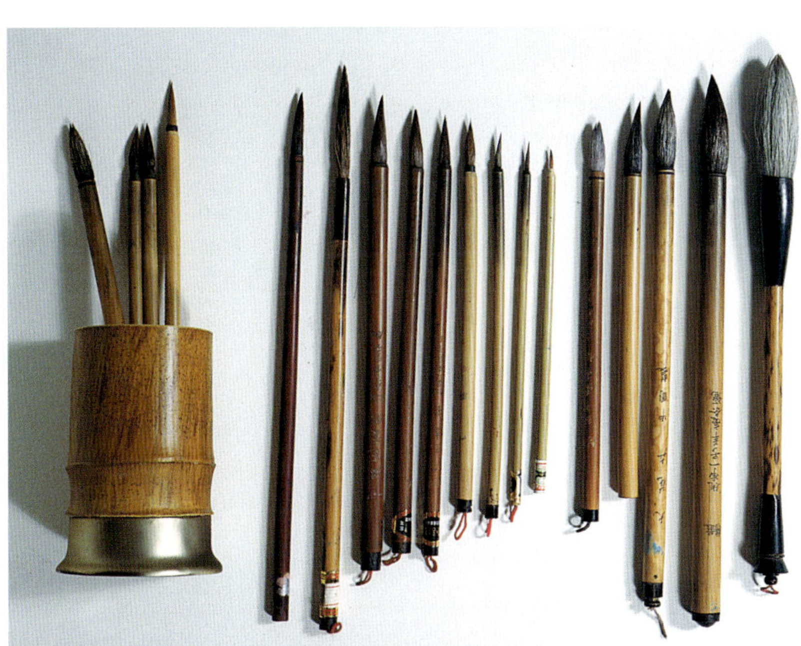

Chinese Brushes
The five brushes on the right are soft brushes, while the others are hard and medium. I use the middle four small brushes a lot when I paint detail-style paintings. A brush container is pictured on the left.

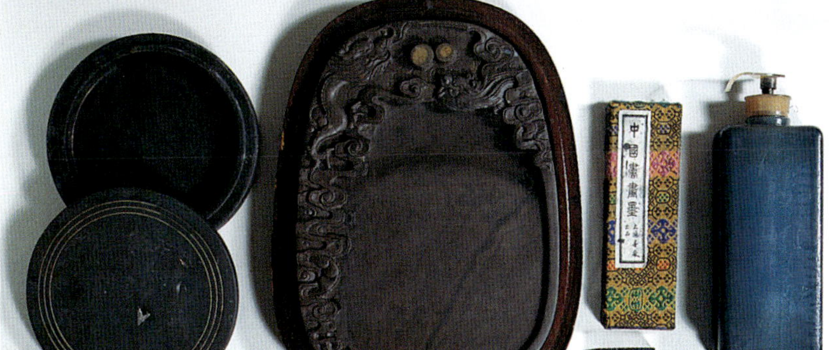

Ink Stones and Inks
A. A common ink stone (10cm [4in] diameter) and its cover.
B. A Twan ink stone with two 'eyes' near its top, along with a cloud-pattern relief sculpture. The stone has a wooden base and cover, though the cover is not shown here.
C. An ink stick with only one-third of its original length left. (Its box is above.)
D. The China ink bottle.

Colours

Similar to watercolours, modern Chinese paints come in tubes. I use Chinese painting colour, produced by SIIC Marie Painting Materials Co., Ltd, Shanghai. I use nine of the pigments frequently: blue (light blue), burnt sienna, carmine (deep red), cinnabar, gamboge (yellow), green (light green), indigo, vermilion and white. The colours are water based and made of plants and minerals, along with glue. Do not use regular watercolour pigments, as they will blend during the process of stretching the painting.

Chops and Rouge

Chops are used for sealing paintings and balancing compositions, and are usually made of soapstone. An artist often has one name chop and a few leisure chops, which are inscribed with short phrases or poems. I carved about ten chops for myself 15 years ago. You can have your own chops made at many Chinese art galleries, where artists can help you to translate your English name phonetically into a Chinese name and carve it on a soapstone.

Rouge is oil-based red colour used for stamping, and comes in various-sized jars with covers so that it won't dry out.

Other Materials

Besides the materials already discussed, you'll need a few other things:

- A china palette or several small white china dishes to use as palettes (a watercolour palette can also be used)
- A painting mat made from smooth, 3mm (⅛in) thick, light-coloured fabric to cover your painting table
- One or two watercolour brush washers (or containers of water)
- A brush container
- A brush holder for resting your brush
- A pair of paperweights for levelling the Shuan paper, as it is not as flat as watercolour paper

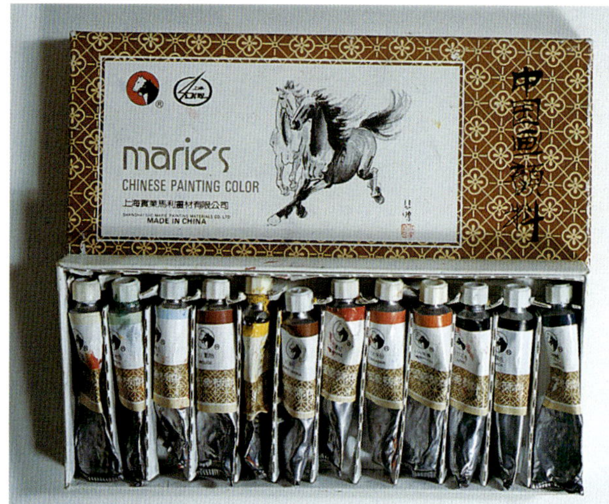

Chinese Colours

Typical Chinese painting colours come in tubes 9cm (3½in) long by 19mm (¾in) in diameter. Another size of Chinese colours not shown here is about half that size, and is sold either in a set or individually. I prefer the larger tubes because they do not harden as quickly as the smaller ones.

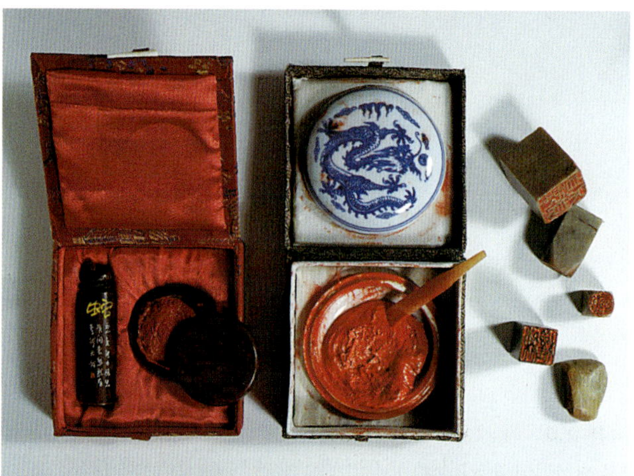

Chops and Rouge

A. This box holds a chop of my daughter's name. Since she was born in the year of the snake, she chose a chop with a little snake at one end.
B. This box holds a large china jar with rouge.
C. Here are several chops I made.

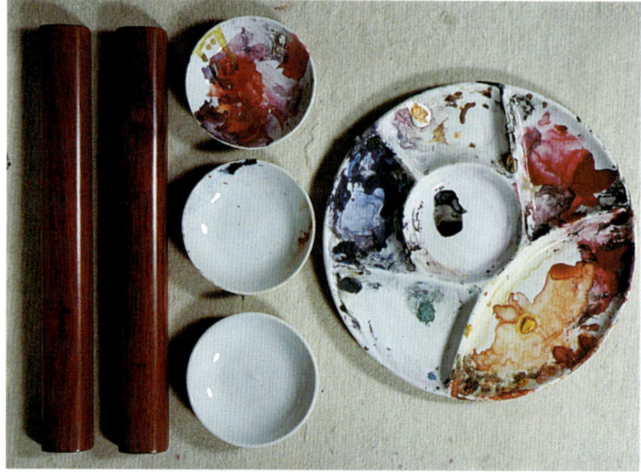

Other Painting Supplies

A. A small painting mat, 51 x 51cm (20 x 20in).
B. Two 4 x 31cm (1½ x 12in) wood paperweights.
C. Three small white china dishes I use to mix colours.
D. Chinese painting palette (china).

USING YOUR MATERIALS

Laying Out Your Materials

You should have a table for Chinese painting. I use a 76 x 183cm (30 x 72in) folding table. There is no one way of laying out the materials on your painting table. Place them according to convenience. I lay them out nicely before I paint. But by the time I finish, they're all over the place!

Holding the Brush

Holding the brush is not the same as holding a pen or pencil. When you hold the brush correctly, you can achieve the desired brushstrokes much easier. Hold the brush with your thumb, index and middle finger. When your fingers hold up the brush, there is a hollow space between your fingers and your palm. This allows the brush to move freely while it is tight in your fingers.

In my Chinese painting workshops, many students hold their brushes correctly for an hour or so then go back to the way they hold a pen because they feel tired. Keep practising for a while; you will get used to the correct way. Interestingly, since I have done Chinese painting for a long time, when I paint details in watercolour, I hold my watercolour brushes in the same way I hold a Chinese brush. I feel it is easier to achieve the best results.

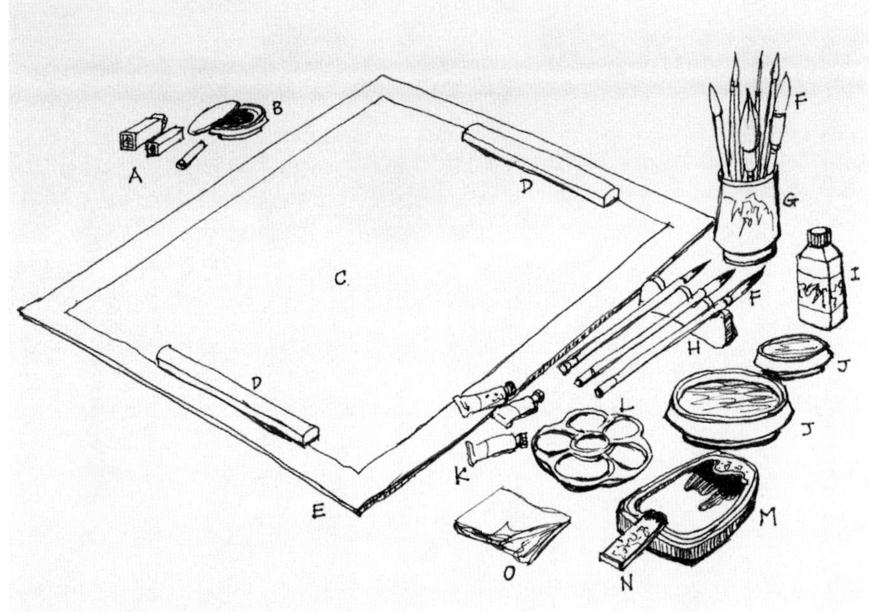

Laying Out Your Materials

Here's how I lay out my materials as I prepare to paint – though by the time I'm finished, things tend to be scattered quite a bit.

A. Chop	I. Bottle ink
B. Rouge	J. Brush washer
C. Paper	K. Colours
D. Paperweights	L. Palette
E. Painting mat	M. Ink stone
F. Brushes	N. Ink stick
G. Brush container	O. Paper towel
H. Brush holder	

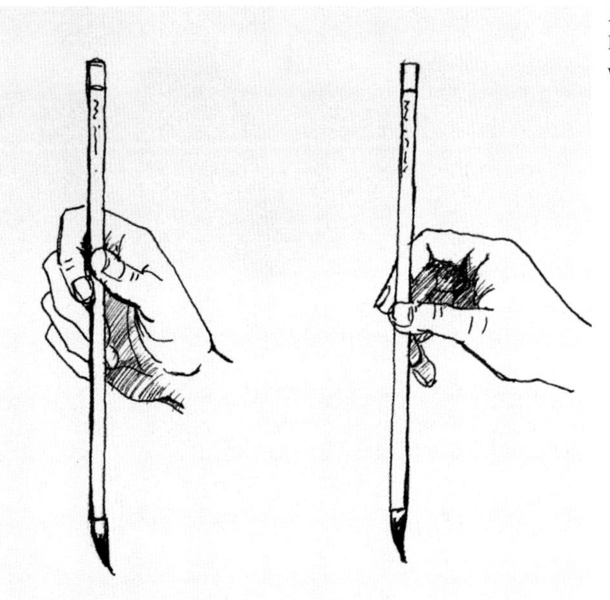

Holding the Brush

Here's the correct way to hold a brush.

BRUSHSTROKES

Good brushstrokes should be confident, without uncertainty. They should have proper tone and the right amount of moisture. They should be strong, energetic and elastic to suggest texture.

Let's use the bird painting to the right as a way to explain brushstrokes. I painted the bird and bamboo with sure, vivid strokes. The strokes are a combination of dry and wet textures in different tones. They appropriately suggest the bird's feather texture, its activity and the movement of the bamboo.

Proper Brush Angle

There are two proper brush angles. One is vertical, approximately 90° from the painting surface. This position is called 'centre brush'. The other angle is less than 80°. It is referred to as 'side brush'. When you hold the brush vertically, you are able to create fine, rounded, uniform and elastic strokes. The side-brush method is used for outlining and detailing, as well as for painting soft-textured objects. When you paint with the side-brush method, you may tilt the brush at different angles. The narrower the angle, the wider the stroke you get. Use side brush to create rough, dry and active strokes and for painting rocks, mountains, tree trunks, weeds and fast-moving objects.

Moisture

The more water in a brush, the damper and smoother the brushstrokes. On the other hand, with less water, you can obtain broken, rough and aged effects.

Pressure

Applying appropriate pressure on a brush is also important. One guideline is for painters to seek quality brushstrokes with the 'power of breaking through the paper'. Such power is achieved by transferring your strong internal energy to the brush, then to the strokes,without actually breaking the paper.

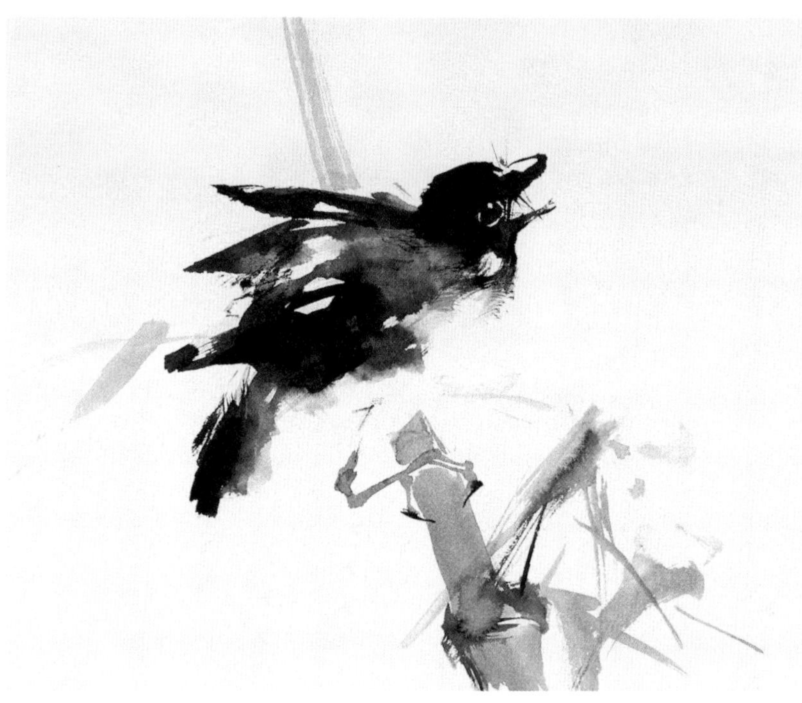

MORNING SONG
28 x 33cm (11 x 13in)
Chinese ink on Academie sketch paper
Spontaneous style

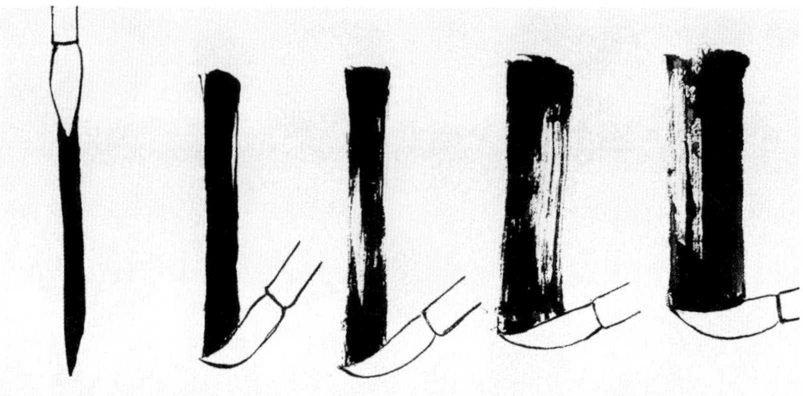

The Angle of the Brush
The brush at left is being held at 90°. The others are being held at various angles.

Stance

It is a good idea to stand when you are painting. Hence you can transfer your energy from your body to your arm and your fingers, then into the brushstrokes. Try to move your arm more often than your fingers because it is easier to control the movement.

Moving Speed

Speed affects the characteristics of your brushstrokes. The faster you move your brush, the more effects will be created by the strokes.

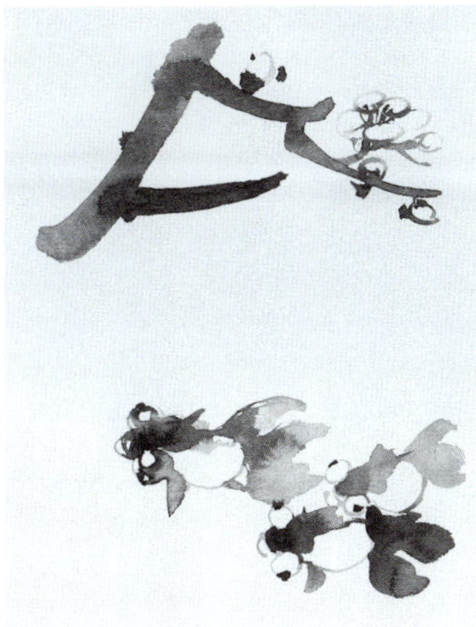

Wet Brushstrokes
A palm branch
with blossoms
and three goldfish
painted using wet
brushstrokes.

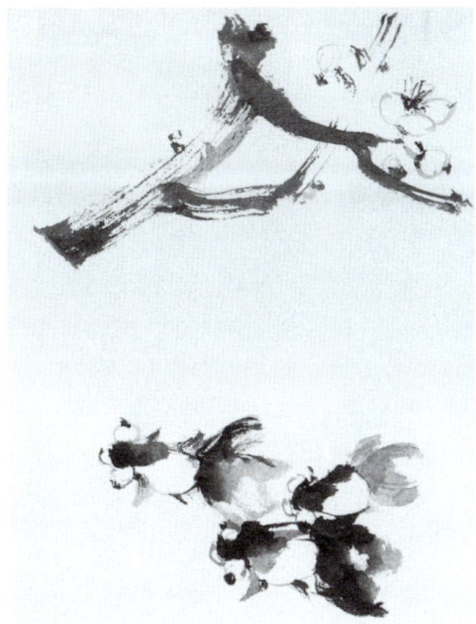

Dry Brushstrokes
The same branch and
goldfish, this time
painted using dry
brushstrokes.

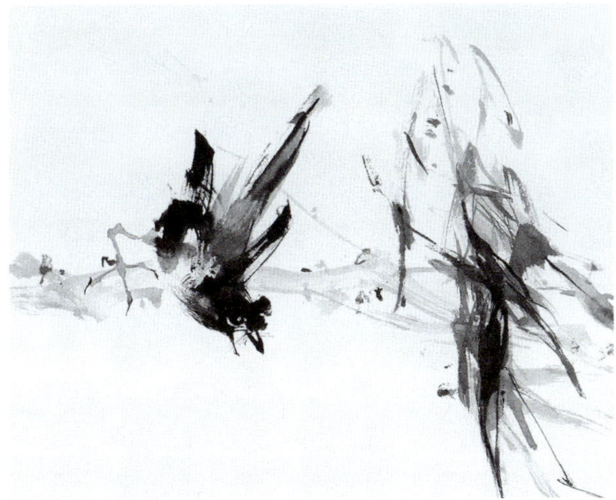

Where Are You?
27 x 33cm (10½ x 13in)
Chinese ink on Academie sketch paper
Spontaneous style

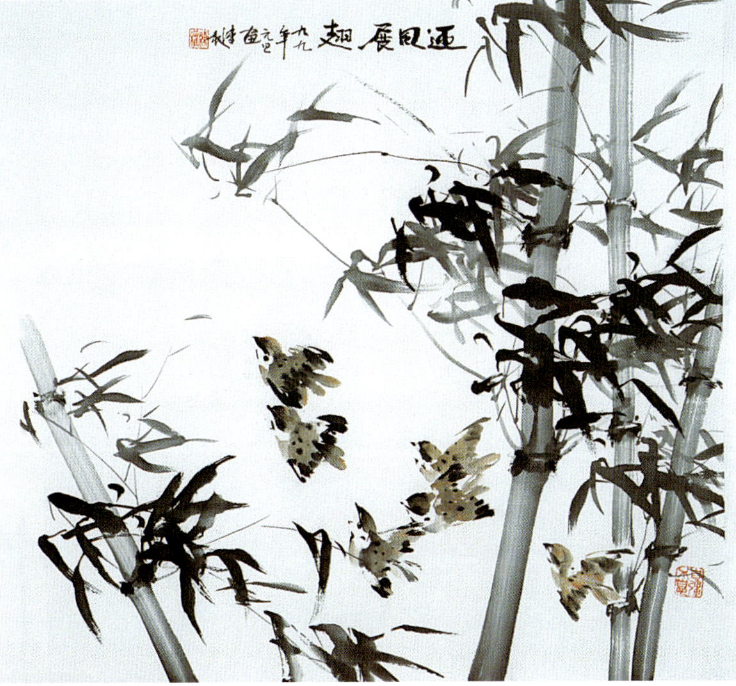

Brushstroke Speed
The bamboo leaves, sparrows' wings and tails are painted with fast-moving strokes to suggest the blowing wind during flight.
Beginning of a Journey
76 x 76cm (30 x 30in)
Chinese ink and colours on double-layer Shuan paper
Spontaneous style

STRETCHING YOUR PAINTINGS

Once you have completed your paintings, they will need to be stretched, as undoubtedly the paper will have wrinkled due to water absorption. Even though stretching Chinese paintings can be tricky, you can do it in a simple way that will give you wonderful results.

What You'll Need

Most of the materials you'll need are fairly common and easy to come by:

❀ One 18cm (7in) cooking pot
❀ A roll of paper towels
❀ A clean 25cm (10in) diameter plate
❀ A 76mm to 152mm (3in to 6in) flat, soft-fur brush
❀ A 19mm (¾in) flat watercolour brush
❀ A water spray bottle
❀ Wheat starch (Use one with a neutral pH so that it will not discolour or disintegrate over time. You can buy it from most art supply stores.)
❀ A stretching surface (I use Plexiglas, or Perspex, because it is smooth and even. I have two sheets of Plexiglas: one is 61 x 91cm [24 x 36in] for small paintings, and the other is 102 x 183cm [40 x 72in] for large paintings.)
❀ A stretching board made from 12mm (½in) thick medium-density fibreboard (MDF) or plywood, the same size or larger than the stretching surface.
❀ A clean, smooth and even mounting surface for drying (I use a 122 x 244cm [4 x 8ft] sheet of MDF.)

Preparing the Stretching Surface

Place the stretching board on a table, and draw rectangular guidelines on it. At a point about 13cm (5in) from both the right and bottom edges, mark the lower right point of the rectangle. From this starting point, draw a 51 x 89cm (20 x 35in) rectangle parallel to the bottom edge and the right side of the board. Use waterproof marker to keep the lines from bleeding onto your artwork.

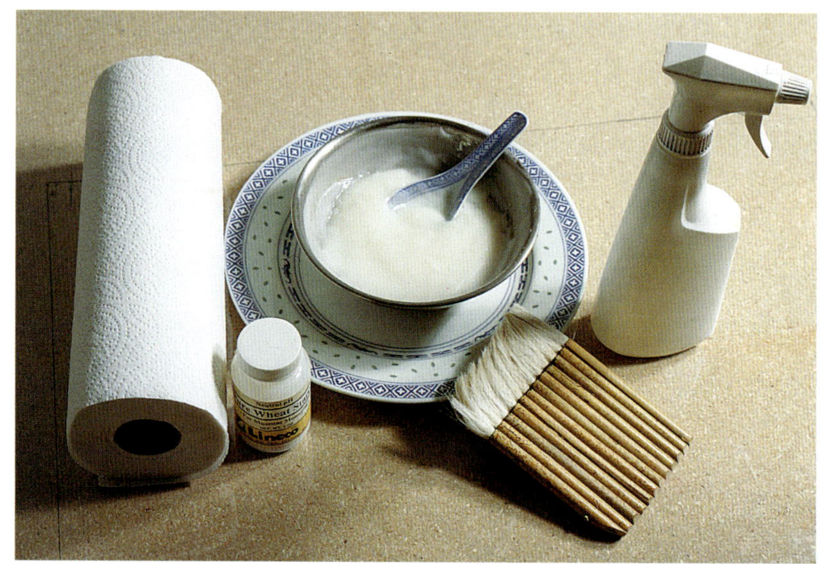

What You'll Need
A roll of paper towel, one bottle of neutral pH pure wheat starch, an 18cm (7in) stainless steel bowl with cooked gravy, a 25cm (10in) plate, a 13cm (5in) flat brush and a water spray bottle.

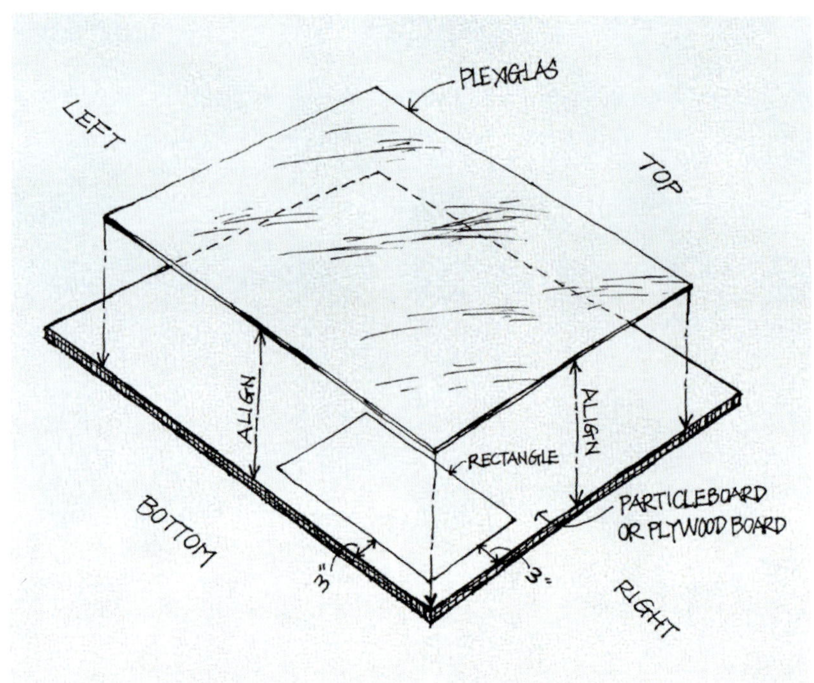

Building the Stretching Board
This diagram shows the stretching board, the rectangle and the stretching surface.

Lay the stretching surface on top of the stretching board. Align both the right and bottom edges of the two surfaces.

Preparing the Stretching Gravy

I usually stretch several paintings at one time. The amount of gravy I am preparing (right) is for eight paintings in a variety of sizes. I needed about 6ml (¼ cup) of starch and 30ml (1¼ cups) of water. In general, the ratio between starch and water is 1 to 5.

Preparing the Rice Paper Backing

The rice paper backing is for attaching to the back of your painting. You can use Korean paper or the same kind of rice paper as for your painting. It should be about 8cm (3in) larger all around than the painting you are working with. For this example, I cut a 58 x 76cm (23 x 30in) piece of raw Shuan paper for the 43 x 61cm (17 x 24in) painting *The Beauty of Freedom.*

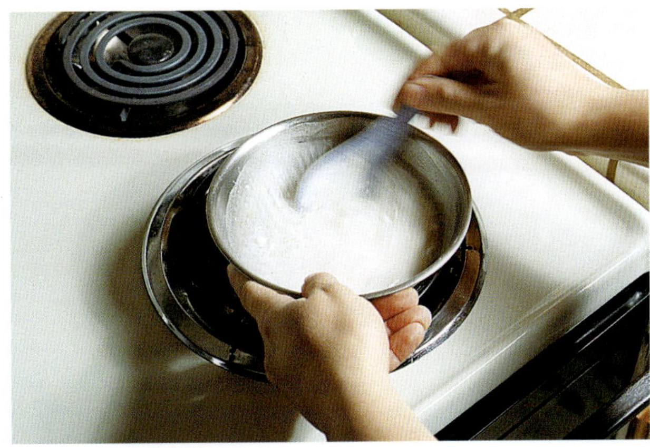

1 *MIX THE STARCH AND WATER*
Stir the starch and water until they are mixed well.

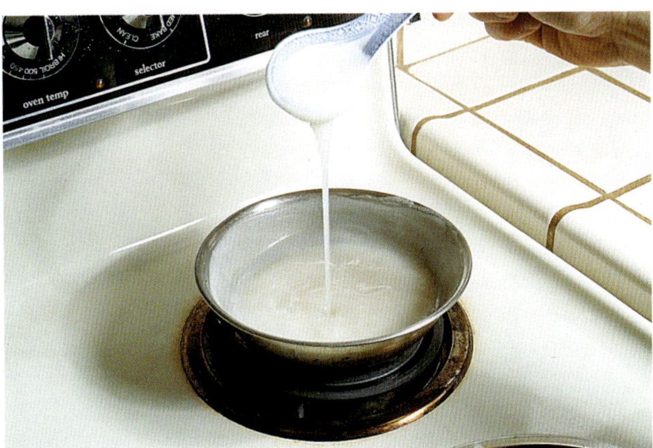

2 *BOIL THE STARCH AND WATER*
Place the bowl on the hob and heat, stirring the liquid slowly. Once the liquid comes to a boil, remove it from the heat.

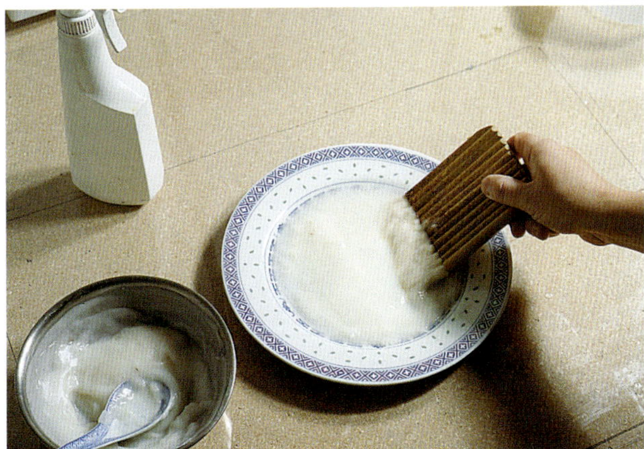

3 *THIN THE GRAVY*
As the gravy cools, it will thicken. Dilute some of it with two parts cold water to three parts gravy, pour the mixture onto a 25cm (10in) plate and stir with a large flat brush. Once the gravy and water are completely mixed, its texture will be similar to cooked clam chowder, as seen in the bowl on the right. Now it is ready to be used for stretching.

Stretching the Painting

The painting will be totally wet during the stretching process. Since Chinese ink and colours are made with special binders that are absorbed into the rice paper's fibres, there will be very little or no blending of colours when the whole painting is soaked. This is in contrast to most watercolours, which do blend.

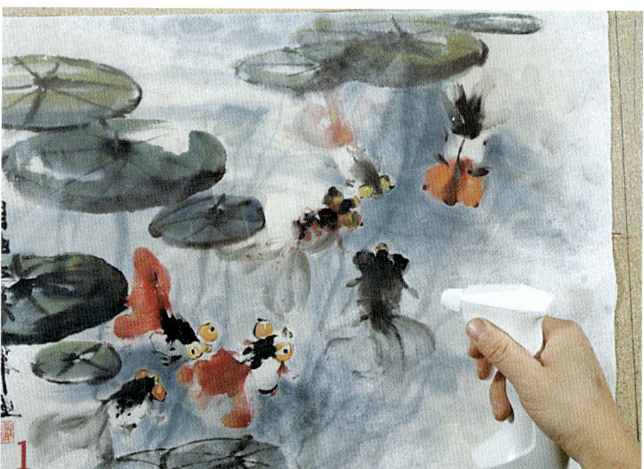

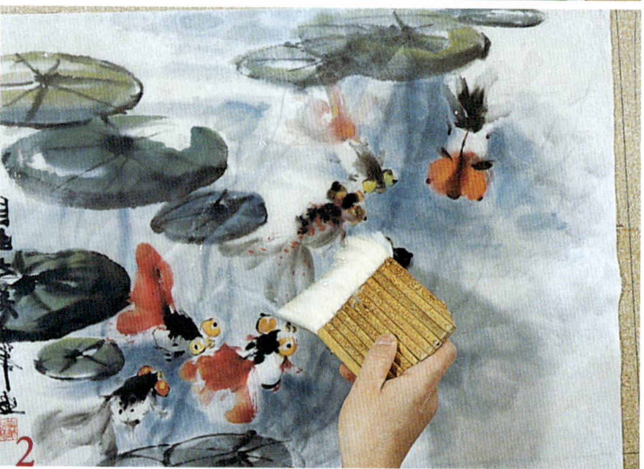

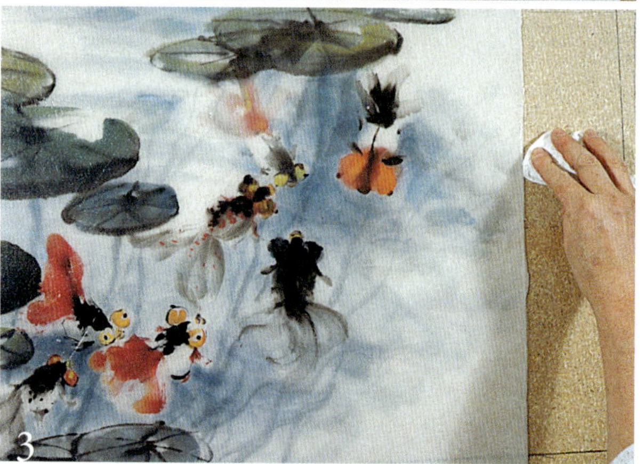

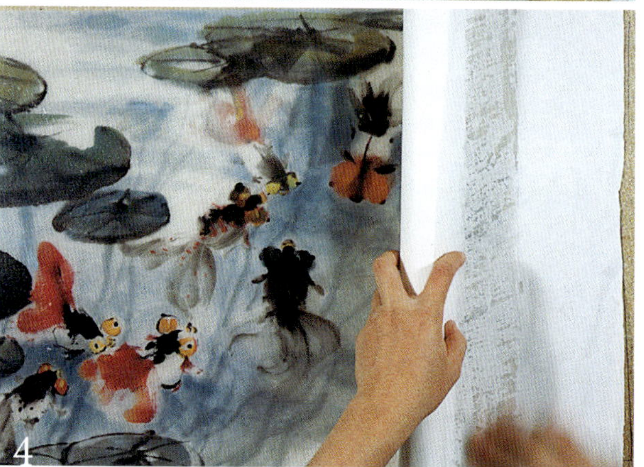

1 Wet the painting

Lay the painting upside down on the stretching surface, and align the right edge of the painting with the right edge of the rectangle. Locate the mid-points of both the painting and the rectangle. Next, use your water bottle to spray water on the painting lightly (don't totally wet it). As the painting softens and expands, use your fingers to carefully pull on the edges to remove any wrinkles. Then continue to spray more water on the painting until it is wet.

2 Apply the diluted gravy

While the painting is wet, soak the bristles of the flat brush with the diluted gravy and apply it to the painting, holding the brush at a 45° angle. Start brushing from the centre of the painting, working outwards to the edges. Do not touch the painting with the bamboo handle of the brush or you will break the painting. If the painting forms large wrinkles, use your fingers to lift up a corner, then slowly release it while carefully brushing the wrinkle towards the uplifted edge. Keep brushing the painting until there are no wrinkles and the painting is flat.

3 Clean up excess gravy

Use a paper or fabric towel to clean up, being careful not to touch the painting. Wash the fabric towel in water after each stretching.

4 Align the backing rice paper

Slide the stretching surface about 8cm (3in) towards the left side. The right edge of the painting is now 8cm (3in) away from the right edge of the rectangle. Roll up the rice paper backing, then align the right edge of the backing paper with the right edge of the rectangle. Measure the mid-points at the right edges to make sure the rice paper backing and the rectangle overlap each other. Next, press a small portion of the backing down to the painting.

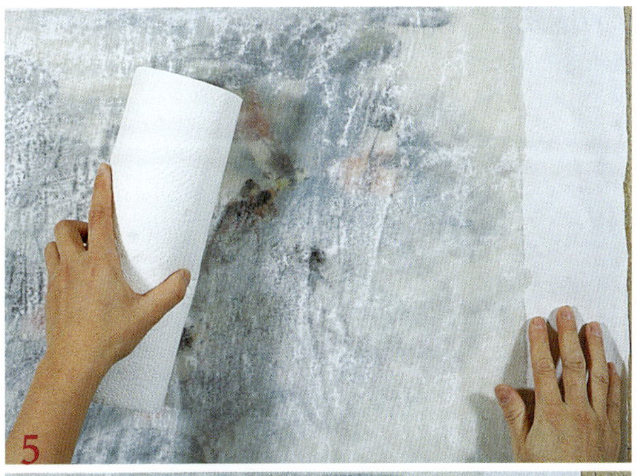

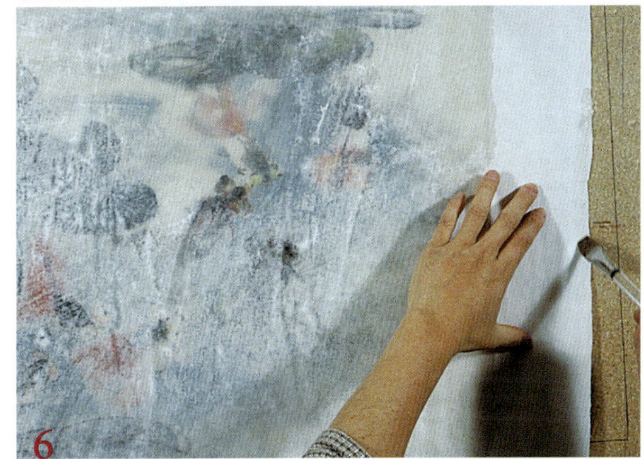

5 ***Attach the rice paper backing***

With your left hand, slowly unroll the backing paper while your right hand continually presses it down onto the painting. Cover the entire painting. Use a paper towel roll immediately, to smooth and reinforce the attachment of the rice paper backing. Lightly press the roll to the backing and slowly work from the centre of the painting towards the edges. Smooth the whole surface of the painting a couple of times.

6 ***Apply thick gravy to the edges***

Use your 19mm (¾in) watercolour brush to apply the thick gravy (not the diluted one) to all edges of the rice paper backing in about a 19mm (¾in) width. Do not drop the gravy on the rest of the backing.

7 ***Lift the rice paper backing and the painting***

Start lifting both the rice paper backing and the painting, starting at one corner and using both hands. Sometimes the backing will not attach to the painting strongly enough to allow you to lift them together. In such cases, release the corner and press it down with your fingers to create a stronger attachment to both the backing and painting. Try to lift the corner again.

8 ***Mount for drying***

After lifting the rice paper backing and the painting together from the stretching surface, paste the edges of the backing on the mounting surface for drying. I use a large sheet of MDF. Make sure all perimeters of the backing are securely attached to the surface.

After a few hours to a full day, depending on the temperature of the room you're working in, everything should be dry. At that time, use a sharp blade to cut under the perimeter of the rice paper, separating the painting and backing from the mounting surface. Finally, the stretched painting is ready for matting and framing.

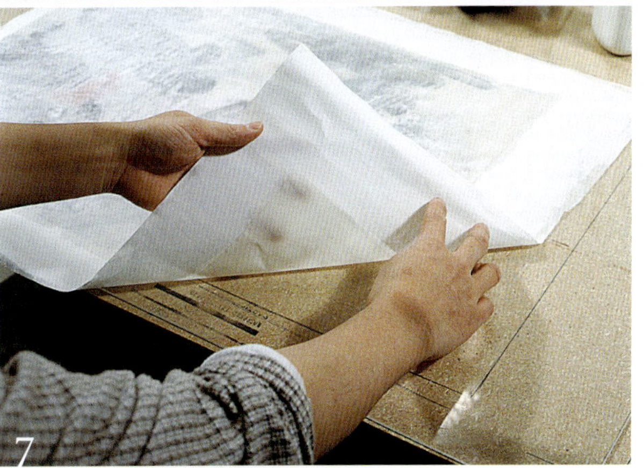

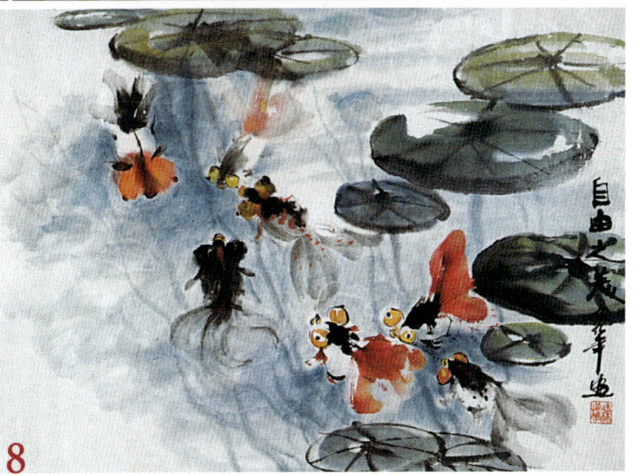

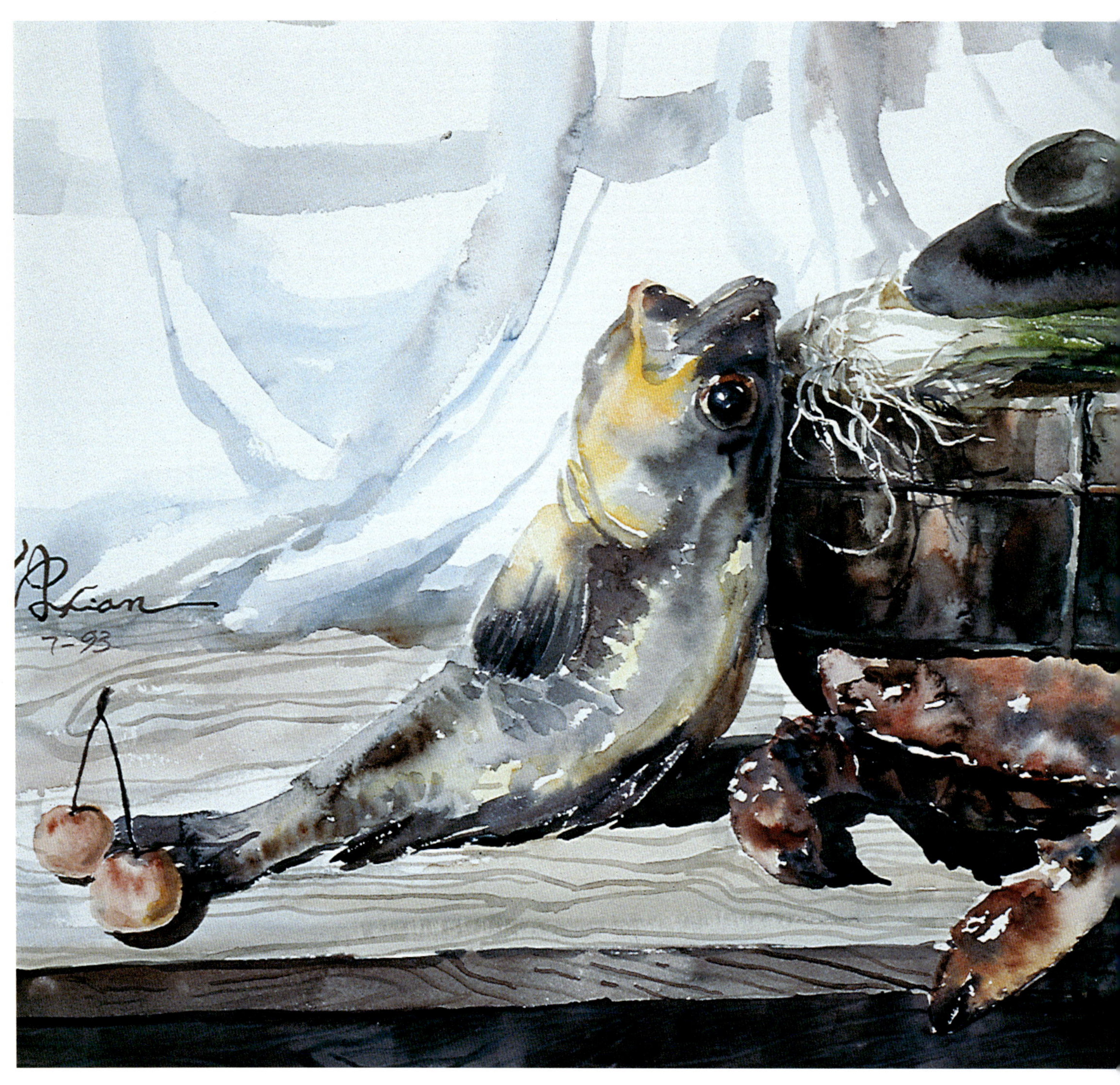

FISH AND CRABS
34 x 51cm (13¼ x 20in)
Chinese ink and colours on double-layer Shuan paper
Spontaneous style

...ION &

...NTING

...CHNIQUES

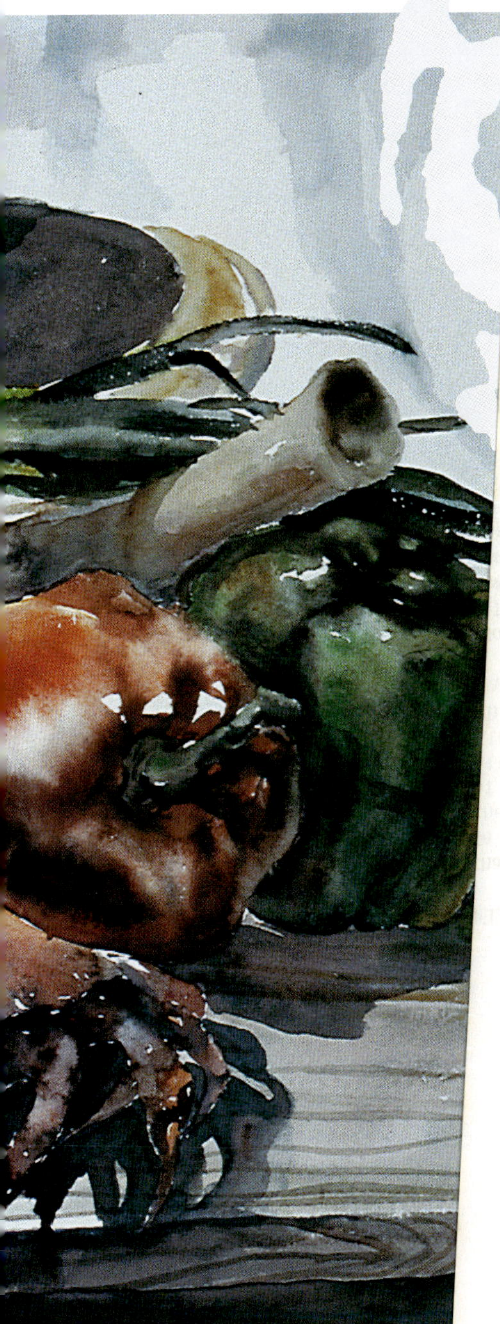

...ntings have unique

...cs. Besides the theory

...ls, special composition

...te to this distinguished

...uce you to the compo-

...ques. I recommend that

...practise the techniques

...ion chapters.

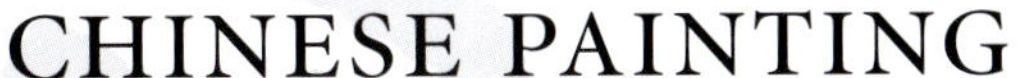

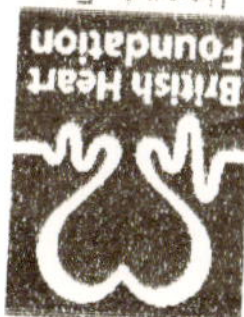

British Heart Foundation
Unit 22 Victoria Centre
Crewe
Cheshire
CW1 2PU

Branch No: C50
Telephone: 01270 580 326

Charity Reg. No England & Wales (225971)
Charity Reg. No Scotland (SC039426)
Vat Registration No. 626 921 824

SALE REF 6750   1 153161   16/08/2014 13:52

Today you were served by TINA

Non Fiction Books
184   1x   2.50   2.50

TOTAL   ITEMS   1   2.50

CASH   £3.00
CASH   -£0.50

Thank you for shopping with us today.
Through your support, you have
made a difference to the fight against
heart disease.
Please keep your receipt as proof of
purchase.

COMPOSITION METHODS

Chinese painting composition is special in terms of linear perspective; priority of objects; balance and the relationship between line, point and surface; geometric organization; and, finally, placement of calligraphy and chops.

Linear Perspective

Linear perspective is the primary composition method in Chinese painting. It does not create camera-defined views; rather, it generates multi-vanishing-point scenes. For example, when you are close to a large, horizontal fish tank, you move from one end to the other to see the fish. If you combine every portion of what you see from every angle to organize a painting, you will create a linear perspective composition painting. (Imagine taking photos while moving from one end of the fish tank to the other, then laying the photos out horizontally, end to end.)

Priority of Objects

You should clearly define the major and minor objects of your paintings. The 'major object' is the focal point of a painting. It should have more details and outstanding colours than the other objects in the piece. 'Minor objects', on the other hand, support the major object. They have fewer details and less intense hues. In most cases, the major object occupies a primary space in a painting. Therefore, it captures viewers' attention. However, the primary object is not necessarily the largest object in a painting or centrally located.

The way of organizing major and minor objects can also be applied to details within individual objects. When painting a bird, for instance, I do not paint its eyes, beak, feathers and legs with the same level of detail; rather, I emphasize one or a few features as focal points of the bird.

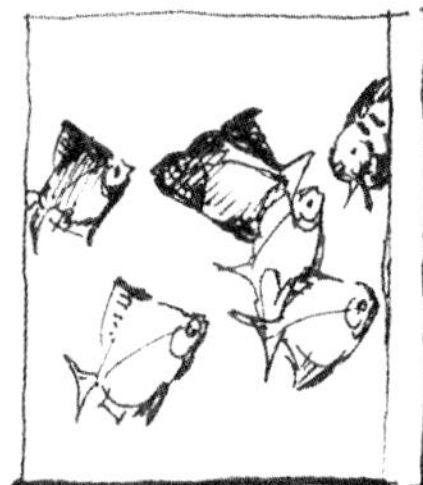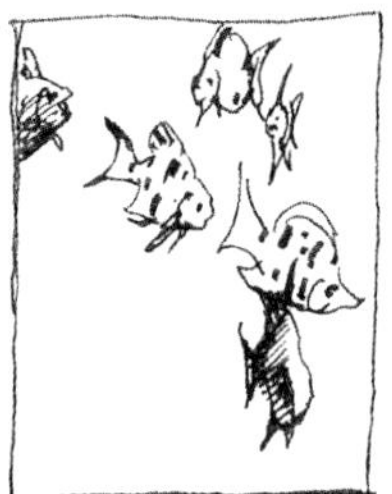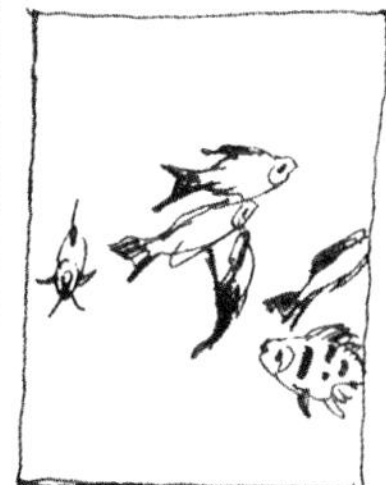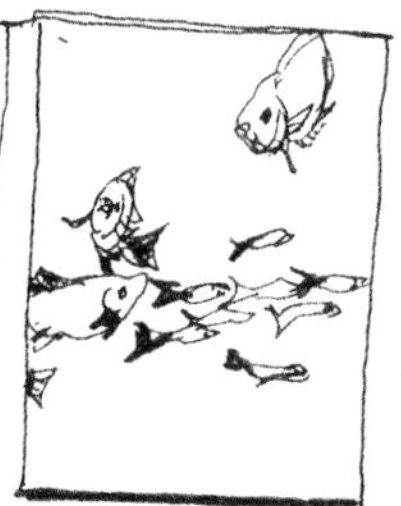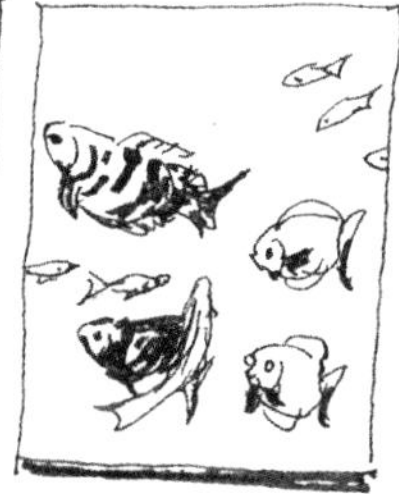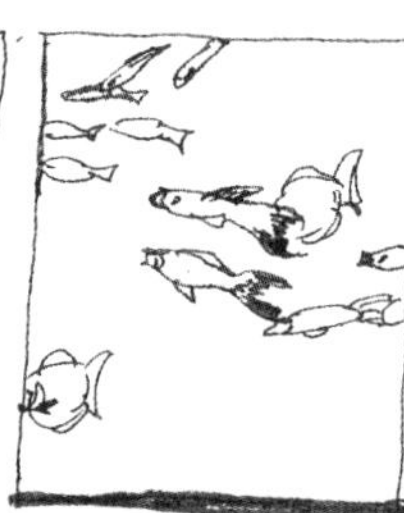

Linear Perspective
These six individual scenes can be put together to form an elongated painting.

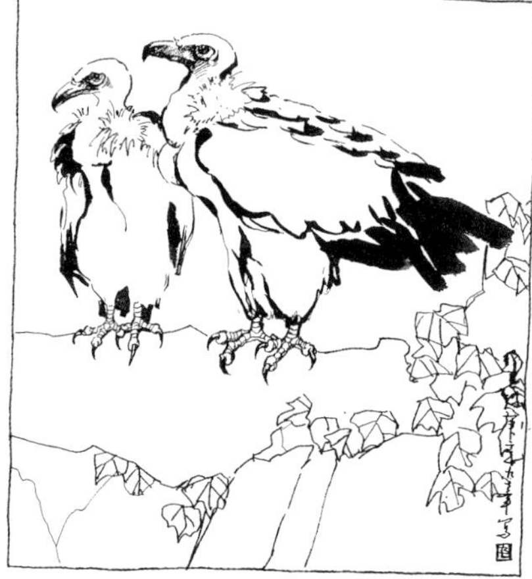

Priority of Features Within an Object
The vultures' heads, eyes and feet are emphasized with more details because they are the primary features that represent the birds' spirits.

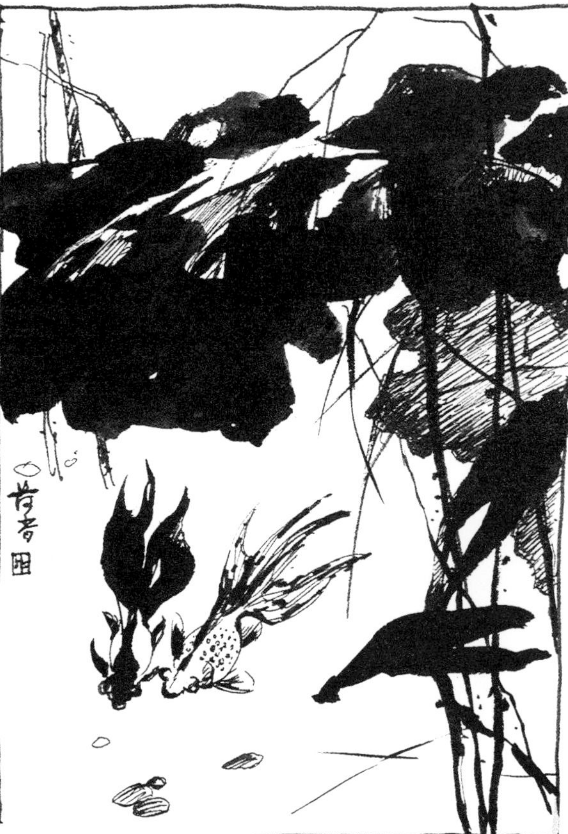

Priority of Objects Within a Painting
The goldfish are the primary objects in this painting, so they feature more detail than the larger lotus leaves.

Establishing Priority

There are five ways to establish priority
and emphasize a major object: make
it larger, direct eye flow, group small
objects, use large to emphasize small and
contrast colour.

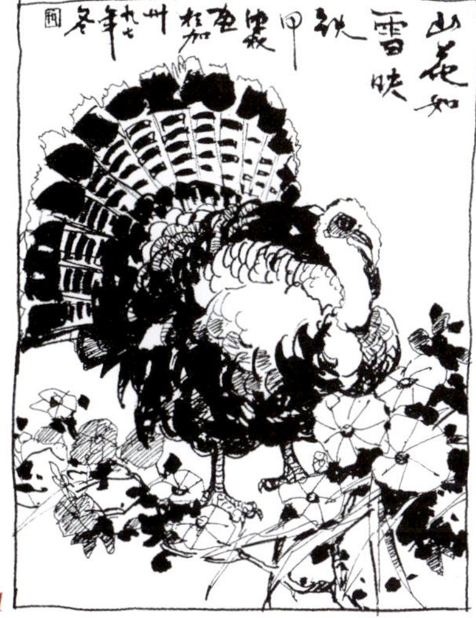

1

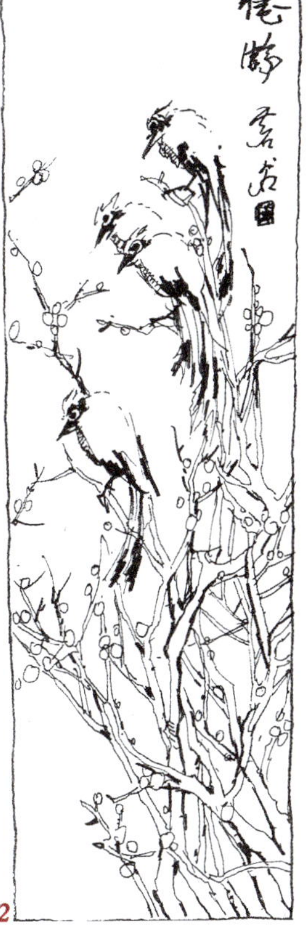

2

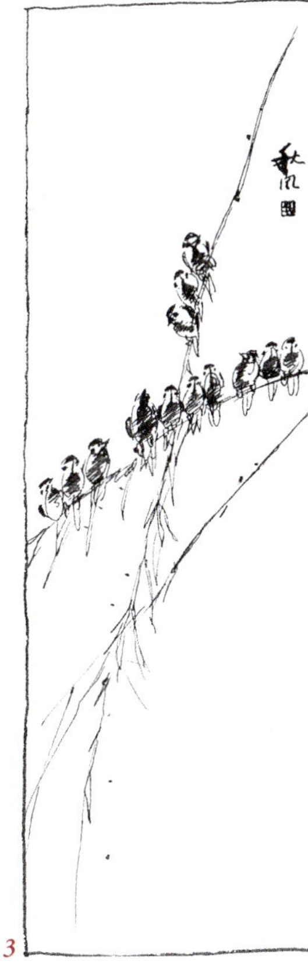

3

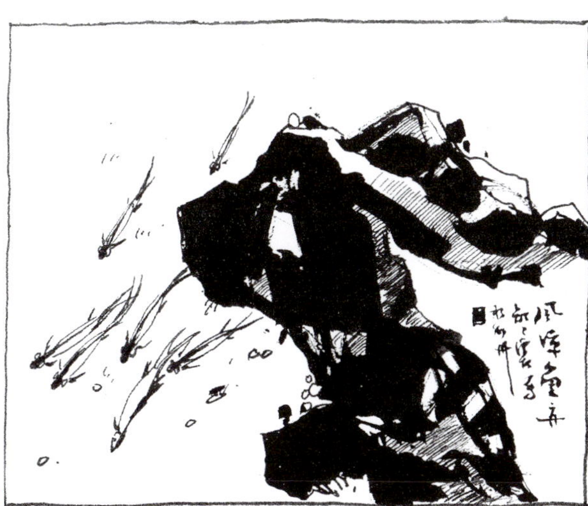

4

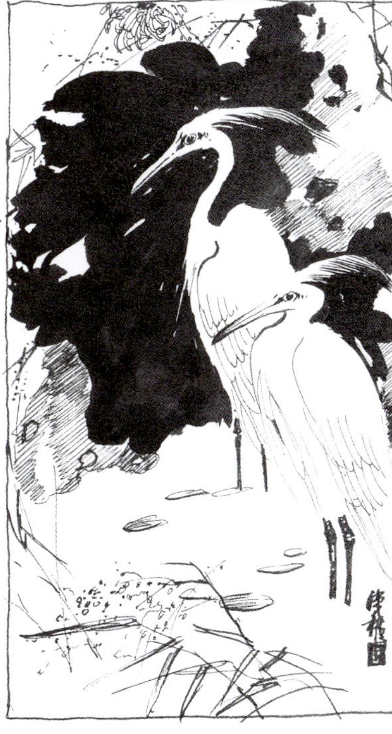

5

*Technique 1: Dominant
Objects* Paint the major object
larger so it dominates the whole
composition. In this painting,
the turkey completely dominates
the composition with its outstanding size. It is the main object. In contrast, the flowers are
smaller. They are minor objects.

*Technique 2: Directing Eye
Flow* Use minor objects to
direct the viewers' eyes towards
the major object. This is useful
when choosing a small-scale object as the major object. Here, the
branches of the flowering tree
point upwards. They guide viewers' eyes towards the primary objects: the birds on the top.

*Technique 3: Group Small
Objects* When a major object
is too small, paint a group of
them as the major object to capture viewers' attention. In this
painting, one sparrow is tiny, but
two groups of sparrows form
primary objects.

*Technique 4: Large
Emphasizes Small* The oppo-
site of technique 1. Use large,
undetailed minor objects to
emphasize the small major
object. The big rock in the fore-
ground of this piece occupies
more than half of the composition, but it is neither active nor
emphasized with details. In contrast, the fish are in motion and
they have more details than the
rock. As a result, the fish are the
primary objects.

*Technique 5: Colour
Contrasting* Dark and light,
black and white, are contrasting
colours. Use them as pairs for
strong effects and to emphasize
major objects. Here, the lotus
leaves in the background are
black, making the primary objects, the white egrets, stand out.

Balance

Balance in Chinese painting is relative. It is not simply a matter of putting objects in the centre of a painting. When you place an object in the centre, the composition is in perfect balance; however, it is not interesting. An objects' weight, colours, activities and surfaces can all determine balance.

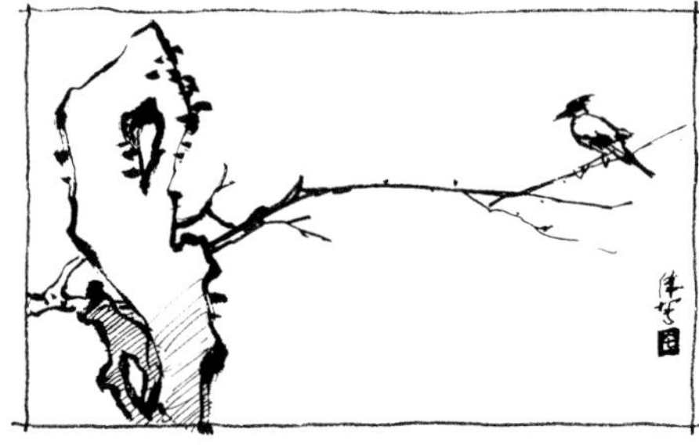

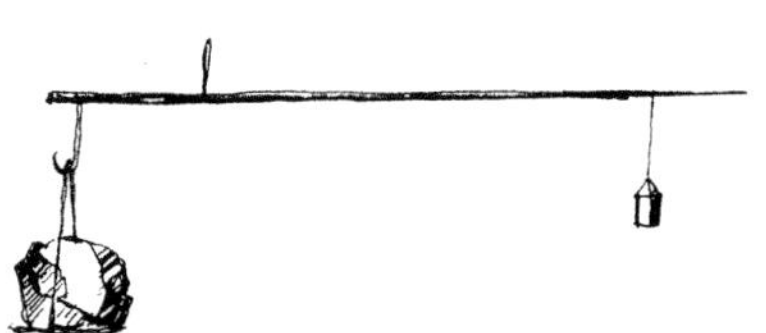

Weight Balance

When you play on a seesaw with a small child, you must move closer to the pivot point in order to achieve balance. In a painting, objects can balance each other in the same way. In this painting, the bird is much smaller and lighter than the rock. Nevertheless, they are visually balanced because the bird occupies much more area than the rock.

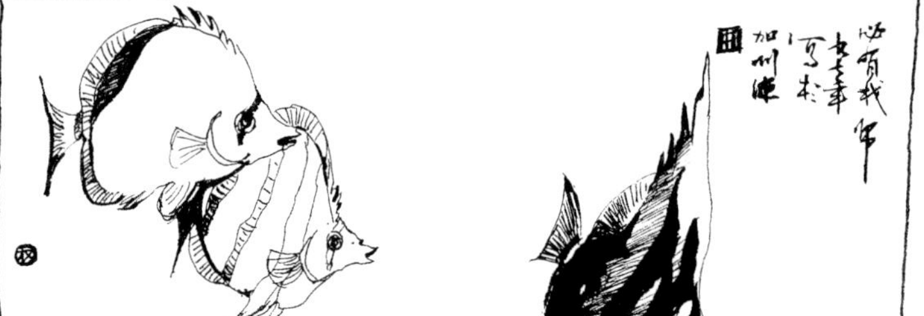

Colour Balance

Colour balance is based on colour contrast. You can use warm colour to balance cool colour, and bright hues to balance dark hues. However, do not give the contrasting colours identical amounts of space. One colour should be dominant. In this sketch, the two white fish on the left balance the black fish on the right. The contrasting perception of the colours achieves balance because black is visually heavier than white.

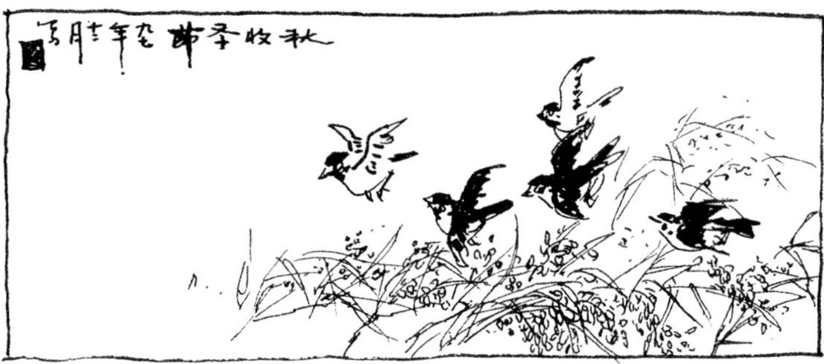

Activity Balance

Active objects tend to occupy more space on a painting than inactive objects. Still objects, such as rocks and trees, are stable and require very little or no movement space. Here, the left side of this sketch has a large open area, but you do not feel it is really empty since the flying birds are moving towards it.

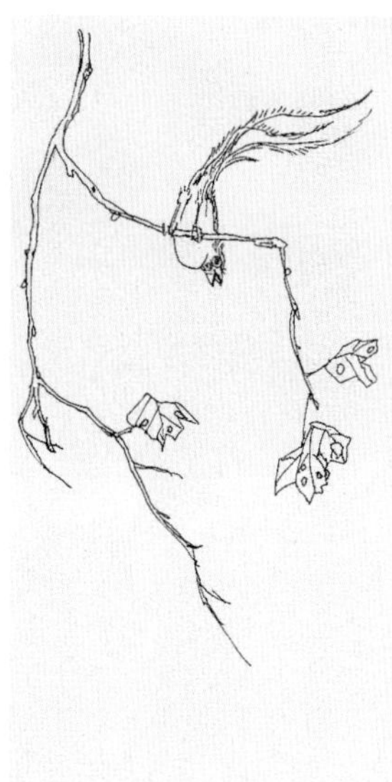

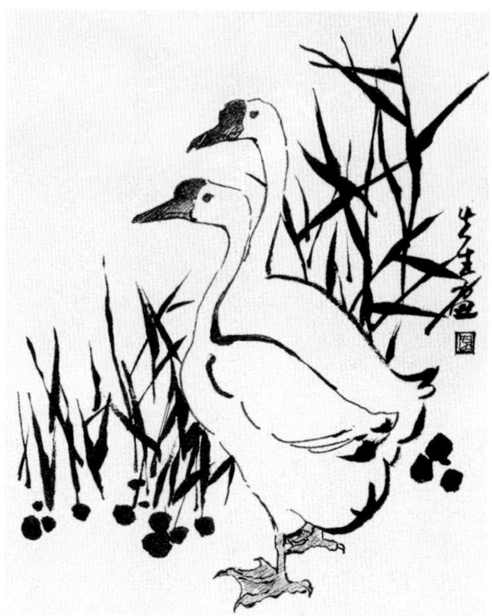

Line, Point and Surface Balance

Even though Chinese painting is mainly line art, points and surfaces are essential elements. A painting that has a combination and integration of these three elements carries more dramatic effect than a line-only painting, because the elements balance each other. In the far left sketch, notice how the subject matter is drawn with lines only, lacking any attractive visual effects. But the manipulation of those lines, points and surfaces, as shown in the sketch on the right, creates a harmonic and beautiful impression.

Geometric Organization

In Chinese painting it is common to group objects into a geometric shape, such as a circle, arc, triangle, rectangle or an S shape,

Though sometimes hidden when viewed up close, the geometric shapes reveal themselves if you view the paintings from a distance.

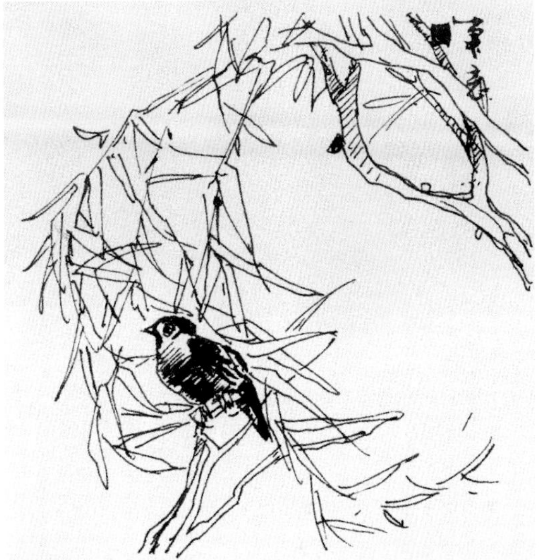

Circular Composition

A circular composition involves arranging objects and their activities in a circular structure. This technique encourages motion of the objects and generates forces towards the centre of a painting. The objects in these two sketches (left and below right) are arranged in circular shapes.

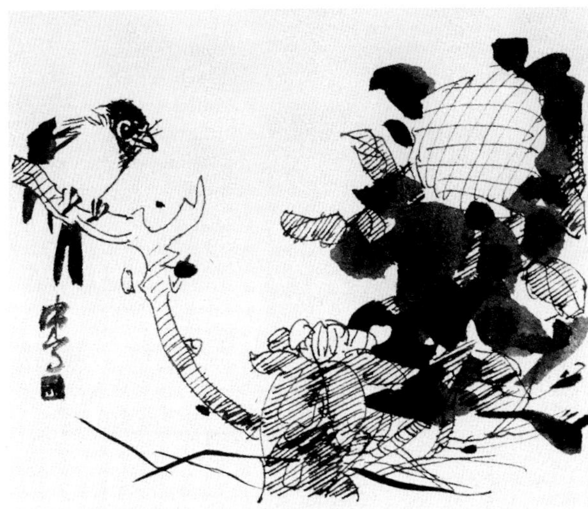

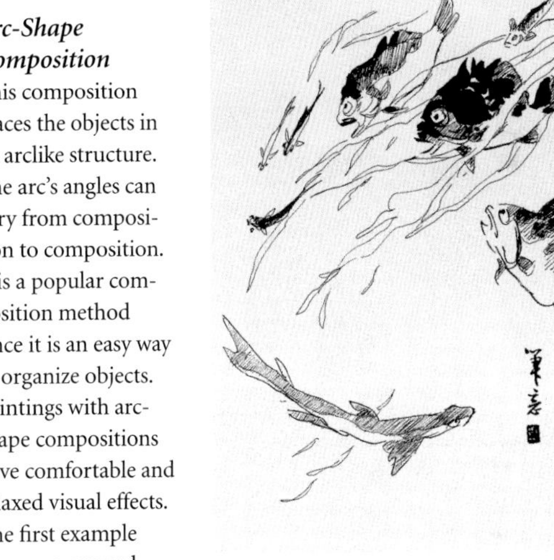

Arc-Shape Composition

This composition places the objects in an arclike structure. The arc's angles can vary from composition to composition. It is a popular composition method since it is an easy way to organize objects. Paintings with arc-shape compositions have comfortable and relaxed visual effects. The first example shows an upward-curving arc that creates dynamic visual tension between the bird and the sun-. flower. The second example shows a downward-curving arc, emphasizing the bird on the top of the geometric shape.

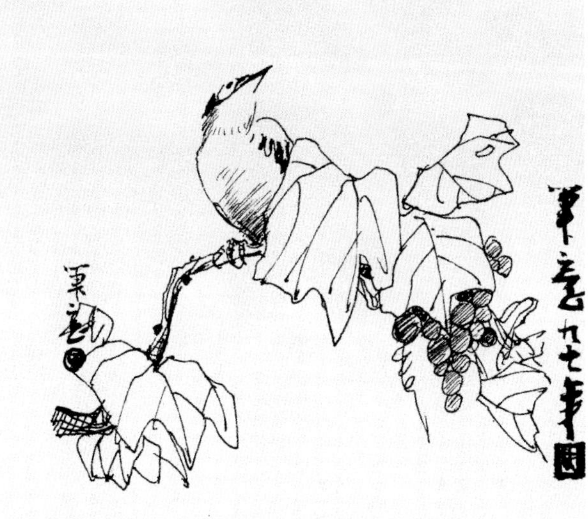

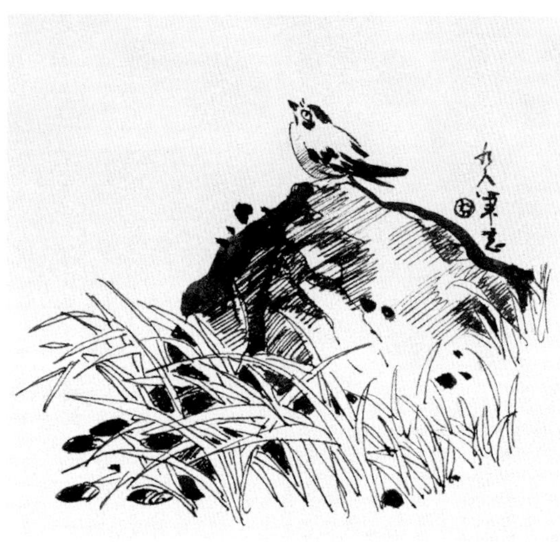

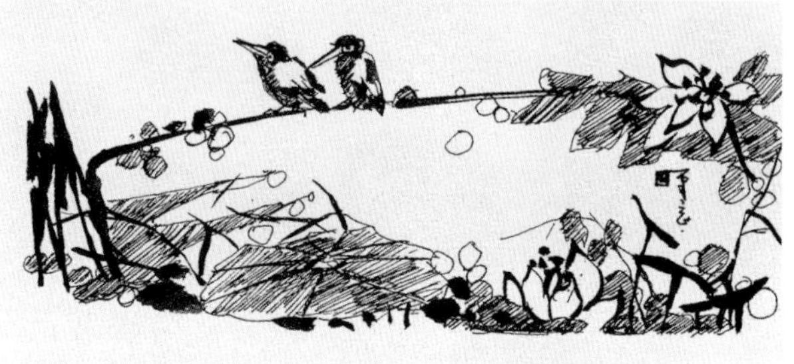

Triangular Composition

A triangular composition gives an impression of stability and inactivity if you place the objects as a pyramid near the centre of the painting. On the other hand, this compositional method depicts dynamic motion if the objects are arranged in a tilted triangular shape. In the first example (left), the rock looks heavy and stable and the bird seems quiet. That is because of the pyramid-shaped composition. In the second composition (lower left), the koi form a tilted triangular shape that enhances the movement of the fish.

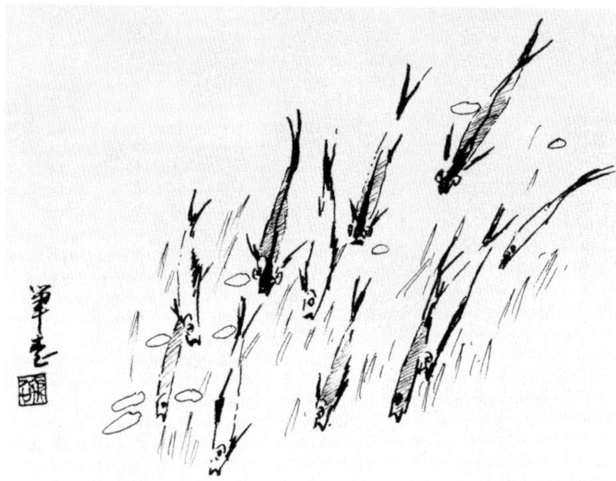

Rectangular Composition

Here objects are placed in a rectangular structure. The objects will appear relatively stable if the rectangle is placed in near alignment with the edges of the painting, as in the first example (above). In the second composition, however, the fish are arranged in a rectangular shape that tilts approximately 40° from the bottom edge of the sketch. The unstable placement of the rectangle further emphasizes the motion of the fish.

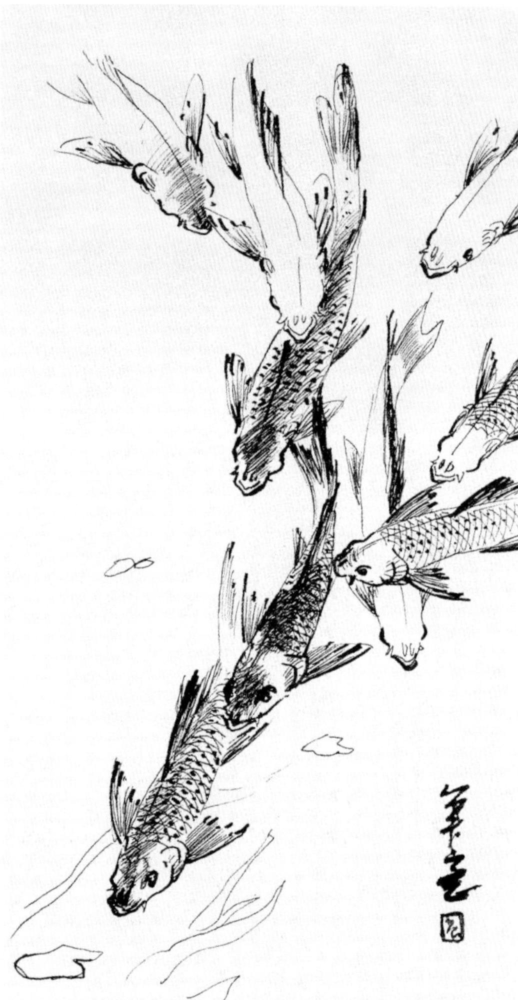

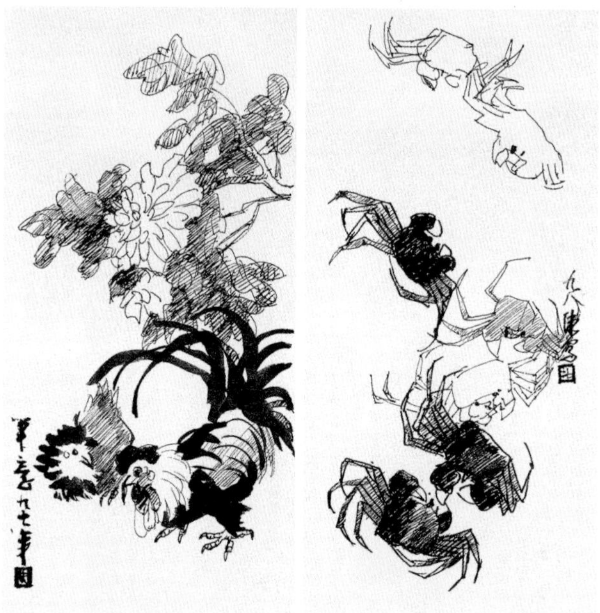

S-Shape Composition

Here objects are placed on an S-shaped path. It is a common composition in elongated paintings in which brief moments of dramatic activity are captured. In the first example, the rooster and hen seem to be communicating and interacting with each other. In the second example, the S-shape makes the normally slow-moving crabs appear more active.

Using Calligraphy and Chops to Balance the Composition

Before the Southern Sung dynasty (AD 1127–1279), artists did not inscribe poems or stamp their seals on paintings. Instead, they hid their signatures in the objects they painted. Inscription and sealing on paintings became favourable for three reasons. First was the development of the spontaneous scholar style. The artists of scholar style advocated the three perfections of calligraphy, poetry and painting. Second, artists left larger unpainted spaces on their paintings that were perfect for inscriptions and seals. Last and most important, artists inscribed phrases and poems to express their ideas, feelings and philosophies in relation to their paintings' images.

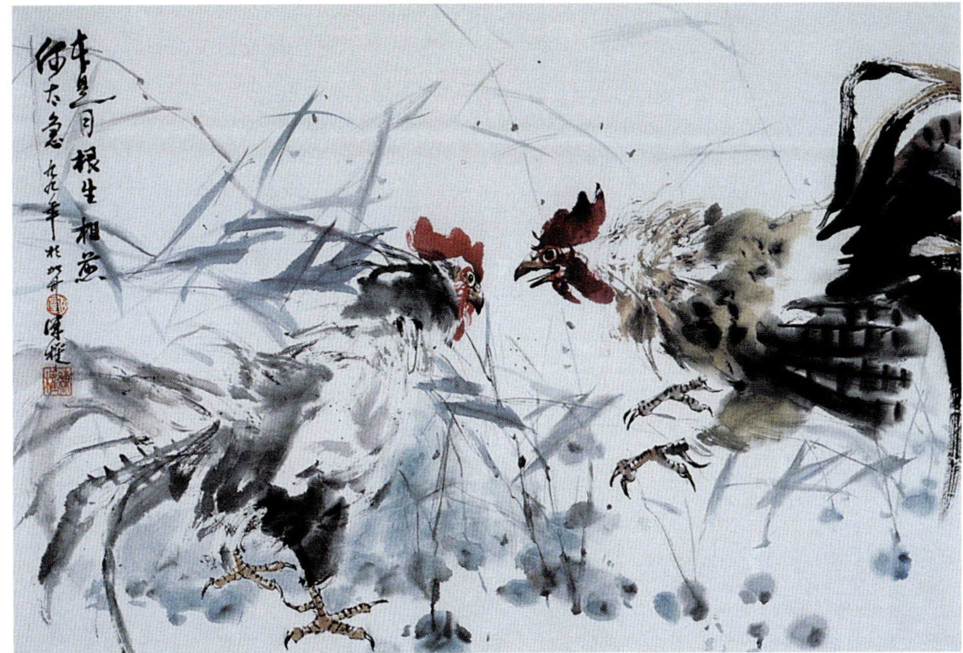

Balancing With Calligraphy

The calligraphy on the upper left balances the composition and expresses my idea. I quoted the last two lines of the famous *Seven-Step Poem* from the Three Kingdoms period, about 1,800 years ago. During this period, a king who was afraid his intelligent brother would try to take over the throne devised this plot against him. The king ordered his brother to chant a poem after walking seven steps. If the brother could not finish on time, the king would kill him. At the final step, his brother chanted the poem:

> *Grinding beans for juice,*
> *To make meat and bean soup.*
> *Burning the bean shells and their stems,*
> *While the beans in the pot are cooked.*
> *Coming from the same root,*
> *Why do they destroy each other so rude?*

Thus the painting is not only art but also an assertion of my point of view on humanity.

TWO FIGHTING ROOSTERS
46 x 69cm (18 x 27in)
Chinese ink and colours on single-layer Shuan paper
Spontaneous style

Breaking the Lines

If you draw lines through each group of objects in a Chinese painting, you will see they cross each other. One of the lines represents the primary force and direction of eye flow in the painting. The others indicate minor forces and secondary objects. The quantity of the lines is usually an odd number. Most of the minor lines break and integrate with the major line to create an interesting composition.

In each of the sketches on this page, a broader line represents a major object, with an arrow indicating the force and direction of flow. The narrower lines represent minor objects.

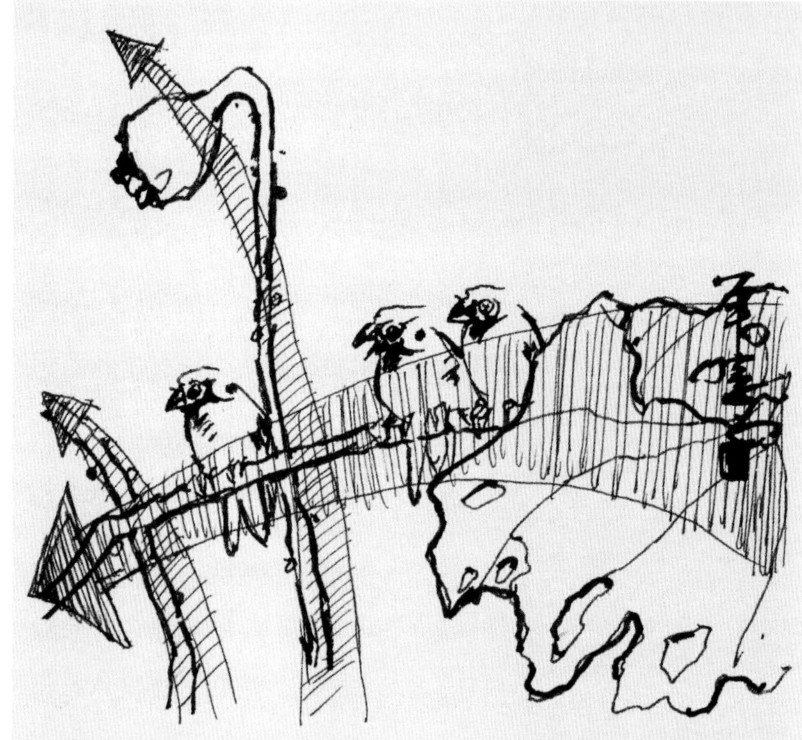

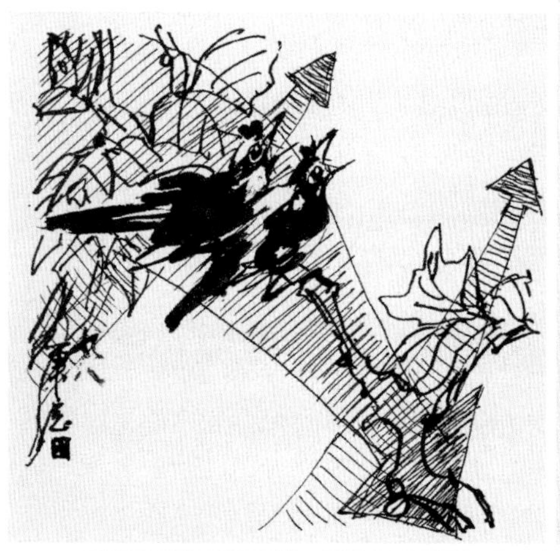

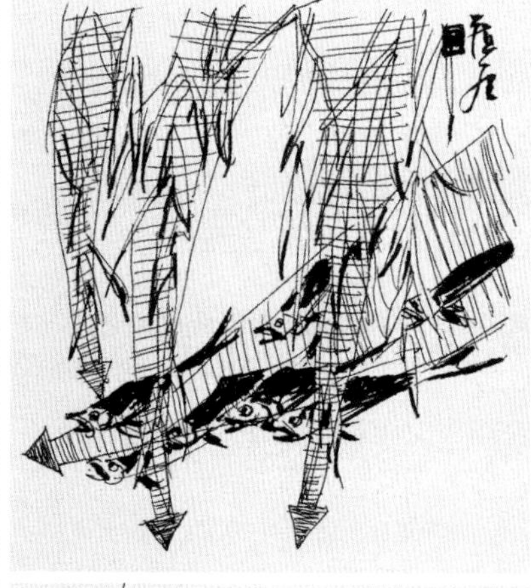

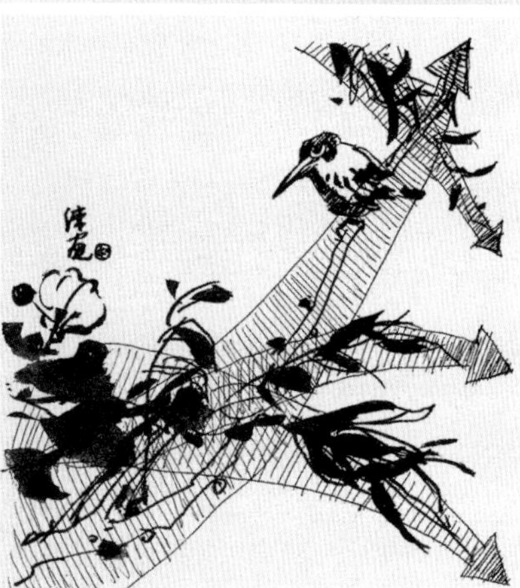

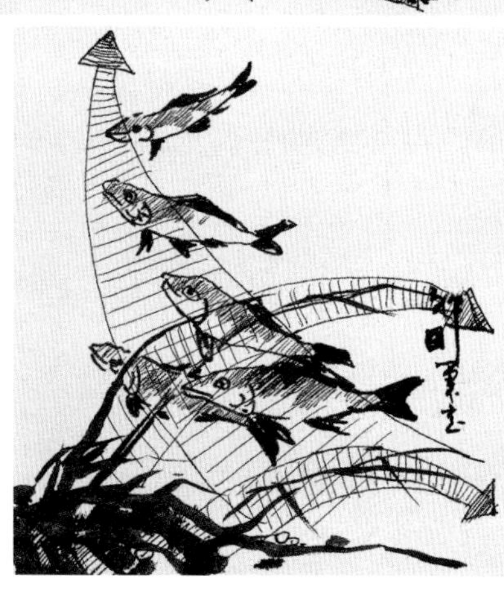

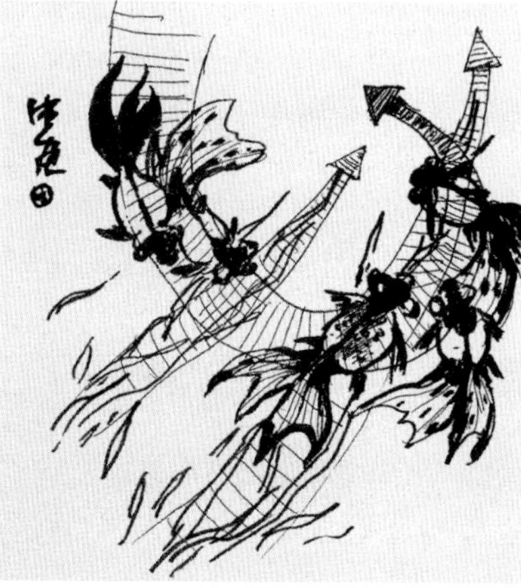

DETAIL-STYLE PAINTING TECHNIQUES

Generally, artists begin detail-style paintings by using light ink to outline objects in a controlled manner. Detail-style painting also takes a much longer time to finish than the spontaneous style. The following are the basic techniques and sequences of detail-style painting. Though each step comes from a different painting, each represents a critical stage in a typical detail-style painting.

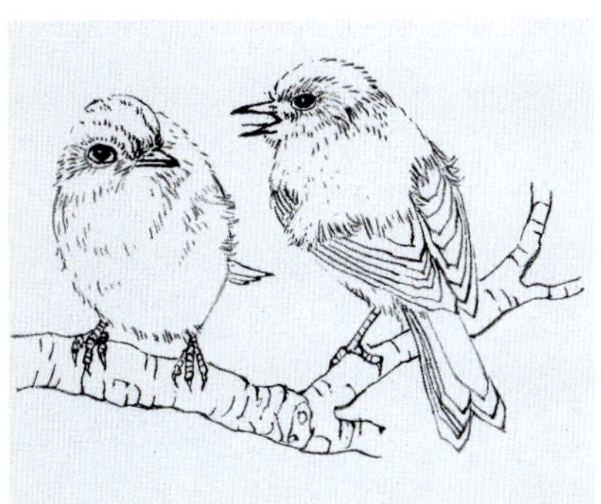

1 *PAINT FIRST OUTLINE*

Use small, pointed hard-fur brushes to paint the outlines of the objects. Hold the brush at the centre-brush angle to paint fluid, elastic and confident strokes. Outline the eyes, beaks and legs with intense ink and the rest with light ink. Paint the brushstrokes according to the feathers' growth directions.

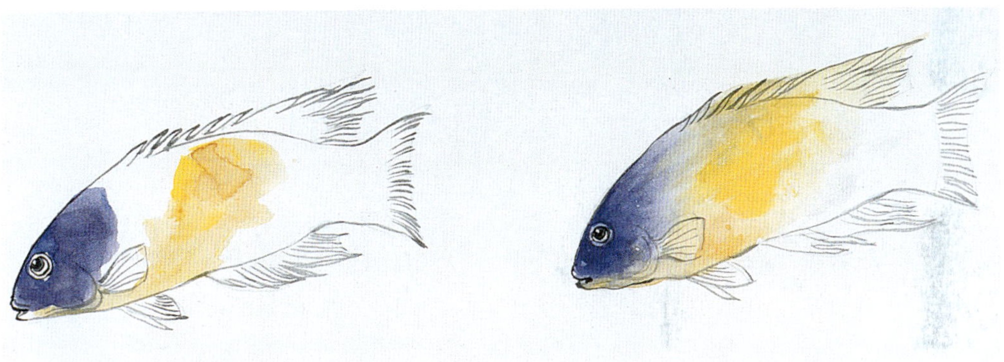

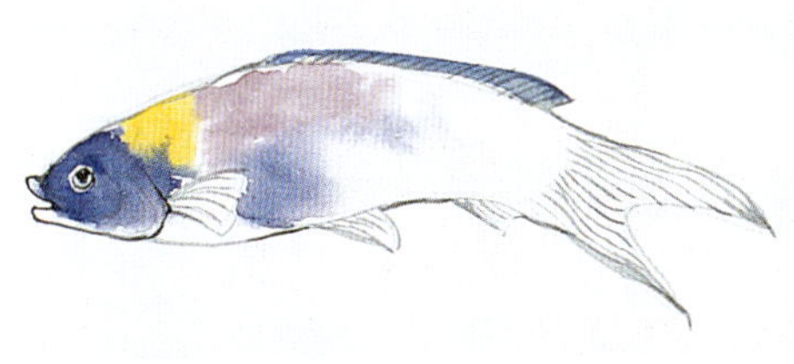

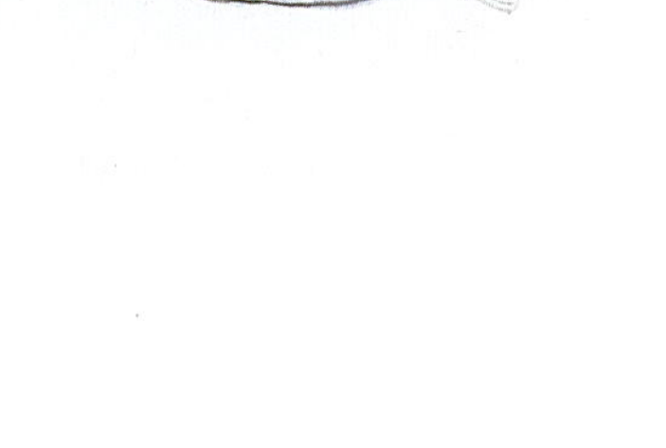

2 *ADD FIRST LAYER OF COLOUR*

When you have finished the first outline process, use light ink and colours to fill the spaces between the outlines as the first layer of colouring. There are two ways to apply the ink and colours. Using the first way, 'dry colouring' (left), apply the ink and colours to a dry area and use clear water to drag and blend them within the outlines. This is similar to watercolour's wet-into-dry technique. For the second method, 'wet colouring' (right), wet the area between the outlines before applying the ink and colours. This is similar to watercolour's wet-into-wet technique. Soft-fur brushes are commonly used for colouring.

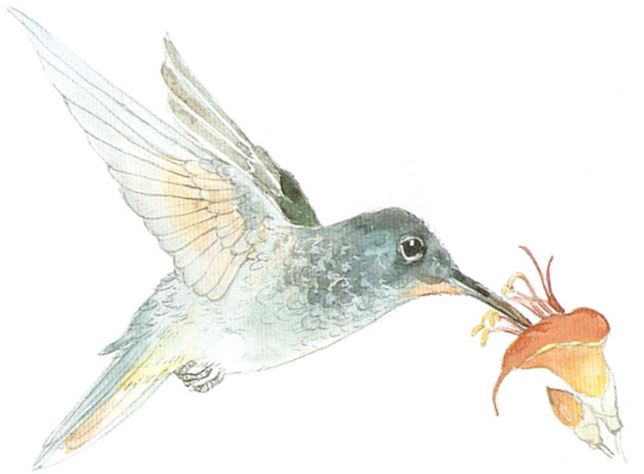

3 *ADD MULTIPLE LAYERS OF COLOUR*

Add multiple layers of colours in order to achieve the appropriate intensity and textures. When the first layer of colour dries, apply a second layer and continue the same process until the desired effects are achieved. I usually apply the ink and colours at least three times. Amazingly, it does not make the paintings dirty as easily as with watercolours. As you can see on the left, the first layer of colour does not reach the desired intensity. But after multiple layers of colour, as shown in the middle painting, everything becomes vibrant and alive.

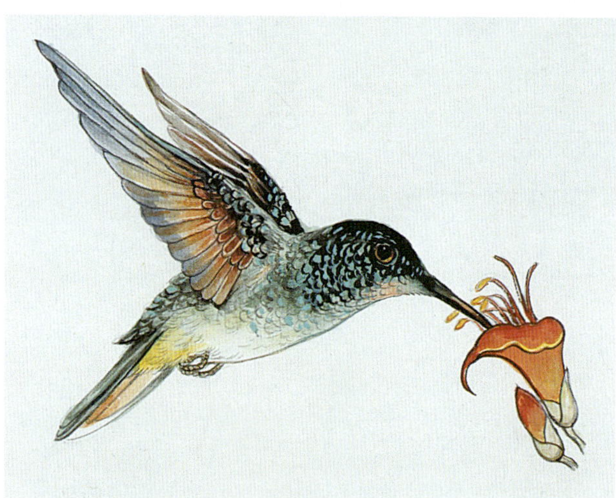

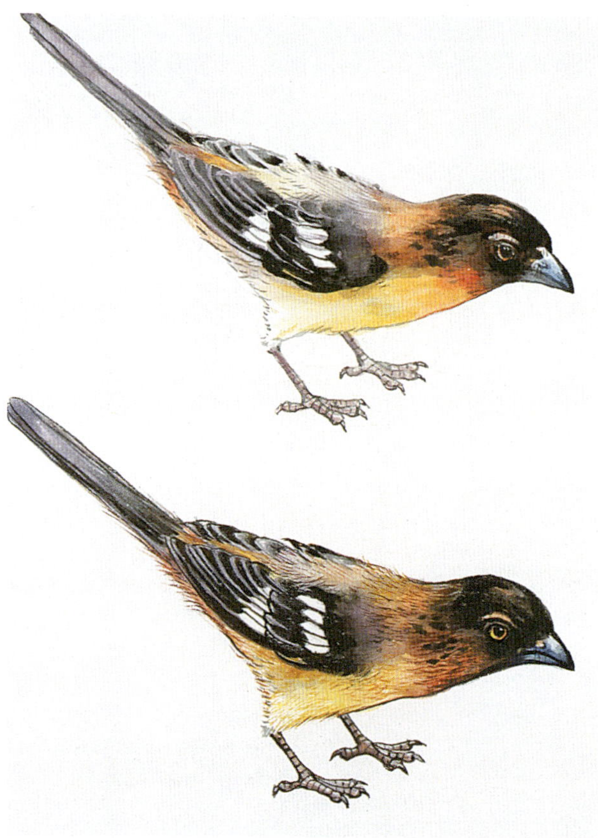

4 *OUTLINE AGAIN*

Some outlines will partly disappear after applying colours, as shown in the top bird (left). Paint the outlines again with ink and colour, as shown in the bottom bird. Use colours that are more intense than the colours painted on the objects. For example, if you paint a tail yellow, use orange combined with light ink for the second outlines. Likewise, if you paint fish scales red, mix rouge with intense ink.

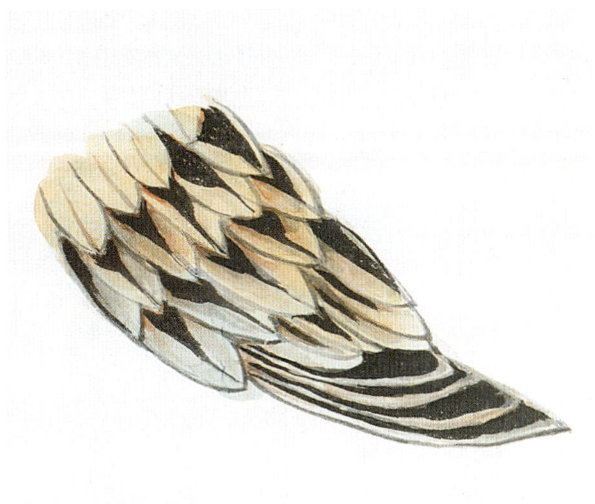

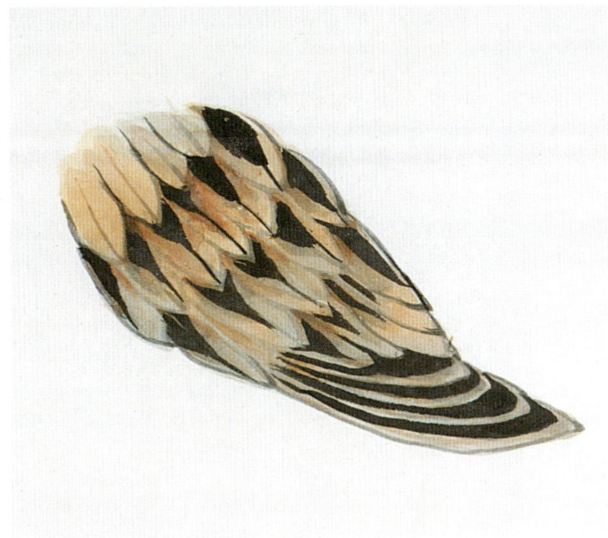

5 Glaze

Adding one or several layers of colours over a large painted area, such as the feathers of wings, is called 'glazing'. It serves the purpose of uniting a variety of colours. Some Chinese colours are transparent if you apply them as thin layers. Among them are yellow, red, carmine, indigo and light ink. The wing on the left is shown before glazing, while the wing on the right illustrates the effects of glazing with a thin layer of cinnabar.

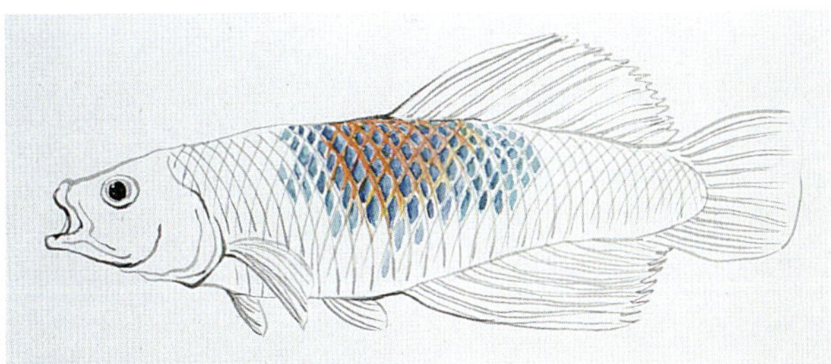

6 Leave white edges

Leave white edges to define small details. For example, when painting fish and birds, leave a narrow white line on the edge of each scale and feather. Then apply less intense colours or ink on the white lines to define the scales and feathers clearly.

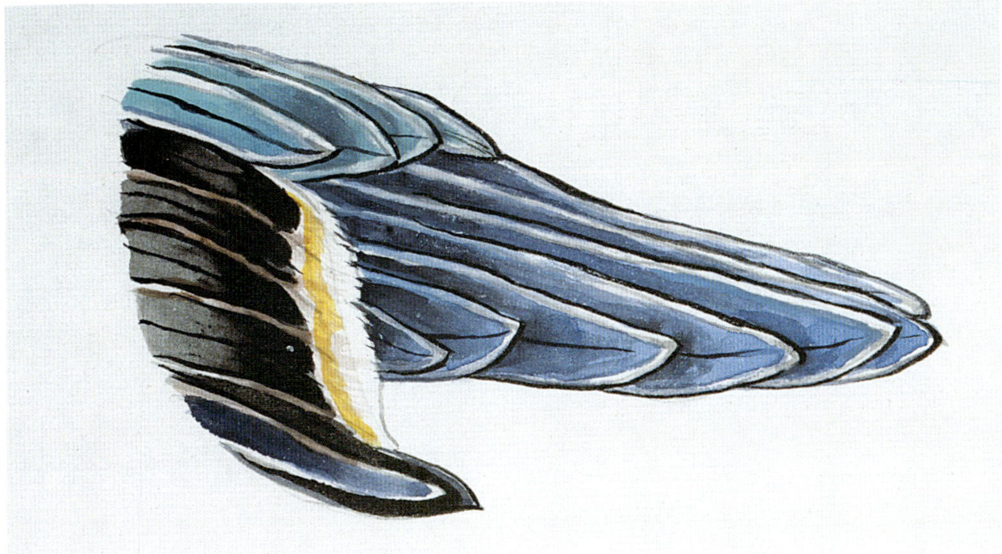

Creating Feather and Fin Textures

There are two methods you can use to create bird feathers and fish fins. The first way is to use a small, pointed brush to paint each feather or fin carefully according to its growth direction. Another way is to form the tip of a used brush into a loose shape and then paint in overlapping strokes to suggest detail.

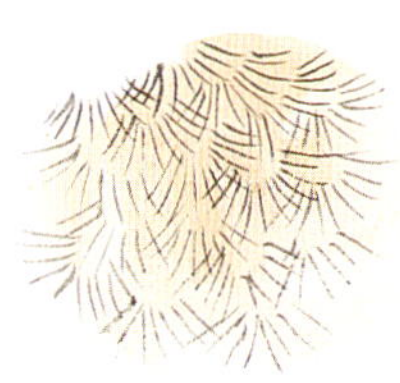

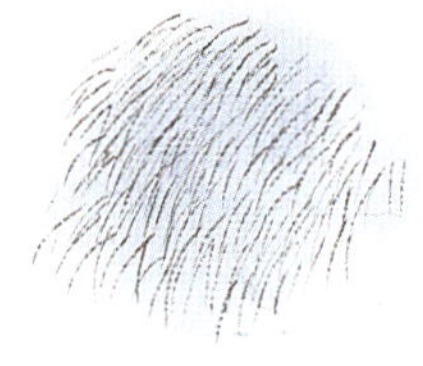

Method 1
Use a small, hard-fur brush and ink to illustrate each feather. Then apply colours over the strokes.

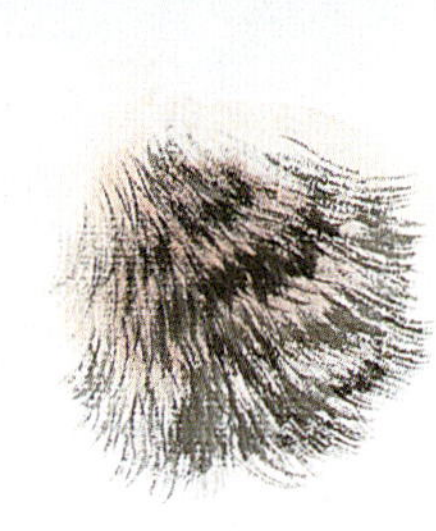

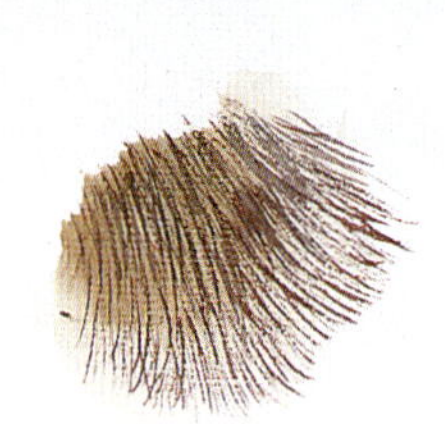

Method 2
Use a loose-tipped brush and ink to paint groups of strokes overlapping each other. Next, apply colours over the strokes.

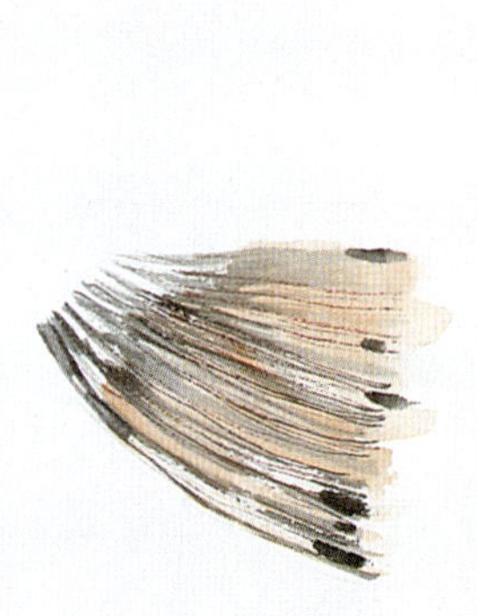

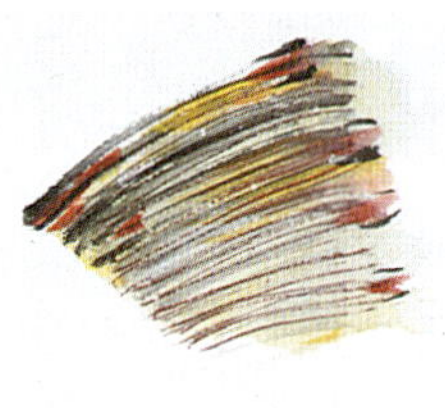

Combining Methods 1 and 2
Use the small, hard-fur brush to paint individual strokes, creating the texture of the fins. Then use the loose-tipped brush to paint over the individual strokes. Finally, paint colours on top of the strokes.

BALD EAGLE IN DETAIL STYLE

This four-step bald eagle painting demonstration will provide you with a better understanding of the techniques and process of detail-style paintings.

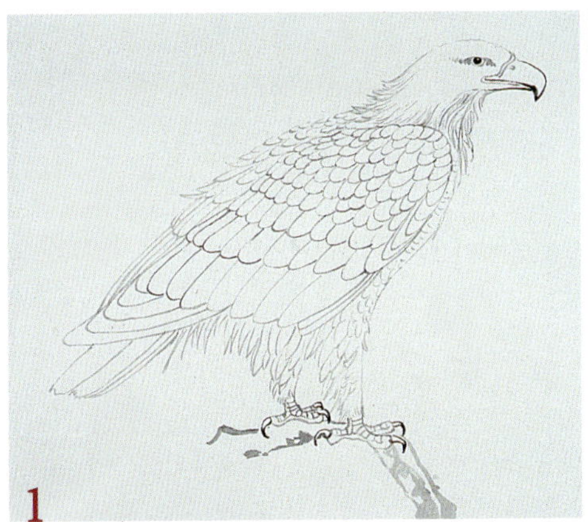

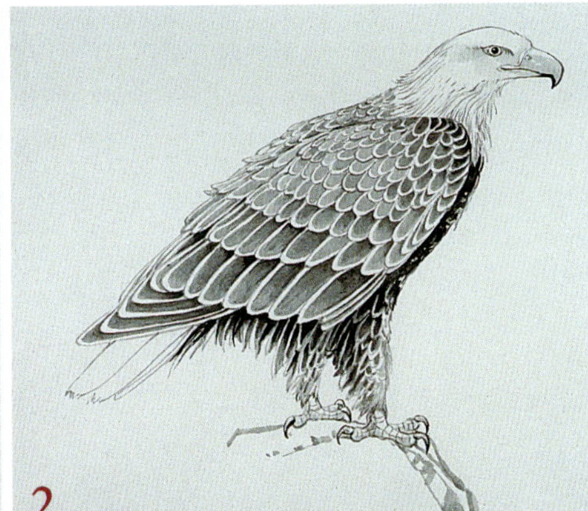

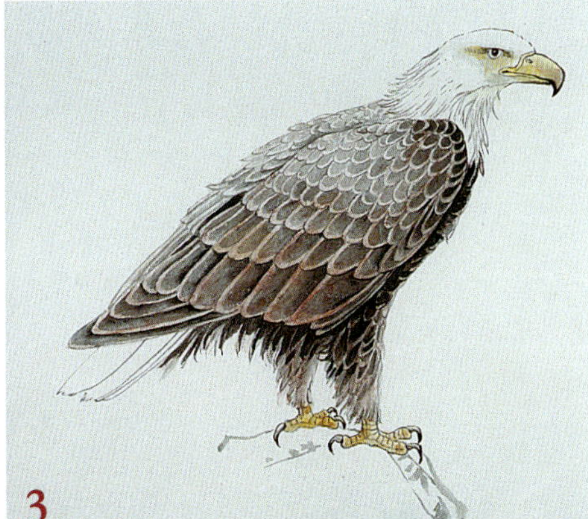

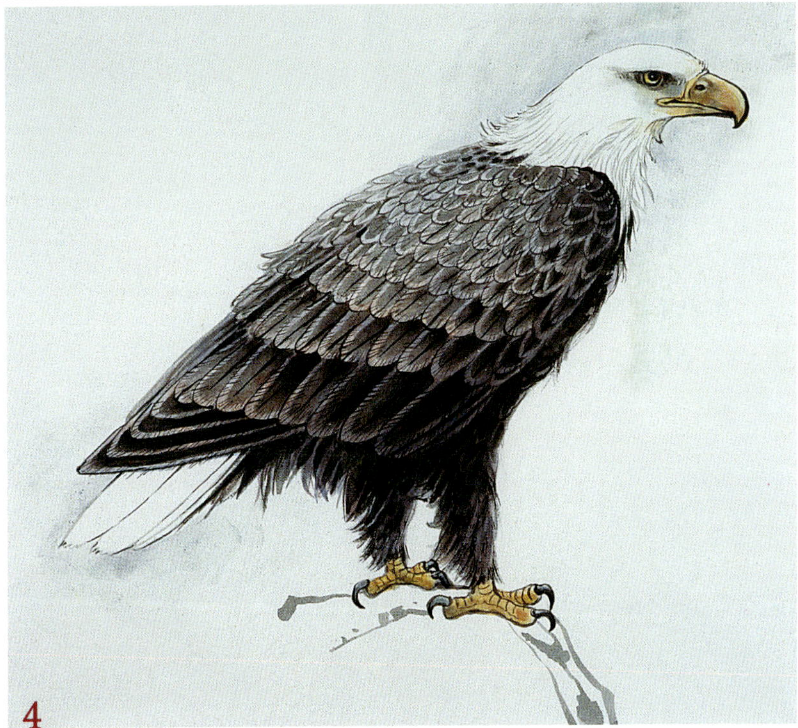

1 PAINT FIRST OUTLINE

Use a small, hard-fur brush to paint the outlines with light ink except for the beak, eye and claws, which should be painted with intense ink.

2 ADD BASE COLOUR

Apply ink as the base colour to define the volumes and shapes of the body parts and each feather. First, use light ink and the dry-colouring method to paint the eagle. Define each feather by carefully leaving white edges. When the first layer of ink is dry, apply more intense ink on top. To paint the gradations on each feather, use a small, hard-fur brush to place intense ink at one end of an individual feather, then use a small, soft-fur brush and water to drag the ink towards the other end.

3 ADD SECOND COLOUR

Use a medium soft-fur brush to paint gamboge (yellow) and vermilion on the beak and claws, and rouge and gamboge on the feathers.

4 APPLY MULTIPLE COLOURS, GLAZES, SECOND OUTLINES AND DETAILS

When dry, repeat the process at least three times until the colours have reached the desired intensity: strong enough to show the textures, yet not muddy. Next, use a large, soft-fur brush to apply a thin layer of indigo on top of the feather area as glazing. Use a similar brush to paint light indigo and ink on the background around the neck and tail so that the white of the paper will stand out. Finally, paint the second outlines and details with a small, hard-fur brush.

SPONTANEOUS-STYLE PAINTING TECHNIQUES

Unlike detail style, which uses vivid colours, spontaneous style uses ink as its primary media. In fact, some artists paint only with ink. Their paintings are called 'water-ink painting'. The manipulation of brushstrokes in spontaneous style is similar to that in calligraphy, to the extent that artists use the term 'writing' to describe painting.

Simplicity is the key word here. Often, objects in the paintings are simplified into minimal brushstrokes using limited colours. This theory comes from Taoist and Buddhist beliefs, that state that simple is beautiful. Consequently, simplicity has become an important aesthetic standard in Chinese painting, especially in the spontaneous style.

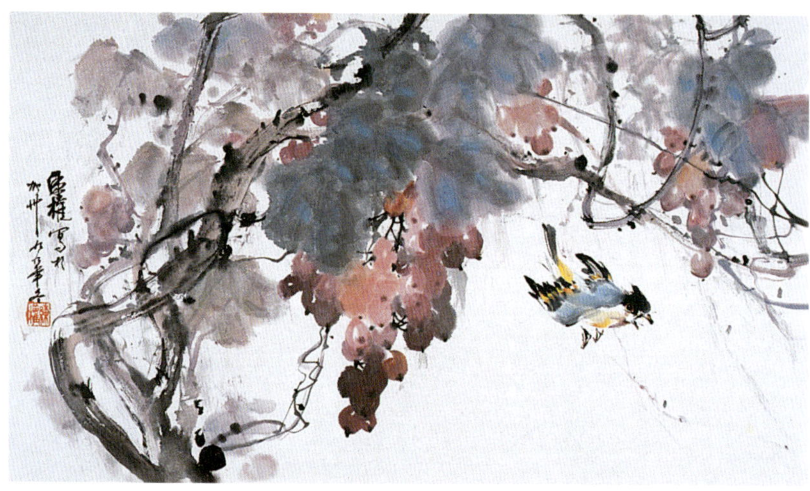

Using Colours in the Spontaneous Style
This painting does not render small details. Instead, it depicts the spirit and essence of the objects with sure, passionate and free strokes similar to calligraphy.
GRAPES AND A
FLYING BIRD
41 x 69cm
(16 x 27in)
Chinese ink and colours on single-layer Shuan paper
Spontaneous style

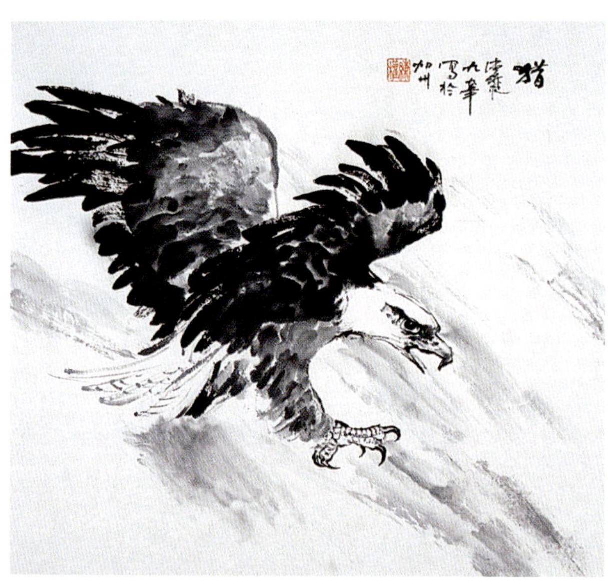

Using Ink in the Spontaneous Style
Water-ink paintings are usually painted in spontaneous style. Artists rely on brushstrokes and different tones of the ink to depict objects.
EAGLE
51cm x 69cm (20in x 27in)
Chinese ink on single-layer Shuan paper
Spontaneous style

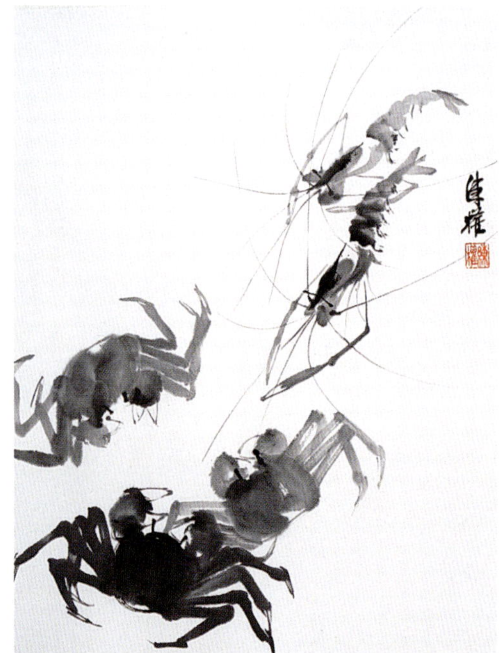

Keeping Things Simple
This is a good example of the simplicity seen in spontaneous-style paintings. Every stroke is taken into consideration in creating the texture, movement and formation of these objects.
CRABS AND SHRIMP
56 x 46cm
(22 x 18in)
Chinese ink on single-layer Shuan paper
Spontaneous style

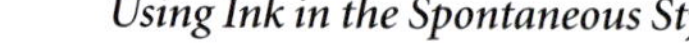

FISH IN SPONTANEOUS STYLE

In contrast to detail style's set painting process, spontaneous style makes use of a variety of methods and steps. Let's paint some fish as an exercise in learning techniques and the common steps of spontaneous-style painting.

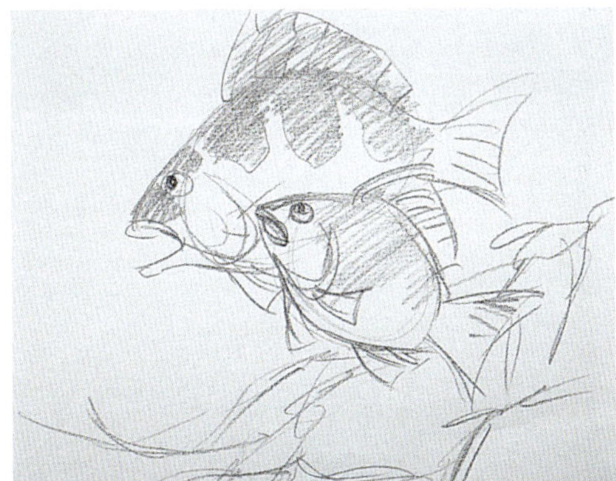

1 ORGANIZE THE COMPOSITION

Spend a few minutes arranging this composition in your head before sketching it on rice paper.

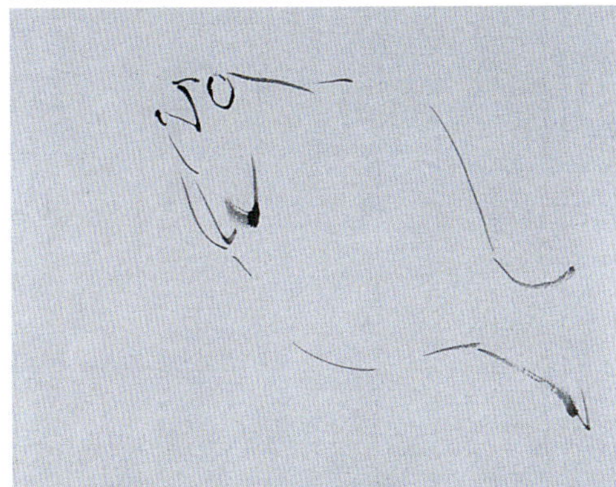

2 MAKE A ROUGH SKETCH

Once you have your composition in mind, start sketching the main outlines of the front fish on Shuan paper. Use a small, medium-fur brush and ink. This step will establish the basic shape of the fish. Sometimes artists do not sketch at all before painting; they adjust the images according to the results during the painting process.

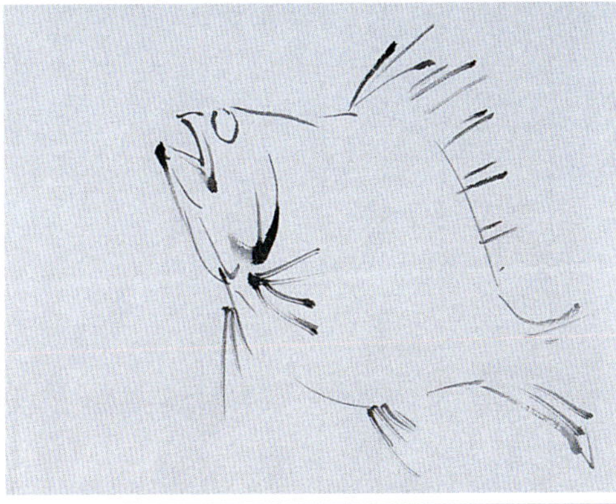

3 PAINT THE MAJOR ELEMENTS AND THE FOCUS AREA IN OUTLINE

Use a medium, hard-fur brush with ink to paint the mouth, gill, fins and tail. Use a medium, soft-fur brush to paint the upper and lower parts of the mouth and the outline of the eye. The brushstrokes should suggest textures and forms. The stroke for the front gill is broader on the bottom and narrower towards the head. It suggests the motions of the gill, which opens wider on the bottom and narrower at the top.

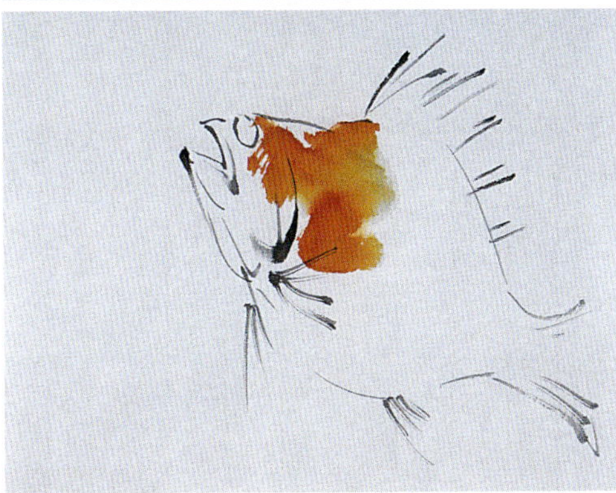

4 ADD COLOUR

Next, use a large, soft-fur brush to apply colours to the head and gill area using the centre-brush method, which will create soft textures. Fill the brush with water and yellow colour. Mix it with vermilion until half of the brush has picked up both colours. Use the tip of the brush to pick up a little rouge. The brush holds three colour zones: yellow, yellow and vermilion and vermilion and rouge. Therefore, each stroke of the brush will contain colour gradations. Apply these colours to the head area.

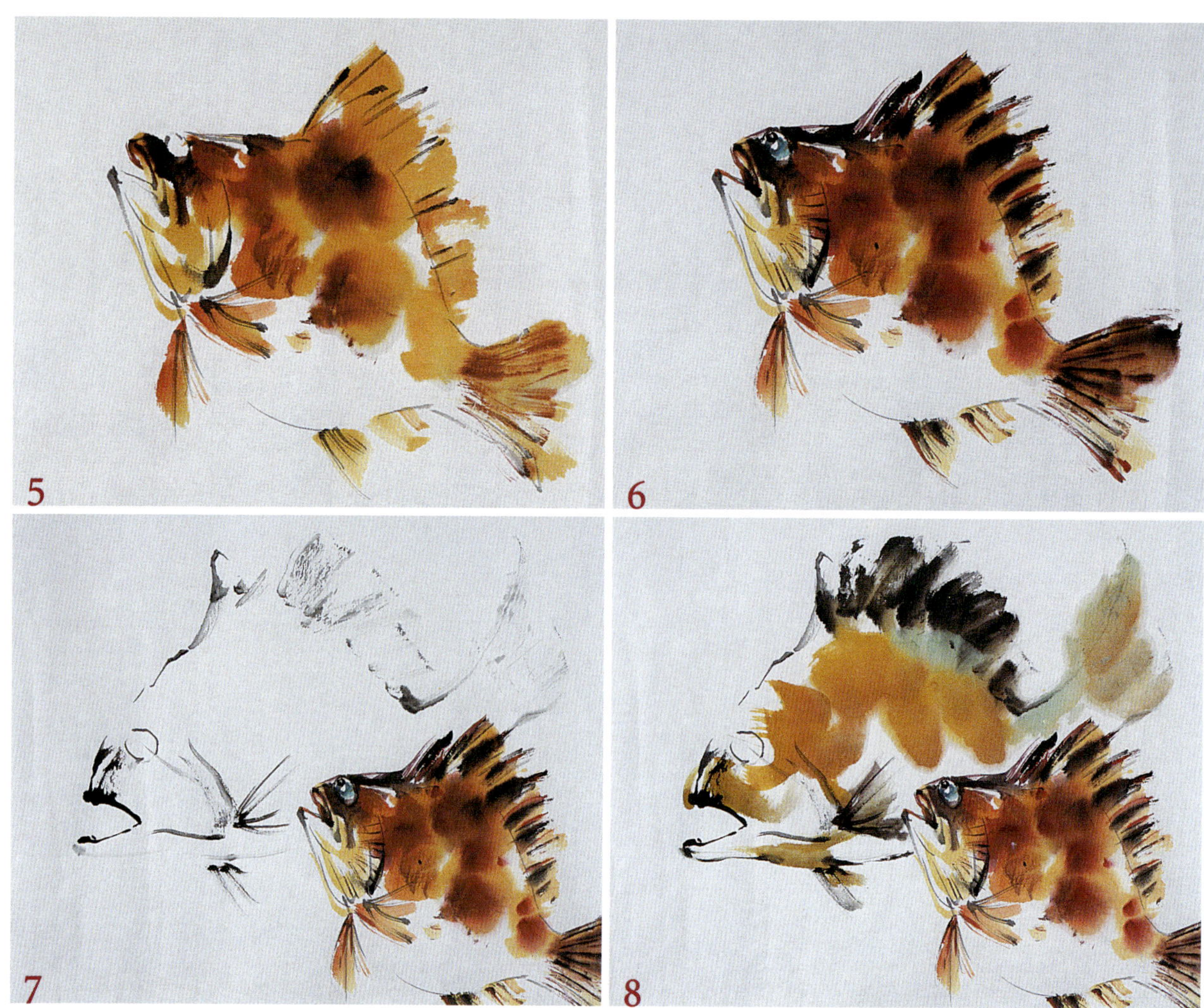

5 PAINT LESS IMPORTANT AREAS

Use the side-brush method to paint the fins and tail with the same colours used in step 4. (Soak the brush with one colour, then add another colour up to the middle. Next, pick up one more colour with the brush tip. This will allow you to create multiple colours with one stroke.) While the colours are wet, use the same brush to get intense rouge and mix it with ink on the tip of the brush. Paint on top of the coloured areas on the body and tail to create dark red spots.

6 FURTHER DEFINE TEXTURES AND DETAILS

While the colours are wet, use a medium, hard-fur brush, intense ink and the side-brush method to further define textures of the fins and tail. When almost dry, use intense ink to add more details to the head, gill and mouth. Finally, use a small, medium-fur brush to complete the eye.

7 PAINT THE OUTLINES OF THE SECOND FISH

Use a medium hard-fur brush and ink to paint the outlines of the second fish. Paint the mouth and outlines of the tail using the centre-brush method. Paint the fins and the gill with the side-brush method.

8 ADD COLOUR TO THE SECOND FISH

Wet the large, soft-fur brush and pick up some yellow. Mix the yellow with vermilion to paint the body using the centre-brush method. Immediately, use the tip to pick up some blue to paint the fins, tail and upper part of the body. While the colours are wet, use a large, hard-fur brush with intense ink to paint the fins using the side-brush method.

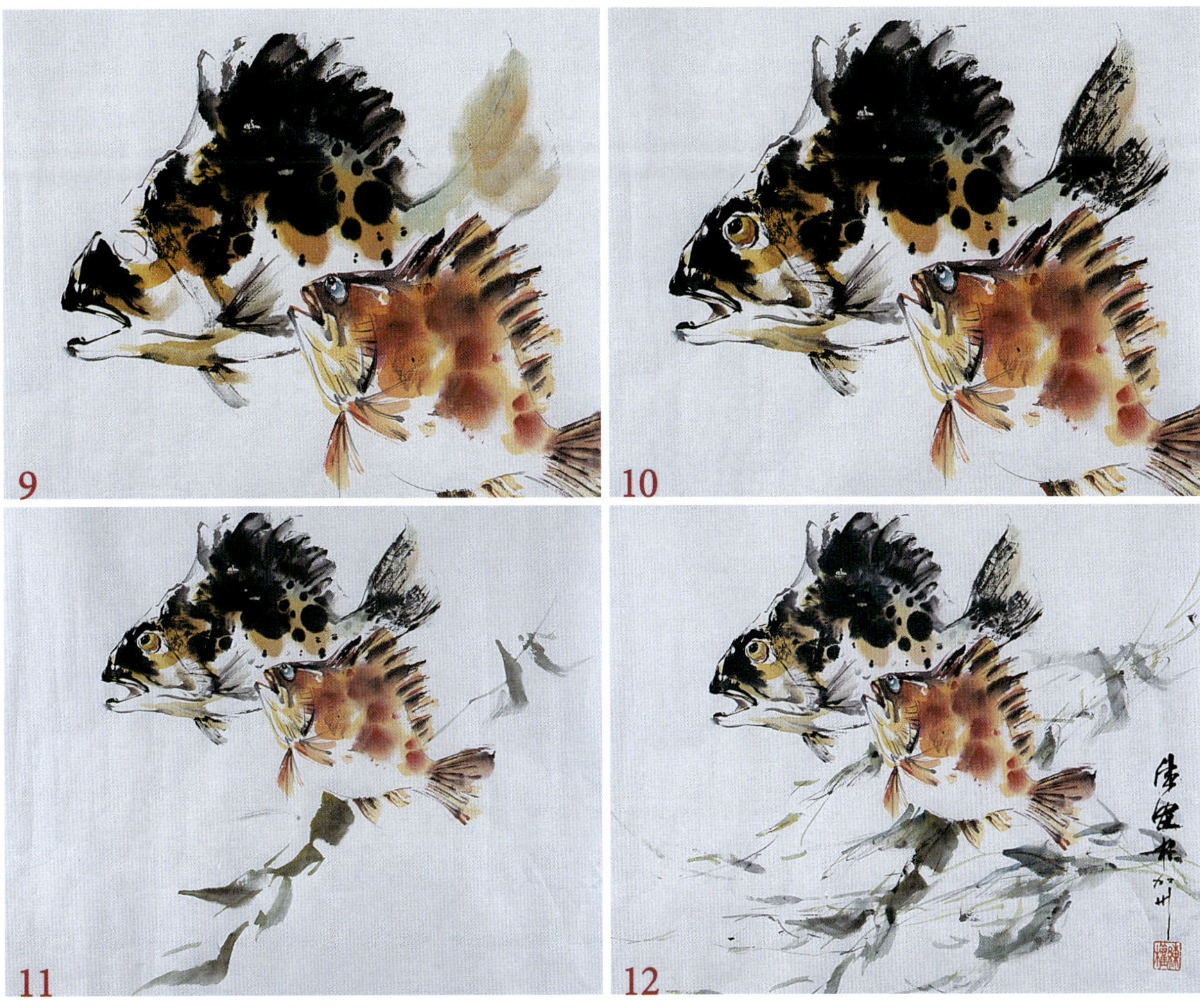

9 ADD DETAILS TO THE SECOND FISH

Continue to paint the dark spots on the fish's body with the same brush and intense ink. Define the area on the eye and mouth when the colours are almost dry.

10 ADD DETAILS TO THE GILLS

Use the same brush with ink to define details on the gill. Next, use the colouring brush and a very small amount of rouge on its tip to paint the eyeball. Finally, use a small, hard-fur brush with very intense ink to paint the pupil, leaving a tiny white area as its reflection.

11 PAINT THE BACKGROUND

To emphasize the motions of the fish, take a large, soft-fur brush and paint the leaves of the seaweed using the side-brush method. Use the brush to mix indigo with yellow and ink. Paint various-sized strokes to represent different sizes of leaves.

12 SIGN AND SEAL

When the colours are still wet, use a medium hard-fur brush and intense ink to paint the veins of the leaves. Finally, sign the painting with intense ink and stamp your chop on it.

TWO BODIES
43 x 43cm (17 x 17in)
Chinese ink and colours on single-layer Shuan paper
Spontaneous style

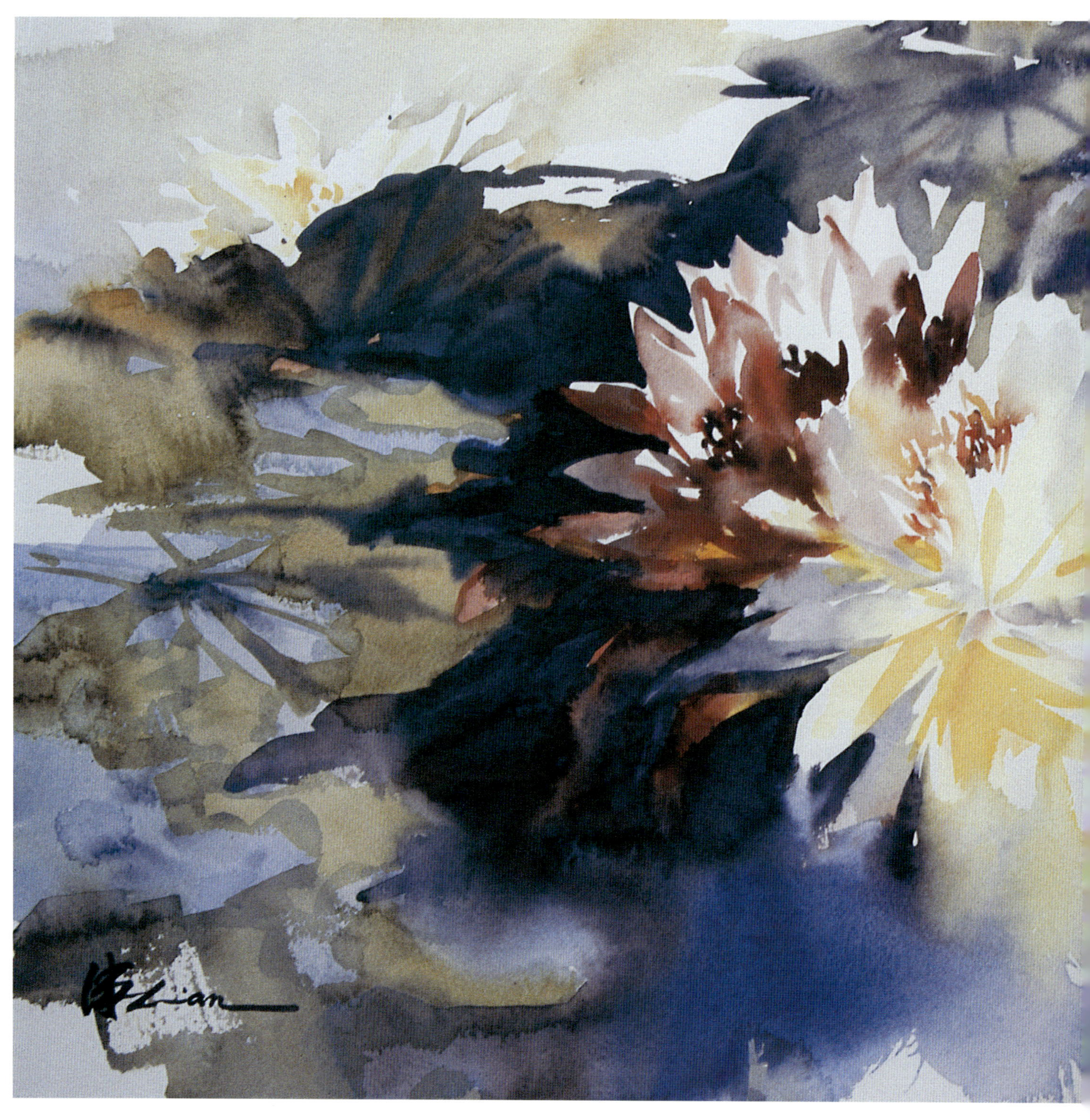

WATER LILY
36 x 53cm (14 x 21in)
Chinese ink and colours on double-layer Shuan paper
Spontaneous style

FROM **CHINESE PAINTING** TO **WATERCOLOUR**

3 Once during a watercolour demonstration, a student asked me whether I was creating a watercolour or Chinese painting. Obviously, my watercolour is strongly influenced by Chinese painting, to the extent that I unconsciously integrate Chinese painting techniques and theories with watercolour painting. I do not think it is important to differentiate a painting style, but it is essential to create paintings from the heart and soul. Colours, brushes and papers are only tools, which we use to express our true selves.

When I was in China, I mainly painted in the Chinese style. After I moved to the United States, I learned to love painting with watercolours. For me, it is the closest medium there is to Chinese painting with regards to materials, techniques and theories. Having a background in Chinese painting has helped me to master watercolour.

MY EXPERIMENTS AND THEORIES ON WATERCOLOUR PAINTING

Educated in both Eastern and Western arts, I have my own points of view on watercolour. They are not necessarily the same as other artists'.

Ink-Pouring Influences on My Watercolour

Ten years ago, I started colour pouring and blending, a method derived from ink pouring. With the help of masking fluid, pouring three primary colours on watercolour paper and directing their blending can create magnificent effects. Such dreamy, harmonic and powerful expression is what I have long been searching for in my paintings.

I have two different ways of painting with colour-pouring-and-blending techniques. The first starts with applying masking fluid to large areas that I want to preserve for details, then pouring the colours. The second starts with painting the objects, then pouring the colours to paint the background.

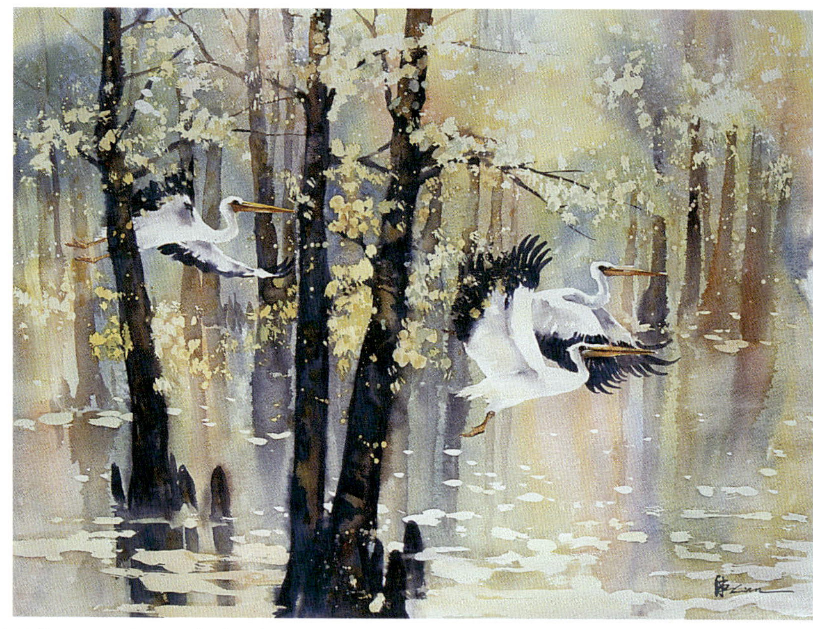

Colour-Pouring-and-Blending Technique
Use masking fluid to block out the birds, tree leaves and water highlights. Wait for the masking fluid to dry. Pour the three primary colours to paint the water, the tree trunks and the background. When the colours dry, lift the masking fluid and paint the details of the egrets, tree and water highlights.
THREE PELICANS
53 x 74cm (21 x 29in)
Watercolour on Arches 300gsm (140lb) cold-pressed watercolour paper
Colour pouring and blending

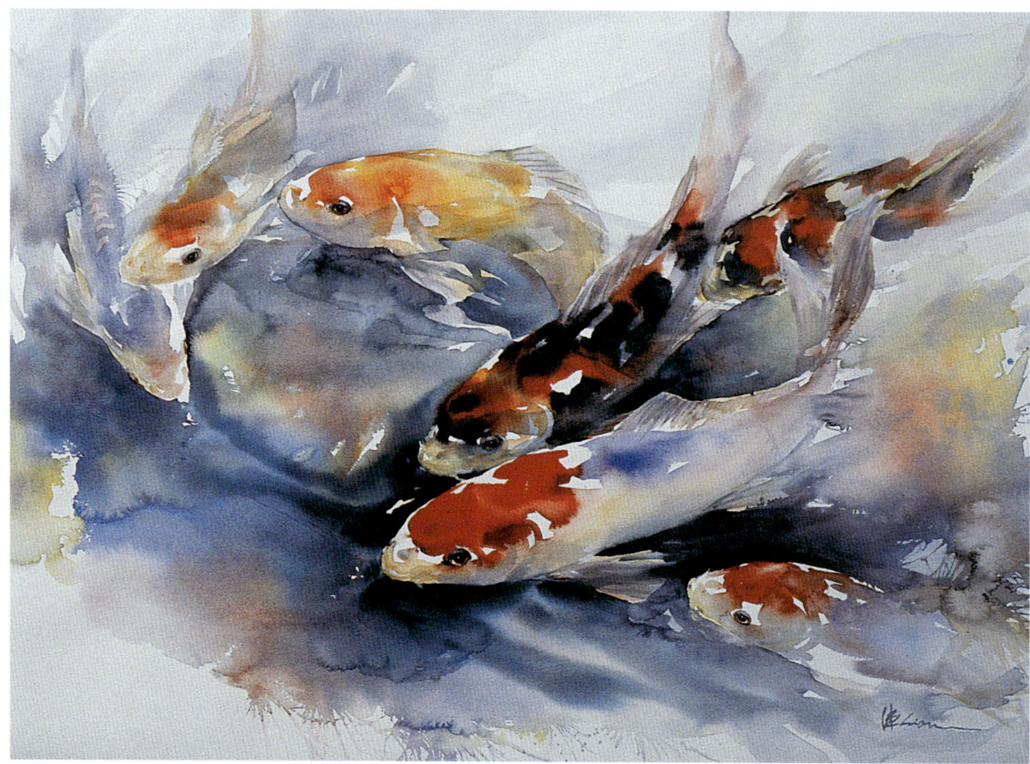

Colour-Pouring-and-Blending Technique
Apply masking fluid only on the fish's eyes before painting. When the masking fluid is dry, paint the koi. Then pour the three primary colours around the fish to paint the water. The whites on the koi bodies are unpainted areas.
KOI
53 x 74cm (21 x 29in)
Watercolour on Arches 300gsm (140lb) cold-press watercolour paper
Colour pouring and blending

*Three Colours – Enough to
Create a Beautiful World*

Most of the time, I paint with the three primary colours. Almost all the watercolour paintings and demonstrations in this book are built from the primary colours. My workshop students are surprised that I have only a few colours and brushes in a little box. In fact, many of my students bring more colours to my classes than I do. After my workshop, they are happy to know that they do not need to spend a lot of money on colours.

There are several reasons for limiting the colours used. First, I love the Taoist and Buddhist idea of simplicity. It is one of the most important goals that many famous artists have attempted to achieve in both Eastern and Western cultures. The legendary modern Chinese painting master Chi Bai Shi painted with limited strokes and colours. His shrimp and crab paintings, for example, use the minimum of strokes that capture the spirits of the objects. Similarly, Picasso once spent several months sketching a cow. He started with detail sketching and gradually dropped the details. At the end, he simplified his sketch with a few lines to depict the cow. Interestingly, children's artworks are also very simple. They tend to focus on the major features of objects.

Second, mixing three primary colours allows me to create other pigments that relate to the originals. Watercolours have amazing blending effects. I let them mix freely on watercolour paper with only minor adjustments. It creates magnificent colours. In addition, I also mix them using traditional watercolour painting techniques. As a result, I am able to get most of the colours I want.

For this book's watercolour demonstrations, 'mixing' yellow, blue and a little red involves using a moist brush to pick up the colours and mix them on your palette. This will create one-colour strokes. To 'get' yellow, blue and a little red, means to fill a moist brush with yellow first, then blue up to its middle and finally red on its tip. This method will result in three-colour strokes, since the colours will not completely mix before being placed on the paper.

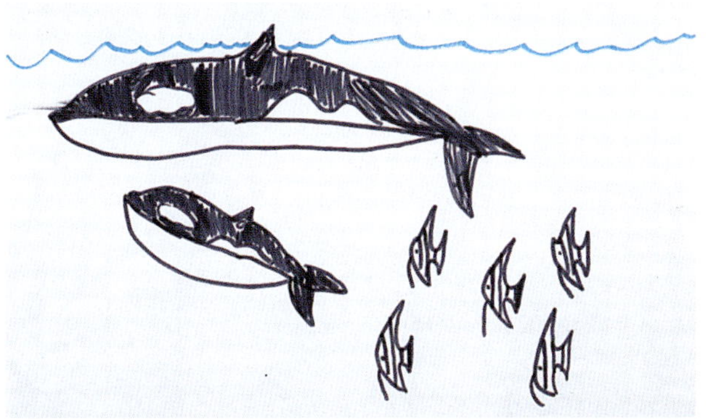

Children's Art 1
My daughter drew this when she was eight. I am amazed by its simplicity and clarity – it uses only a few lines to depict the most important characteristics of the fish.
ORCA WHALE AND BUTTERFLY FISH
23 x 28cm (9 x 11in)
Amery Zhen
Black markers on sketch paper

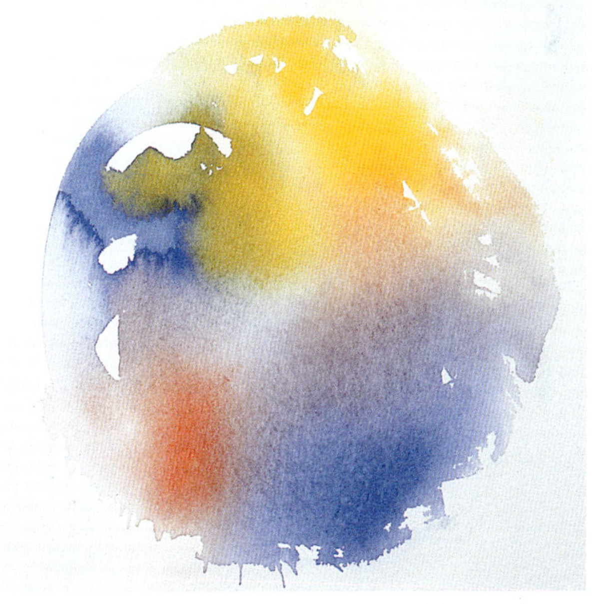

Endless Variety
Here is a sample
of the variety of
colours that can be
acquired from pour-
ing the three primary
watercolours next to
each other.

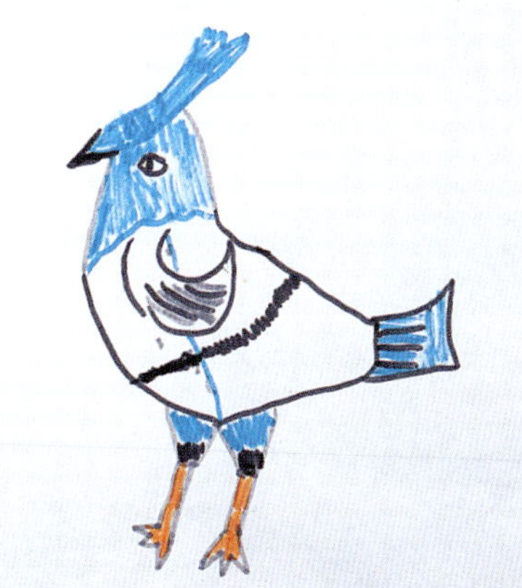

Children's Art 2
I do not know what
kind of bird my
daughter sketched
here. It seems she
didn't care about
that. Again, she used
minimum lines and
colours to paint a
lively bird.
BIRD
18 x 20cm
(7in x 8in)
Amery Zhen
Colour markers on
sketch paper

Colour is not the only essential element in watercolour painting. Brushstrokes and composition are also important.

I refuse to be dictated by an object's real colours. I like to create my own colour schemes from my impressions. When I paint colourful goldfish, for example, I do not copy the actual colours on each fish from what I have seen. I endeavour to capture an overall impression of their colours. Therefore, I paint from either my memory or a few glances. I want to create my own fish. I believe depicting a real fish is a camera's job. People call some of the goldfish in my paintings 'Lian's goldfish' because they can not find the same species elsewhere.

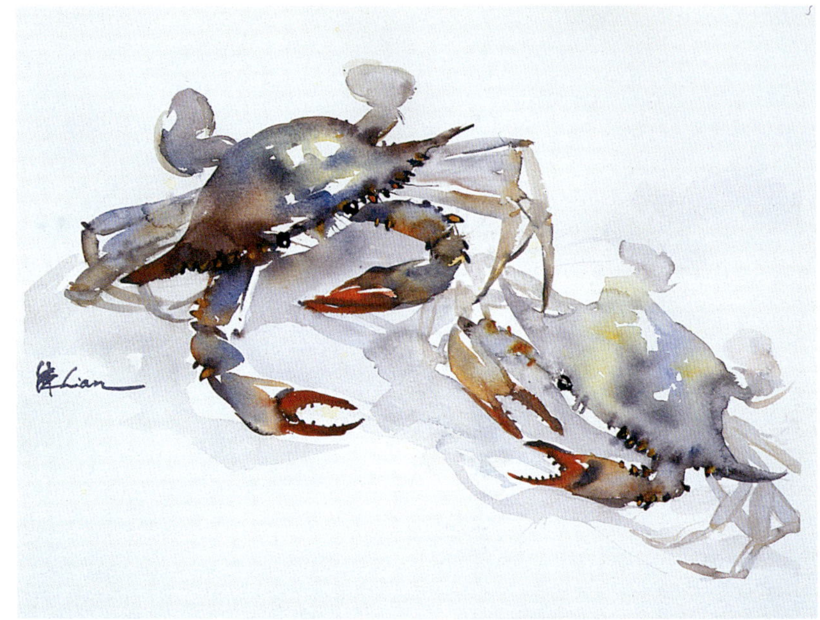

Essence of Brushstrokes
Brushstrokes play an important role in depicting objects' textures and motions in this painting. Those brushstrokes are most obviously shown on the legs and claws.
TWO CRABS
25 x 38cm (10 x 15in)
Watercolour on Arches 300gsm (140lb) cold-pressed watercolour paper
Colour pouring and blending

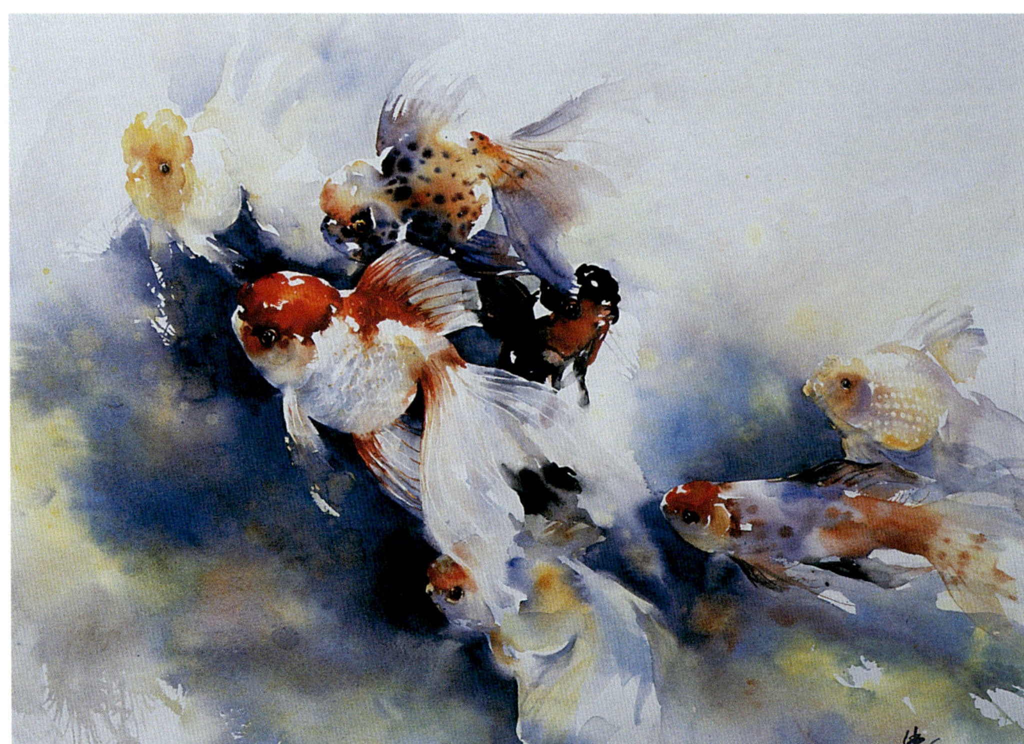

My Goldfish
The colours of the three goldfish in this painting are my own creation, from the red-crown on the bottom and the black-red and black-spot behind the centre large goldfish.
GOLDFISH
53 x 74cm (21 x 29in)
Watercolour on Arches 300gsm (140lb) cold-pressed watercolour paper
Colour pouring and blending

Free Lighting

Traditionally, light is not a major element in Chinese painting, since Chinese painting focuses on depicting objects' shapes rather than their three dimensions. Chinese artists ignore unnecessary details, such as highlights and gradations, and use alternative methods to suggest light effects. Depicting a night scene, for instance, they paint a moon on the sky as an allusion to night, instead of painting a dark sky.

In combining both Chinese and Western lighting effects, I have created my own style I refer to as 'free lighting'. When painting a fish, for example, I do not carefully define its highlight, shadow and reflection areas; rather, I leave white randomly on its head and body to suggest its volume and lighting effects. The highlights could be on the upper part of the fish's head and body, as well as on the middle and lower parts. As a result, there are multiple light sources.

In addition, I do not always paint shadows nor follow the lighting directions to paint them. I only consider painting shadows when they are critical in defining volume and composition. Otherwise, I use background to function as shadows.

From time to time, I also try to capture diffuse lighting and backlighting effects. Objects under diffuse lighting situations do not have strong shadows. They appear soft because the lights illuminate from different directions. Diffusing lights create a warm, lovely and dreamy environment. Similarly, backlighting gives a profound and spiritual impression. Nature does not control me, yet I want to recreate it in my paintings.

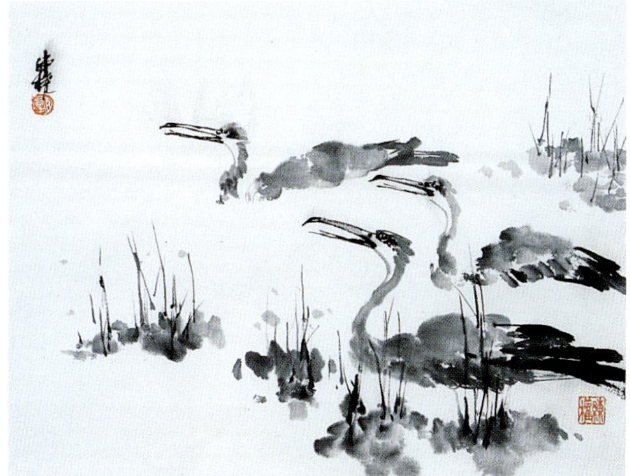

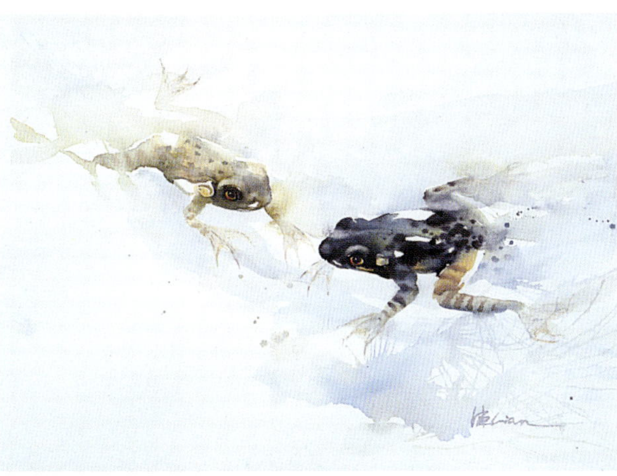

Free Lighting, Example 1
The highlights on the camerons' bodies are kept white between the minimal strokes. The other unpainted areas represent water. Even though there is no sky, light beams or shadows, viewers can feel the bright environment.
THREE CAMERONS
38 x 56cm (15 x 22in)
Chinese ink on single-layer Shuan paper
Spontaneous style

Free Lighting, Example 2
There are multiple light sources in this painting. The highlights on the backs of the frogs indicate a light source coming from the top, while the highlights on the mouths suggest another light source at the bottom. In addition, the highlight on the left leg of the frog on the right is from a light source on the right. Shadow is not necessary because the water helps to define the volume of the frogs.
TWO FROGS
25 x 36cm (10 x 14in)
Watercolour on Arches 300gsm (140lb) cold-pressed watercolour paper
Colour pouring and blending

Combination of Diffused Lighting and Backlighting
This scene features soft backlighting. Also, it contains diffused lighting effects because the snow strongly reflects the lights. Therefore, I did not paint strong shadows.
LOVE DANCING
74 x 53cm (29 x 21in)
Watercolour on Arches 300gsm (140lb) cold-pressed watercolour paper
Colour pouring and blending

No Mistakes

'No mistakes' is an optimistic attitude that allows me to release the pressures of forcing myself to create a masterpiece every time I paint. It does not mean I do not make mistakes during painting; instead it refers to my attitude towards the mistakes. When I make mistakes, I try to turn them into creations.

In my workshops and classes, I have seen students so upset about their paintings that they lose their interest in learning. Painting is supposed to be fun, not stressful and boring. Taoism advocates a belief that everything in the universe has a purpose and is natural. I think making mistakes while painting is natural.

When to Stop

When to stop is a tough question to answer. Some artists tend to overpaint because they are searching for realistic and perfect representations. I am no exception.

Take a look at the examples on this page. I had planned to use this hummingbird painting as a demonstration in this book. Starting from the beginning, I took pictures to record the painting process. Towards the end of painting, I realized that I had overworked the bird in the upper right corner.

If you do not know when the best time to stop is, take photographs to record your painting process, then analyze them. Most likely, you will realize that you should have stopped just a few steps before taking the last photo.

Another way to learn when to stop is to review watercolour demonstrations in books and magazines. Be critical and analytical. Even master watercolourists may not stop at the right moment. As an outsider, you can easily tell when to stop and will learn from their experiences.

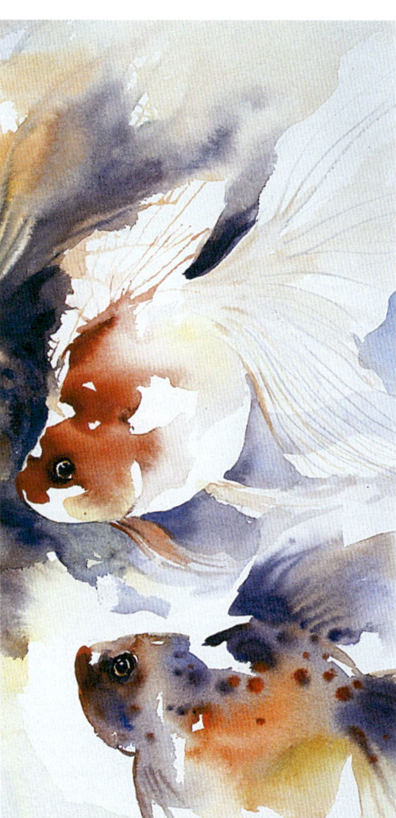

A Mistake With a Happy Result
During the painting process, I blow the colours on the background to direct their flowing and mixing. Here, my blowing was so strong that some colours spilled over into the dorsal fin of the goldfish. It was not the result I wanted, yet it looked like the texture of the fin. Also, it suggested the motions of the fish. Therefore, I kept the colours.

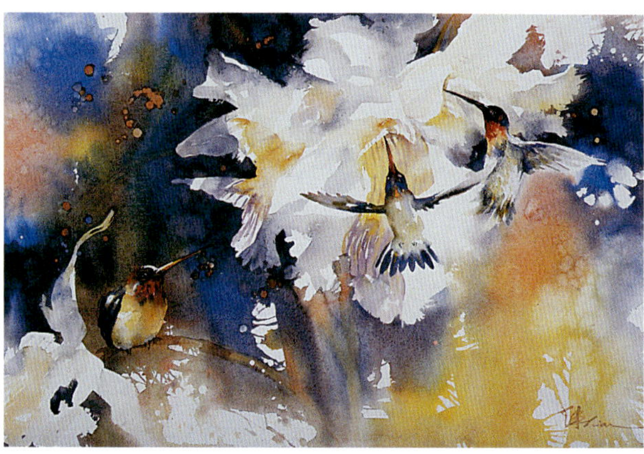

Best Time to Stop Painting
I took this picture several minutes before the bird was overpainted. It was the best time to stop.
THREE HUMMINGBIRDS AND LILY FLOWERS
36 x 51cm (14 x 20in)
Watercolour on Arches 300gsm (140lb) cold-pressed watercolour paper
Colour pouring and blending

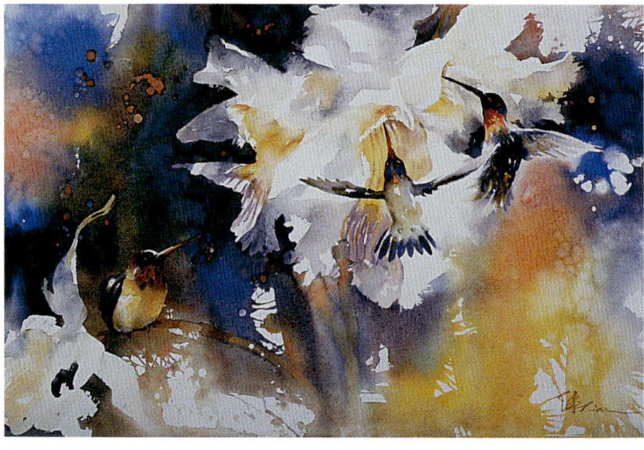

Overworked Painting
This picture shows the overworked bird on the upper right corner.
THREE HUMMINGBIRDS AND LILY FLOWERS
36 x 51cm (14 x 20in)
Watercolour on Arches 300gsm (140lb) cold-pressed watercolour paper
Colour pouring and blending

VARYING THE COMPOSITION

My watercolour painting composition is the integration of Chinese painting's free organization and Western art's perspective theory. When I arrange objects in my painting, I use whatever methods and theories meet my needs.

Perspective

Perspective in my watercolour is free and loose, especially in bird and fish paintings. I have done architectural renderings in college and at work. The renderings have to be so perfect in perspective that they look dry and mechanical. This is not the effect I want my paintings to have. I want my paintings to be free and creative. To achieve my goal, I free myself from accurate perspective.

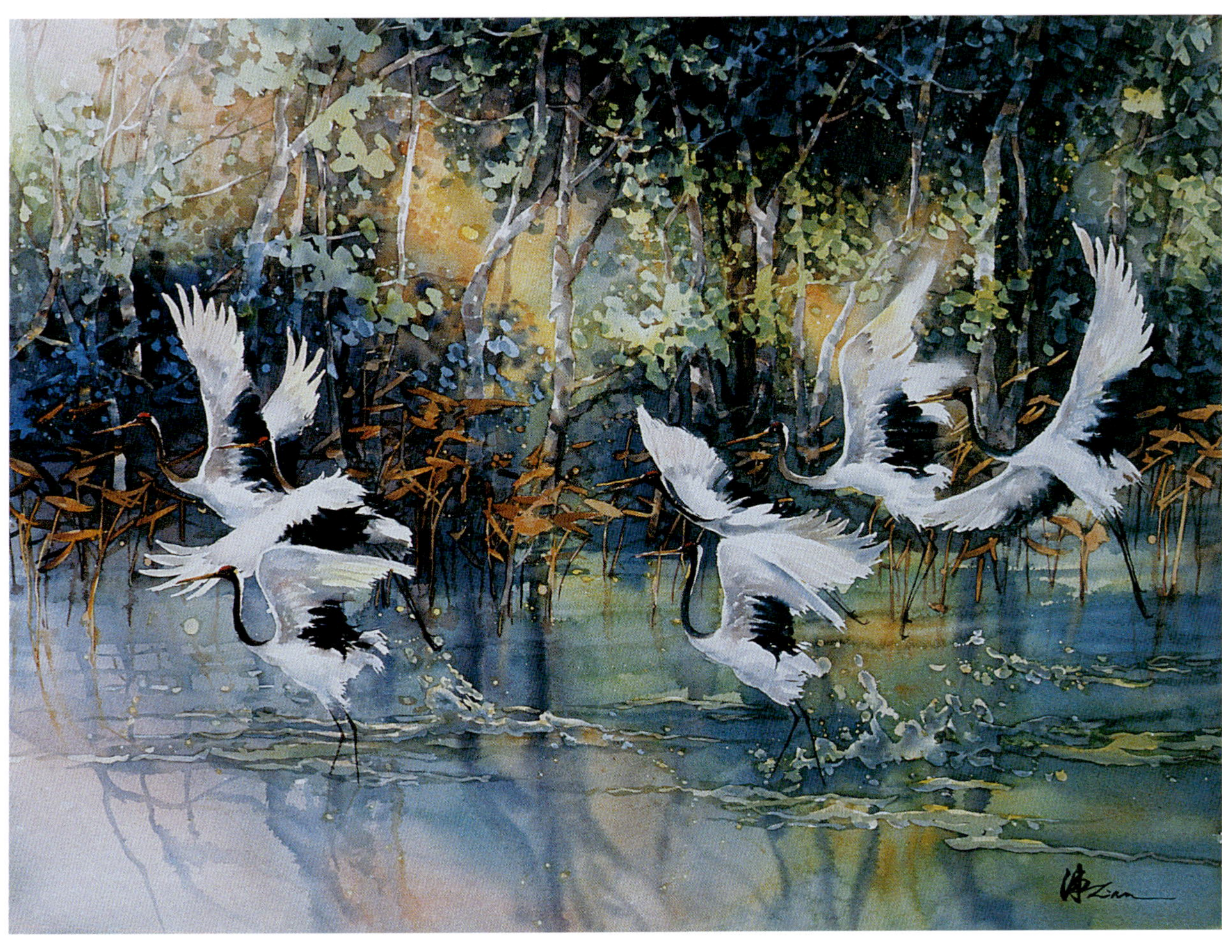

Linear Perspective
This is a linear or moving perspective painting. The trees and weeds are placed horizontally in the background without concentration on perspective. It emphasizes the crane's flying motion. Also, the cranes are arranged with individually defined perspectives.

MORNING FLY
53 x 74cm (21 x 29in)
Watercolour on Arches 300gsm (140lb) cold-pressed watercolour paper
Colour pouring and blending

Geometric Structure

As I do in my Chinese paintings, I group objects in geometric structures in my watercolour compositions. Let us take three variations of a single painting as examples. *Three Angels,* is a painting of three angelfish with different colours. I arranged their bodies together on an arc-shaped path that helps to further emphasize their motion. The angle of the arc could be narrower or wider. However, if it becomes too close to a horizontal line, the painting will lose its dynamic effect.

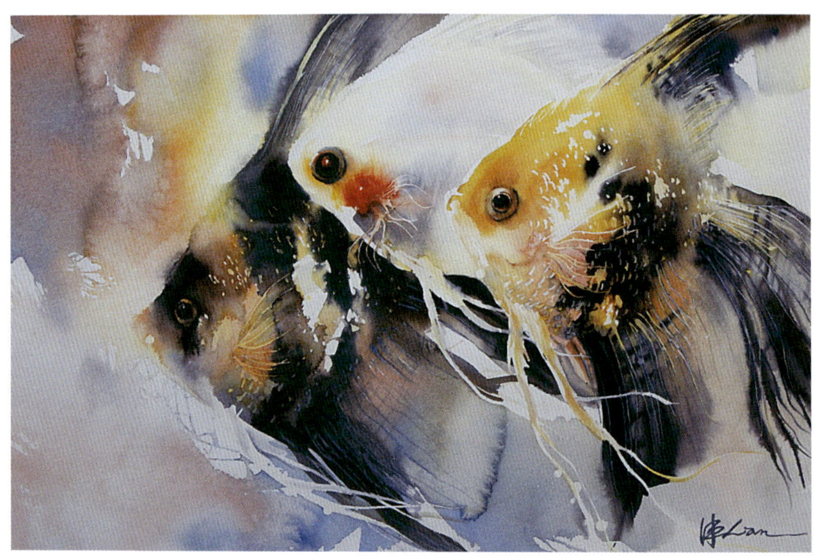

Arc-Shape Composition
Imagine a line drawn through the fish eyes to the tail of the yellow fish at front.
THREE ANGELS
38 x 53cm (15 x 21in)
Watercolour on Arches 300gsm (140lb) cold-pressed watercolour paper
Colour pouring and blending

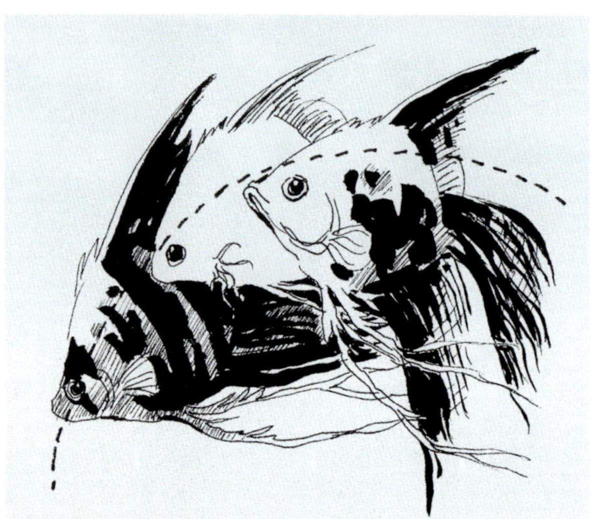

Same Fish Placed on a Narrower Arc
A narrower arc creates a stronger motion effect.

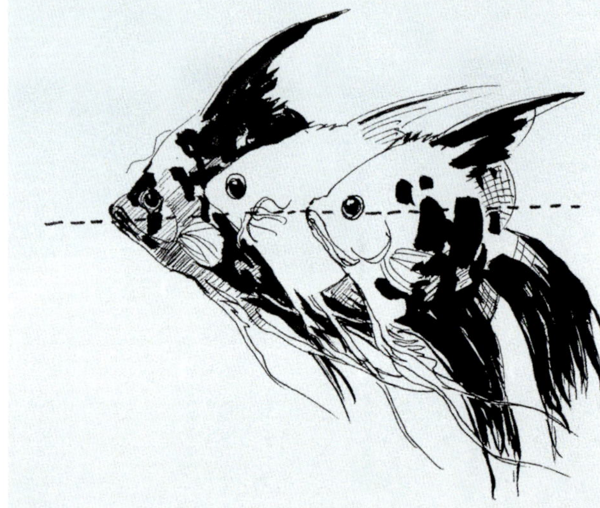

Same Fish Placed on a Wide-Open Arc
A wide-open arc resembles a horizontal line. In this composition, the fish are not in dynamic motion.

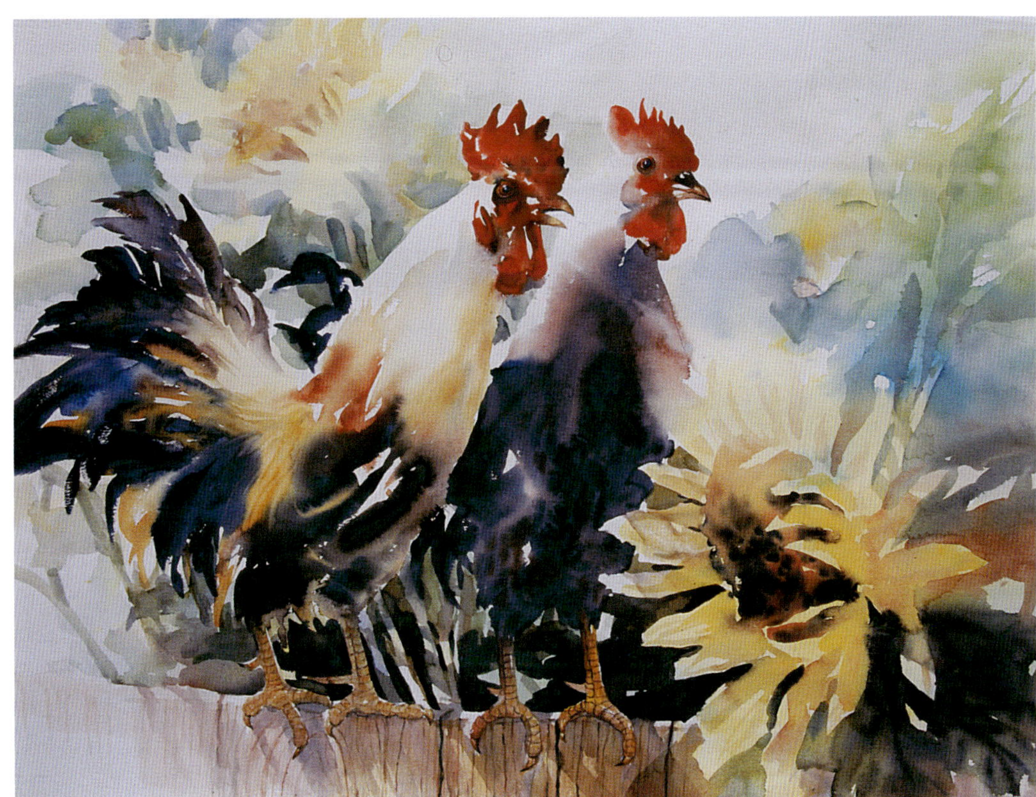

This painting has a triangular composition. The two heads of the roosters form the top angle, while the tails on the left and the sunflower on the right are the two other angles. Since the triangular shape is like a pyramid near the centre of the painting, it provides a sense of stability to the roosters that are standing on the wooden fence. If I move the sunflower from bottom right to middle right, the triangular composition will disappear. The roosters and the sunflower would be too close together.

ROOSTER AND SUNFLOWERS
53 x 74cm
(21 x 29in)
Watercolour on Arches 300gsm (140lb) cold-pressed watercolour paper
Colour pouring and blending

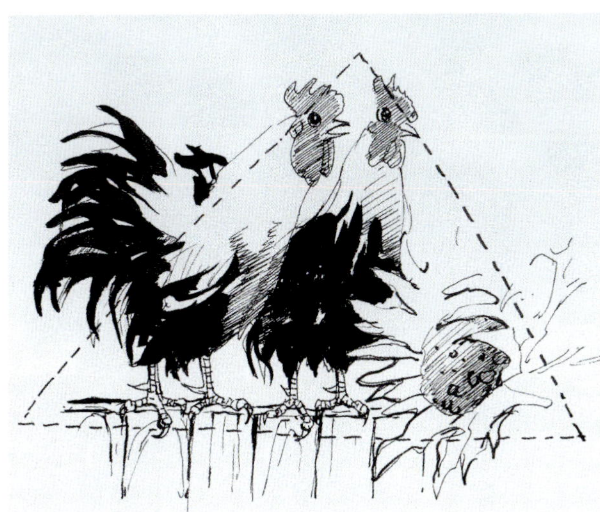

This sketch shows the triangular composition.

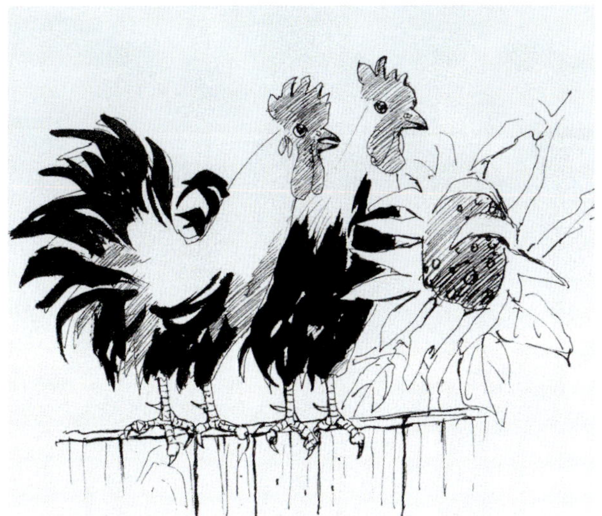

Without the triangular structure, the objects lack vitality.

Three Ways to Compose Geometrically

Using geometric structures is a simple and easy method to organize compositions. There are three ways to make composition sketches using geometric shapes: arrange objects on a path, arrange objects within one shape or arrange objects within multiple shapes.

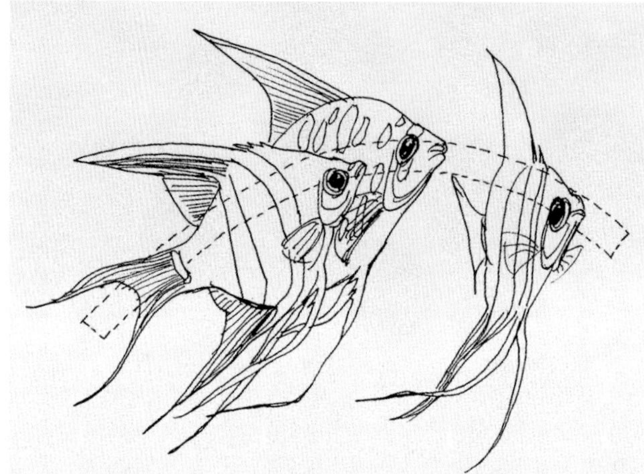

Method 1: Arrange Objects on a Path of a Geometric Shape
Start by drawing a geometric shape, such as an arc or a circle. Then place major objects on the path of the shape. The fish shown here are arranged on the paths of different arc shapes.

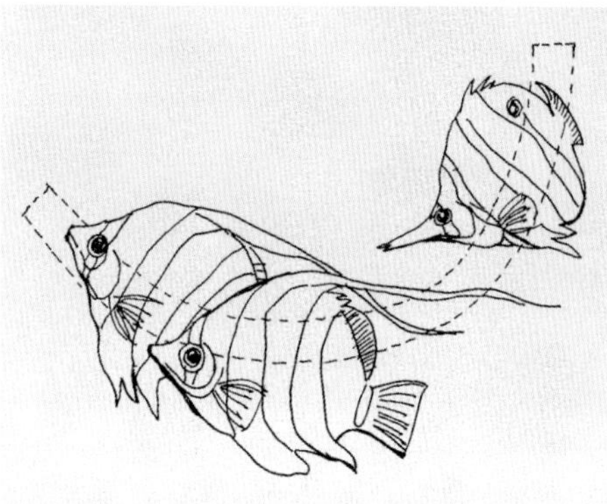

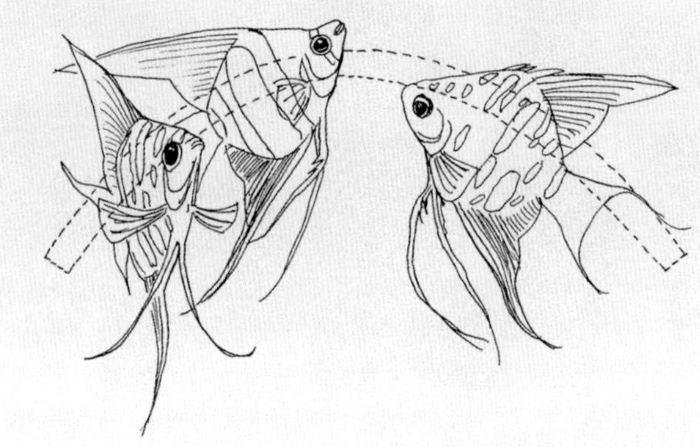

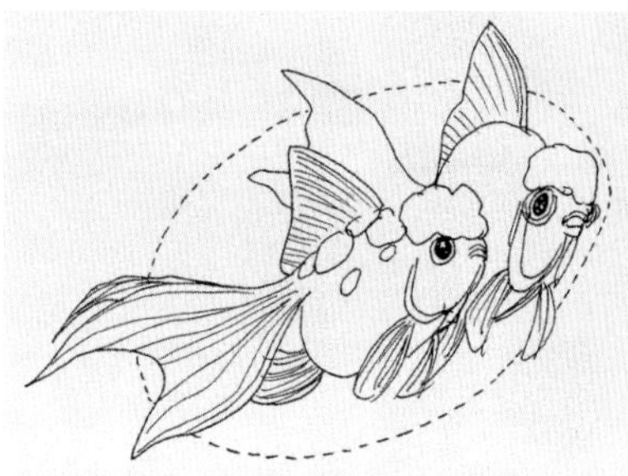

Method 2: Arrange Objects Within One Geometric Shape
Sketch a geometric shape first, then organize objects within the shape. This is handy for a composition featuring two or three major objects. The goldfish shown here are in oval shapes.

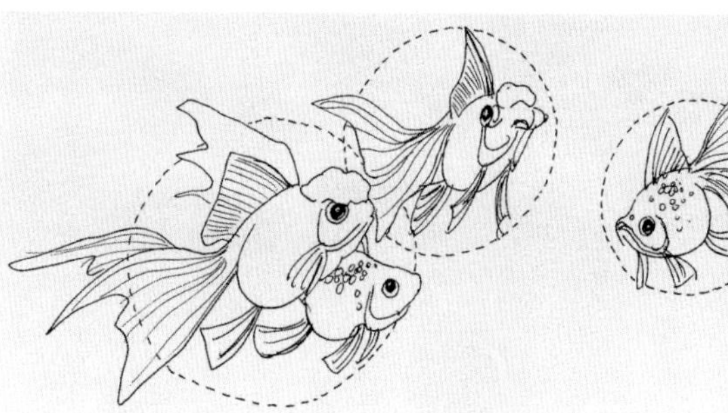

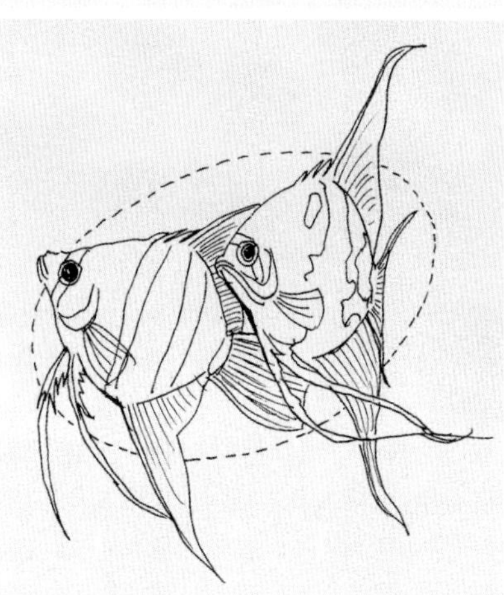

Method 3: Arrange Objects Within Multiple Geometric Shapes
Sketch two or more geometric shapes at the beginning. The shapes can be the same or different. Next, organize the objects within the shapes. It is common to place the major objects in the large shape and minor objects in the small shapes. I use this method for paintings containing three or more objects.

Leaving White for Balance

One similarity between Chinese painting and watercolour is the method of leaving some areas of each painting white, unpainted. In watercolour, the unpainted areas can serve the purpose of balancing composition and highlighting. In addition, they are the spaces for viewers to input their ideas and imaginations. The viewers will 'finish' the paintings.

I think a painting with proper unpainted areas is comparable to the ruins of the Colosseum in Rome. Both of them are physically incomplete yet more attractive and beautiful because of this. Their incompleteness piques curiosity and imagination.

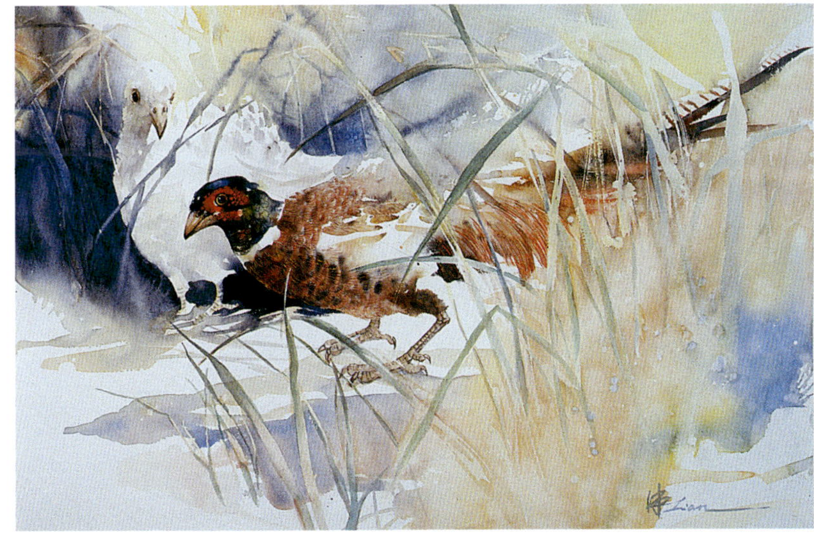

Leaving White Areas, Example 1
The white areas on this painting provide strong contrasting effects between the colourful bird in front and the white bird behind, and between the intense background and the white bird. The white also provides balance between the colours. In addition, the white on the body of the front bird suggests shape and highlights.
TWO PHEASANTS
36 x 53cm (14 x 21in)
Watercolour on Arches 300gsm (140lb) cold-pressed watercolour paper
Colour pouring and blending

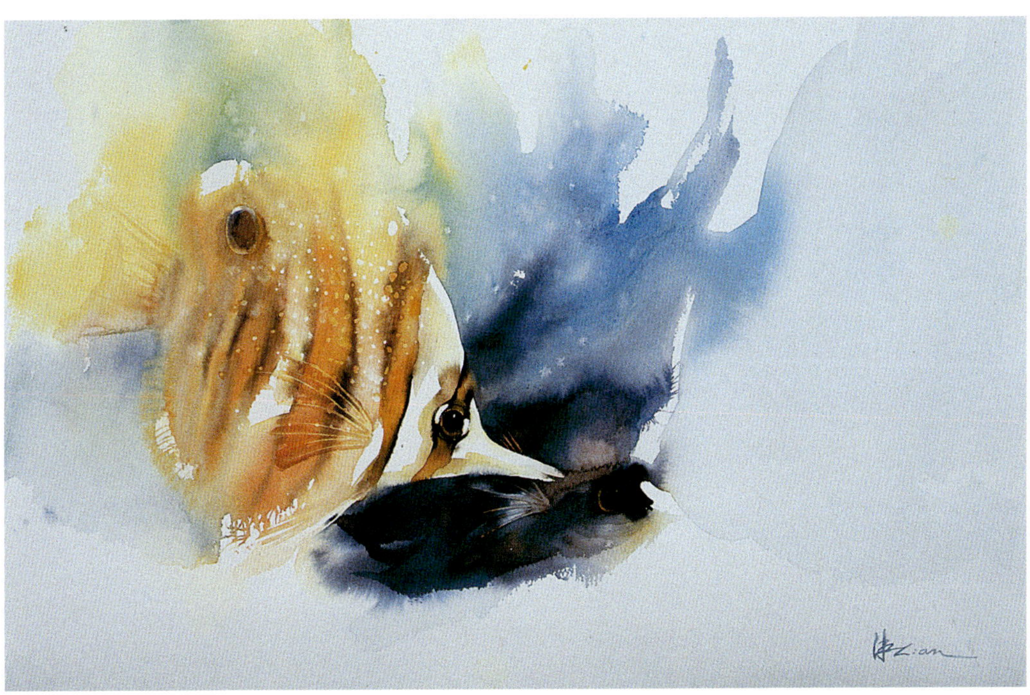

Leaving White Areas, Example 2
There are a lot of unpainted areas on this painting. They contrast and balance the dark colour of the fish. The white on the fish suggest highlights and the shapes of the fish.
TWO BUTTERFLY FISH
36 x 53cm (14 x 21in)
Watercolour on Arches 300gsm (140lb) cold-pressed watercolour paper
Colour pouring and blending

Focal Point

When people talk to each other, they usually look at each other's eyes. The eyes become the focal points in the action. Similarly, a painting has one or a few focal points. They are the larger primary objects painted with the most details, brightest colours and dramatic gestures. Even though there may be only two fish or birds in a painting, one of them should be more outstanding. A painting without a focal point resembles a person talking without a topic.

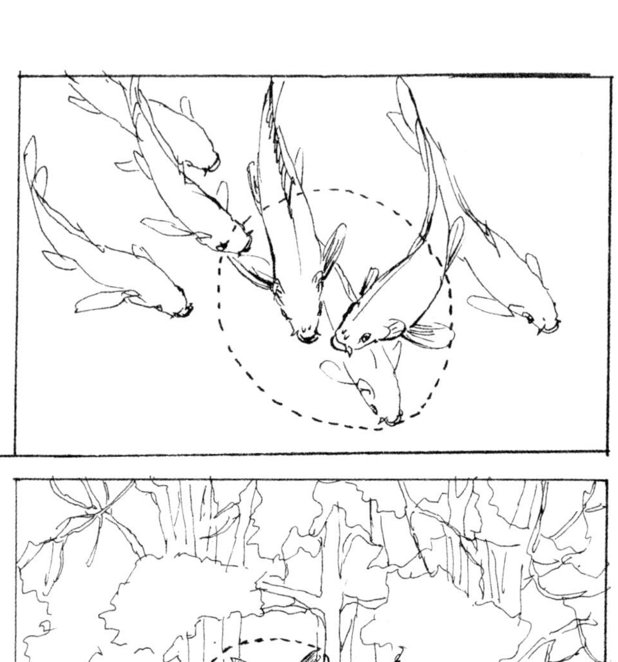

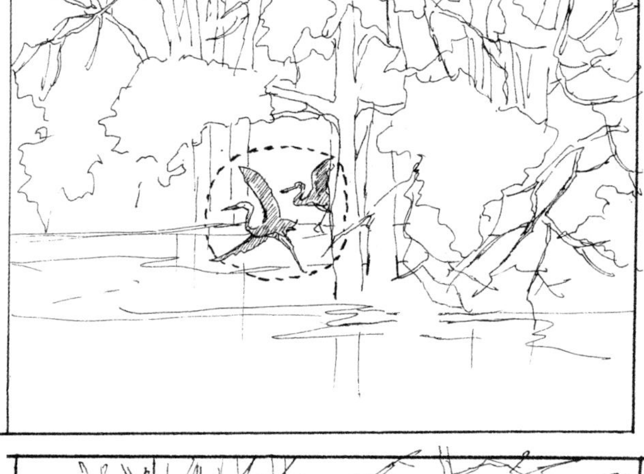

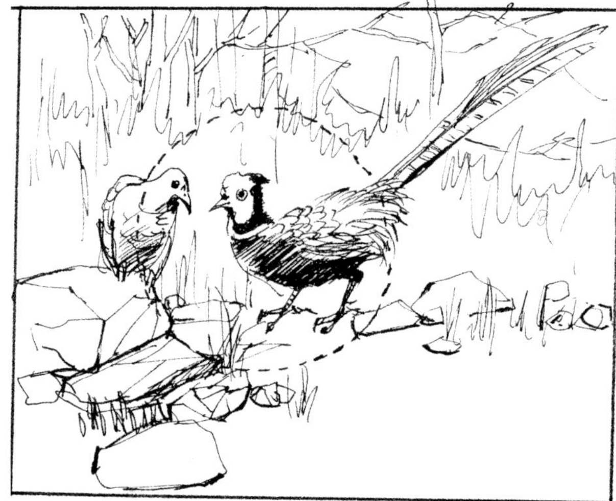

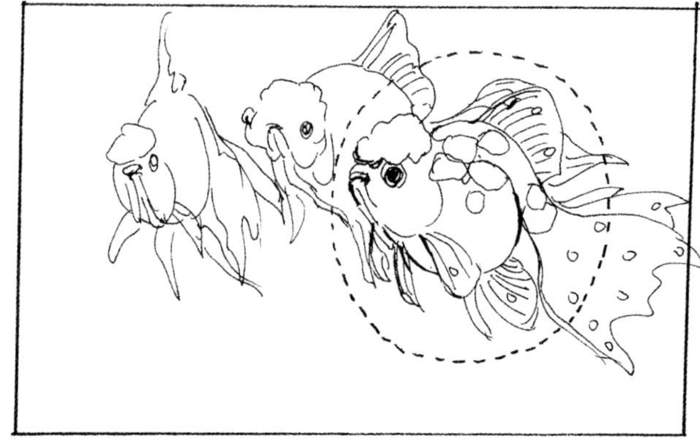

The dotted circles on these sketches represent the focal points of each composition.

Placing Your Signature

Some artists sign their paintings for authenticity purposes. Their signatures do not help to improve their paintings and are at worst distracting. I consider my signature as part of the whole composition, and it should blend in with the colours and brushstrokes. My signature for watercolour paintings is my first name in Chinese and English. Often, I sign it near a bottom corner depending on the compositional balance.

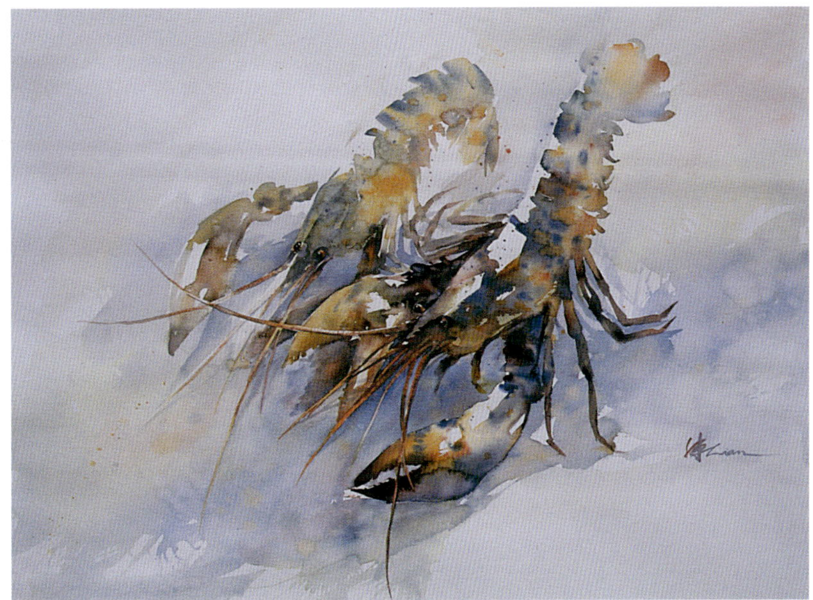

Minimizing a Signature's Impact on a Painting
The lobsters are moving towards the left, leaving an empty space on the right. Thus I signed my name on the lower right corner. The signature is next to a leg, as if an extension of it. As a result, it does not carry away the tension from the lobsters.
TWO LOBSTERS
53 x 74cm (21 x 29in)
Watercolour on Arches 300gsm (140lb)
cold-pressed watercolour paper
Colour pouring and blending

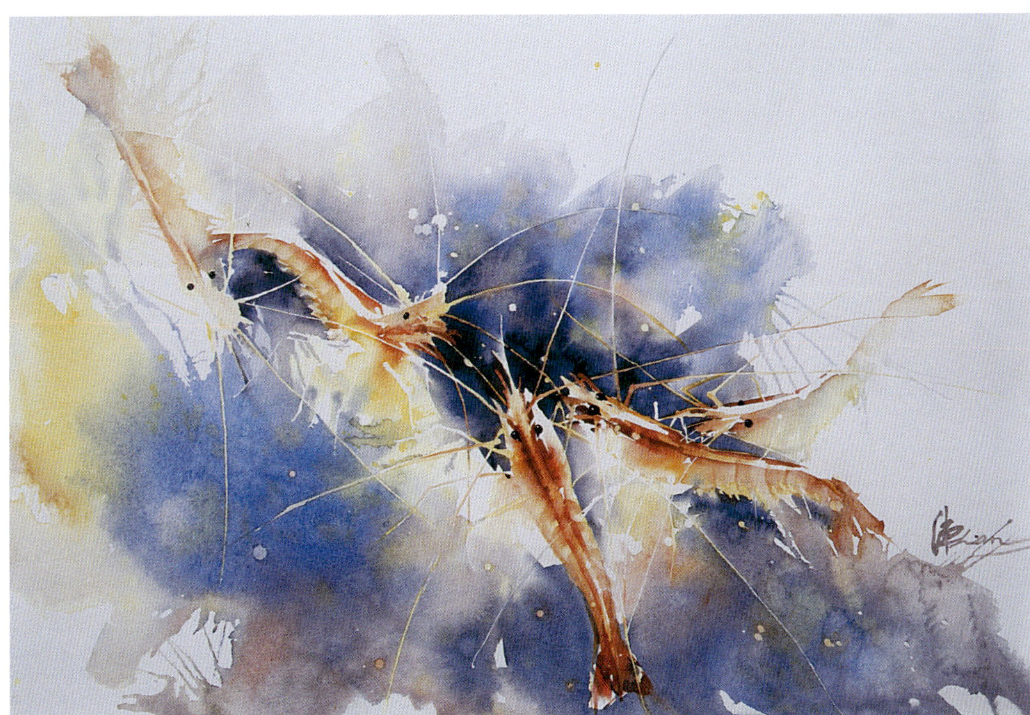

Integrating Your Signature Into the Painting
I follow the background strokes and colours to sign my name. It becomes part of the painting.
SHRIMP
36 x 53cm
(14 x 21in)
Watercolour on Arches 300gsm (140lb) cold-pressed watercolour paper
Colour pouring and blending

SPECIAL MATERIALS FOR WATERCOLOUR

I use common watercolour materials found in major art supply stores. I believe that having more and complicated materials is not necessary to make my paintings look better. Some materials can create special effects, such as salt used to produce rain and snow impressions. However, I do not want to over-manipulate such materials because they can overshadow my personal style.

Papers

I used Arches 300gsm (140lb) cold-pressed watercolour paper for all the watercolour paintings and demonstrations in this book. I always buy full sheets in packs. When I want to paint smaller paintings, I cut the sheets to the desired size. Occasionally, I use heavy paper, such as Arches 640gsm (300lb) paper. If you are a beginner, I suggest you try different kinds of papers. You will then find one that you like best.

Brushes

I use flat and round sable brushes. Their sizes range from small to large. The flat brushes, for example, range from 3 to 51mm (⅛ to 2in). The round brushes are from No. 4 to No. 10.

Paints

The three primary colours that I use are cadmium red deep from Winsor & Newton and ultramarine blue and cadmium yellow light from Utrecht. Occasionally, I use other colours, such as violet, cadmium yellow deep and cobalt blue. Colours from different manufacturers may be slightly different despite having the same name.

Palette

I use a John Pike palette for indoor paintings and a smaller palette for outdoor sketches. Often, I put one pigment in two compartments on a palette. One compartment is for mixing and the other is for pure colouring. It's nice to arrange colours from warm to cold or vice versa so that it's easier to keep them clean when mixing.

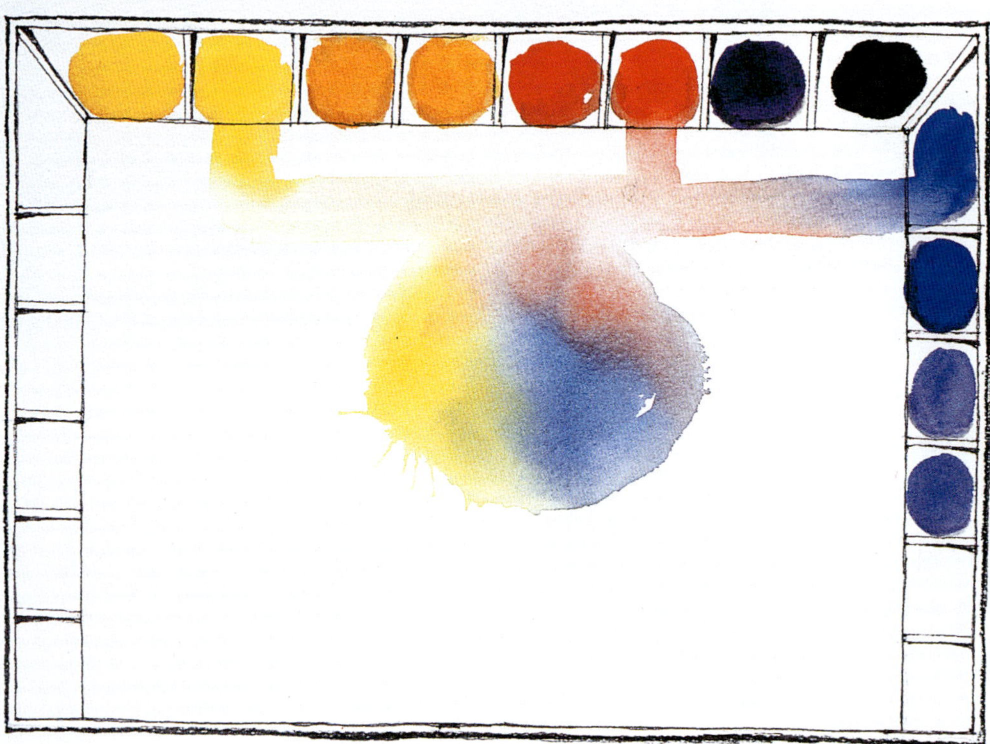

Arranged Colours on My Palette
This is my colour layout on a John Pike palette. Warm colours are on the left and cool colours are on the right. Each colour occupies two compartments.

Masking Fluid

Masking fluid is necessary for painting with the colour-pouring-and-blending technique. I use Winsor & Newton light yellow art masking fluid, but since the yellow fluid doesn't show clearly on film, I used a pink masking fluid from another manufacturer for the demonstrations in this book.

When a bottle of masking fluid is more than half used, it gets thick. Put half or one capful of clear water into the bottle to dilute the fluid.

Incredible Nib and Bamboo Pen

The 'Incredible Nib' looks like a pen with a nib at each end. It is used to apply masking fluid to small areas. Bamboo pens are also good for the same purpose. In one of my watercolour workshops, a student cut some bamboo from his garden to make bamboo pens for everyone in the class. I still use two of his bamboo pens today. For larger areas, use an old No. 6 (or larger) round brush. Wash the Nib, pen or brush immediately after you finish masking.

Other Materials

For sketching, keep a soft-lead pencil, such as a No. 2 and B series. I also have at least three small white dishes for mixing pure colours, packing tape for taping down the watercolour paper, one or two brush washers (containers of water), a roll of paper towels, one or two fabric towels for cleaning, a couple of waste containers and a hair dryer. Also keep a roll of masking tape close to hand to lift the masking fluid after your painting is dry. Cut the tape into 3 to 5 cm (1 to 2in) long pieces, then press it onto the masking fluid. Pull up the tape to remove the fluid.

My Painting Table

Formally speaking, my painting table is not a table. I put a 91 x 122cm (3 x 4ft) smooth three-ply wooden board on a small, portable bookshelf to make my table. The advantages of having such a table are that it is handy to move it around and the bookshelf can hold painting materials.

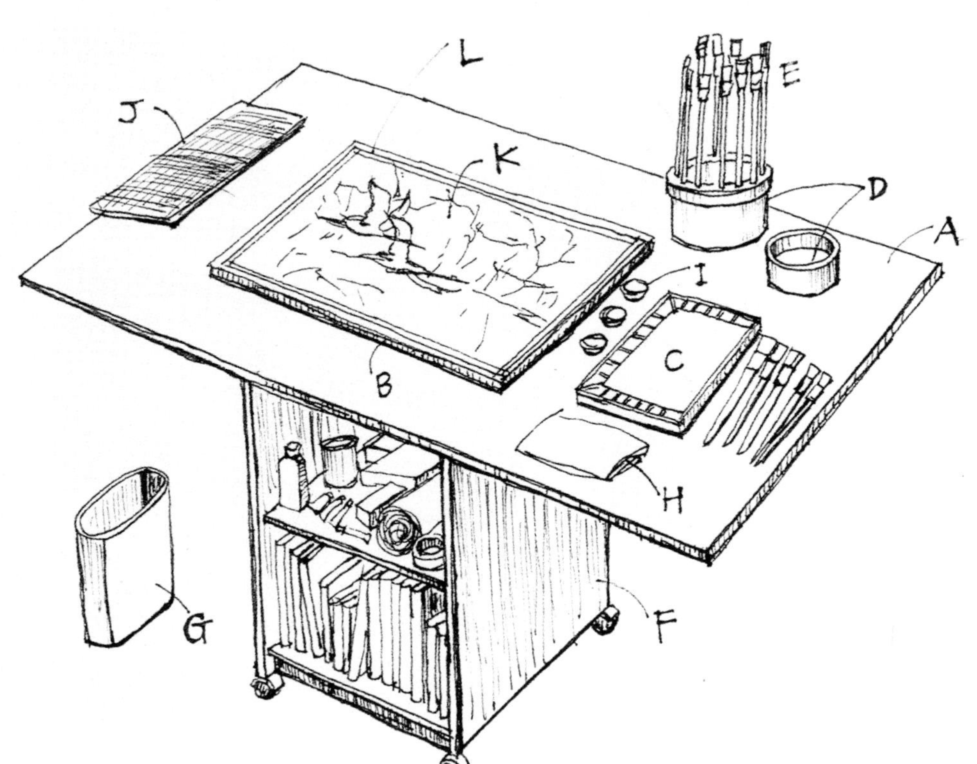

My Painting Table and Materials Layout
A. Plywood boards 91 x 122cm (3 x 4ft)
B. Smaller plywood boards 41 x 58cm (16 x 23in)
C. Palette
D. Brush washers (containers of water)
E. Brushes
F. Bookshelf
G. Waste container
H. Paper towels
I. Small dishes
J. Fabric towel
K. Watercolour paper with its edges taped to the board
L. The taped edge

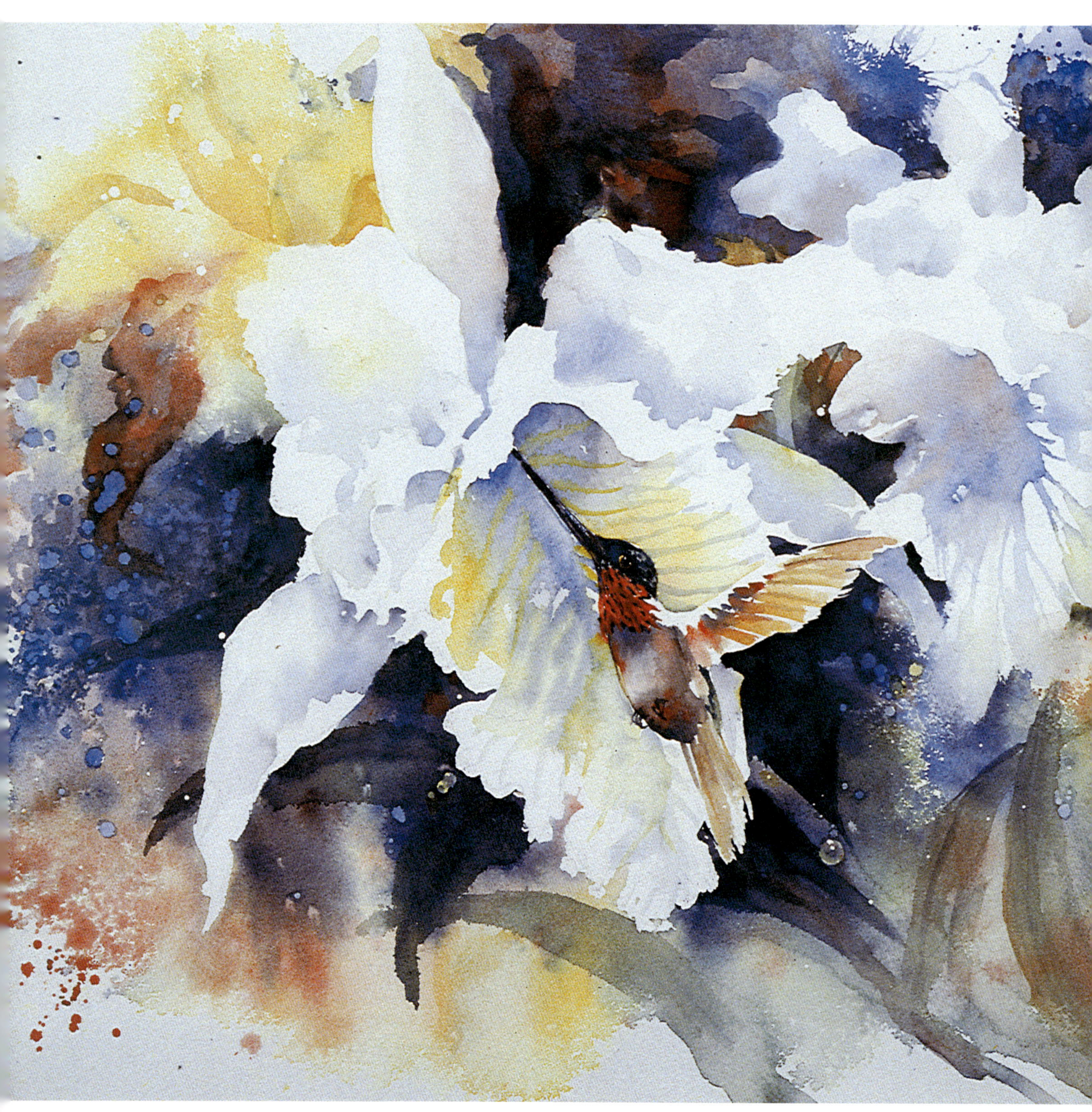

HUMMINGBIRDS AND ORCHID FLOWERS
36 x 53cm (14 x 21in)
Watercolour on Arches 300gsm (140lb)
cold-pressed watercolour paper
Colour pouring and blending

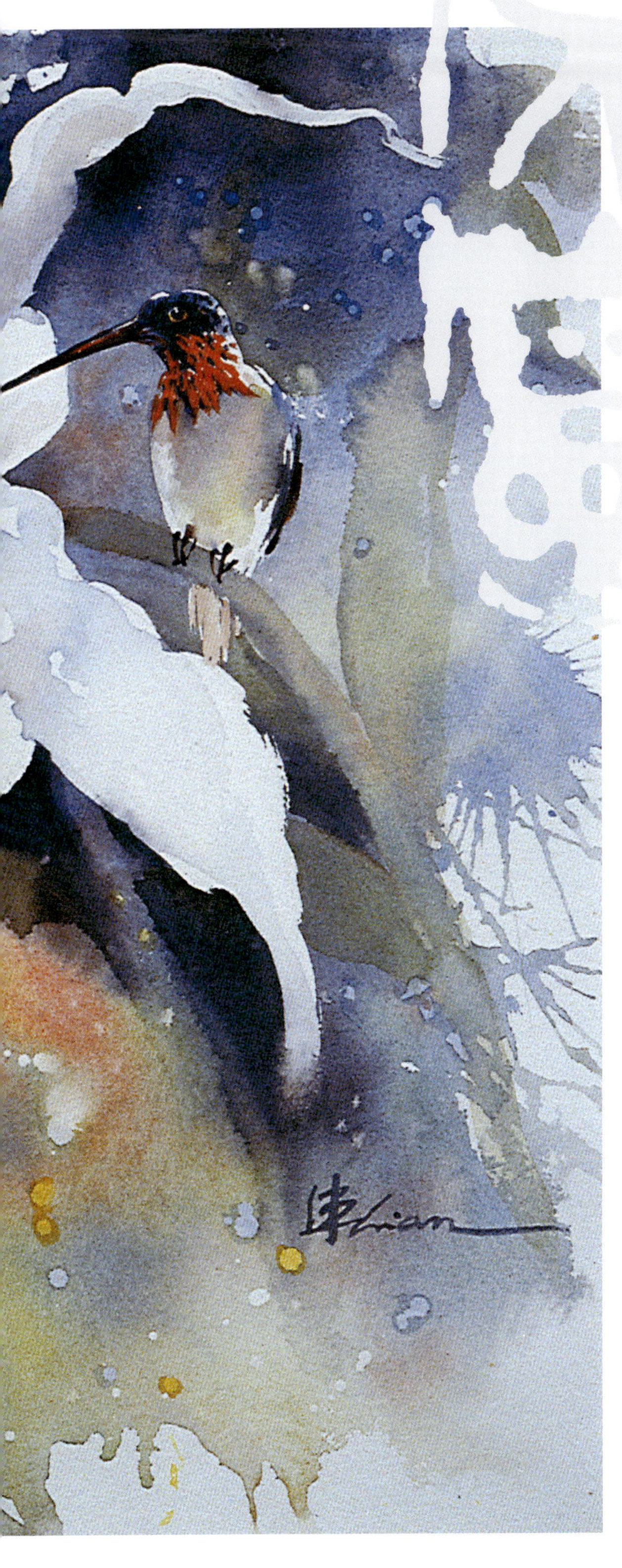

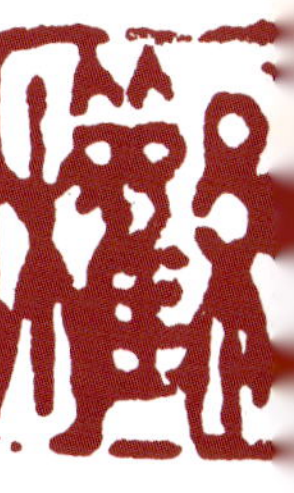

4 PAINTING BIRDS

With an overview of theories and techniques on both my Chinese paintings and water-colours, you'll be able to start painting birds, flowers and landscapes by following the painting steps in the featured demonstrations. In the Chinese painting demonstrations, I will show you how to paint in detail style, spontaneous style and half-detail, half-spontaneous style. In the water colour demonstrations, I will show you my colour-pouring-and-blending techniques.

ANATOMY OF BIRDS

A bird's skeleton dictates its shape. Studying the skeleton, therefore, can help you to capture the right proportions. However, I do not think it is necessary to remember all the terminology; rather, relate the skeleton to human beings. For instance, the wings correspond to arms and hands, and the legs and feet to human legs and feet.

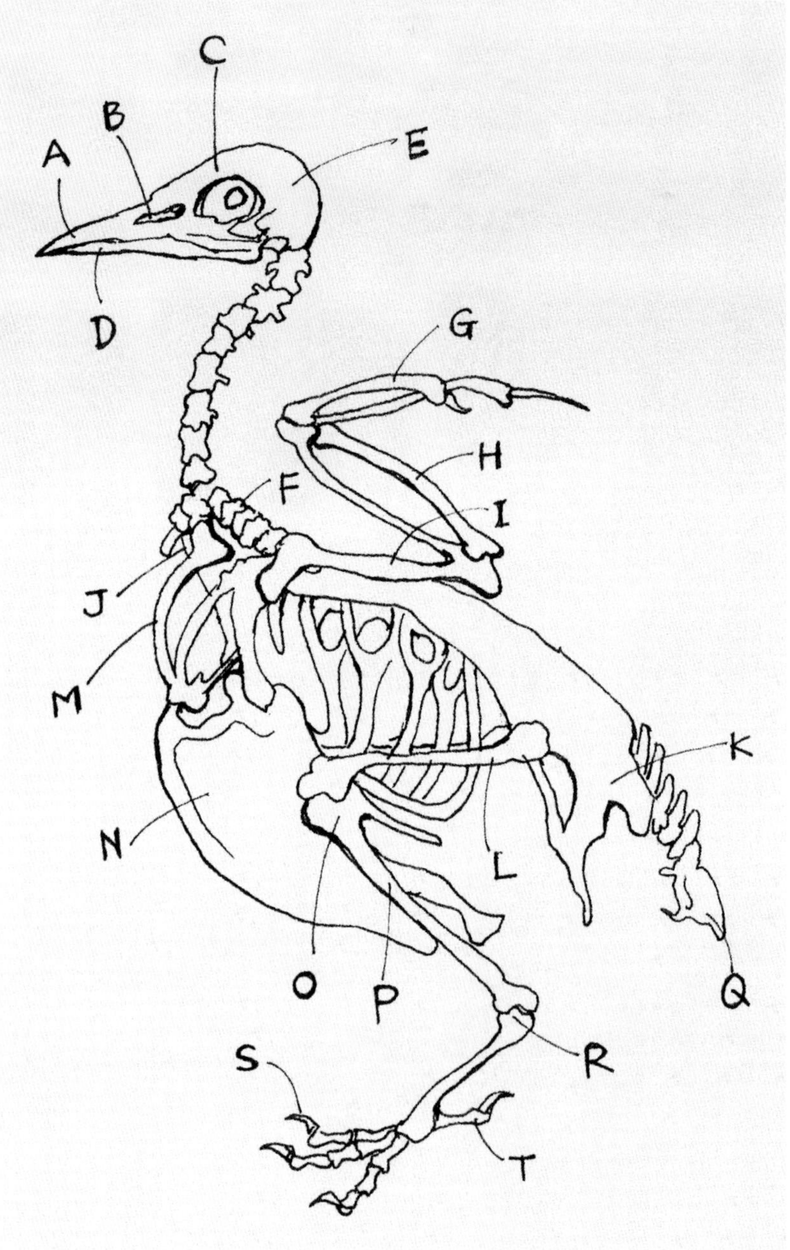

Bird Skeleton
This is a typical flying bird skeleton. Having a huge keel is an obvious feature of a flying bird. The keel is the projection from the breastbone that anchors the wing muscles. Along with the backbone, it forms the egg-shaped body. In comparison, the human chest bone is flat and proportionally smaller.

A. Upper jawbone	K. Hip girdle
B. Nostril	L. Thighbone
C. Eye socket	M. Wishbone
D. Lower jawbone	N. Keel
E. Skull	O. Knee joint
F. Backbone	P. Lower leg bone
G. Metacarpus	Q. Bony stump
H. Ulna	R. Ankle
I. Humerus	S. Claw
J. Coracoid bone	T. Hind toe

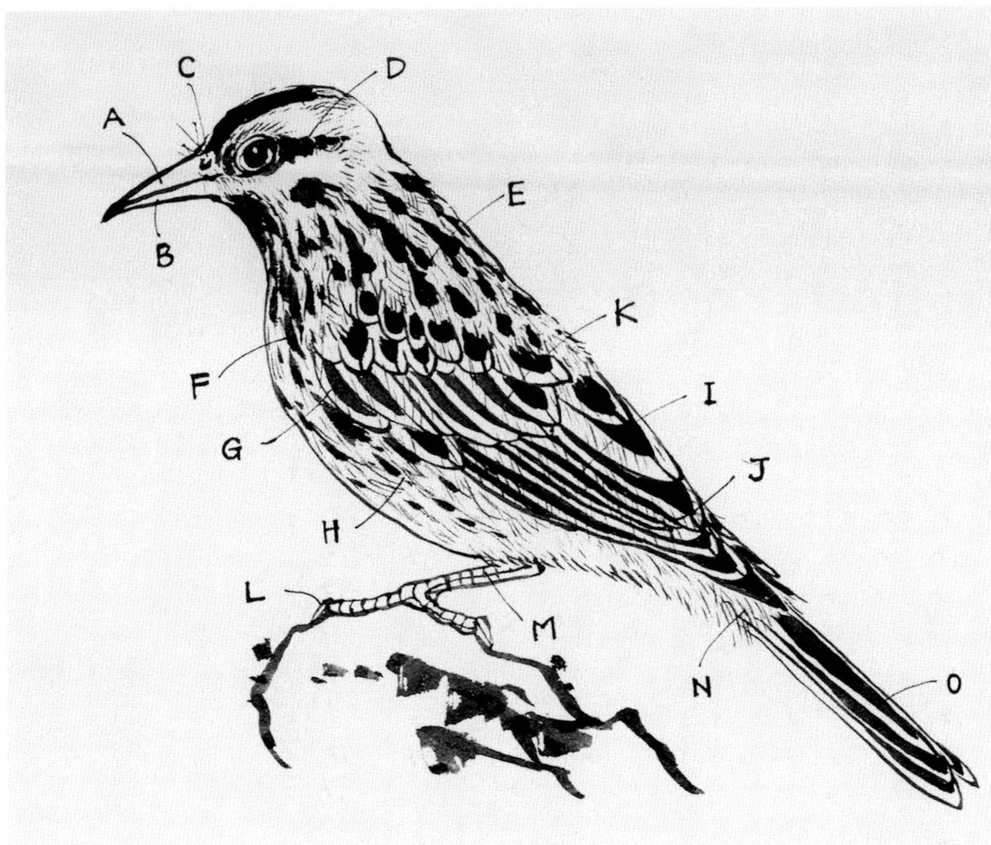

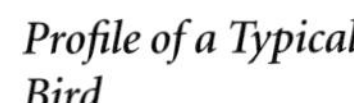

Profile of a Typical Bird

This is a sparrow in profile. Its features relate to its bones.

A. Upper jawbone
B. Lower jawbone
C. Nostril
D. Ear (hidden beneath feathers)
E. Nape
F. Breast
G. Alula
H. Flank
I. Secondary flight feathers
J. Primary flight feathers
K. Wing coverts
L. Toe
M. Tarsus
N. Tail coverts
O. Tail

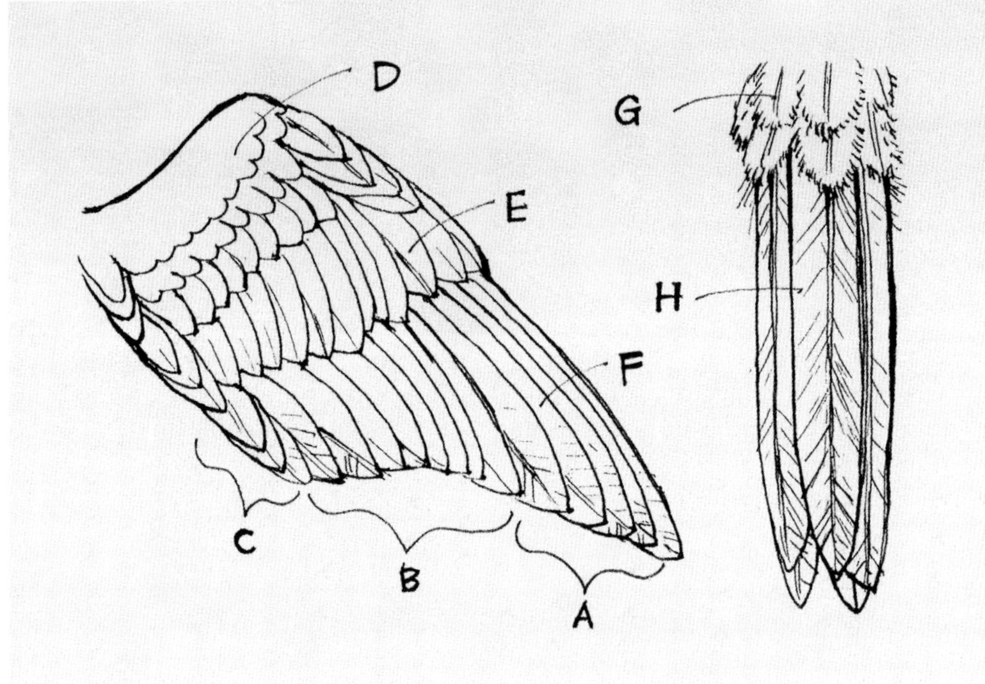

Feathers

Many birds' feathers are in arrangement similar to that shown in this sketch. Interestingly, flying birds do not have true tails. Instead, their tail feathers are attached to a bony stump.

A. and F. Primary flight feathers
B. Secondary flight feathers
C. Tertiary flight feathers
D. Lesser coverts
E. Main coverts
G. Tail coverts
H. Tail feathers

FEATURES OF BIRDS

To adapt to different environments, birds
have evolved a variety of features. The
following illustrations depict the characteristics and features of six different
groups of birds that I often paint .

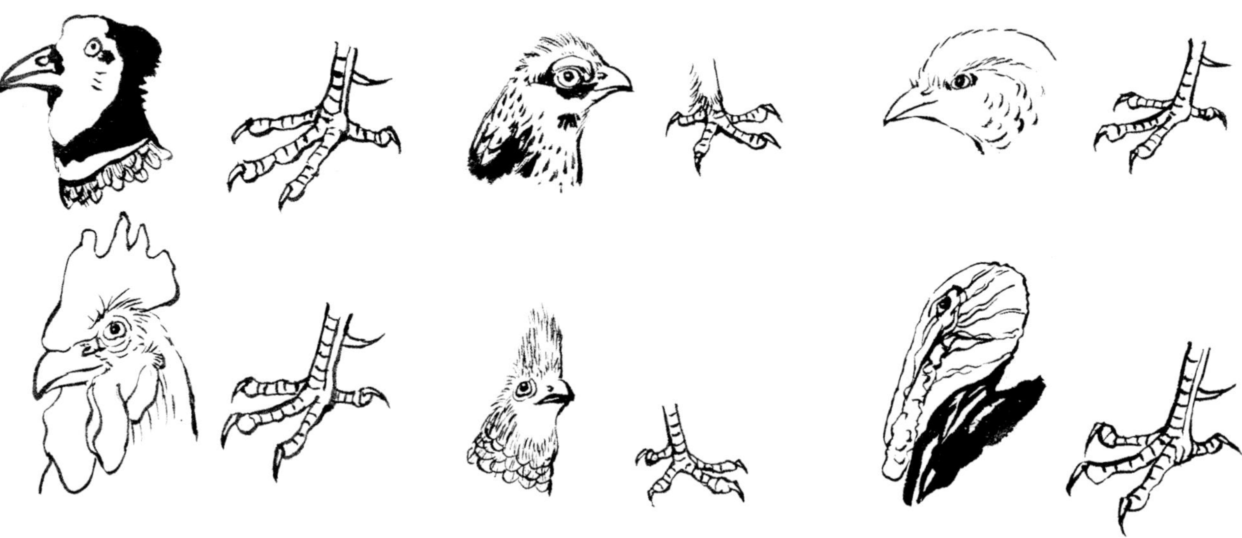

Upland Ground Birds
Chickens, turkey, pheasant, quail and peacocks are upland ground birds.
These birds are good at walking but weak at flying. Therefore, they have
stronger legs and smaller wings compared to many other birds. Their
beaks are short and their claws are sharp. Most male birds have colourful
feathers. In the top row, you see a pheasant, bobwhite and grouse. In the
bottom row are a rooster, scale quail and turkey.

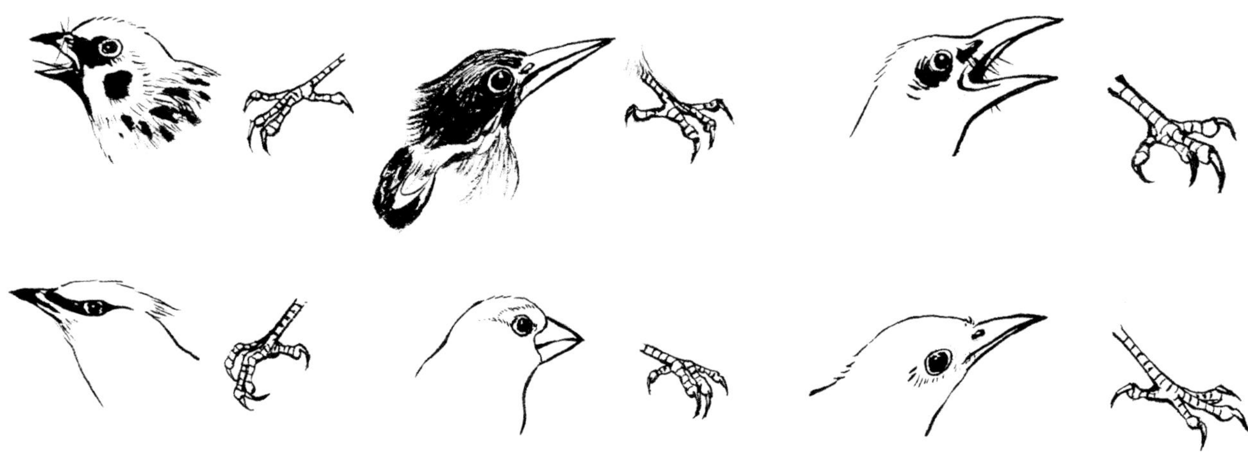

Songbirds
Many songbirds are smaller than other kinds of birds. Among them are
hummingbirds, sparrows, longspurs, finches, waxwings, blue jays, king-
fishers and cardinals. Compared to other kinds of birds, songbirds have
strong wings and are very active. Most of them have small beaks, legs and
claws. In the top row, you see a sparrow, kingfisher and crow. In the bottom are a blue jay, grosbeak and waxwing.

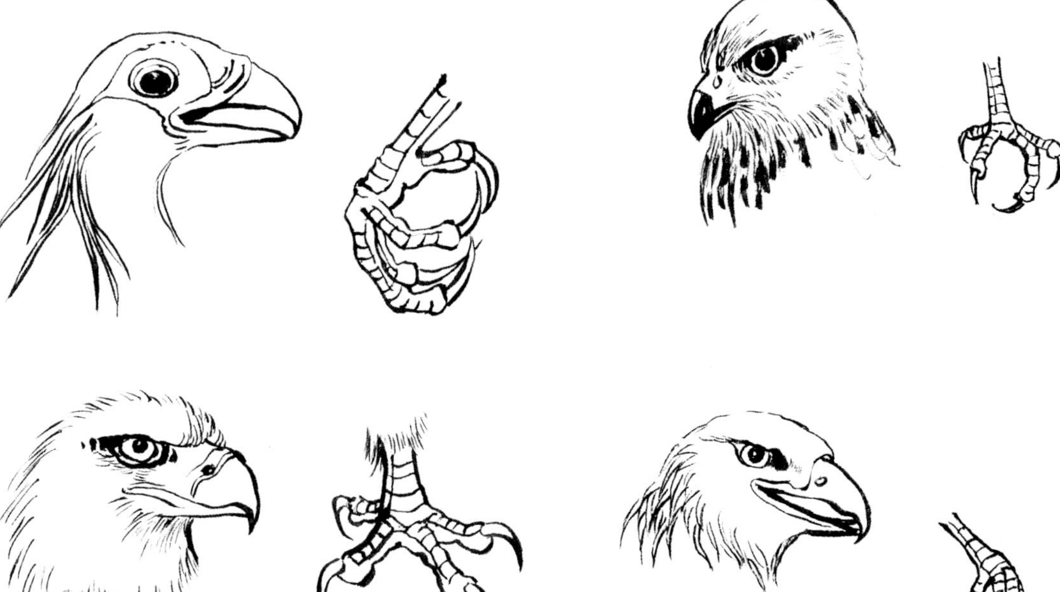

Hawklike Birds

Hawks, eagles and vultures are grouped as hawklike birds. They are built for hunting. Therefore, they are large in size, and have big wings, sharply hooked bills, strong legs and sharp claws. In the top row, you see a vulture and marsh hawk. In the bottom are a bald eagle and golden eagle.

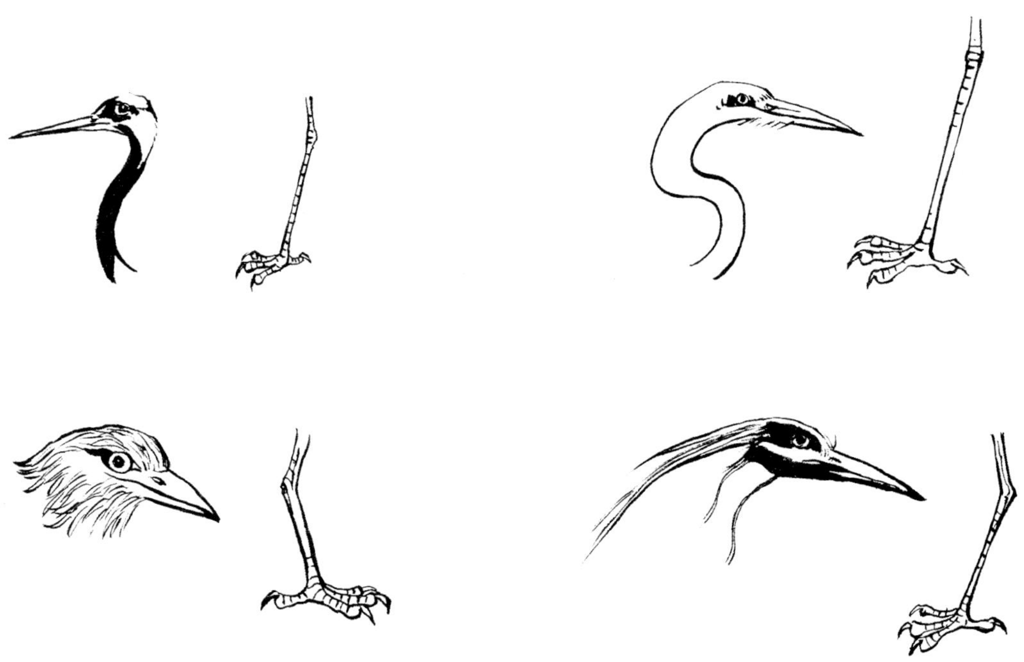

Long-Legged Birds

Long-legged birds are waterbirds with long legs adapted for wading. These birds also have long beaks and long necks. However, their tails are short. Interestingly, even though they live in water environments, they do not swim. In the top row, you see a red crown crane and white egret. In the bottom are two different kinds of herons.

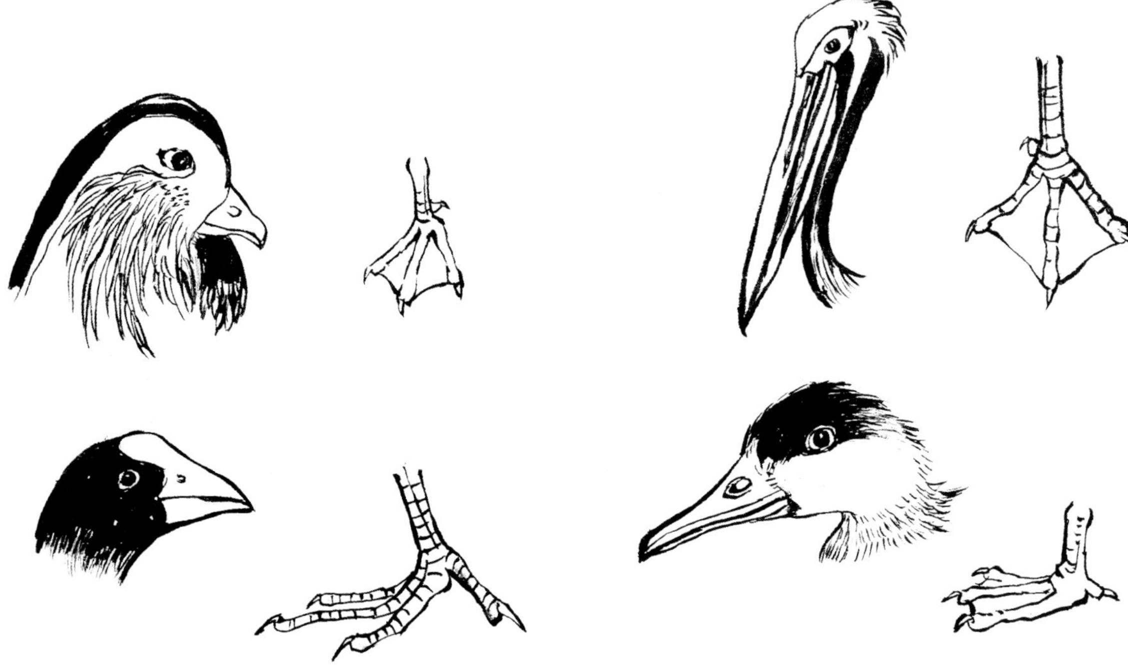

Ducklike Birds

Ducks, geese, swans and pelicans are ducklike birds. They have flat beaks, boat-shaped bodies and webbed toes (or scaly flanges). Their legs are located farther back than on other birds, to enhance their swimming ability. In the top row, you see a wood duck and pelican. In the bottom are a coot and duck.

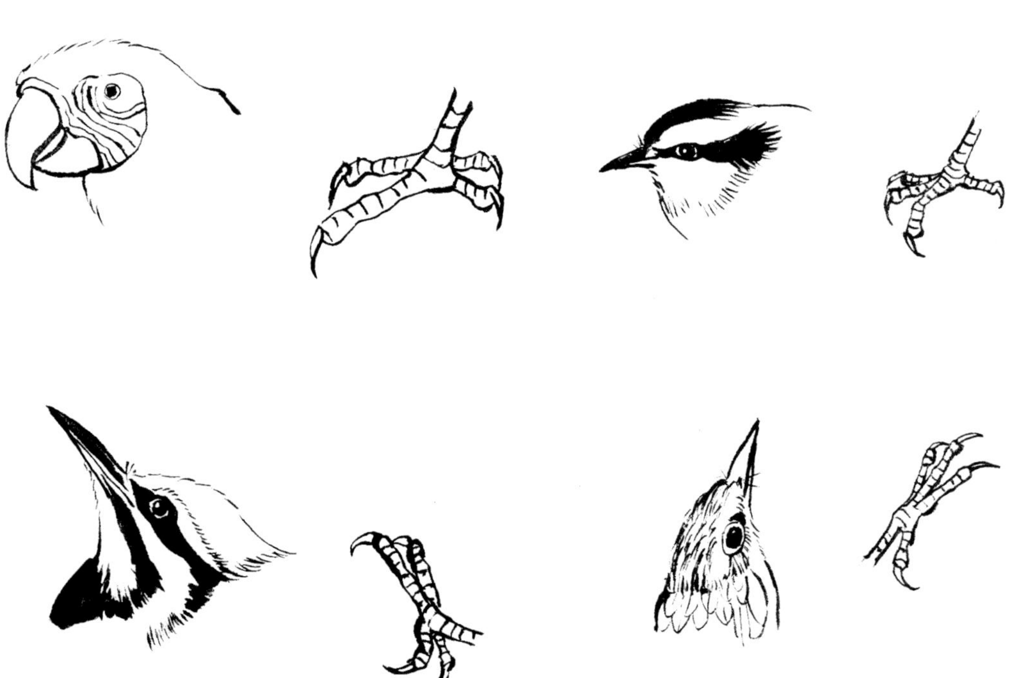

Tree-Climbing Birds

Among the tree-climbing birds are woodpeckers, nuthatches and parrots. Many of them have the distinguishing feature of standing on branches of trees with two toes in front and the other two towards the back. Their beaks are strong and sharp for cracking nuts and wood. In the top row, you see a parrot and nuthatch. In the bottom are a woodpecker and creeper.

A SIMPLE WAY TO SKETCH BIRDS

To sketch birds, relate them to geometric shapes. Interestingly, birds hatch from eggs and their bodies resemble eggs. Their tails are either a square or a fan shape and their beaks are triangular. Despite their movements and positions, their egg-shaped bodies change little. Start by drawing their bodies. Once you have established this, you can easily add their heads, beaks, wings and tails.

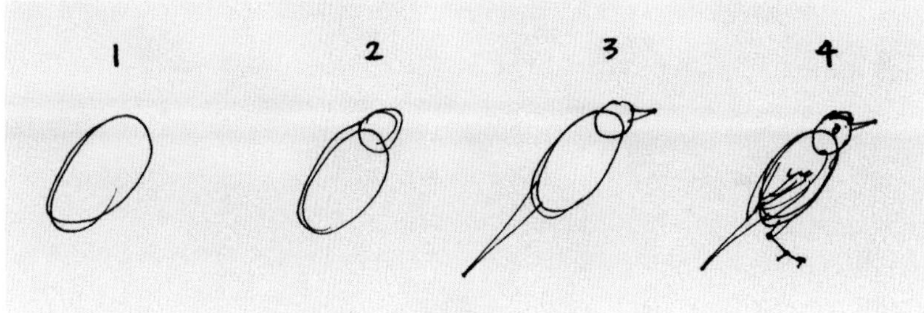

Four Simple Steps for Sketching a Bird
First, draw an egg shape as a bird's body. Second, add a small egg to represent the bird's head. Third, add a narrow triangle as a tail on one end of the big egg, and draw a smaller triangle on the smaller egg as the beak. Fourth, add eyes, wings and legs.

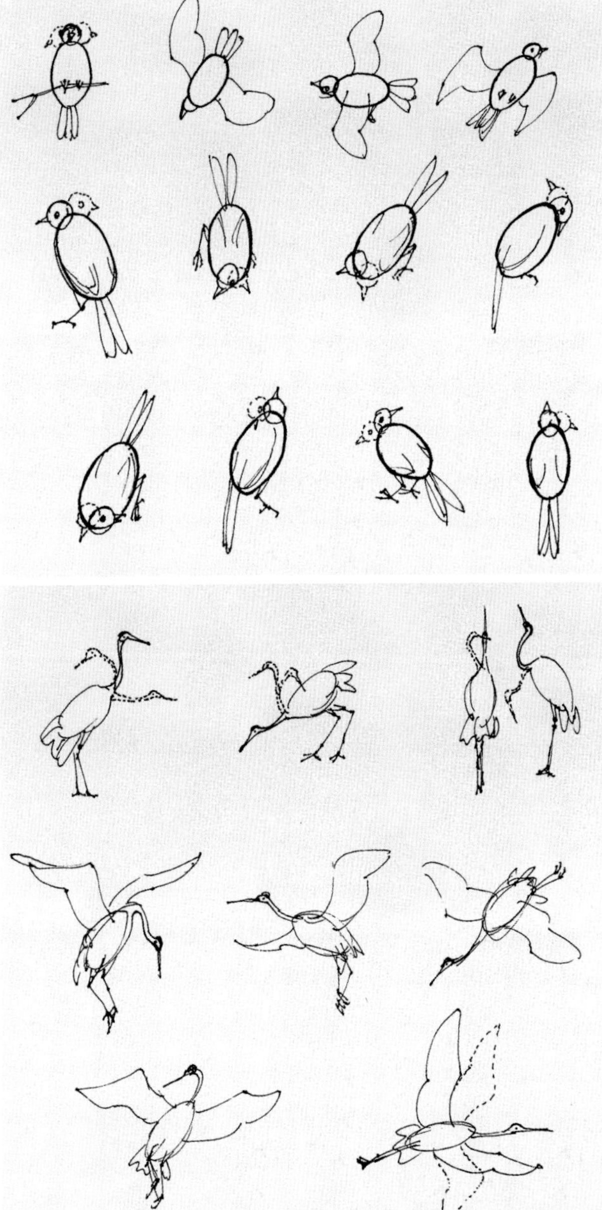

Sketch Birds in a Variety of Positions and Movements
Birds' heads, necks, wings, tails and legs are the most flexible parts. In contrast, their bodies are stable. Therefore, you should always sketch their bodies first, then move on to the other parts.

Various Positions and Movements of Cranes
The crane is one of my favourite birds. To capture its proportions, start by drawing its body.

PAINTING PHEASANTS IN DETAIL STYLE

This demonstration is a full exploration of traditional detail-style painting. Its composition is an S shape. The top leaves of the tree lie at the beginning of the S; the body of the front pheasant and the large rock are at the centre part of the S; the water and the rocks at the bottom left locate the other end of the S. This S-shape composition enhances the motion of the water in contrast to the stillness of the pheasants.

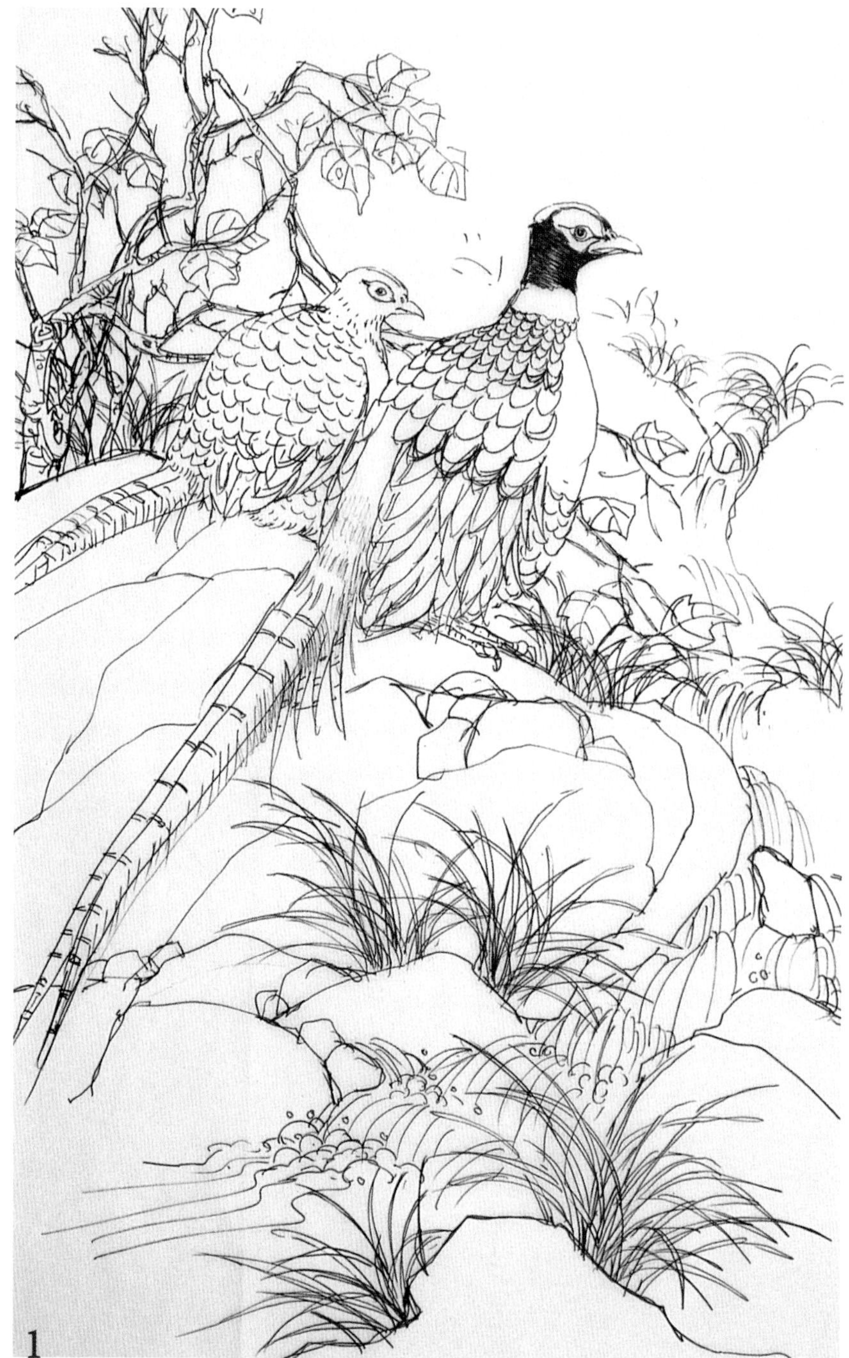

1 SKETCH WITH PENCIL AND INK PEN
On a 69 x 41cm (27 x 16in) piece of tracing paper, sketch the images with a pencil. Next, lay a piece of mature Shuan paper on top. Trace the image with an ink pen. Add more details to the objects. Then tape the ink drawing onto a foamcore board.

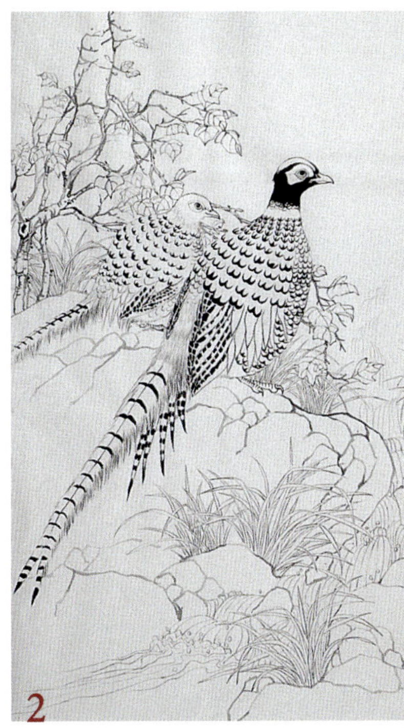 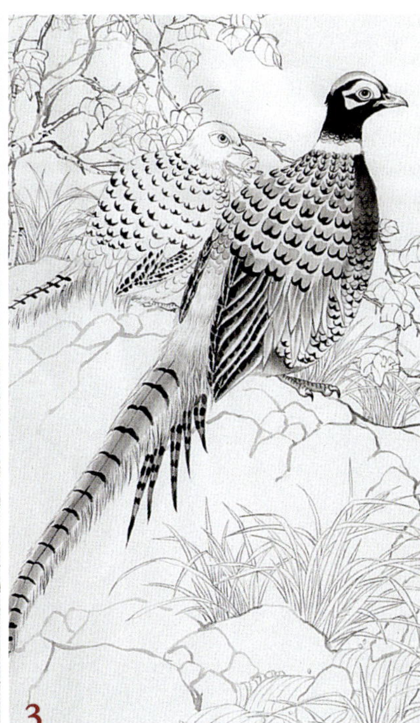 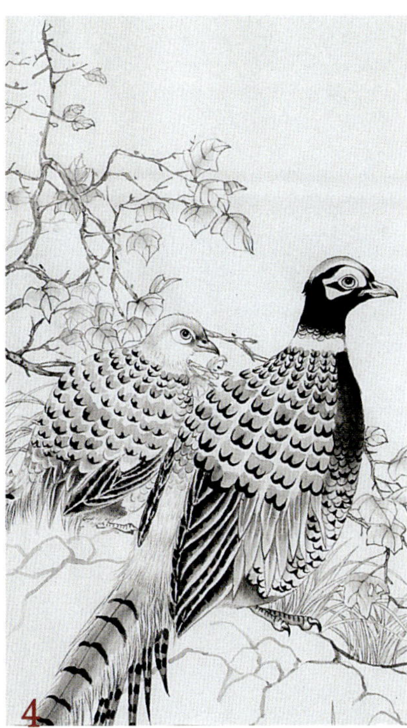

2 *Paint first outline*

Use an extra-small brush and intense ink to outline the male pheasant's beak, eye, coverts and back feathers. Outline the rest of the bird with light ink. Outline the female pheasant in the same way. Next, outline the weeds on the bottom near the centre of the painting with light ink, then the two groups of weeds directly above. Use a small brush to outline the rocks. Next, use the same brush to paint the tree trunk and branches with the side-brush method. Use the extra-small brush to outline the tree leaves. Finally, outline the water and the weeds behind the rocks and the tree.

3 *Tone the male bird with ink*

Paint the male bird's beak, head and eye first, then its body. Use a small brush to apply the ink, then immediately use a medium brush to blend it with water. Leave white for each flight and tail feather and for the toes and claws. After the first layer of ink is dry, tone the bird one more time in the same way.

4 *Tone the female bird and the tree and weeds*

Tone the female bird a couple of times as you did with the male bird. Then use a small brush to tone the tree trunk and branches, leaving white on the centre area of the trunk and upper parts of the branches. Next, use a small brush to apply medium ink on the centre vein and the beginning part of each leaf. Immediately blend the ink into the outside edges with water. Paint two to three leaves at a time. Tone the weeds behind with an extra-small brush. Apply darker ink on the bottom part of the leaves, then blend the ink to their tips. For the overlapping areas, tone the back leaves darker.

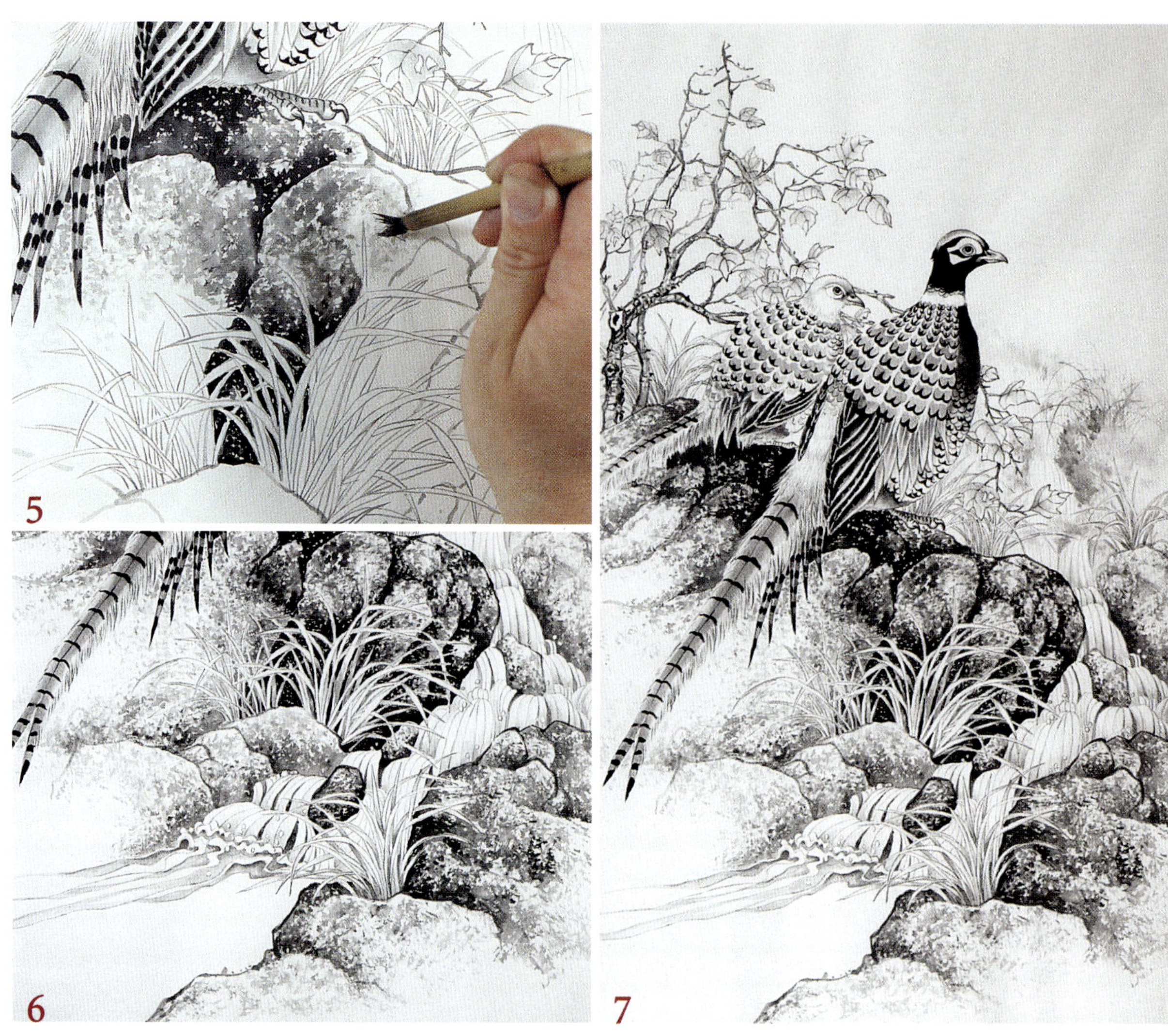

5 PAINT THE TEXTURE OF THE ROCKS

Make a medium brush into a split tip. To do this, press a wet brush on a paper towel to absorb the water. When most of the water is gone, the brush tip will split into multitips. With a small amount of ink, paint the rocks using the side-brush method. Apply light ink first, then medium, then intense ink last. Do not paint the weeds and the water.

6 TONE WEEDS AND WATER WITH INK

Tone the weeds as described in steps 3 and 4. Use a small brush to apply medium ink at the bottom of each water wave. Immediately use another brush to get a small amount of water to blend the ink into the middle part. Leave white on the top portion.

7 TONE THE DISTANT OBJECTS

Use a medium brush to tone the rocks and water in the background with light ink. While the ink is damp, use an extra-small brush to paint the weeds. Each brushstroke depicts one leaf. Now the painting is ready for colouring.

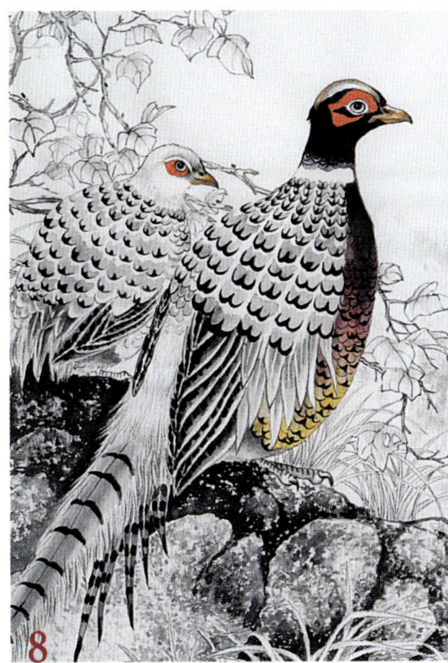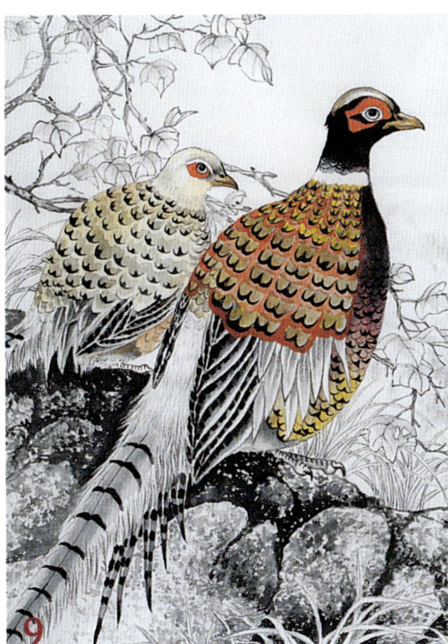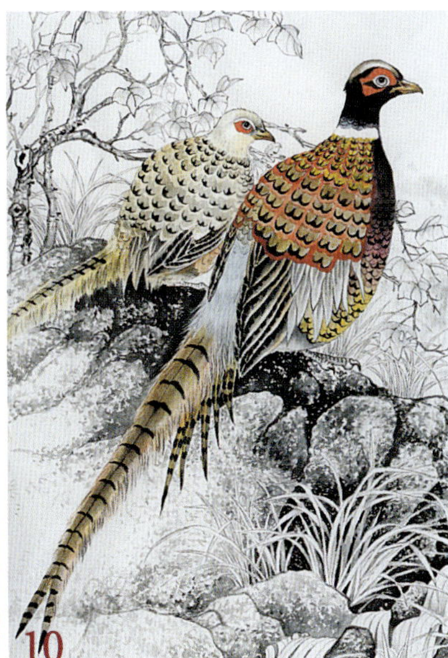

8 COLOUR THE BIRDS

Use a small brush to apply intense cinnabar around the eyes. Apply yellow on the beaks. While they are wet, apply burnt sienna on the tips and bottom portions of the jawbones. Paint the top of the male's head with burnt sienna. On the left side of the neck above the white ring, apply phthalocyanine blue and blend it to the rouge on the right. Next, use a medium brush to apply rouge on the right side of the neck and the chest. Immediately, apply yellow to the abdomen and blend it into the rouge.

9 CONTINUE COLOURING THE BIRDS

Use a medium brush to paint yellow on the male bird's head and lesser coverts. Use a small brush to paint intense cinnabar on its main coverts. Paint light yellow on the female bird's head, neck and body.

10 CONTINUE COLOURING THE BIRDS

Use a medium brush to paint the tail covert feathers on the male bird with blue. Next, apply burnt sienna on the flight feathers for both birds. Also, paint their large tail feathers with yellow and burnt sienna. Define the tail feathers' fringes with light cinnabar.

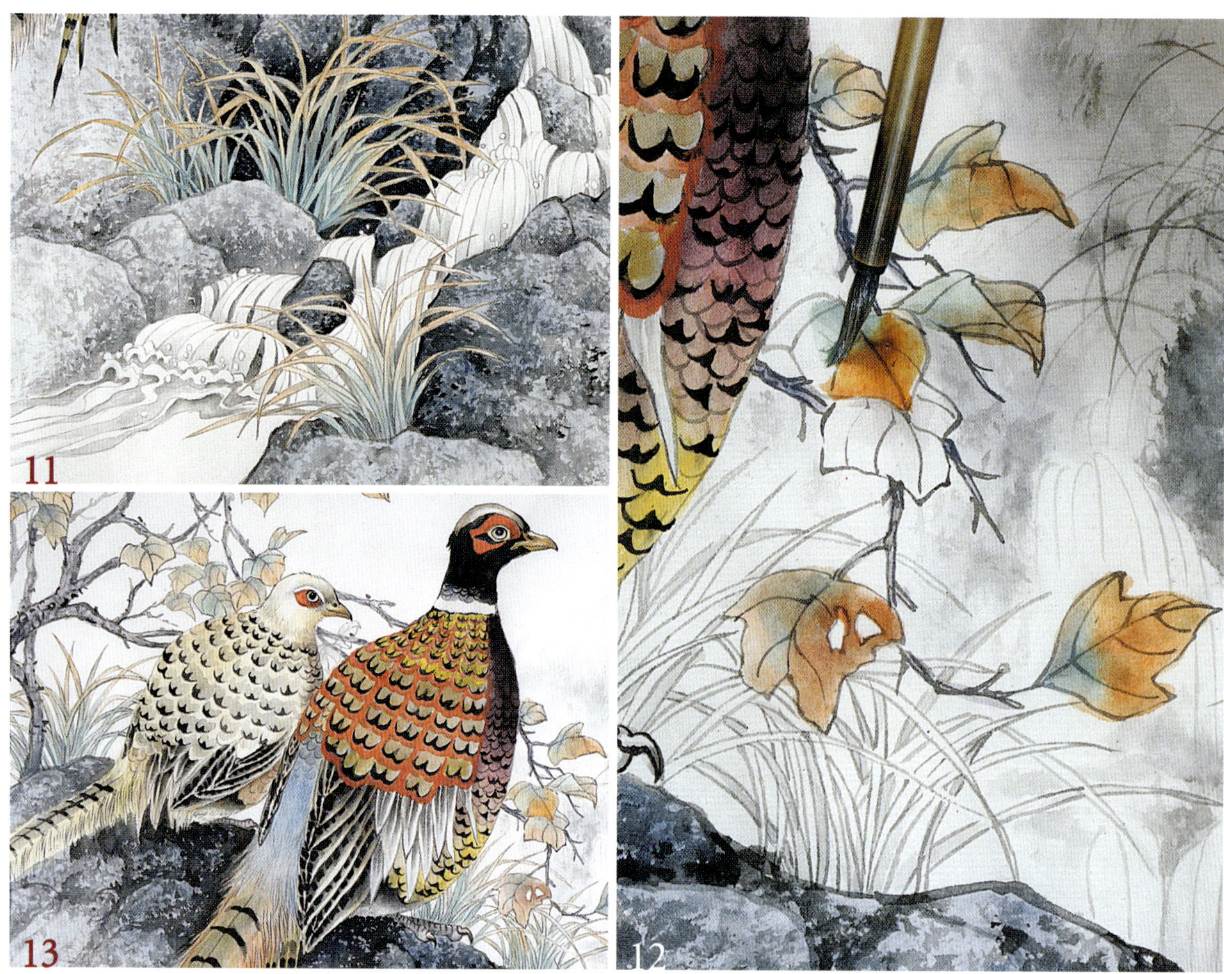

11 *COLOUR THE ROCKS AND WEEDS*

Use a large brush to paint the rocks with light blue. Next, use a small brush to apply green to the bottom portion of each leaf. While the colour is wet, use another small brush to apply cermilion from its tip to the green. Finally, blend the two colours with a small, moist brush.

12 *COLOUR THE TREE LEAVES, BRANCHES AND TRUNKS*

Paint the leaves one by one using small brushes. Apply cinnabar on the tip and centre area of a leaf. Immediately apply green on the area near the stem and drag the green into the cinnabar. Finally, blend the colours with water. To paint the trunk and branches, use a medium brush to mix light indigo and rouge into light blue-purple. Then apply it on the branches and trunks.

13 *APPLY A SECOND LAYER OF COLOURS ON THE MALE BIRD*

In order to build up stronger saturation on the male's feathers, you need to apply a second layer of colours. Use the same brushes, colours and techniques as with the first layer of colouring to paint the feathers again.

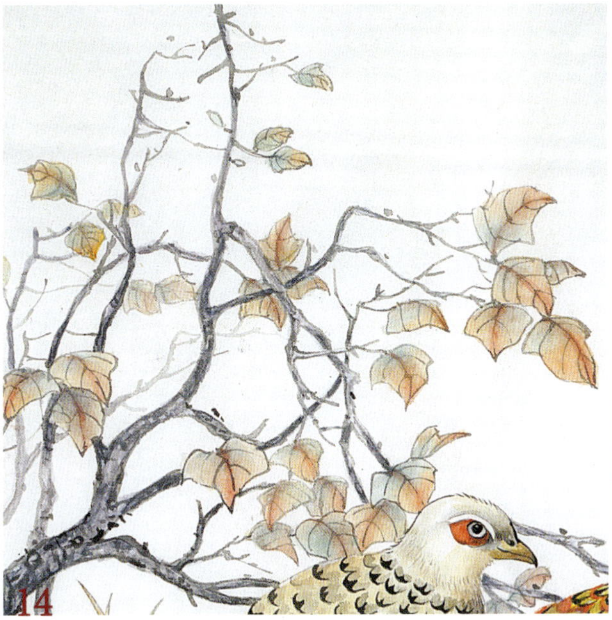
14

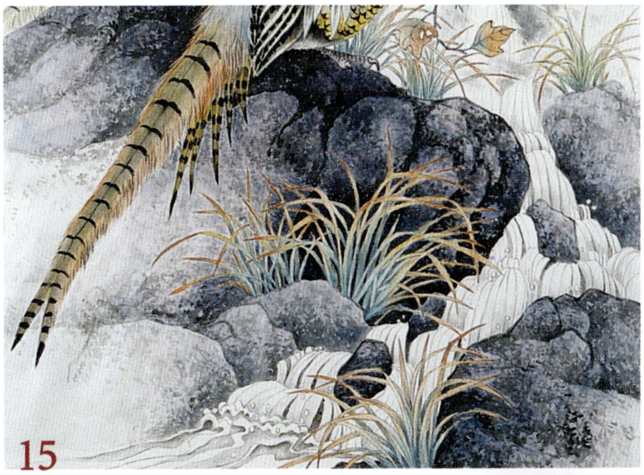
15

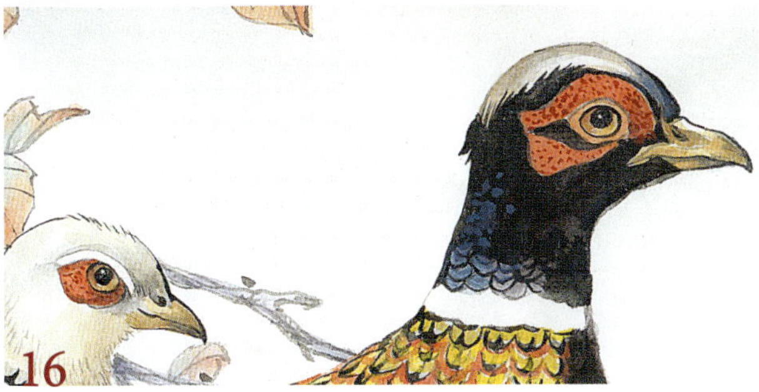
16

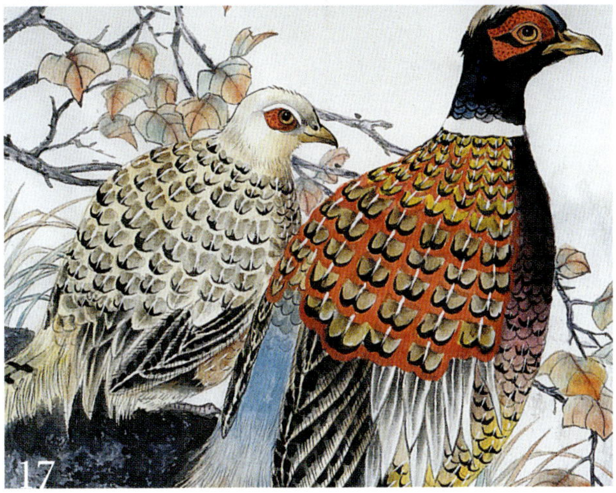
17

14 Apply a second layer of colour to the tree leaves

Use a small brush to apply cinnabar to a leaf. While the colour is wet, use a small, moist brush to blend it to the edges of the leaf. Paint the leaves one by one.

15 Apply a second layer of colour to the weeds and multiple colours on the rocks

Use the same brushes and colours as described in step 11 to apply a second layer of colour on the weeds. Then use an extra-small brush to paint the tip of each leaf with light rouge. Next, use a large brush to paint the rocks with light blue. When the colour is dry, apply the blue again. Finally, apply a thin layer of rouge.

16 Add details to the birds' head and neck

Use a small brush and intense rouge to paint some dots around the eyes. Use an extra-small brush to paint light yellow on the eyeball. Then use the same brush to apply burnt sienna to the upper portion of the eyeball while the yellow is wet. At the left side of the neck above the white ring of the male bird, apply intense blue.

17 Add details to the feathers

Use a small brush to paint the centre part of each covert with dark brown mixed from intense ink and burnt sienna. When the colour is dry, use a small brush to paint an intense white stroke on the centre of each of the feathers. Then use an extra-small brush to paint small, diagonal, intense ink strokes on each primary flight feather.

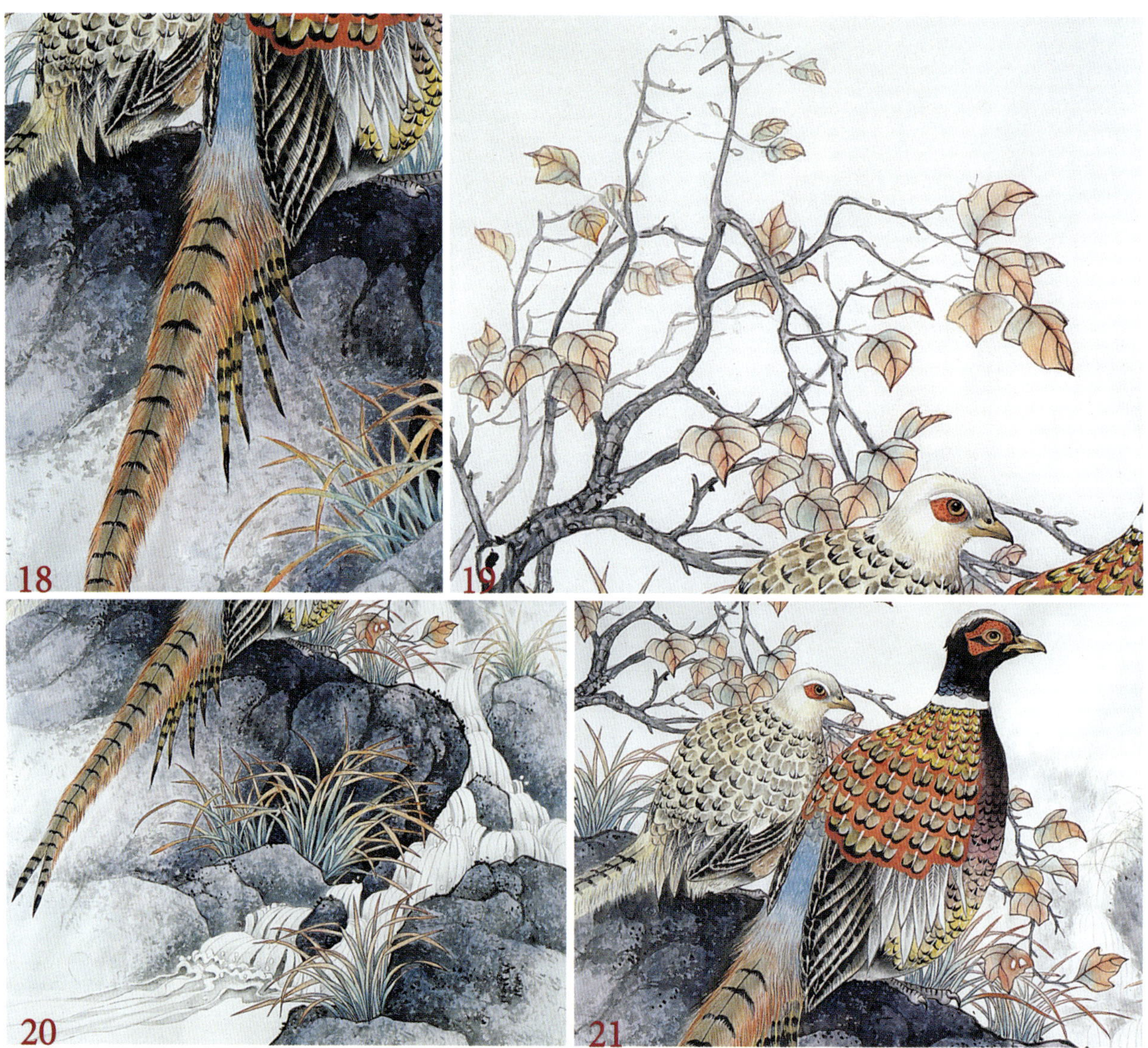

18 Add details to the tails

Use an extra-small brush to call out the small tail covert feathers with white. On the large tail feathers, paint small strokes on the bottom of each black stripe with intense white. Also, add tiny strokes on the edges of the large tail feathers with intense cinnabar.

19 Paint the second outline on the tree

Use extra-small brushes to outline the trunk and branches with ink that is darker than the first outlines. Mix ink and rouge to outline the leaves. Try to match the first outline strokes.

20 Paint the second outline on the rocks and weeds

Use a medium brush to outline the rocks with ink that is darker than the previous outlines. Add some intense ink dots randomly on the rocks, a technique known as 'calling out the moss'. Mix rouge and ink to outline the upper part of the weeds. Mix ink and indigo to outline their lower portions.

21 Paint the second outline on the birds

Use an extra-small brush to outline the beaks, heads, necks, feet, claws and feathers with intense ink. Outline the body of the male bird with rouge and ink. Outline the body of the female bird with burnt sienna and light ink.

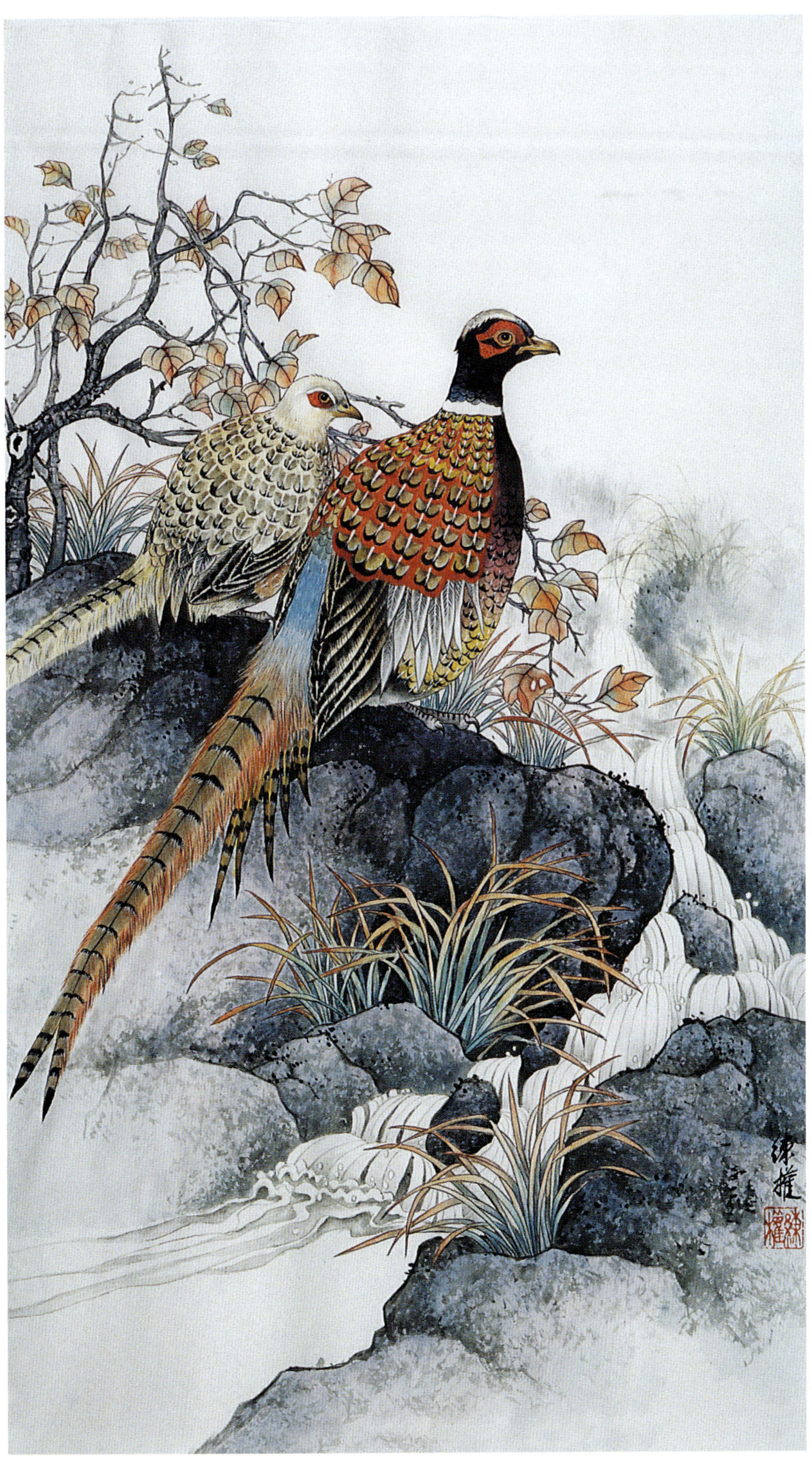

22 SIGN AND SEAL
YOUR PAINTING
Sign your name to
the lower right cor-
ner and stamp your
chop below it. Be-
cause your signature
and chop are not
needed for balance
in this composition,
hide them in the
rocks.
PHEASANTS
69 x 41cm
(27 x 16in)
Chinese ink and
colours on mature
Shuan paper
Detail style

PAINTING AN EGRET IN HALF-DETAIL, HALF-SPONTANEOUS STYLE

This painting has a triangular composition. The wing on the left, the top portion of the bamboo post and the lotus leaves behind form the tip of the triangular shape. The net, the lotus leaf, the signature and the chop on the lower right form the right side of the triangular shape. Likewise, the net and lotus leaves on the left form the left side.

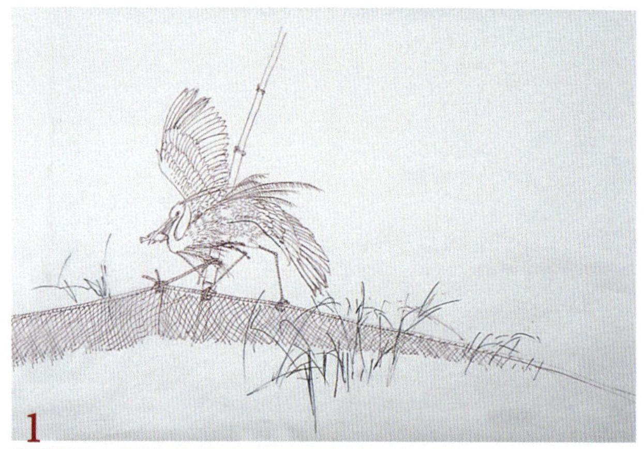

1 Sketch on tracing paper

Place a 43 x 61cm (17 x 24in) piece of tracing paper on foamcore board and tape down its corners. Sketch the images with pens.

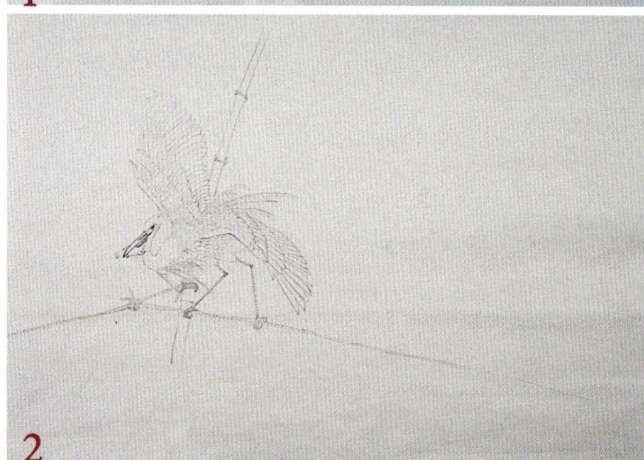

2 Paint first outline

Lay a 43 x 61cm (17 x 24in) piece of mature Shuan paper on top of the sketch and tape its corners onto the board. Use an extra-small brush to paint the outlines of the bird first, then move to the net ropes and finally to the bamboo post. Paint the beak and eye of the egret with intense ink and the rest with light ink.

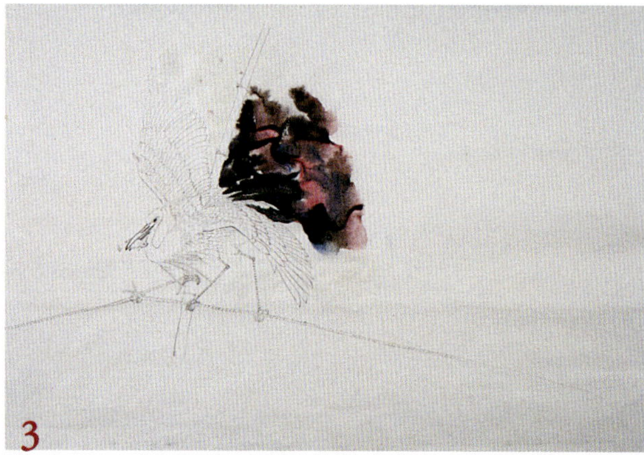

3 Paint the background at right

Use a large brush to wet the right background without wetting the bird. Immediately, apply intense ink next to the bird with a medium brush. In addition, apply medium rouge and phthalocyanine blue onto the ink with another large brush. Let the colours blend into each other.

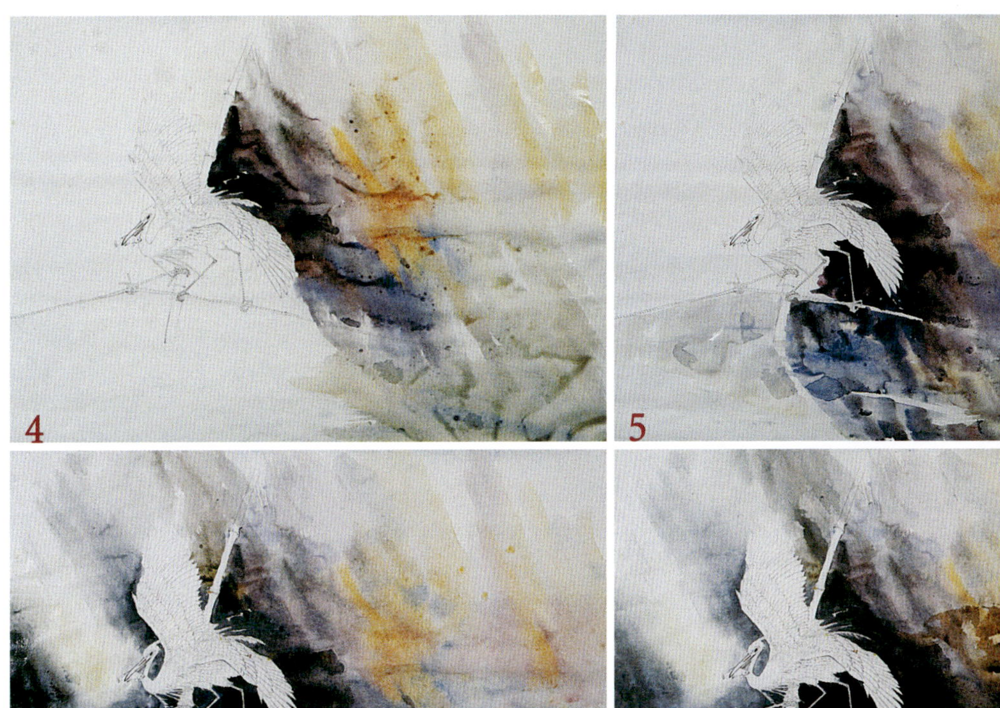

4 CONTINUE TO PAINT THE BACKGROUND AT RIGHT

Use a small brush to guide the colours for defining the edge of the
wing and bamboo. Wet the background at far right. Then use a large
brush to apply yellow and cinnabar to the centre and upper portions.
Next, apply phthalocyanine blue to the lower part to create the water
effect. Use a large brush to blend the colours.

5 DEFINE THE SHAPE OF THE EGRET

Apply intense ink between the legs and the front wing with a medium
brush. Then use a small brush to define the outlines of the feet, the
body and front wing by dragging the ink towards the outlines of the
bird. Use a large brush to add rouge on the right and lower centre of
the background.

6 PAINT THE BACKGROUND AT LEFT AND CONTINUE
TO DEFINE THE SHAPE OF THE EGRET

Wet the background at left, then apply ink and indigo. Leave white
above the bird's head. At the edge of the rear wing, drag the colours
diagonally to the upper left with a large brush. The diagonal strokes
will create the illusion of rain.

7 PAINT THE LOTUS LEAF NEXT TO THE FRONT WING

Fill a large brush with rouge, then add intense ink to its tip. Hold
the brush sideways and move it quickly from the centre of the leaf
to its edge so that you create an effect called 'fly white', the white areas
on the leaf.

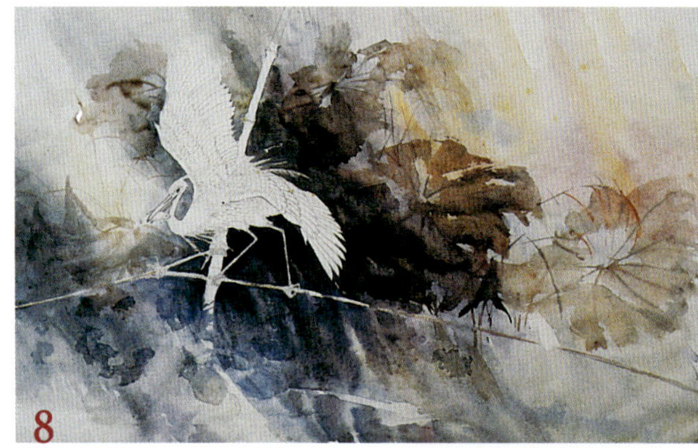

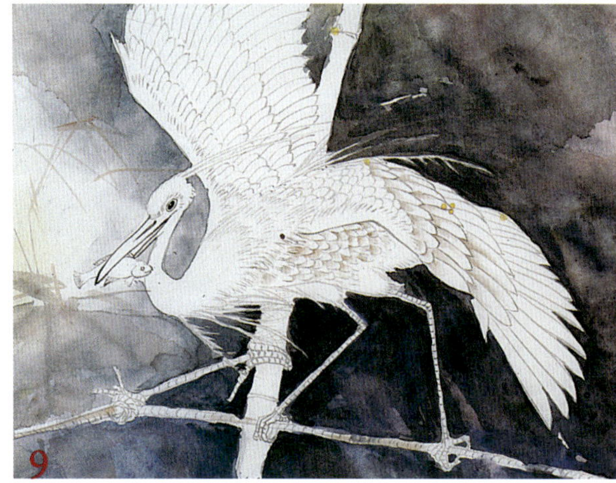

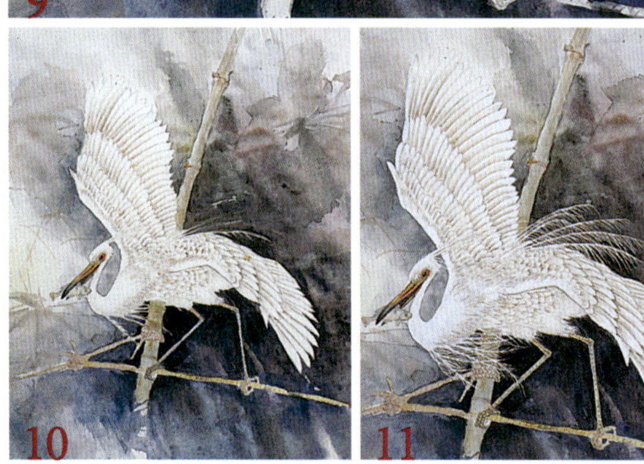

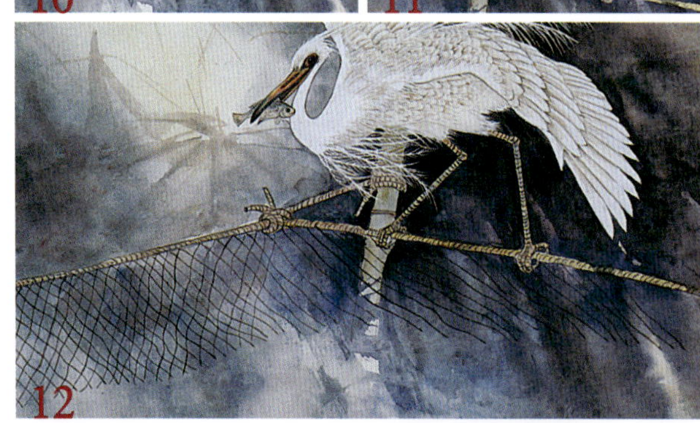

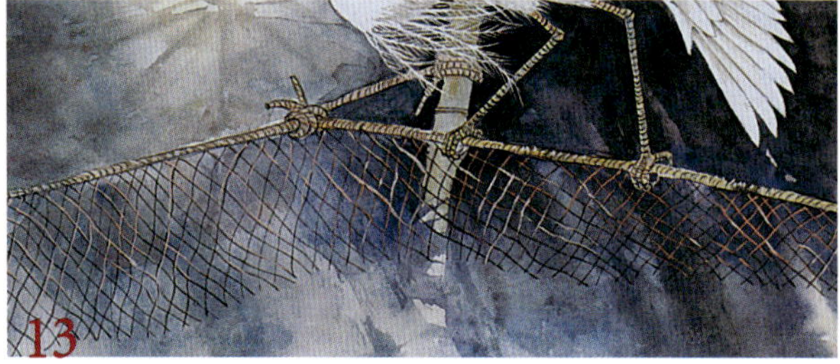

8 Paint the other lotus leaves and weeds

Use the same brush to paint the leaf above with lighter rouge and ink. Paint the other leaves with light rouge, yellow and a little ink. When it's raining, lotus leaves hold water in their central areas. Thus, leave the lighter background colours at their centre. To finish the leaves, use a medium brush to paint the veins with medium ink and rouge. Next, use a small brush to mix ink and vermilion. Paint the weeds while the colours on the leaves and background are damp.

9 Paint the egret's feathers

Use a small brush to mix burnt sienna and light ink. Apply the colours at the beginning of each feather. Then use another small brush to blend the colours towards the tip with water. Paint the feathers one by one.

10 Paint the other areas of the bird, bamboo post, net ropes and fish

After you are finished painting the feathers, use a small brush to paint the beak and eye with yellow. Then apply vermilion to the beak and around the eye. Add rouge to the tip of the beak, then apply light blue at the tip and nostril. Next, use a small brush to paint the feet with blue and vermilion. Use a medium brush to mix yellow, blue and burnt sienna to paint the bamboo post. Paint the ropes with yellow and vermilion. Paint the fish with yellow, vermilion and blue.

11 Add detail to the feathers and paint the breeding plumage

Use an extra-small brush to paint the centre line of each feather and the breeding plumage (narrow, fringed feathers) with very intense white. Apply your brushstrokes from the bird's body outwards. In addition, paint white at the tips and edges of the other feathers. Next, use an extra-small brush to mix yellow, vermilion and white to outline and call out the texture of the feet.

12 Paint the net and apply second outline on the bird, the fish and the ropes

Use an extra-small brush to paint the net with intense ink. Next, paint the second outlines using intense ink on the bird's eye, beak and feet; using burnt sienna and ink on the neck; using indigo and ink on the fish; and using burnt sienna and ink on the ropes.

13 Paint water drops on the net

Use an extra-small brush to mix vermilion and white. Randomly apply the colour to the threads of the net.

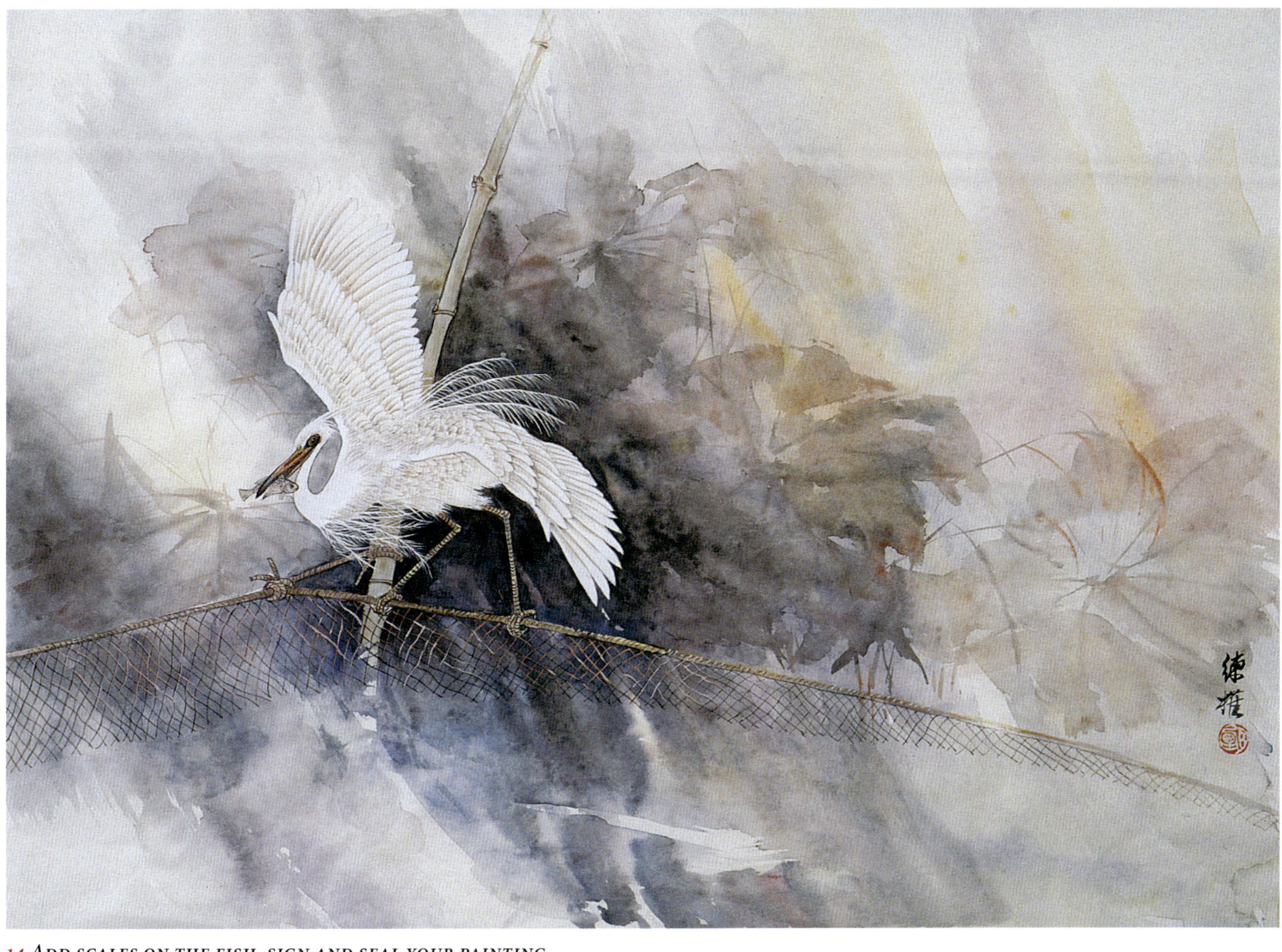

14 ***ADD SCALES ON THE FISH, SIGN AND SEAL YOUR PAINTING***

Use an extra-small brush to mix vermilion and white. Paint small dots
on the fish as scales. Finally, sign your name and stamp your chop on
the lower right corner. They will balance the bird on the left.

FISHING IN THE RAIN
43 x 61cm (17 x 24in)
Chinese ink and colours on mature Shuan paper
Half-detail, half-spontaneous style

PAINTING PEACOCKS IN SPONTANEOUS STYLE

Most accomplished Chinese artists do not sketch their spontaneous compositions before they paint. However, you can use a charcoal stick to sketch your images on Shuan paper before you paint. Do not draw details because spontaneous-style paintings tend to lack careful organization. You may change objects' shapes and colours during the painting process according to the developing composition and your mood and style of expression.

The composition of this painting is a reverse C shape. Even though the peonies are at the front, the colourful male peacock is the focal point. In contrast to other spontaneous-style paintings in this book, this painting features more details.

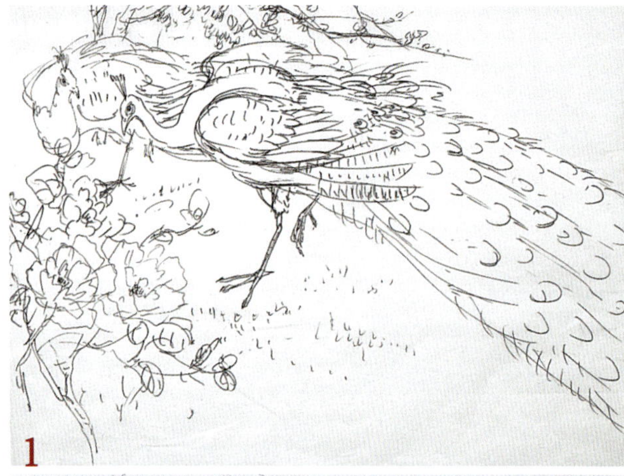

1 SKETCH ON TRACING PAPER

Sketch the images and composition on a 46 x 69cm (18 x 27in) piece of tracing paper with an ink pen. Keep in mind that you do not have to paint all the objects you have sketched. In fact, the flower tree behind the birds is not in my finished painting.

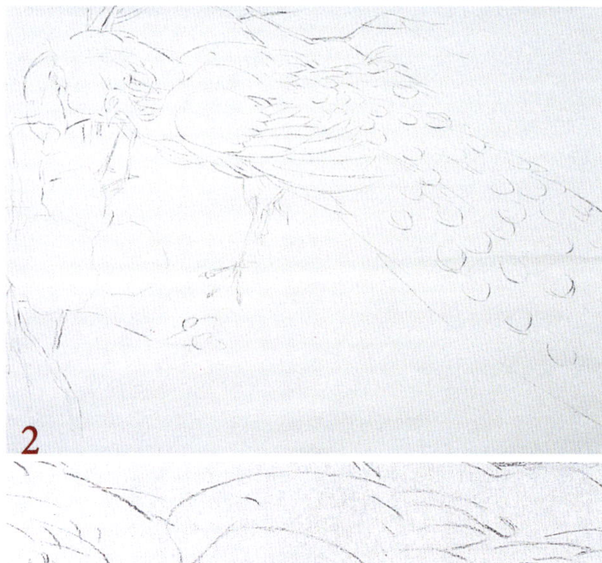

2 SKETCH ON THE SHUAN PAPER

Place a piece of double-layer Shuan paper the same size as the tracing paper on top of the sketch, then trace the images with a charcoal stick. Draw only the main outlines of the objects. When you have finished tracing, scrape off any excess charcoal.

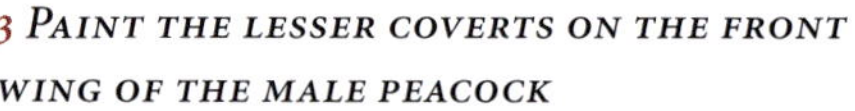

3 PAINT THE LESSER COVERTS ON THE FRONT WING OF THE MALE PEACOCK

Use a large brush to mix yellow and indigo, then add intense ink to its tip. Paint a few brushstrokes using the centre-brush method. Next, make the brush into a split tip. Use ink to paint the split brushstrokes. Then use another large brush to mix rouge, light ink and yellow to paint the lesser coverts at left.

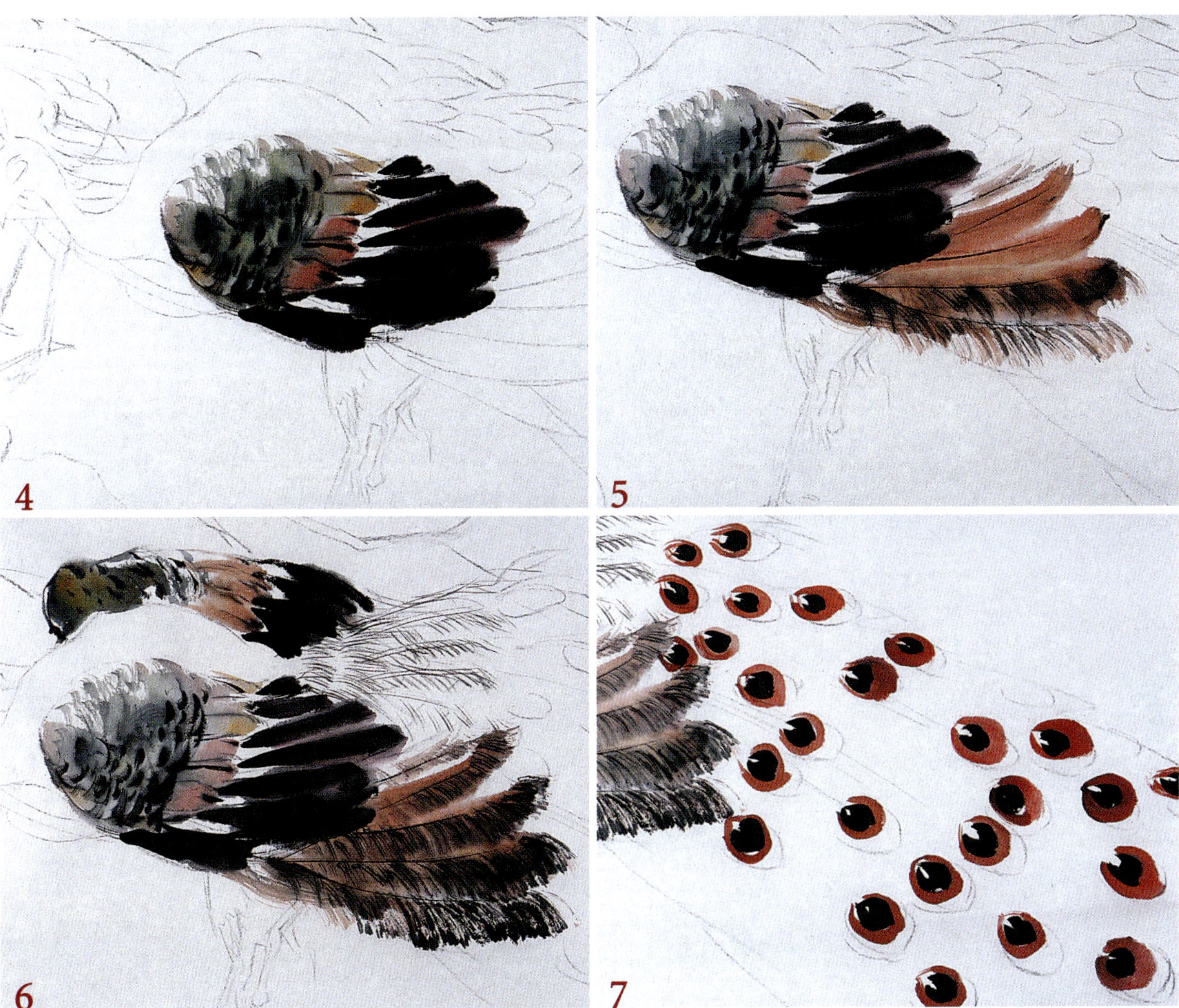

4 PAINT THE MAIN COVERTS

Use a large brush to mix intense ink and a little rouge to paint the main coverts. Then paint an intense ink stroke on the centre of each lesser covert.

5 PAINT THE FLIGHT FEATHERS

Use a large brush to paint the flight feathers with vermilion and light ink. Paint the brushstrokes from the tip of the feathers to the main coverts. Each stroke depicts one feather. When the feathers are halfway dry, use a small brush to paint a stroke at the centre of each flight feather with intense ink. Also, use a medium split-tip brush to paint the texture with ink and vermilion.

6 PAINT THE REAR WING AND THE TAIL COVERTS

Paint the rear wing in the same way as the front wing. Then use a small brush to paint the tail coverts with ink.

7 PAINT THE CIRCULAR PATTERNS OF THE TAIL

Use a medium brush to paint the black spots with intense ink. Next, use another medium brush to mix carmine and rouge to paint the strokes around the black spots.

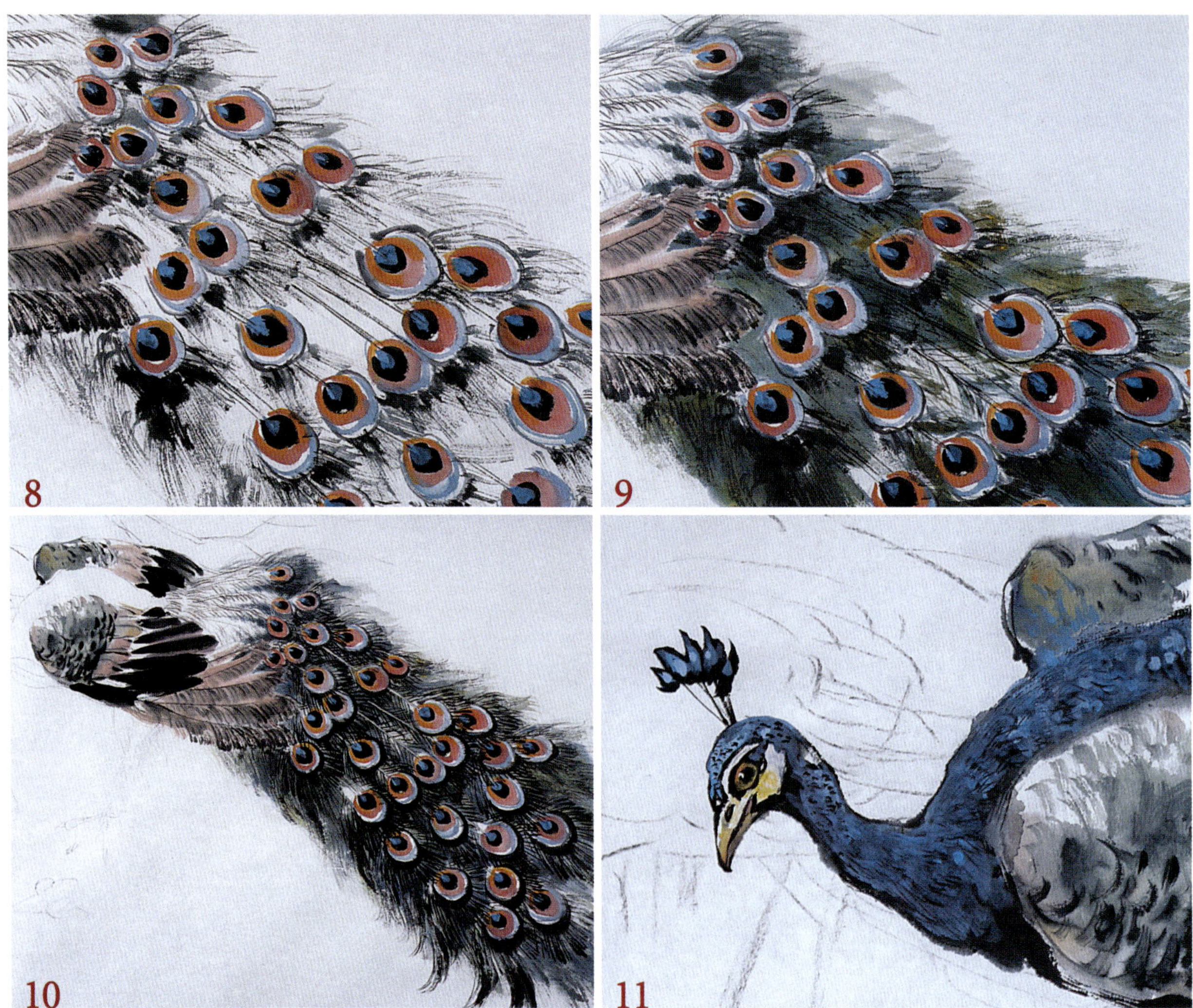

**8 FINISH THE CIRCULAR PATTERNS AND PAINT
THE TEXTURE OF THE TAIL FEATHERS**

Use a medium brush to paint the outlines of the circular patterns with
ink. Then paint light blue inside the outlines. Next, apply intense blue
at the centre of the circles. Paint vermilion and yellow on top of the
dark red strokes on each pattern. Next, use a split-tip brush to paint
the tail feathers with ink, moving your brush outwards from the edges
of the circular patterns.

9 COLOUR THE TAIL FEATHERS

Use a big brush to mix phthalocyanine blue, yellow and ink to paint
the tail feathers. Use lighter colours on the upper part of the tail.

10 ADD DETAILS TO THE TAIL FEATHERS

When the colours are halfway dry, use a small brush to paint intense
ink strokes diagonally outwards from each circular pattern. Also, apply
white to the centres of the feathers.

11 PAINT THE HEAD, NECK AND BACK

Use a medium brush to apply intense ink to the head, neck and
back. Also outline the eye, the face and the beak. While the ink is
wet, apply blue on top of the head, neck and back. Then use a small
brush to paint small feathers with intense ink. Next, colour the
eye, face and beak with yellow. Add cinnabar to the eye. Apply cinnabar
and ink to the beak.

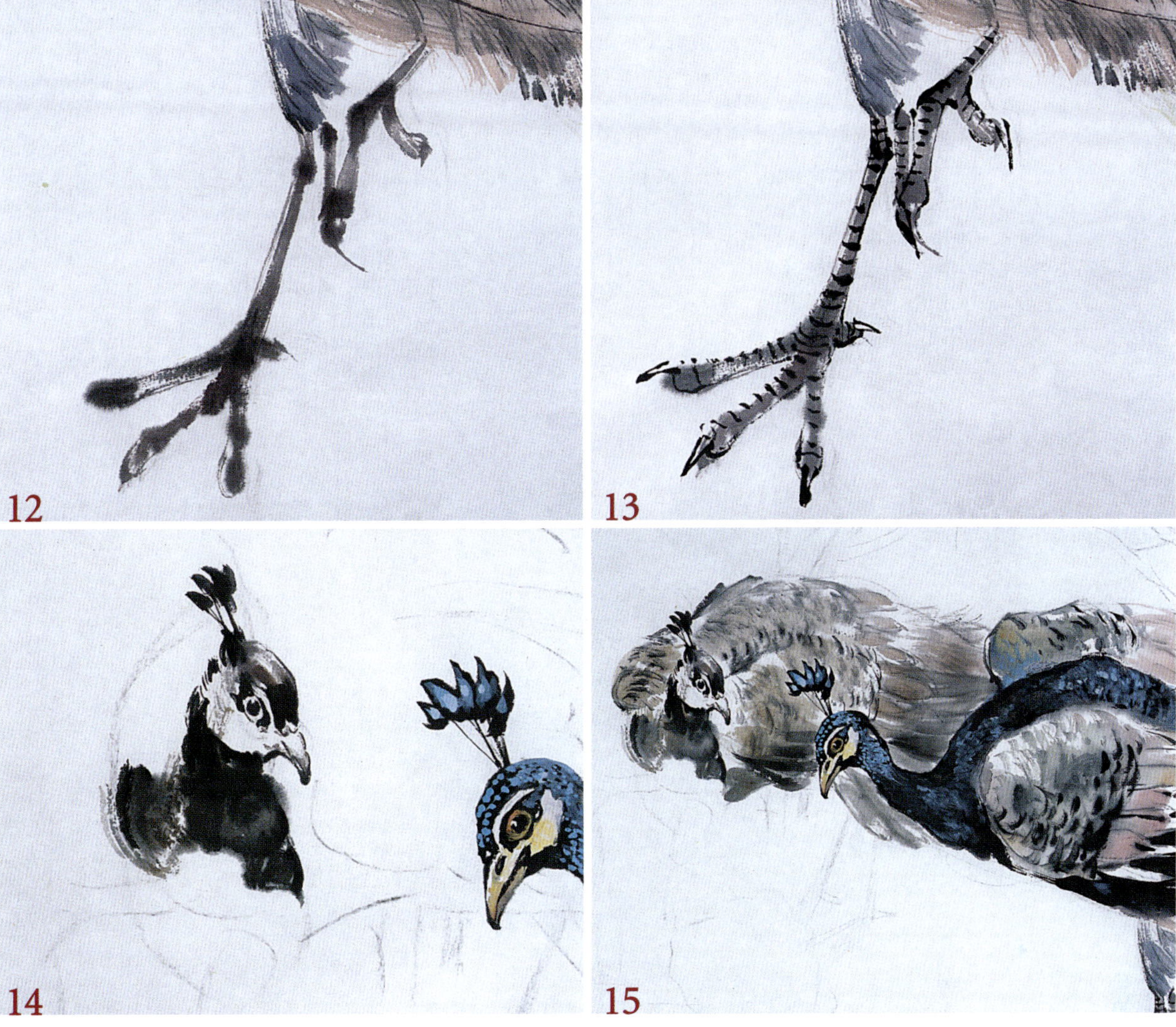

12 Paint the feet

Use a medium brush to mix ink and burnt sienna. Hold your brush in
the centre-brush position and paint several strokes for the feet.

13 Paint the texture of the feet and paint the claws

When the colours are halfway dry, use a small brush to define the
texture of the feet with intense ink. Also paint the claws.

14 Paint the head and neck of the female bird

Use a medium brush to outline the female bird's beak and eye with
intense ink. Then mix ink and burnt sienna to paint the head and neck
with centre-brush strokes.

15 Paint the body of the bird

Use a large brush and light burnt sienna to paint the body and wings.
While the colour is wet, define the feathers with medium and intense
ink. Also, mix cinnabar and light ink to paint the main coverts.

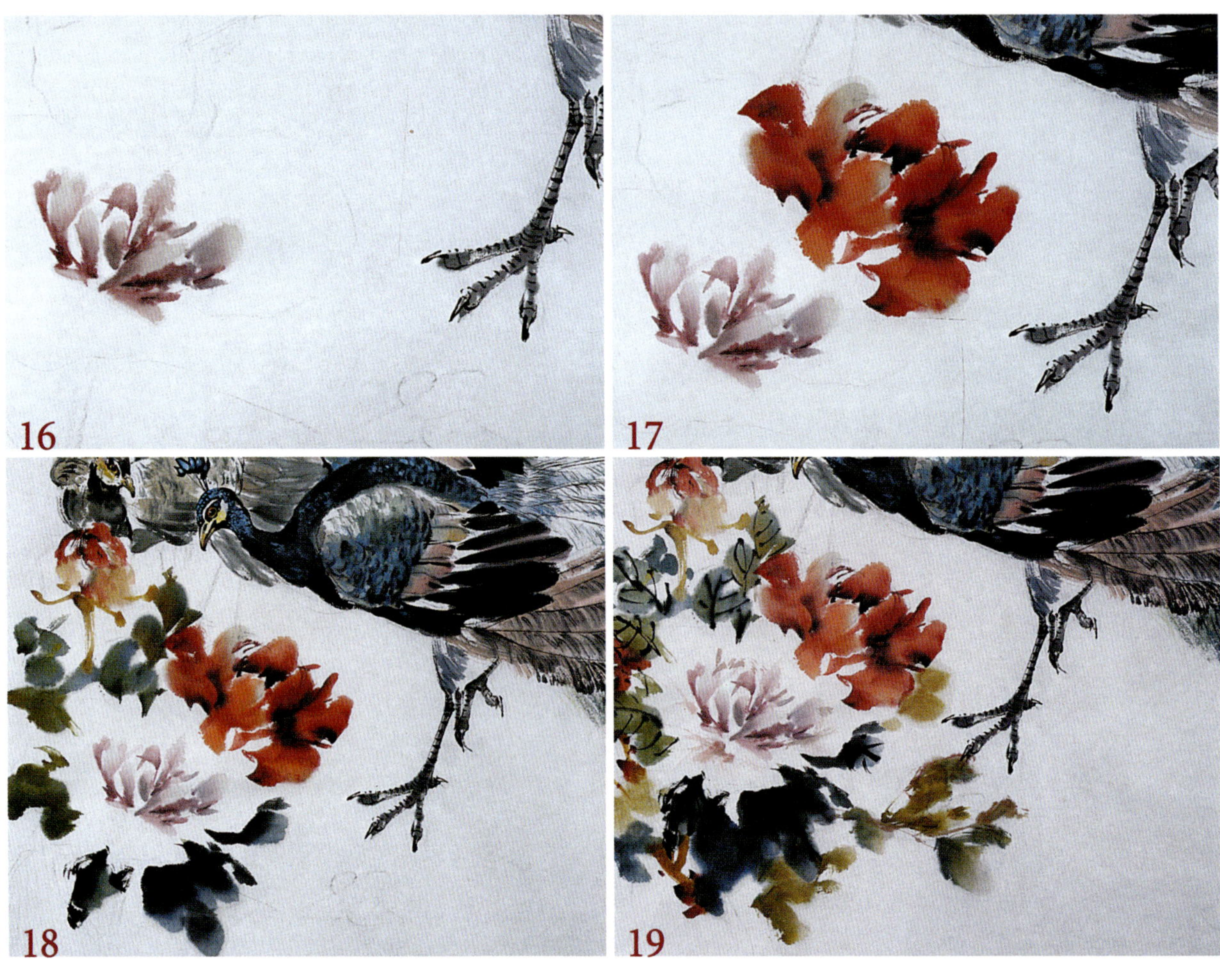

16 *Paint the pink petals of the peony*

Soak a large brush with white. Load carmine up to its middle portion
and rouge at its tip. Use the side-brush method to paint the peony
petals. Place the tip of your brush pointing towards the centre of the
flower. Paint one or two strokes to depict a petal.

17 *Paint the red petals*

Soak a large brush with cinnabar, then carmine up to its middle portion. Mix rouge and ink with its tip. Paint the petals with the side-brush
method, pointing your brush tip towards the centre of the flower. Leave
white on the top area of the pink petals to depict white petals.

18 *Paint the red bud and leaves*

Use a large brush to mix vermilion and yellow. Paint three centre-brush
strokes at the bottom of the bud. Immediately use the large brush
used for painting the red petals to paint the upper part of the bud.
Next, dip a large brush in indigo. Get intense ink on its middle and tip
area to paint the leaves at the bottom of the pink-white flower. Use the
same brush to mix yellow, indigo and ink. Hold your brush using the
side-brush method to paint the other leaves.

19 *Paint more leaves and red buds*

Use the same brush and colours to paint more leaves. When they are
halfway dry, paint the veins with ink. Next, use the brush used to paint
red petals to paint two more red buds behind the leaves. Use a medium brush to mix vermilion, yellow and ink. Then paint the stem at
lower left with the centre-brush method.

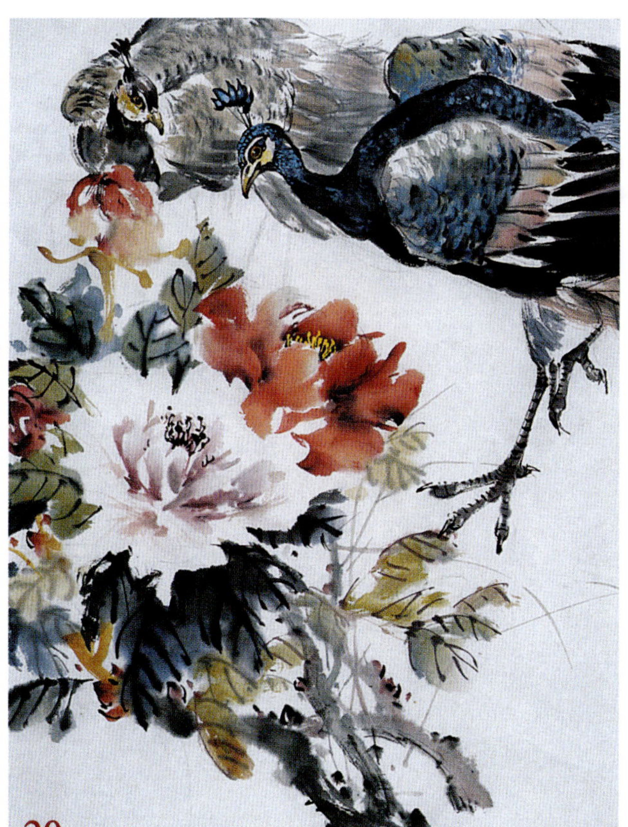

20 *Paint the trunks, stamen and long grasses*

Use a large brush to mix ink and a little carmine to paint the trunks with the side-brush method. While the trunks are wet, randomly add some intense ink dots and carmine spots on the trunks to emphasize their textures. Next, use a small brush to mix yellow and white to paint the stamen on the red flower. Mix carmine and intense ink to paint the stamen on the pink-white flower. To paint the lone grasses, use a small brush to mix light ink and carmine and make long strokes. Hold your brush in the centre-brush method, and move it from the bottom of the grasses to their tips.

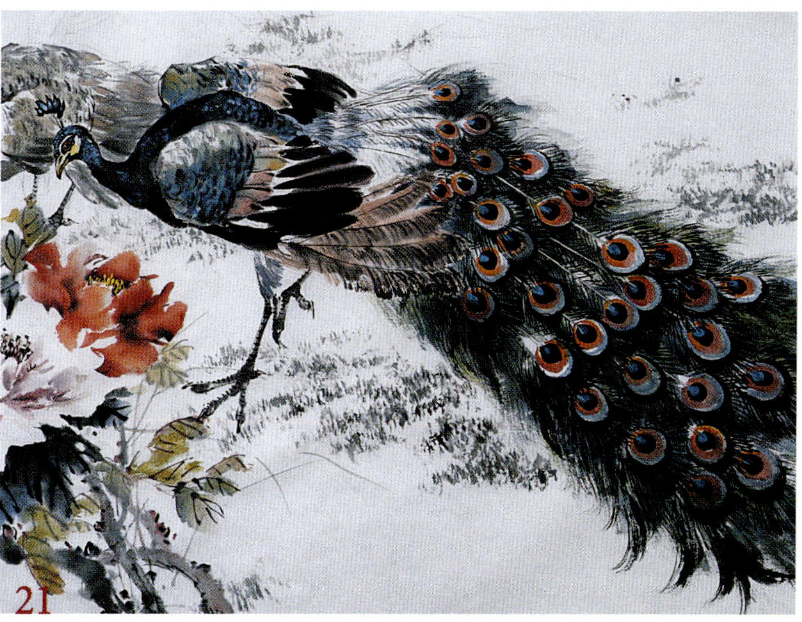

21 *Paint the small grasses on the ground*

Use a split-tip medium brush to paint short strokes with different intensities of ink. Overlap the strokes to create the grass texture.

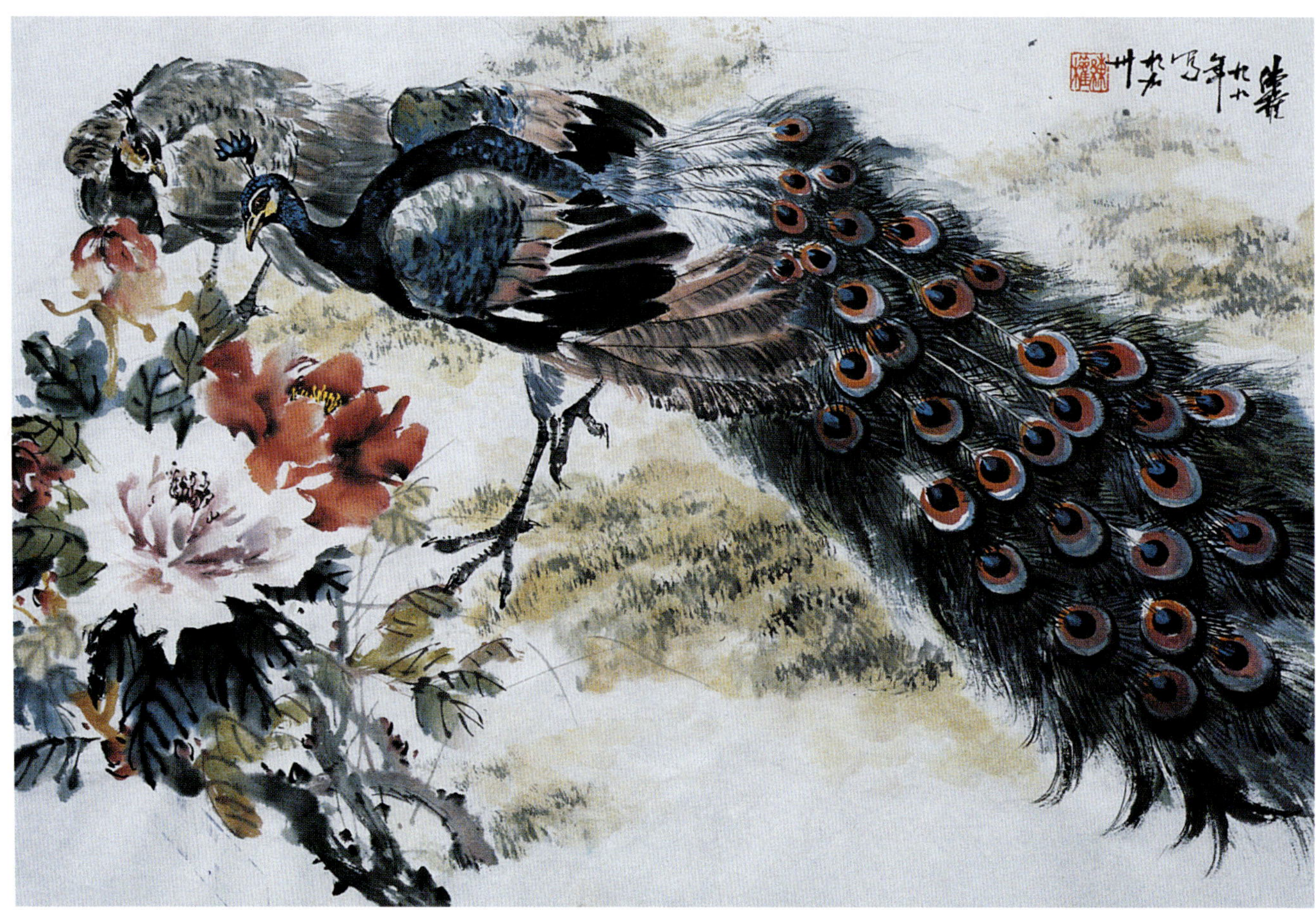

**22 *Apply colours on the grasses, sign and
seal your painting***

Use a large brush to mix burnt sienna and light ink to colour the
grasses. Apply less intense colours on the distant grasses. Finally, sign
your name, the date and the place of the painting.

PEACOCKS AND PEONY
46 x 69cm (18 x 27in)
Chinese ink and colours on double-layer Shuan paper
Spontaneous style

PAINTING DUCKS

I used only the three primary colours for all the watercolour demonstrations. They are cadmium red deep from Winsor & Newton and cadmium yellow light and ultramarine blue from Utrecht. I will refer to these colours as red, yellow and blue in the demonstrations. The paper is Arches 300gsm (140lb) cold-pressed watercolour paper. The masking material is Grumbacher's Miskit Liquid Watercolour Frisket.

Before painting, I used masking tape to tape about 1cm (½in) at the four edges of the paper to a three-ply plywood that was larger than the paper. The 3 or 4cm (1 or 1½in) brown masking tape is best because it holds the paper firmly.

As you work, feel free to change the objects and composition according to the results you get at each stage. Remember, there are no mistakes.

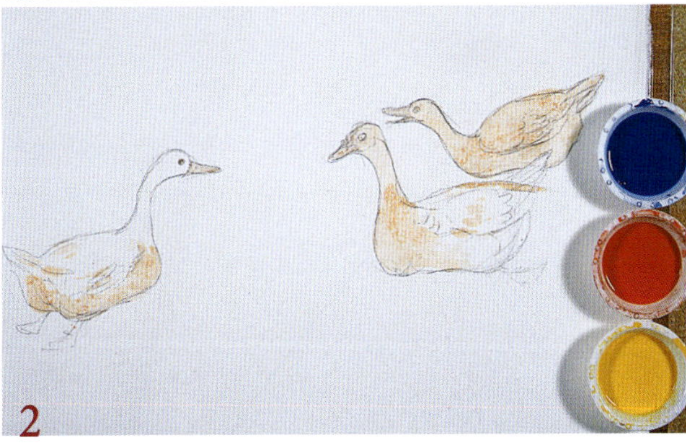

1 SKETCH THE DUCKS

Use a soft pencil to sketch the ducks on a 36 x 53cm (14 x 21in) Arches 300gsm (140lb) cold-pressed watercolour paper. Do not draw details.

2 MASK THE DUCKS AND PREPARE COLOURS

Apply the masking fluid to the ducks. To prepare the colours, add about 6ml (¼ cup) of clean water to each dish. Then add pigment approximately the size of the bristles of a No. 6 round brush from each tube into the separate dishes (one colour per dish). (The amount of water and pigment you need depends on the size of your painting and the intensity of colour you want.) Use three small brushes to stir the colours until they blend with the water, using one brush per colour.

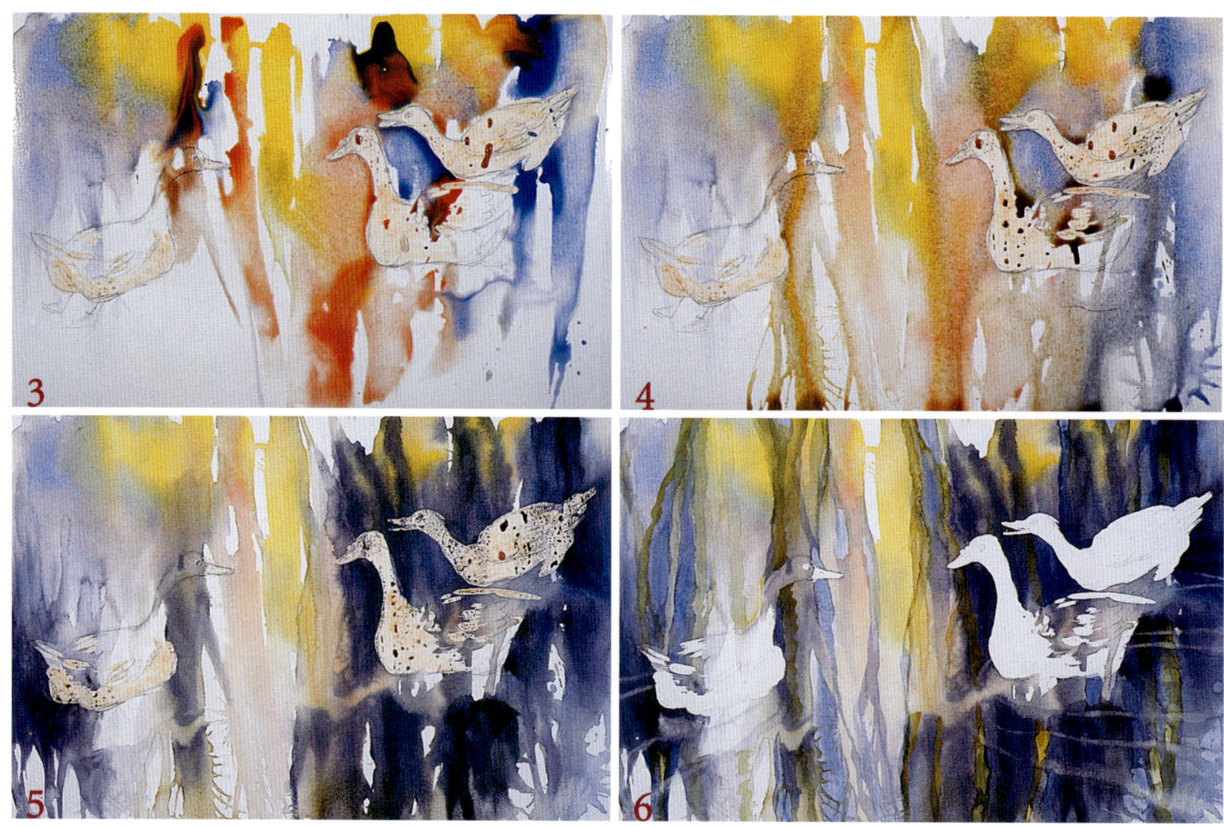

3 Dry the masking fluid and pour the colours

Wait for the masking fluid to dry or use a hair dryer to dry it. Use a water sprayer to lightly wet the painting. Pour the yellow paint at the upper middle, where the sunlight reflects. Pour the blue paint on the right and left. Finally, pour the red paint below the yellow.

4 Direct the flow of the colours

Tilt the upper edge of the painting up about 13cm (5in) so that the colours flow towards the bottom. Blow the colours at the middle bottom and right bottom to get the radiation effects.

5 Paint the water and reflections

While the colours are wet, use a 25mm (1in) flat brush to mix intense blue and a little red. Paint the water around the ducks. The intense colours will cause the ducks to appear to pop out from the paper, especially the white duck at the upper right. Use a moist No. 8 round brush to lift colours to create the reflections of the two ducks at front.

6 Create movement of water and reflections of trees, and lift the masking fluid

When the colours are almost dry, use a 19mm (¾in) flat brush to mix yellow and blue into green to paint the reflections of the trees. Next, use a No. 10 round brush to paint vertical strokes with blue. This will further emphasize the water. Before the colours dry, use a moist No. 6 round brush to lift colours off the water for waves. When the painting is totally dry (I use a hair dryer to dry it), use masking tape to remove the masking fluid.

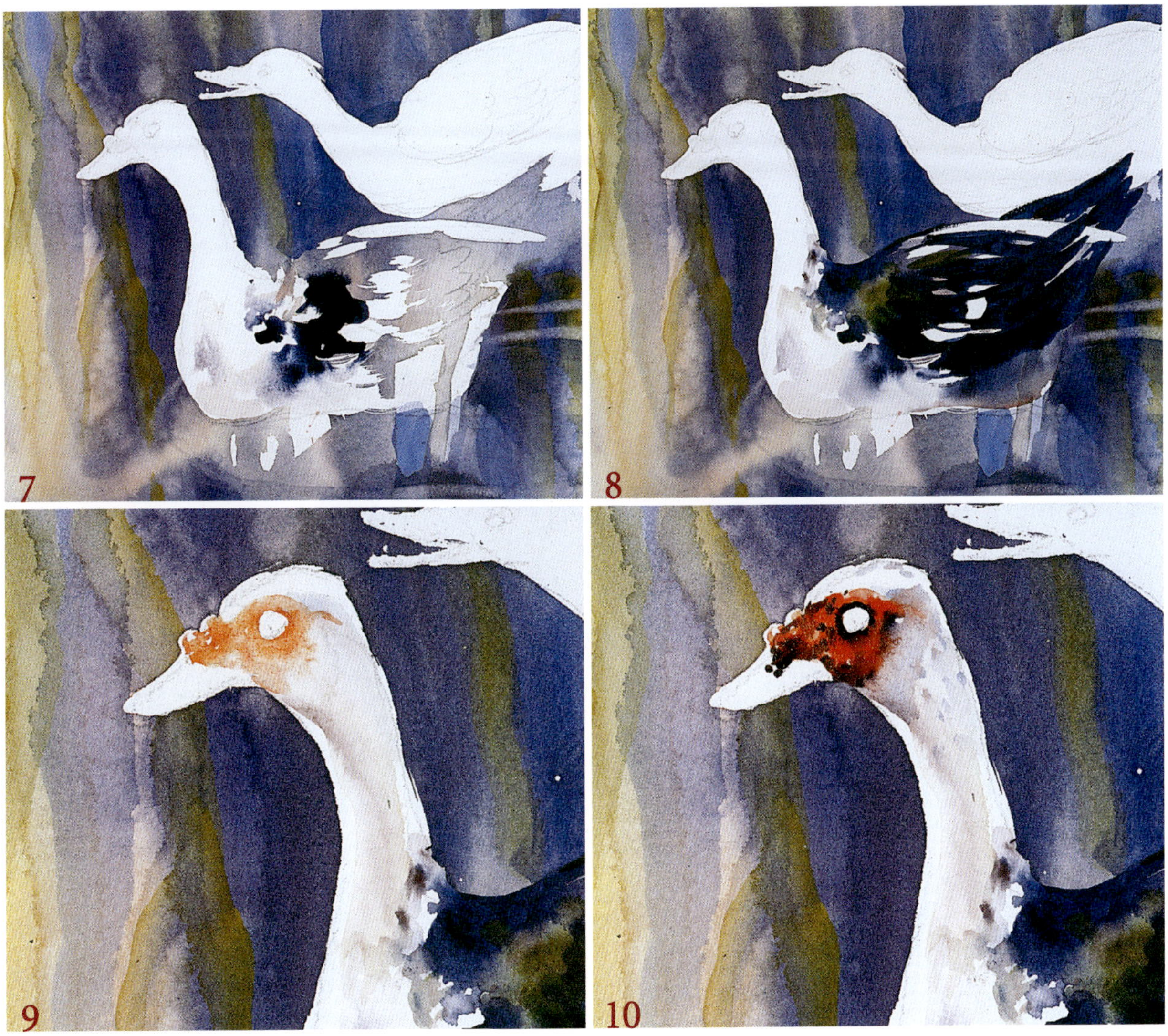

7 Paint the duck at front right

Use a 19mm (¾in) round brush to wet the duck's body with water.
Mix very intense blue and red into black to paint the front wing. Let
the colour blend into the water to create soft feather effects. Paint the
chest with light purple mixed from light blue and light red.

8 Continue painting the duck

Use the 19mm (¾in) flat brush to paint the back, wings and tail with
dark blue, mixing from intense red and blue. Leave white for the white
feathers. While the colours are wet, use a No. 10 round brush to apply
yellow on the back to create the green feathers.

9 Paint the head and neck

The duck's neck and head are mainly white. Use a No. 10 round brush
to wet them with water. Mix light red and blue to paint the neck. Mix
yellow and red, making orange, to paint the face and nostril, leaving a
white circle for its eye.

10 Apply more colours on the head and face

While the orange is wet, use a No. 10 round brush to get intense red
and paint on top of the orange. Immediately use the same brush to
get intense blue on its tip to paint the dots on the red area. Also,
outline the eye circle again.

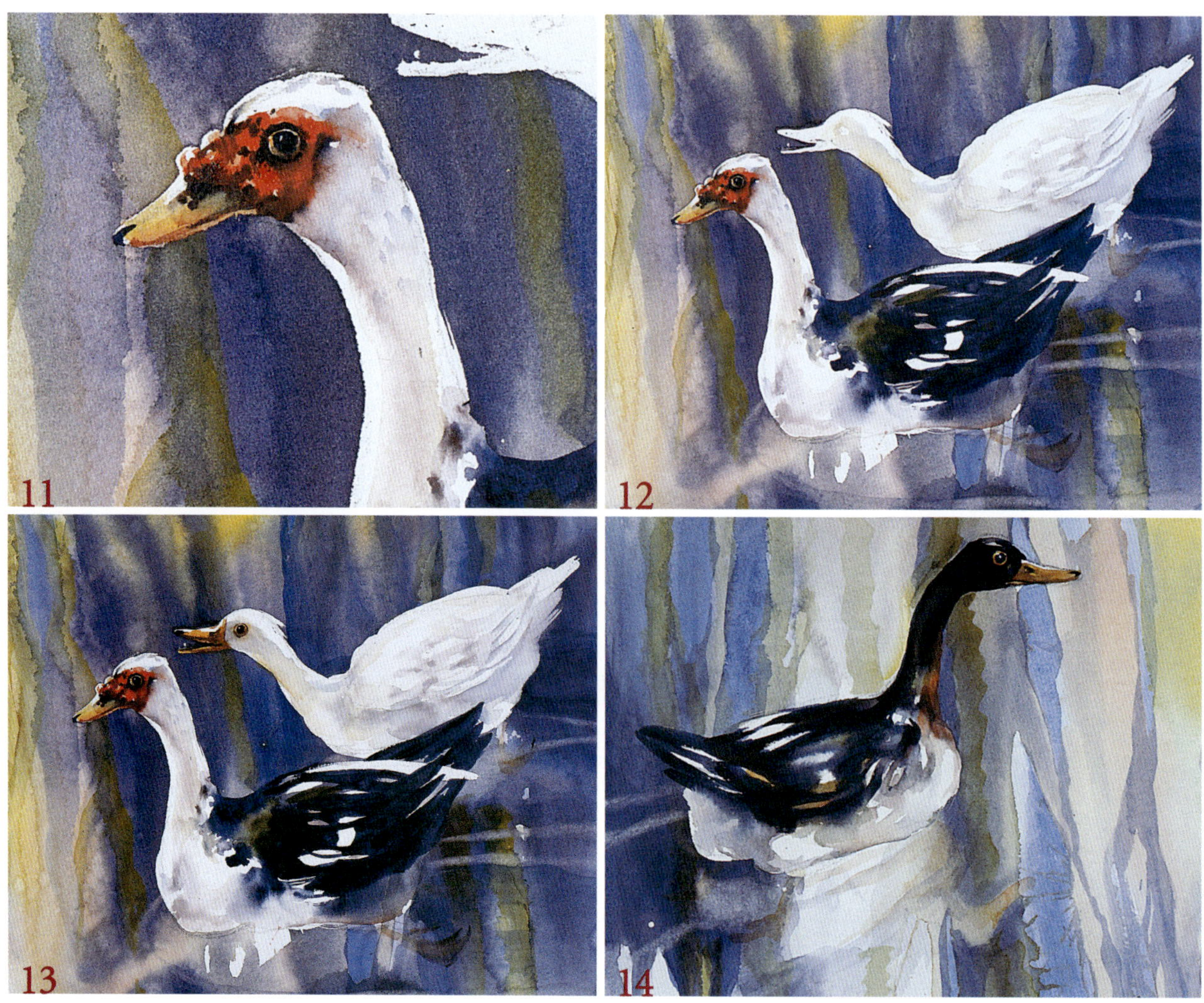

11 PAINT THE BEAK AND EYE

Use a No. 6 round brush to apply yellow to the eyeball and beak. Drag the colours from the nostril area to the upper jawbone. Paint the edges of the jawbones with red. Next, mix the red and blue into black to paint the pupil, leaving a white spot as the highlight.

12 PAINT THE BODY AND WINGS OF THE SECOND DUCK

Use a 19mm (¾in) flat brush to apply light yellow on its neck and back. Paint light purple on its body and wings. Leave a lot of white. In the area between its front wing and body, paint more intense purple.

13 PAINT THE BEAK AND EYE

Use a No. 6 round brush to mix yellow and red into orange. Paint the jawbones and eyeball. Leave white on top of the upper jawbone and at the upper pupil. While the colours are wet, use the same brush to mix a little blue and red to define the jawbones and outline the eye. Finally, get very intense blue and a little red to paint the pupil.

14 PAINT THE DUCK AT LEFT

Use a No. 10 round brush to lightly wet the head, neck and body. Leave the white feathers untouched. Paint the middle and bottom part of the neck with red. Mix intense red and blue to paint the other part of the neck and the head. Next, use a 19mm (¾in) flat brush to mix intense blue and red to paint the feathers on the back and wings. Use another wet 19mm (¾in) flat brush to drag the colours into the lower part of the body with water. Paint its eye and beak as in step 13.

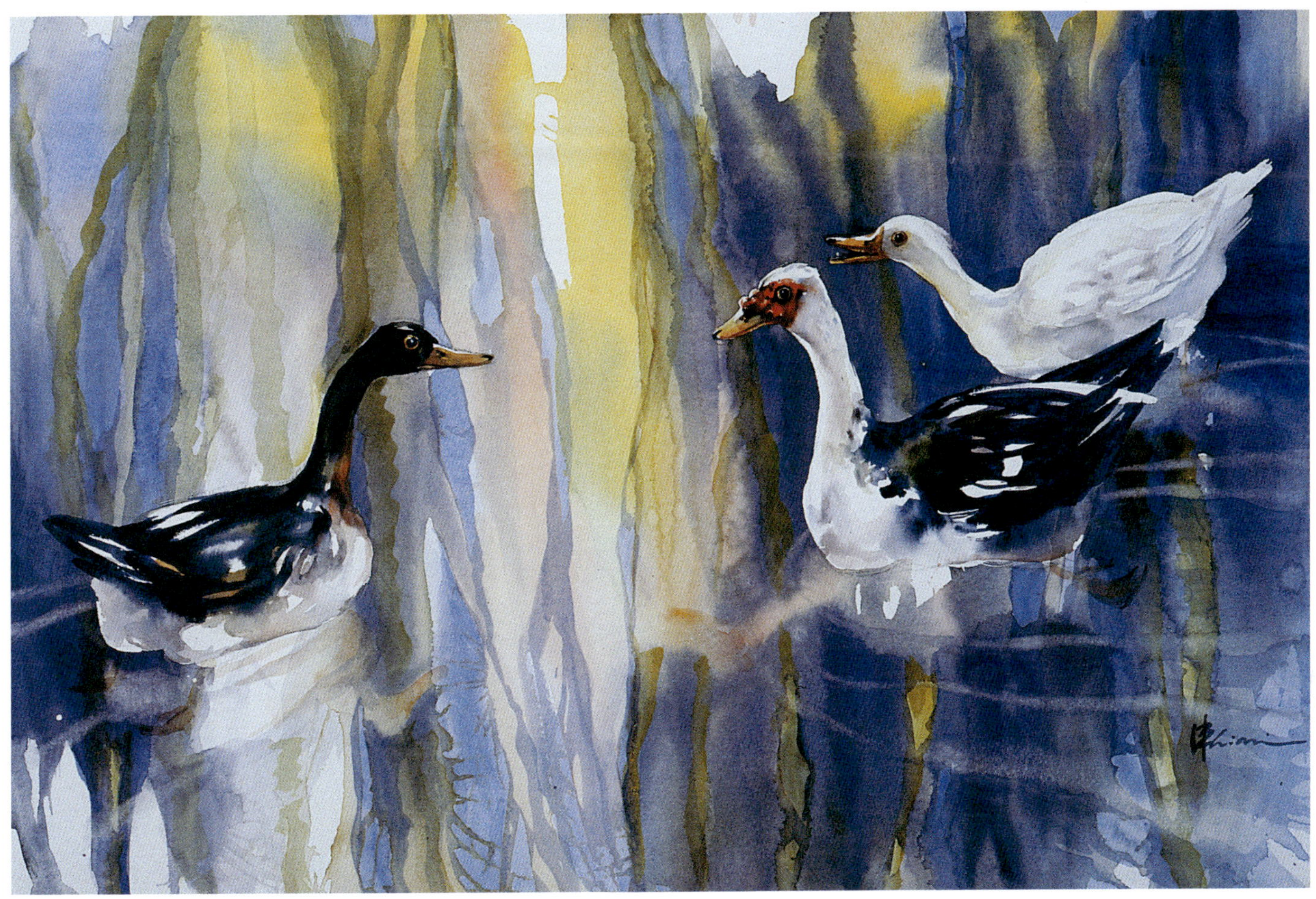

15 *Sign your painting*

Sign your name on the bottom right of your painting. Your painting
will be different from mine even though we used the same colours and
techniques. This is because the colours blend differently after you pour
them on your painting. I have never been able to paint two paintings
the same or even very similar. Actually, when I paint using the colour-
pouring-and-blending method, I do not know what exact result I will
have before I finish.

SUNSET AT SWAMP
36 x 53cm (14 x 21in)
Three primary colours on Arches 300gsm
(140lb) cold-pressed watercolour paper
Colour pouring and blending

PAINTING CRANES

This painting will use a lot of masking fluid to preserve the sky, cranes and snow. If
you stretch your paper before you paint, you can use masking tape instead of the fluid
to block out the snow area at the bottom of the painting. However, do not use the
masking tape if you do not pre-stretch the watercolour paper: the upper portion of
the paper will be very wet and will contract strongly when it is dry, while the lower
portion of the paper will not contract since it is taped with masking tape, therefore
causing the finished painting to warp.

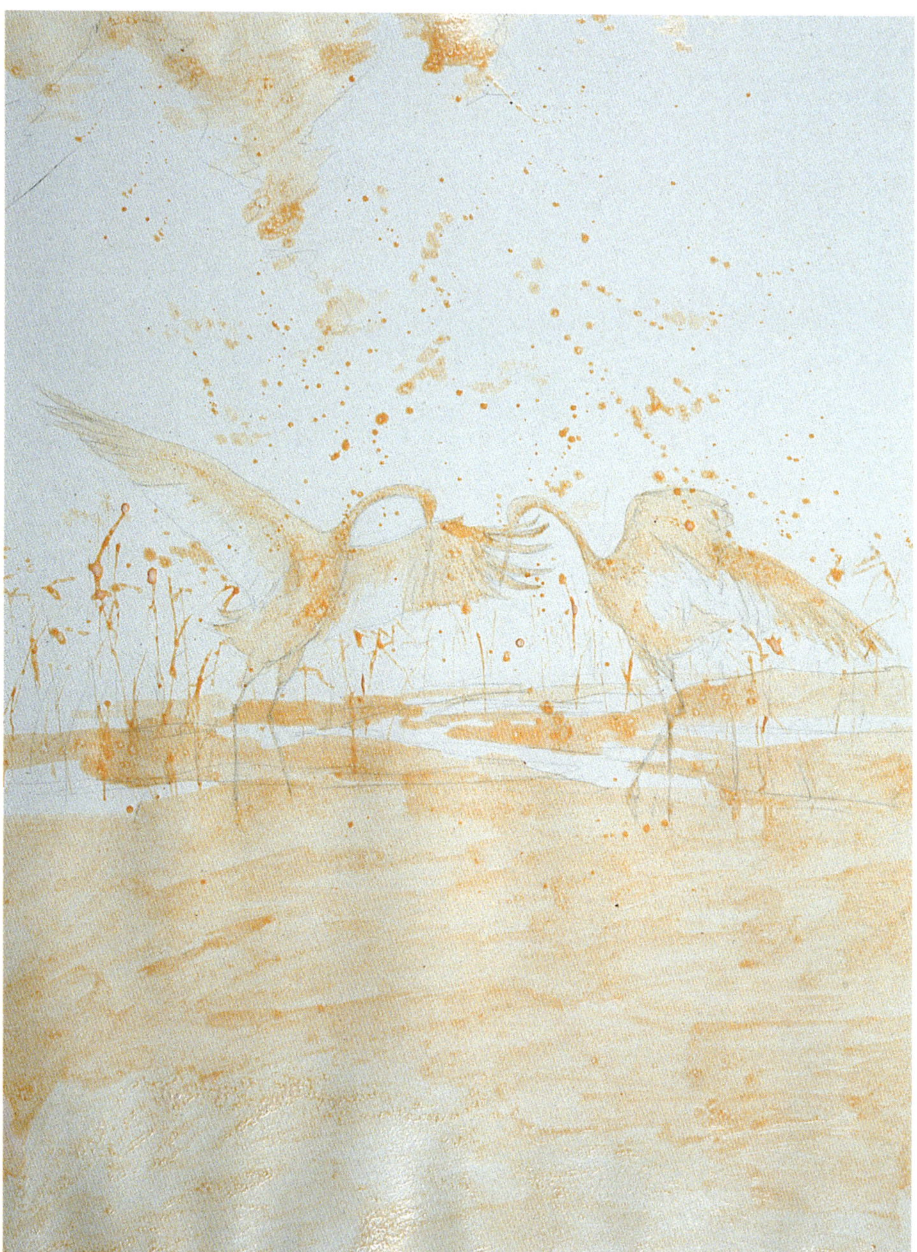

1 *SKETCH THE IMAGES AND APPLY MISKIT*

Use a pencil to sketch the images on your 74 x 53cm (29 x 21in) Arches
300gsm (140lb) cold-pressed watercolour paper. Apply masking fluid
to the sky at top, to the birds and grasses at middle and to the snow
at bottom. Splatter the fluid on the tree area diagonally from upper left
to lower right, for snowflakes.

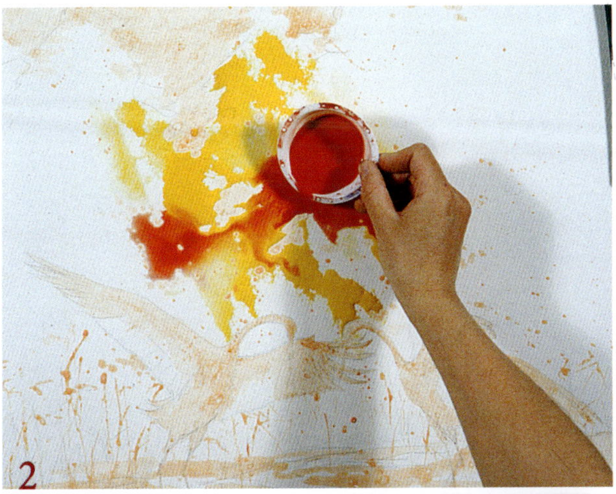

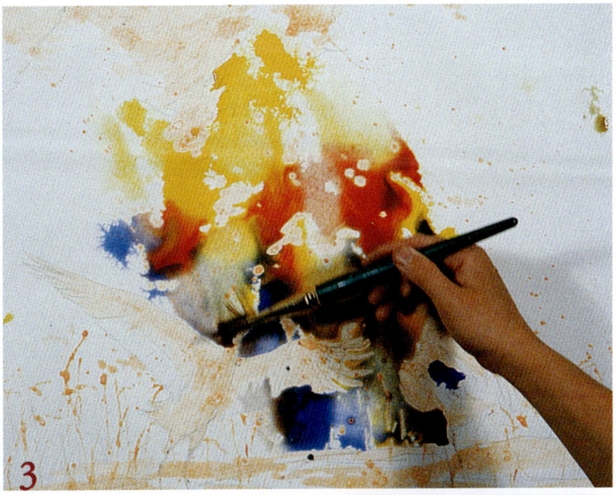

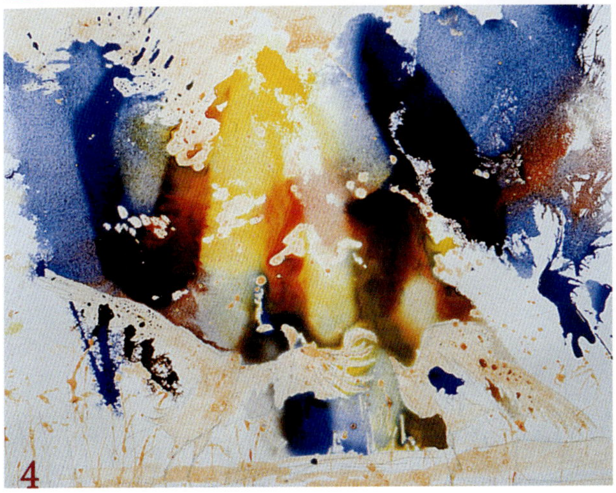

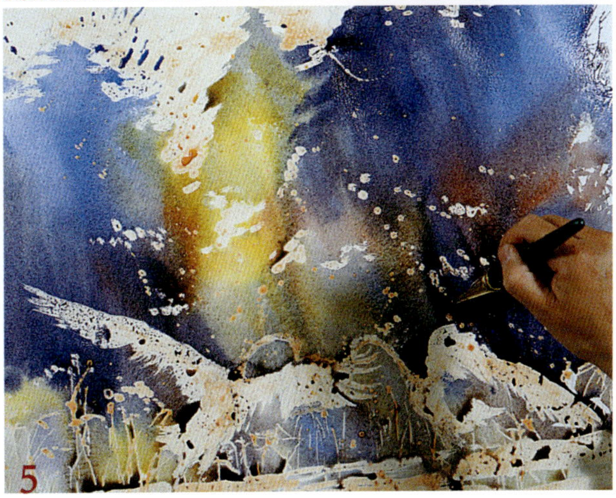

2 WET THE PAINTING AND POUR THE COLOURS

Use a hair dryer to dry the masking fluid. Prepare the colours as described in step 2 of the duck demonstration (page 87), preparing about twice as much colour as previously used. Wet the painting with a water sprayer. Next, pour the yellow and red on the upper centre area where sunlight is shining through the trees.

3 DIRECT THE COLOURS

Pour the blue on the lower part of the yellow and red. Use a 38mm (1½in) flat brush to direct the colours towards the birds. Also, guide the colours to touch each other so they can blend gracefully.

4 POUR MORE COLOURS

On the upper left of your painting, pour some blue. On the upper right corner, pour blue and red. Blow the colours on the right towards the right edge of your painting to create abstract trees. Spray more water on the middle right and middle left to guide the colours down.

5 DIRECT THE FLOW OF THE COLOUR, PAINT THE TREES AND GRASSES

Tilt your painting board towards you with the upper left corner highest. The colours will flow diagonally from the upper left towards the lower right. This creates diagonal patterns on the trees, the illusion of wind movement and falling snowflakes. Next, put an 8 to 10cm (3 to 4in) high object under the top left corner of your board to keep the colours flowing in the same direction. While the colours are wet, use a 38mm (1½in) flat brush to add intense blue and red to the trees.

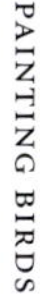

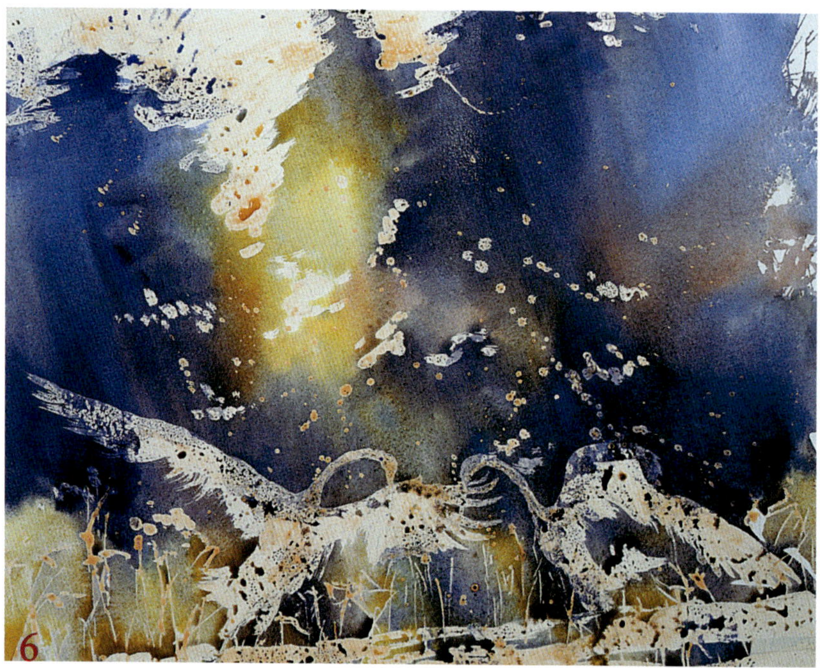

6 Define the trees and grasses and apply salt

Continue to use the 38mm (1½in) brush to define the shapes of trees with intense blue and red. (Note: 'intense' colour refers to adding a little water to the pigment, whereas 'very intense' refers to a pigment without water. 'Light' colour means to use more water to dilute the colour.) Paint the area against the upper portions of the wings darker to accentuate the white feathers of the cranes. Pour more yellow on the grass area in the middle of the painting. Apply about 40 to 50 crystals of cooking salt on the trees. Put more of them in the central area, around the head of the bird on the left.

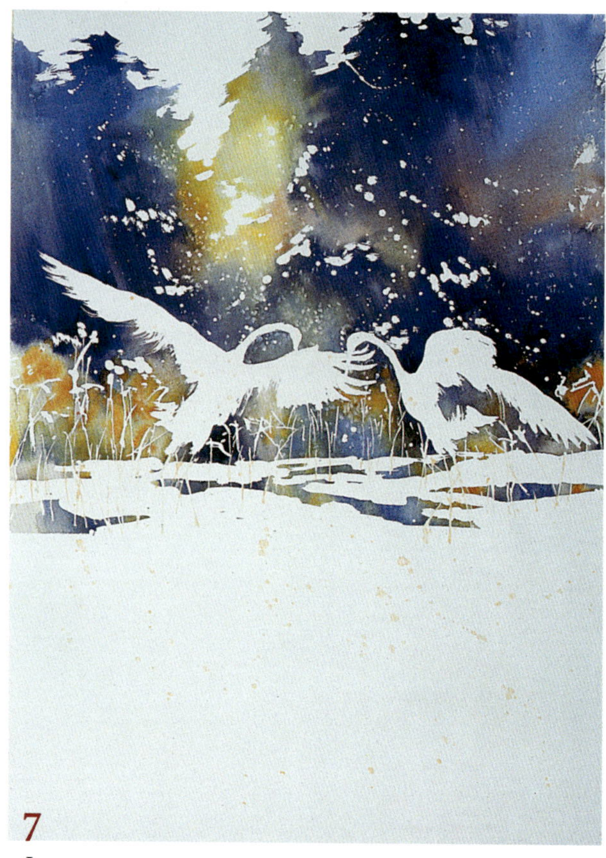

7 Lift the masking fluid and splatter small spots of fluid a second time

Dry the painting with a hair dryer. Lift the masking fluid using masking tape. Next, use an old round brush to randomly splatter the fluid on the snow and the birds. Use the Incredible Nib to apply the fluid on the lower portions of the grasses. Dry the masking fluid with a hair dryer.

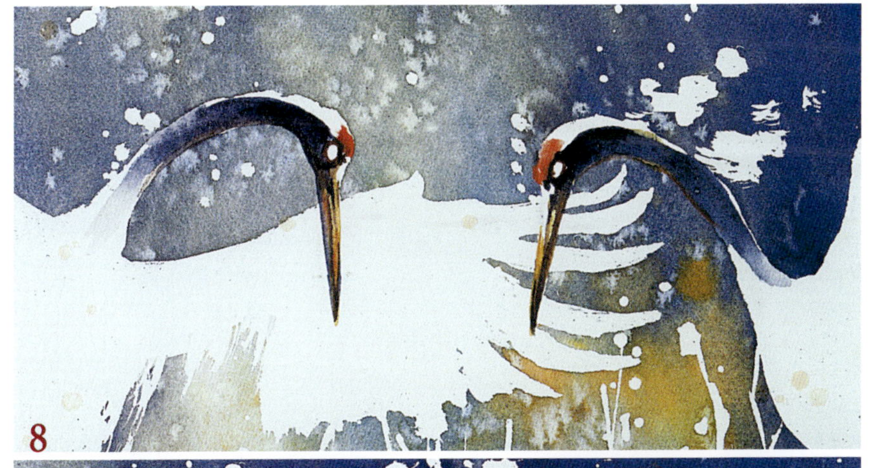

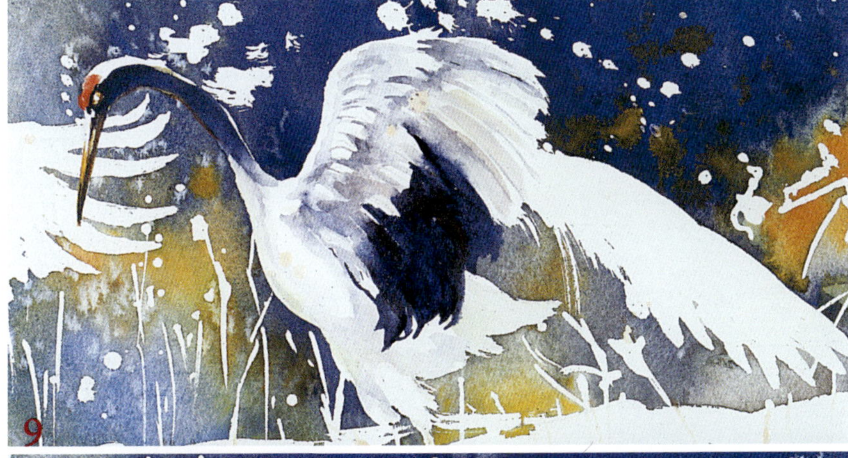

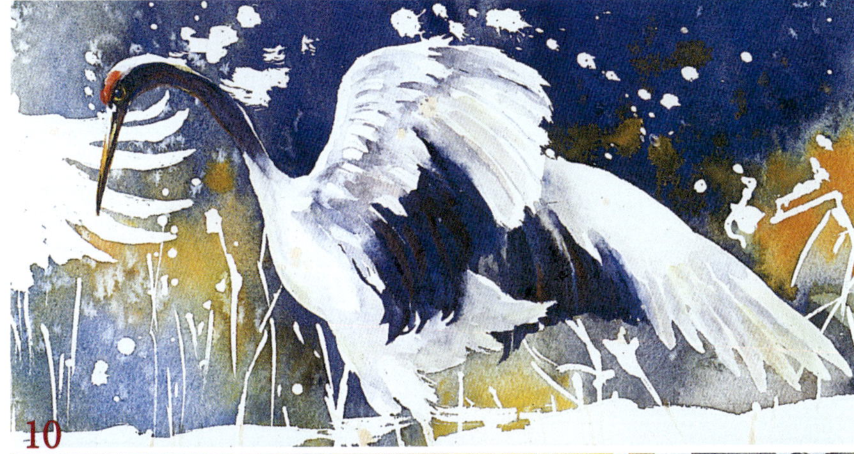

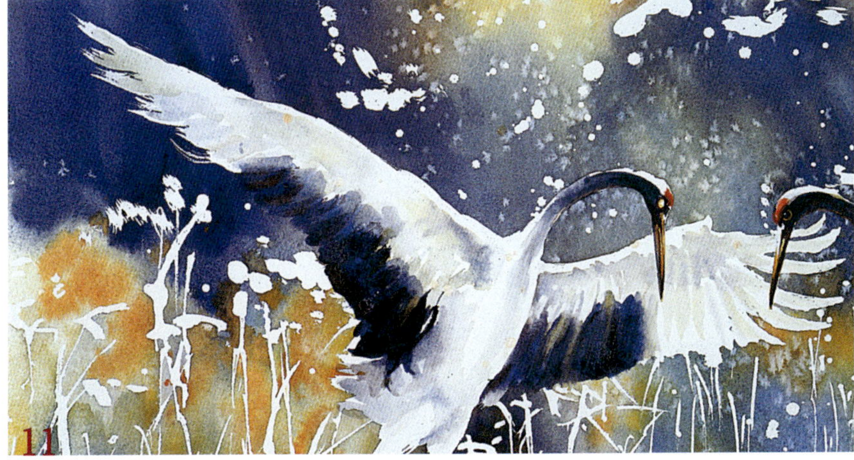

8 *PAINT THE HEADS, BEAKS AND NECKS OF THE BIRDS*

Use a No. 6 round brush to apply yellow on the beaks, then apply red on the middles and tips of the beaks. Wet the tops of the heads with water. Paint the combs with very intense red. Next, use a No. 10 round brush to wet the necks without touching the upper edges. Mix intense red and blue to paint the wet area. Use the No. 6 round brush to mix intense red, yellow and a little blue into dark brown to define the beak.

9 *PAINT THE FRONT WING OF THE CRANE AT RIGHT*

Use a No. 6 round brush to wet the small coverts. Apply light blue and light red to define the feathers. Paint light yellow on the primary flight feathers. Wet the black feather area with a No. 10 round brush. Use a No. 8 round brush to mix very intense blue and red (do not mix them completely). Paint the black feathers in a few strokes.

10 *PAINT THE REAR WING, THE TAIL AND THE BODY*

Paint the right crane's rear wing in the same way as the front wing. Leave more white. Wet the chest and abdomen with a No.10 round brush. Apply light purple to define the chest, the thighs and the tail. Drag the colours from the black feathers into the tail feathers.

11 *PAINT THE WINGS AND BODY OF THE CRANE AT LEFT*

Paint the wings and body in the same way as done for the bird at right (see steps 9 and 10). When painting the flight feathers of the rear wing, leave white between the feathers.

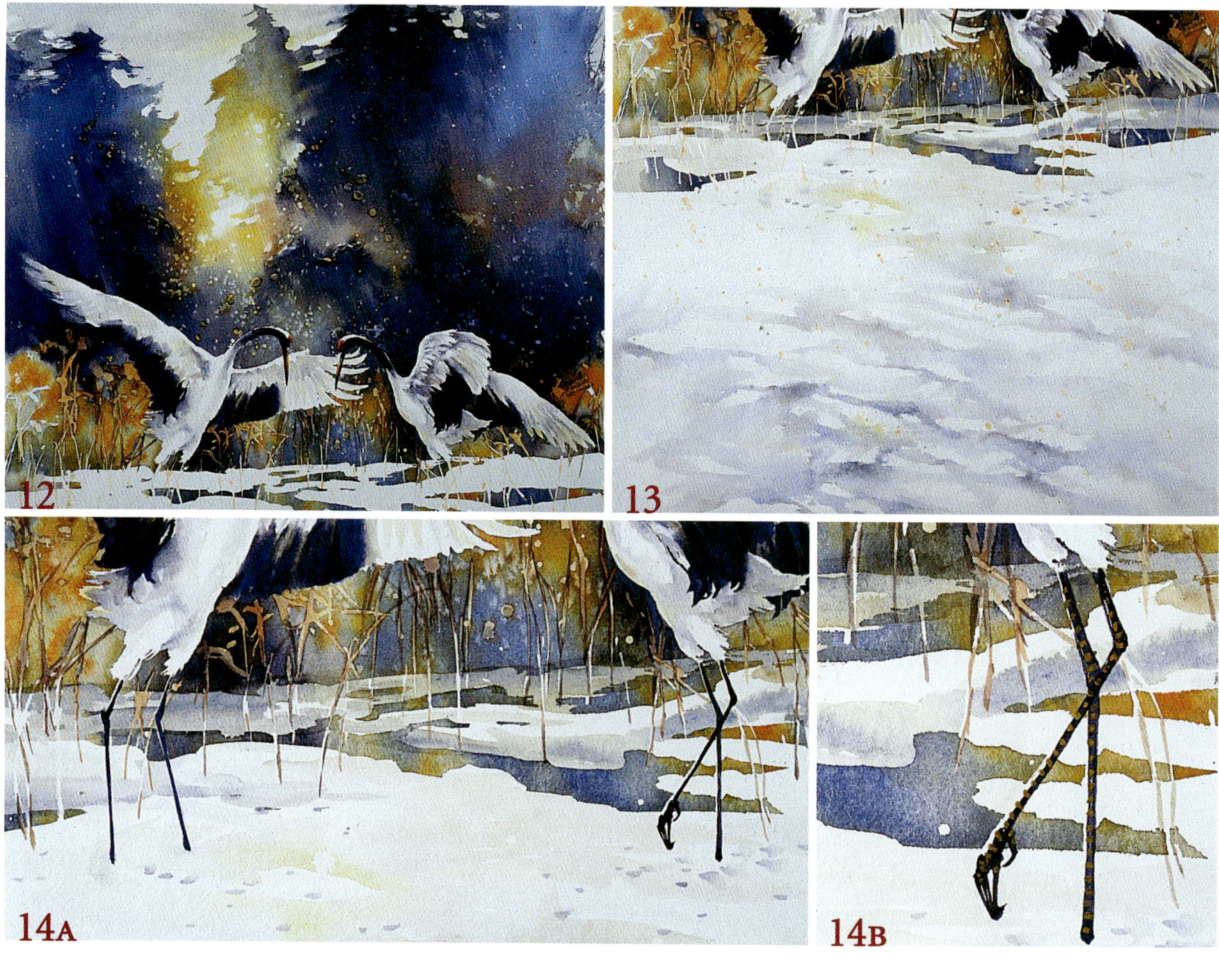

12 *Fill in colours for the white spots, paint the grasses and the sky*

Use a No. 6 round brush to apply red and yellow to the white spots near the sunlight and to those on the grass area. Apply blue to the white spots on the trees. Mix intense red and yellow to paint the grasses. Use a 25mm (1in) flat brush to wet the upper area of the sky. Apply light yellow in the centre area. Also, paint light red and blue on top. Use a 38mm (1½in) flat brush to drag the colours from the treetops into the sky using water.

13 *Paint the snow*

Lightly spray water on the snow area. Use a 25mm (1in) flat brush to paint the snow with different intensities of blue. In the centre area below the cranes, apply light yellow and red on top of the blue while the blue is wet. Then use a 19mm (¾in) flat brush to blend the colours with water. This will create sunlight reflections on the snow.

14 A & B *Lift the masking tape, paint the grasses and the feet*

Lift the masking fluid. Use a No. 6 round brush to mix red, yellow and a little blue into brown. Paint the lower portions of the grasses. Leave white to depict the snow on the stems. Next, use the same brush to paint the feet with very intense blue and red. While the colours are wet, paint intense yellow strokes to define the texture.

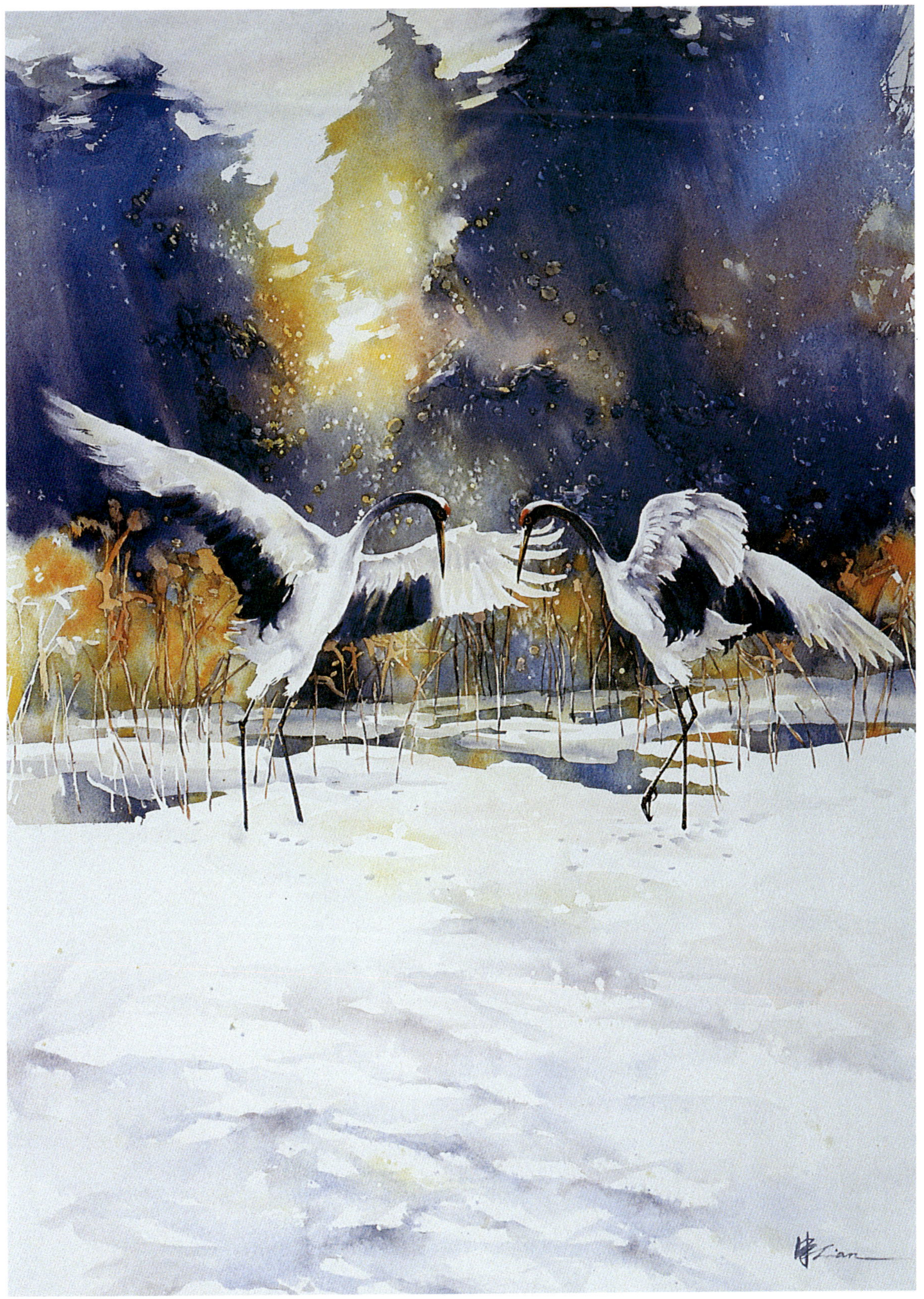

15 SIGN YOUR PAINTING

Sign your name at bottom right to balance the composition.

HARMONY
74 x 53cm (29 x 21in)
Watercolour on Arches 300gsm (140lb) cold-pressed watercolour paper
Colour pouring and blending

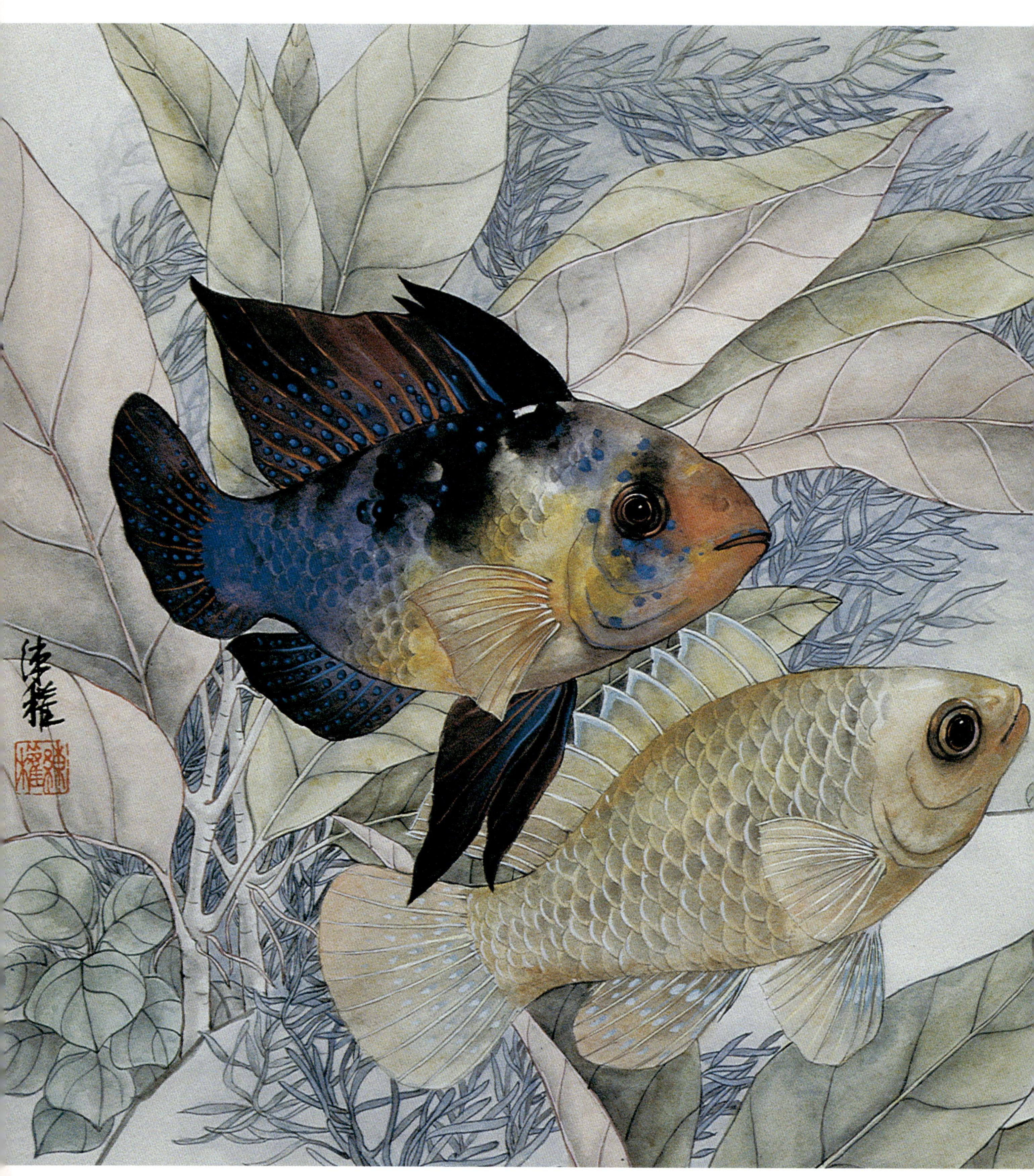

TWO CICHLIDS
51 x 41cm (20 x 16in)
Chinese ink and colours on mature Shuan paper
Detail style

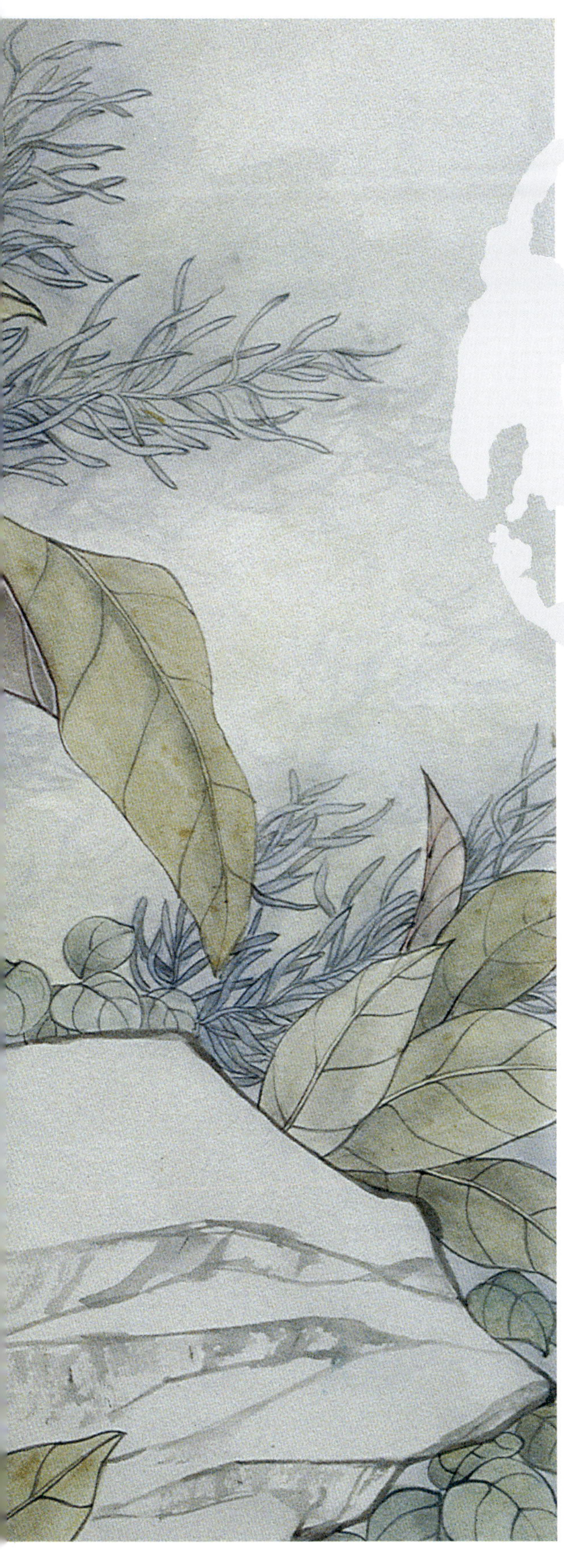

5

It is important to capture the essence of fish when you paint them. Their creative shapes, magnificent colours, and graceful movements are wonderful features to depict. When I am painting fish, I focus on the integration between fish and water. Fish and water are inseparable naturally and spiritually. Therefore, fish is water and water is fish.

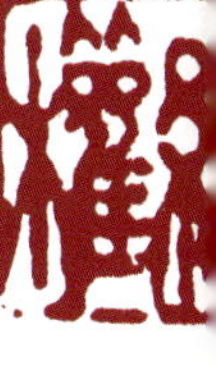

ANATOMY OF FISH

The fish I usually paint are teleosts, or bony fish. Among them are goldfish, angelfish, koi, butterfly fish and coral fish. Even though they live in different environments, they have similar skeletons that have two major functions: first, to form supporting frameworks for the internal organs and tissues, and second, to provide a series of flexible joints and attachment points for muscles to enable the fish to move. From the artist's viewpoint, it is not important to paint a fish exactly like a particular species, such as the ones I have mentioned. Keep in mind that you are painting, not illustrating. Do not let the fish control you. Feel free to rearrange and change fish colours and shapes to suit your creativity. When I paint goldfish, for example, I often choose the most beautiful features from all kinds of goldfish. As a result, I create my own goldfish.

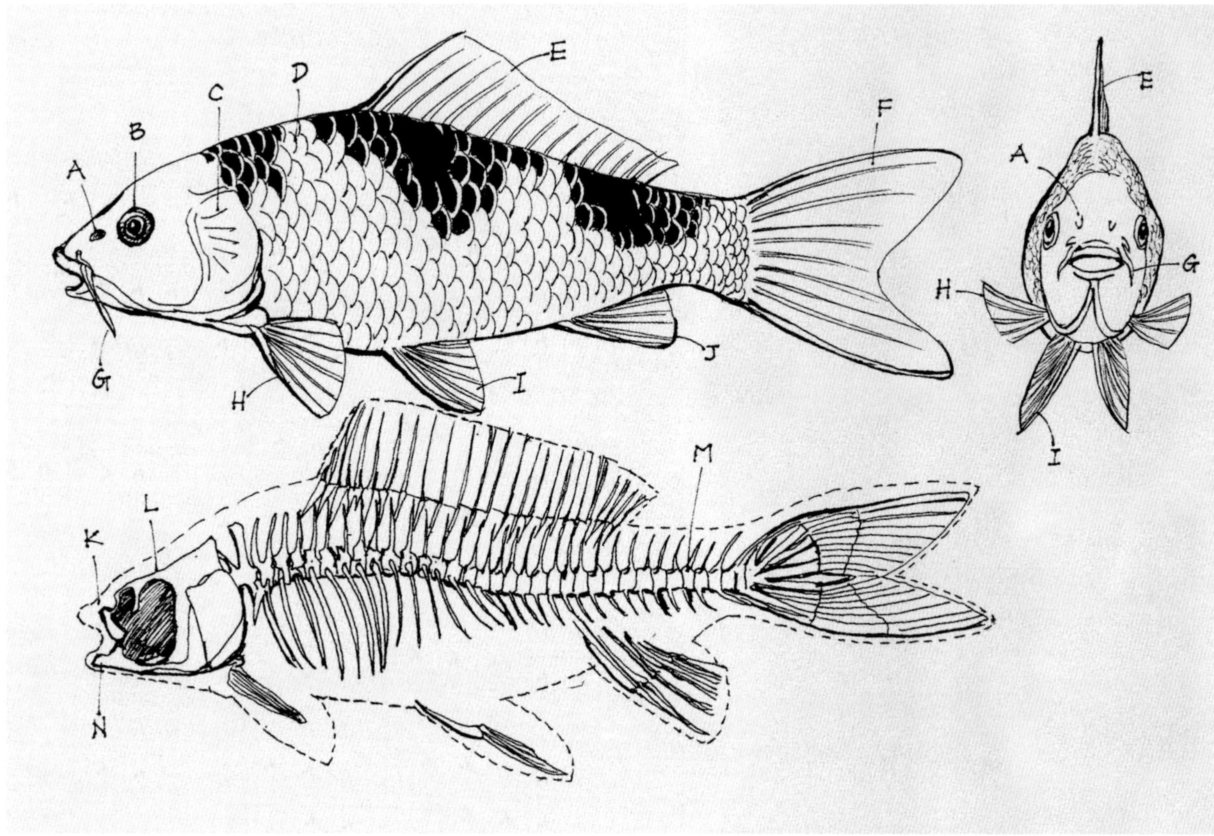

Fish Skeleton
This is a koi skeleton, along with side and front views of a live koi.
They clearly show how the skeleton forms the fish's framework,
which supports and articulates its body.
A. Nostril
B. Eye
C. Gill
D. Scale
E. Dorsal fin
F. Tail
G. Barbels
H. Pectoral fin
I. Ventral fin
J. Anal fin
K. Upper jaw
L. Skull
M. Spine
N. Lower jaw

FEATURES OF FISH

Koi

Despite the beautiful colour patterns, koi are still carp from an anatomical viewpoint. Their cylindrical bodies are broader at the front and narrower at the rear. This shape minimizes turbulence as the fish moves through the water. The widest point of a koi is between the pectoral fins and the beginning of the dorsal fin. A koi may grow up to 76cm (30in) long and weigh about 10kg (22lb).

A koi's pectoral and ventral fins are in pairs. Its dorsal and anal fins are single fins. The dorsal fin works in the same way as the keel of a ship to keep the fish upright. When a koi swims fast, its dorsal fin is low and the other fins are close to its body to create a streamlined effect. When its pectoral and ventral fins counteract the gills' action (which tends to create forward movement), the fish is motionless.

The face of the koi extends to the tip of its head. As a result, it has an inferior mouth. There are paired barbels on its upper lip. These are sense organs that help the fish locate food. Like many fish, a koi does not have eyelids. There are two nostrils in front of its eyes. These sense hormones released by other organisms and fish.

The koi's scales are transparent, overlap one another and become larger as the fish gets older. Scales do not provide colour for a koi. Instead, the amount of reflective tissue in the skin beneath the scales determines the various colours. The less reflective the scales, the more intense a koi's colour will be. The pigments found in the tissues are red, orange, yellow, brown and black.

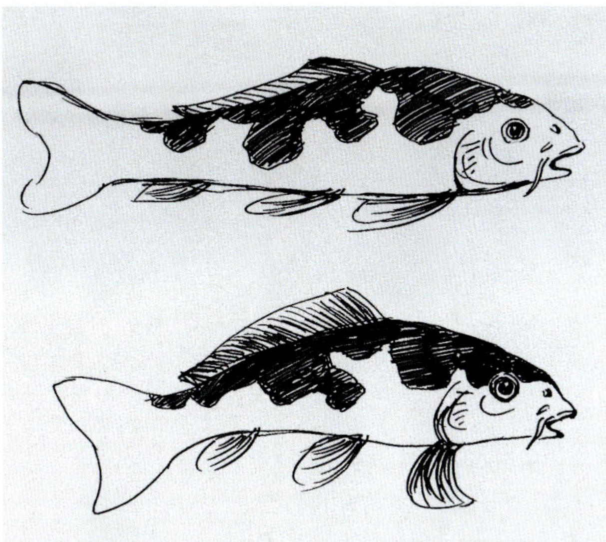

Koi
At top left is a speeding koi. Notice how the dorsal fin is low and the other fins are narrow. The other koi is stationary, with its pectoral fins moving forwards.

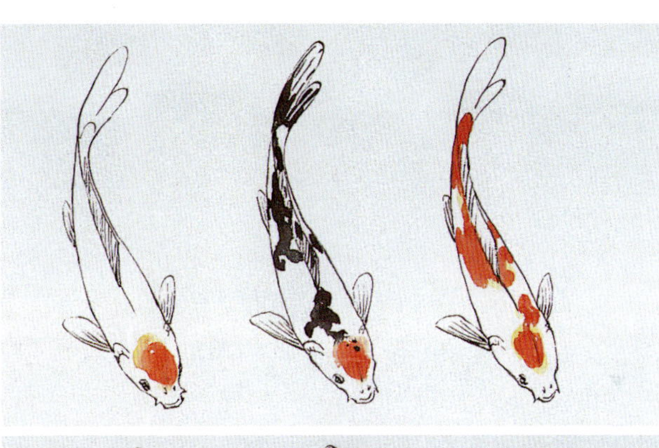

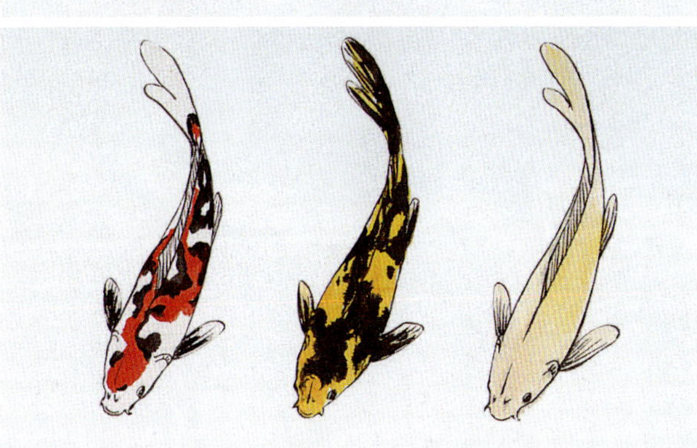

Koi Colouring
Here are some of the common colours and patterns on koi.

Goldfish

Goldfish also belong to the carp family. One major difference between goldfish and koi is that goldfish do not have barbels. In addition, goldfish are much smaller than koi. Most of them have deep, ball-shaped bodies. They can reach lengths of 20 to 25cm (8 to 10in) in about six years.

Similar to koi, goldfish have scales that are transparent. Pigment cells underneath the skin provide coloration for the fish. Some of my favourite goldfish are the ryukin, the oranda, the shubunkin, the lionhead, the telescope eye, the bubble eye and the veiltail.

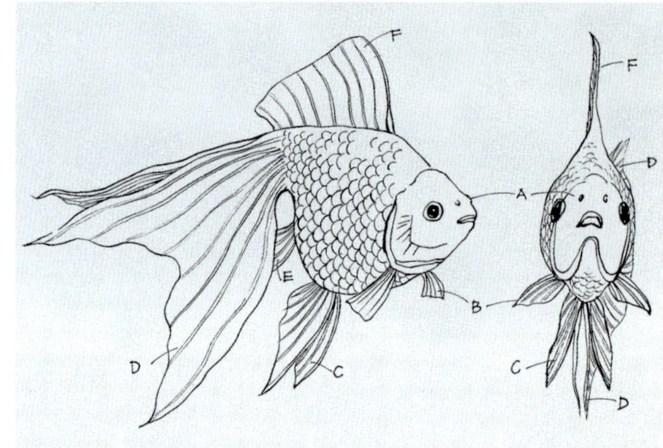

A Typical Goldfish
A. Nostril
B. Pectoral fin
C. Ventral fin
D. Tail
E. Anal fin
F. Dorsal fin

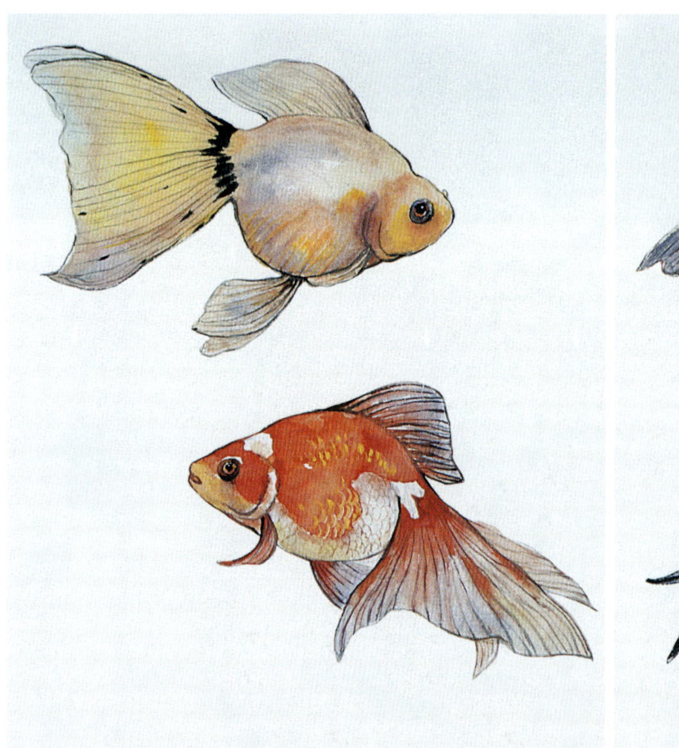

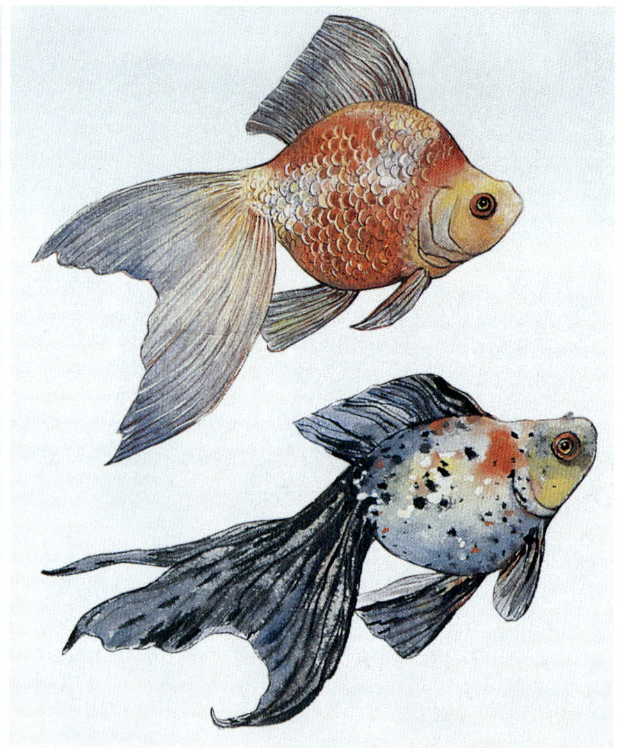

Ryukin and Veiltail Goldfish
A typical ryukin has a short, deep ball-like body and a hump in the shoulder area. Its tail is long and forked. Its fins are also lengthy. The fins and tail are magnificent when the fish is moving. I often choose ryukins as focal points in my goldfish paintings.

The bottom right-hand fish is a veiltail goldfish. It was bred in the United States during the early 1920s. Its special characteristics are the unusually long fins and tail that gracefully display when the fish is moving in water, as if it were a bride dancing in her wedding gown.

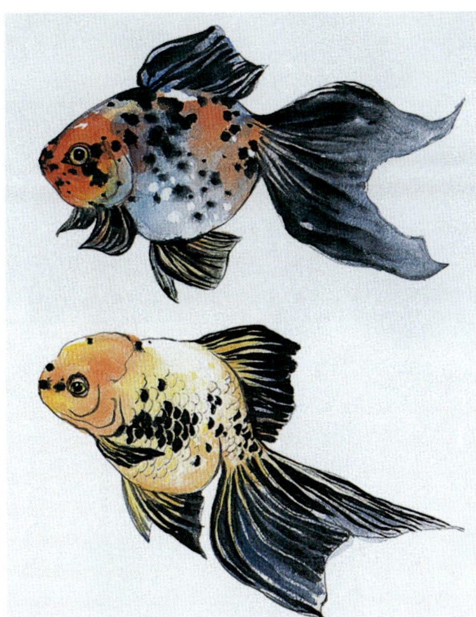
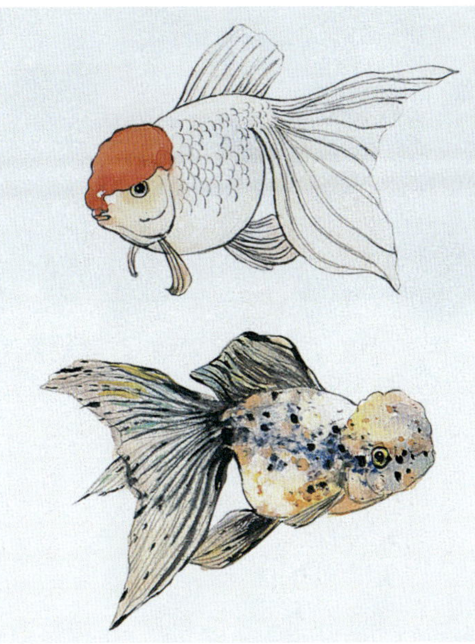

Oranda Goldfish
A very special feature of this fish is its hood, or the out-growth of skin on its head, which encases the whole head except its eyes and mouth. There are various colours of hoods. I like to place a hood as a focal point in my painting compositions.

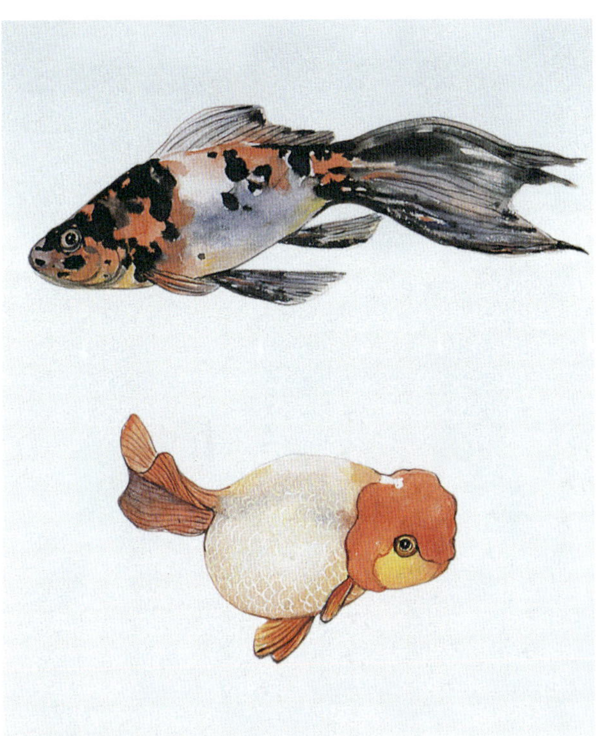
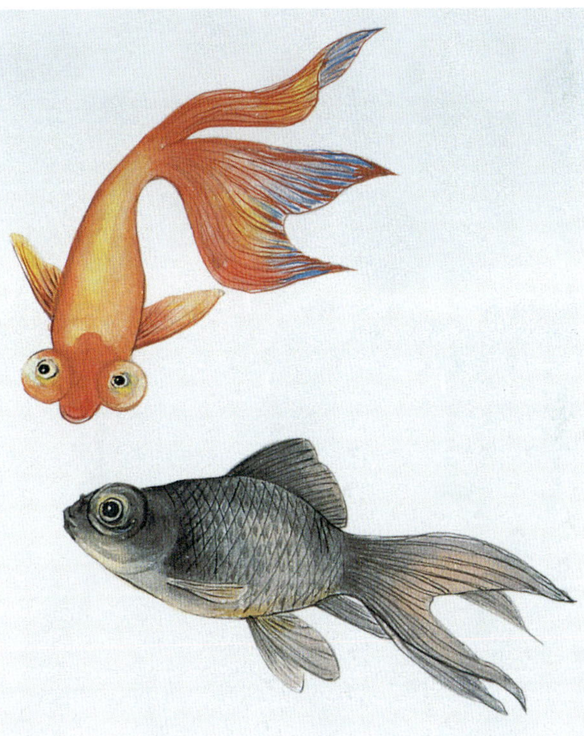

Shubunkin and Lionhead Goldfish
At the top is a shubunkin goldfish, also called a calico goldfish. Unlike other goldfish, it has a slim body that can grow to about 15cm (6in) long. Shubunkins' bodies have patches of red, yellow and black, along with dark inklike speckles on their bright blue or purple flanks.

At the bottom is a lionhead goldfish. Similar to the oranda, it is also hooded. It looks shorter than other goldfish because its fins and tail are very short. It does not have a dorsal fin.

Bubble-Eye and Telescope-Eye Goldfish
At the top is a bubble-eye goldfish. From its name, you can tell the feature of the fish: two big, bubble eyes. Some eyes are even bigger than the fish's body. Bubble-eye goldfish have slim bodies, similar to the shubunkin. The majority of them are red.

At the bottom is a telescope-eye goldfish. Obviously, the goldfish has telescope-like popping eyes. Many of them are brown-black.

Angelfish

Unlike koi and goldfish, angelfish have thin bodies. They look like diamond shapes in head-on views and profiles. Angelfish can grow to 15cm (6in) in length and 25cm (10in) in height. They have huge dorsal and anal fins. Their magnificent long, narrow ventral fins curve into beautiful sweeping arcs when they are in motion.

Typical characteristics are the four vertical black stripes on the flanks of many angelfish. The first stripe runs through the eyes. The second goes from the beginning of the dorsal fin to the vent. The third is the longest, travelling from the end of the dorsal fin through the body and down to the end of the anal fin. Finally, the fourth stripe lies at the beginning of the tail.

My favourite angelfish are the veiltail, black lace-veil, marbled veiltail, ghost, yellow-black and gold crown.

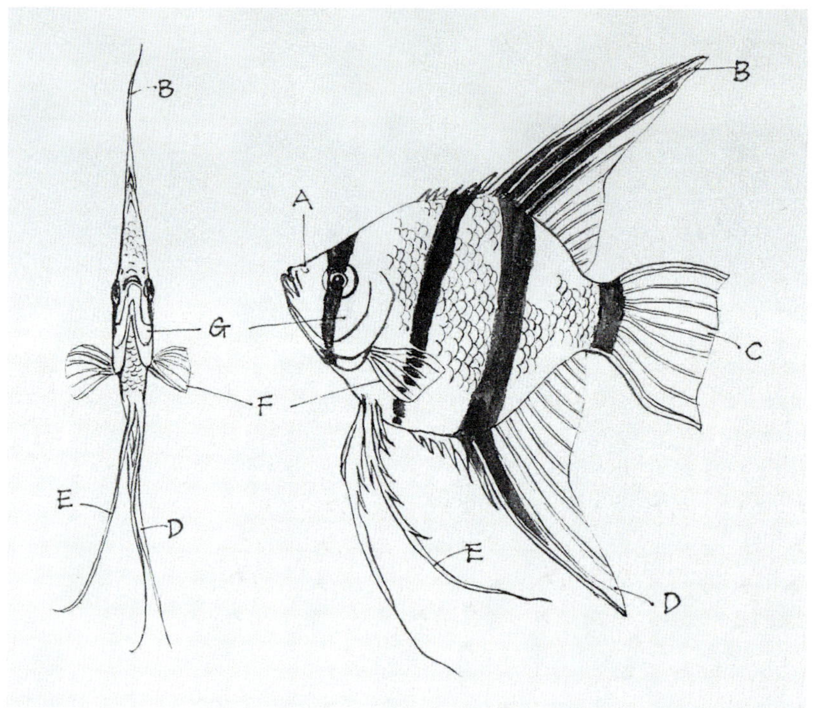

Angelfish
A. Nostril
B. Dorsal fin
C. Tail
D. Anal fin
E. Ventral fin
F. Pectoral fin
G. Gill

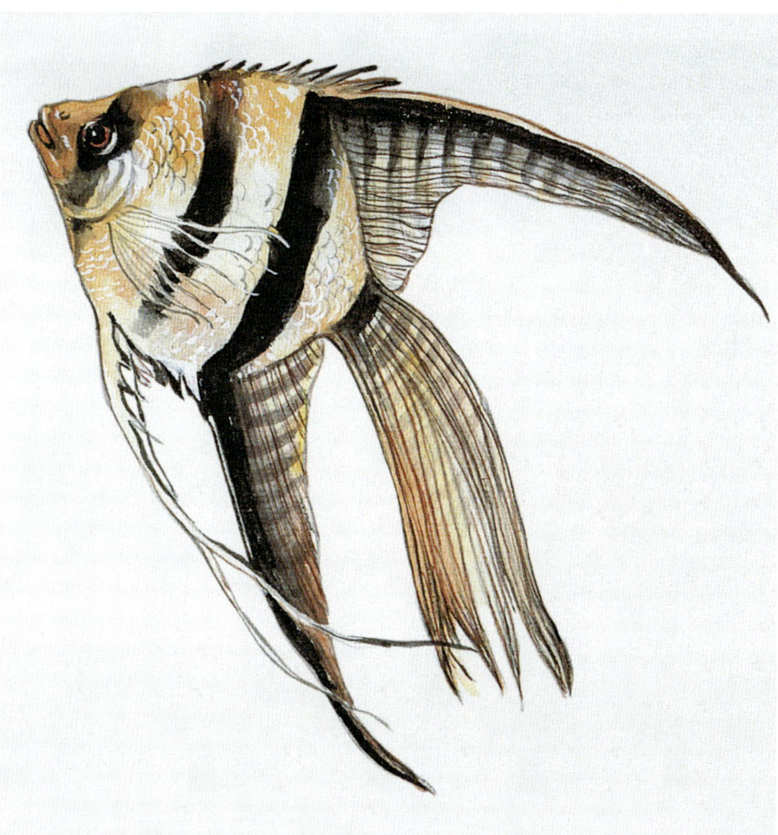

Veiltail Angelfish
This is a common angelfish. The most striking features are its lengthy fins and tail, along with four black stripes on its body. Its head, shoulder and dorsal fin are yellow-orange.

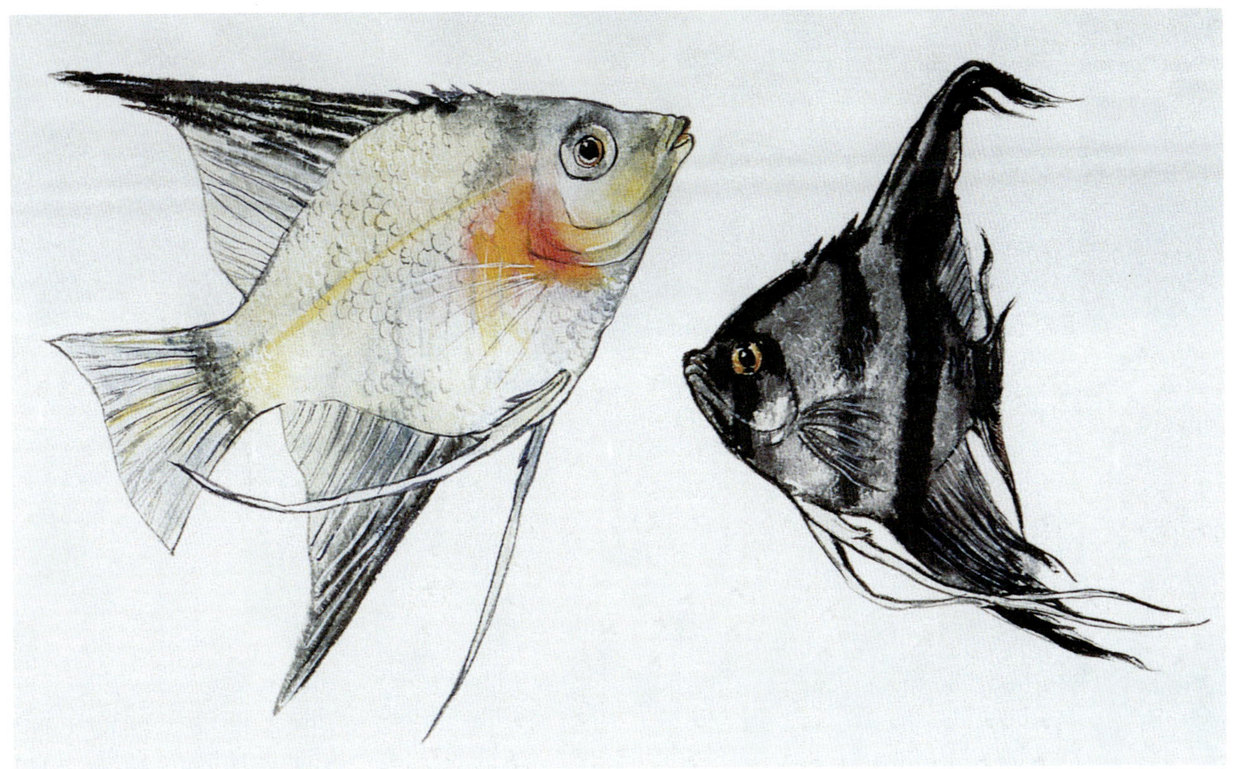

Ghost and Black Lace-Veil Angelfish
Ghost angelfish, like the left fish above, have semi-transparent bodies.
You can even see the bones and stomach through its muscles. The most
distinguishing characteristic is a red area on and around its gill.

Besides having the four black stripes, black-lace angelfish, like the
right fish above, range from light silver-grey to black. I often put a dark-
coloured black lace-veil behind a light-coloured angelfish to achieve
strong contrasting effects.

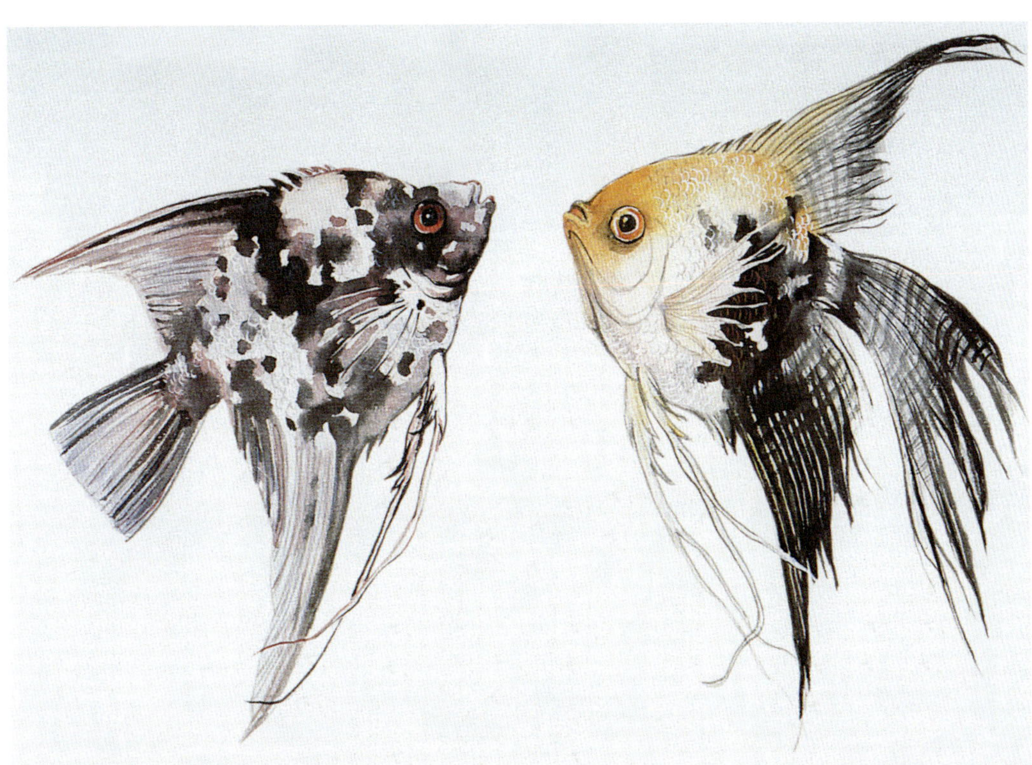

***Marbled Veiltail
and Yellow-Black
Angelfish***
The left fish is a mar-
bled veiltail angelfish.
Instead of having
uniform stripes, it
has random black
patterns on its flanks,
as if the four black
stripes were de-
formed. In addition,
it has unusual hori-
zontal bars on its tail.

At right is the
yellow-black angel-
fish. It is a handsome
fish, featuring yellow-
gold on its upper
body, along with
silver-white on the
lower body. Black
patterns are graceful-
ly distributed on its
fins, flanks and tail.
In addition, it has a
magnificent long tail.

Butterfly Fish

Butterfly fish are tropical fish with beautiful coloration. Their body shapes resemble those of angelfish: slim and flat. Some butterfly fish have dorsal and anal fins that blend into their bodies and extend to their tails. An adult fish is about 15 to 20cm (6 to 8in) long. Their colourful, flat bodies are like butterflies. Some of my favourites included the long-nosed, threadfin, three-banded, black-back, pennant and Philippine pennant.

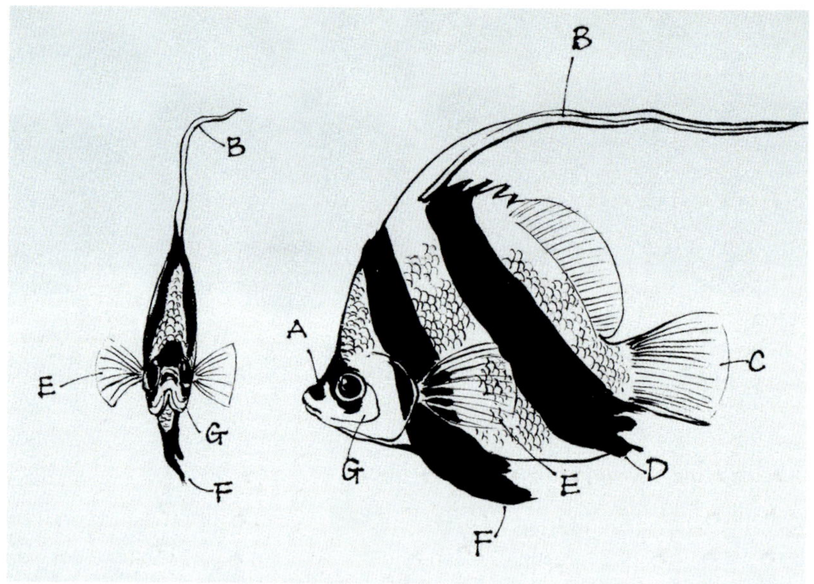

Front and Side Profiles of a Butterfly Fish
A. Nostril
B. Dorsal fin
C. Tail
D. Anal fin
E. Pectoral fin
F. Ventral fin
G. Gill

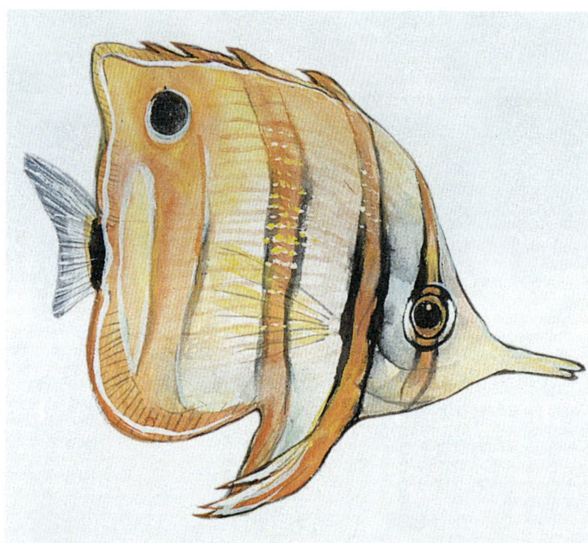

Long-Nosed Butterfly Fish
This is also called a copper-banded butterfly fish. Both names describe the two major features of this fish. In addition, the fish has a black spot on its dorsal fin, similar to the black spots on a butterfly.

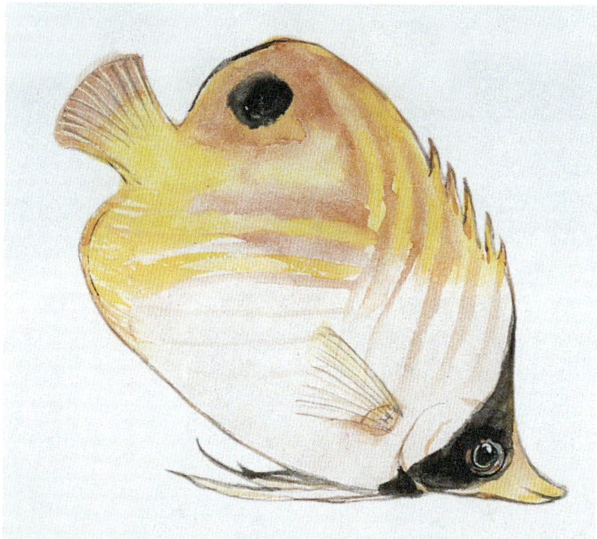

Threadfin Butterfly Fish
Its mouth is shorter than that of the long-nosed. A black band comes down from its head, crosses the eyes and ends at the bottom of its gill. About 16 brown pinstripes lie gorgeously on its body.

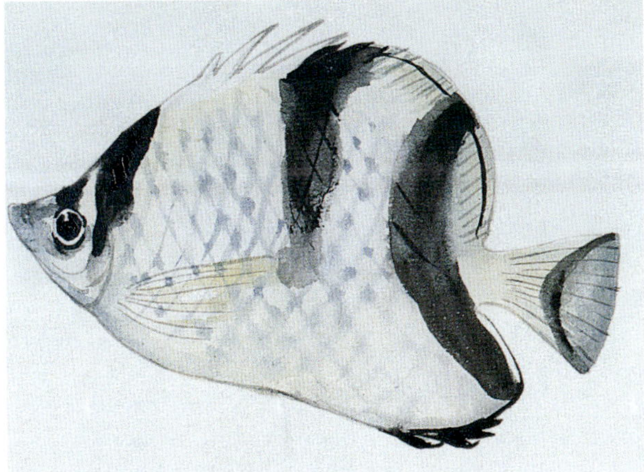

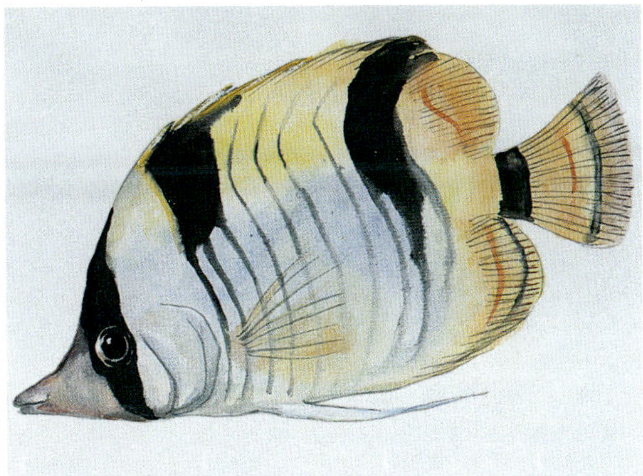

Three-Banded Butterfly Fish

It has three small, threadlike black bands. The first one is on its dorsal fin, the second one is on the anal fin, and the third is on the tail. This butterfly fish has a silver-white body.

Black-Back Butterfly Fish

It has a medium-length mouth and four black bands running vertically along its body, along with some thin black stripes. This fish has beautiful coloration of yellow, orange and light silver-blue.

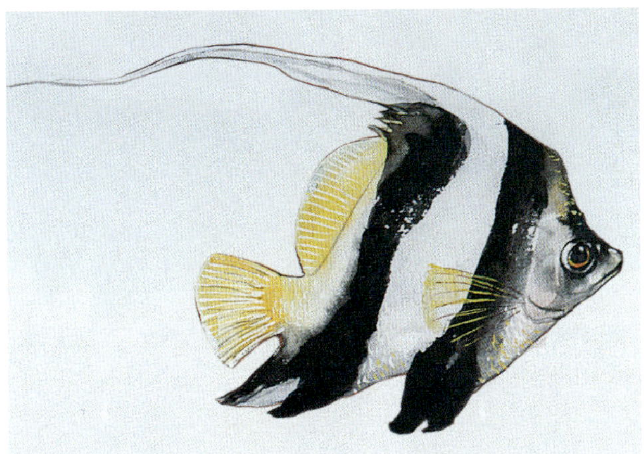

Pennant Butterfly Fish

I like to paint this fish a lot because it has a magnificent long dorsal fin and pretty black bands on its body. In addition, the fish has simple and strong contrasting colours: yellow, black and white.

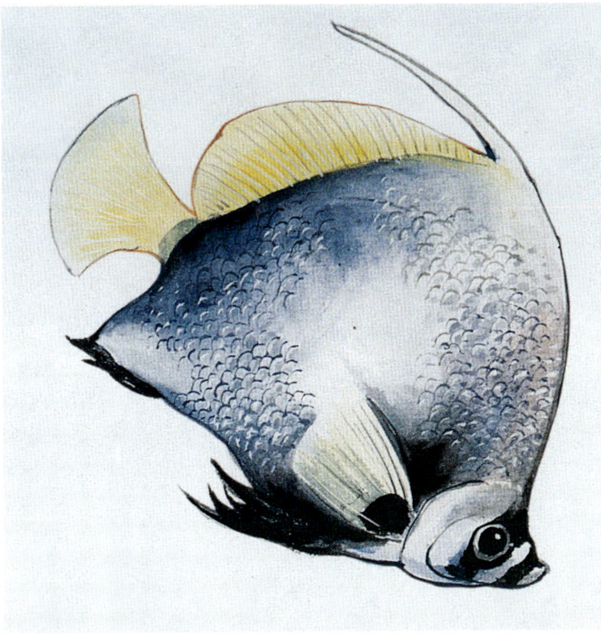

Philippine Pennant Butterfly Fish

Its dorsal fin is shorter than the pennant. It does not have the large black bands; instead, it has two smaller black bands on its head and mouth.

HOW TO SKETCH FISH

The techniques for sketching fish are similar to those for sketching birds. In the beginning, you should relate the fish to geometric shapes instead of focusing on details. It is not easy to get the appropriate proportions and perspectives of the fish, especially when sketching moving fish. You can use a fish model made of metal, plastic or ceramic to help you. I have fish tanks at home, so I can watch the fish a lot. Following are some simple processes for sketching fish.

Sketching Koi

The koi's body relates to a cylinder shape with arcs at both ends. Therefore, start by drawing a cylinder shape. Next, draw a line from one end of the cylinder to the other to indicate the centre line of the fish. The line defines the top of the fish's head, dorsal fin and tail. Once you have established the centre line, sketch the head on one end of the cylinder and the tail on the other. Finally, draw the fins.

What part and how much of the koi you can see are determined by the viewing angles between you and the fish. Pay attention to the angles in order to get proper perspectives.

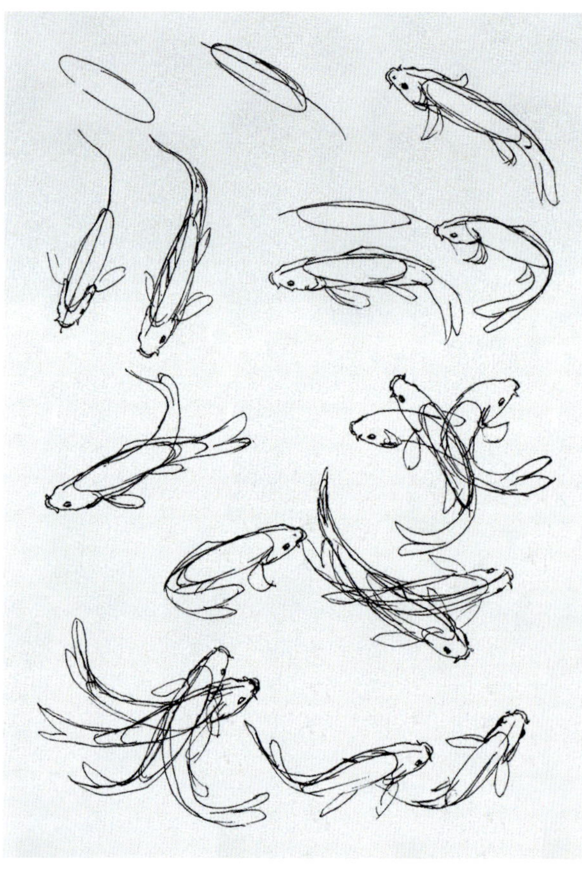

Sketching Koi
These koi sketches show aerial views. The koi displays its colour, shape and movement very well from such angles.

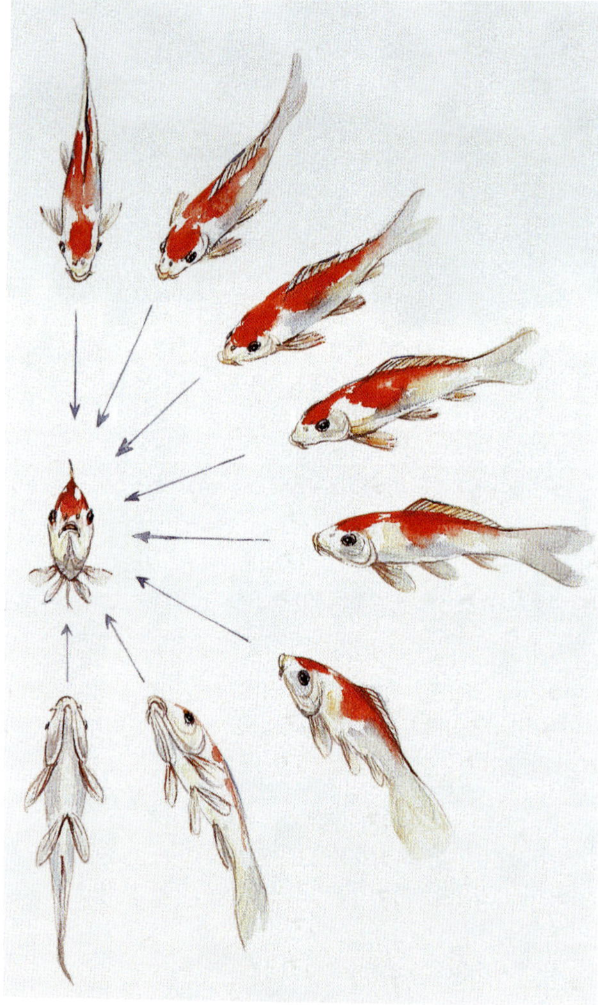

Fish Change as Viewpoint Changes
In this illustration, the arrows indicate viewing angles. The fish at the beginning of each arrow corresponds to the angle.

Sketching Goldfish

First sketch an egg as the body. Next add smaller eggs at one end to establish the gill and head. Place a little circle on one egg as an eye, then sketch the fins and tail. Once you get the overall shape and perspective of the fish, add details.

Sketching Angelfish

Start with a diamond shape to indicate the body and head. Add two triangular shapes on the top and bottom of the diamond as dorsal and anal fins. Next, place another triangle between the fins, representing its tail. Draw a circle on its head as the eye and define the gill. At this point, you have established the basic form of the fish and you can add more details. When sketching a fish swimming towards you, start with a narrower diamond shape. Accordingly, the triangular shapes are also narrower. If the fish is tilted at an angle, the geometric shapes should be tilted, too.

Sketching Butterfly Fish

Sketching a butterfly fish is very similar to sketching an angelfish except that it requires an egg shape rather than a diamond shape for the body.

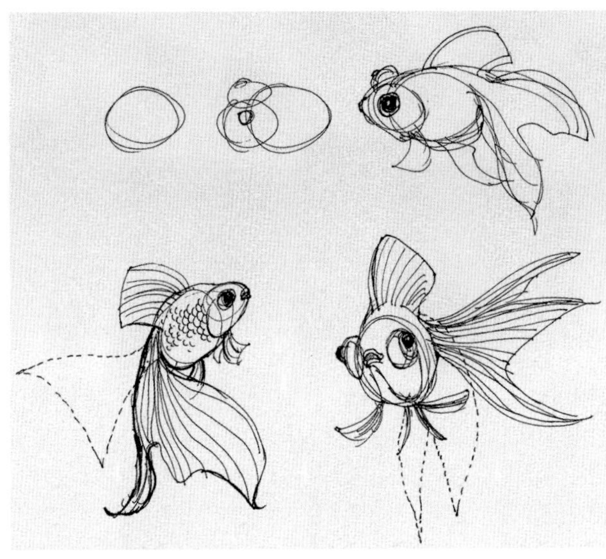

Sketching Goldfish
Here are some simple ways to sketch goldfish.

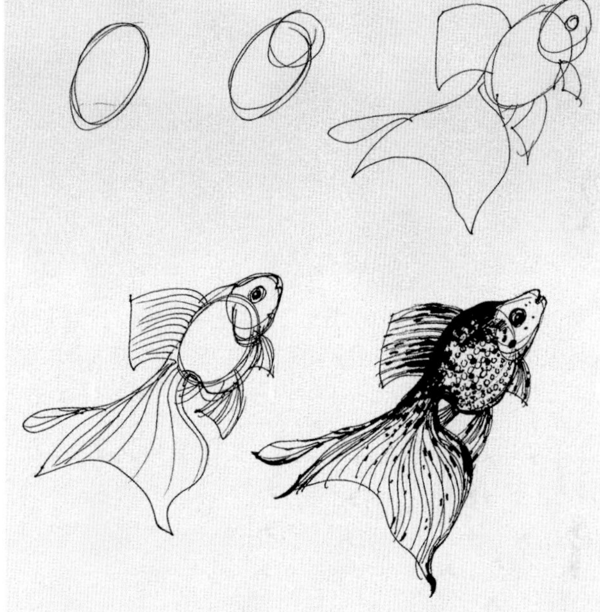

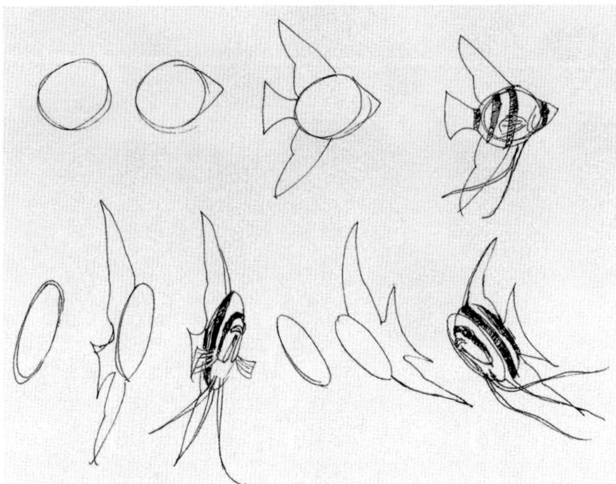

Sketching Angelfish
This shows some simple ways to sketch angelfish.

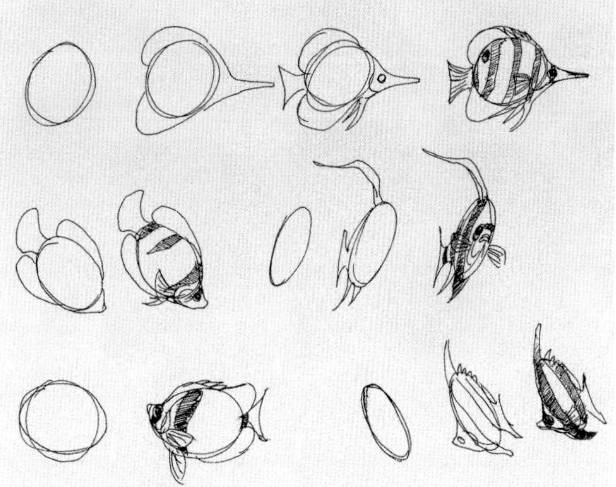

Sketching Butterfly Fish
Here are sketches of butterfly fish at different angles.

PAINTING GOLDFISH IN DETAIL STYLE

This painting has an arc-shape composition. Three fish, the major objects, form an upward curving arc. This helps to emphasize the activity of the fish. The plants in the background form minor vertical forces that break the arc, further enhancing the movement of the fish and water.

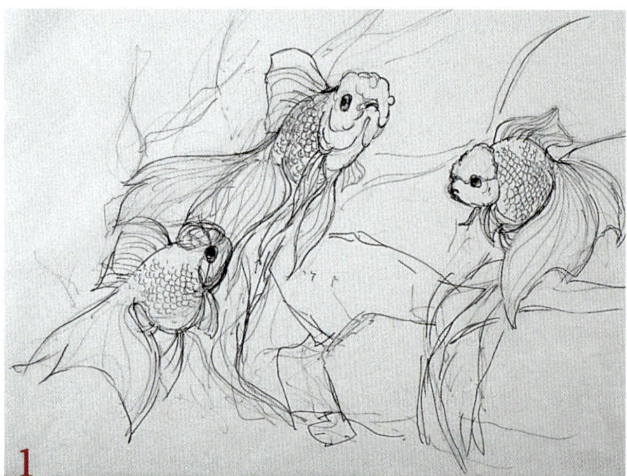

1 SKETCH THE IMAGES

Get a 38 x 48cm (15 x 19in) piece of tracing paper or sketch paper. Roughly sketch the fish and plants with a pencil. Next, use an ink pen to draw the objects again with more details.

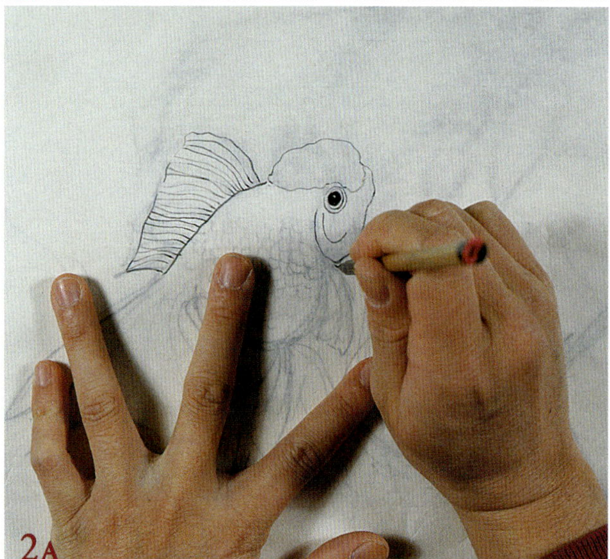

2 A & B OUTLINE THE FISH WITH INK

Place a 38 x 48cm (15 x 19in) piece of mature Shuan paper on top of your sketch and tape its corners down with drafting tape. Use an extra-small brush to outline the fish with ink. Hold the brush according to the centre-brush method. Apply intense ink on the eyes and light ink on the other parts. Paint the fish at bottom left first.

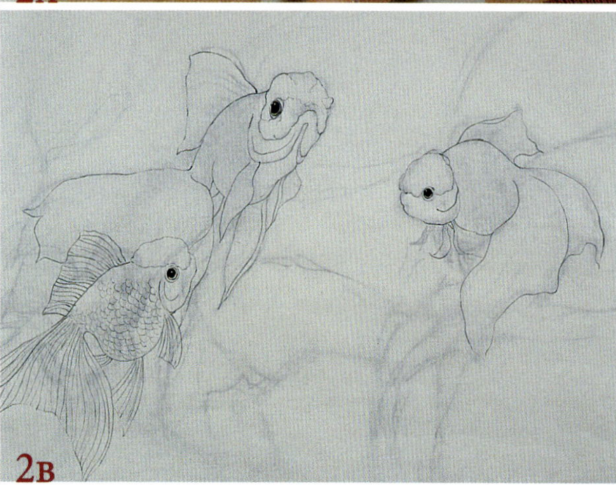

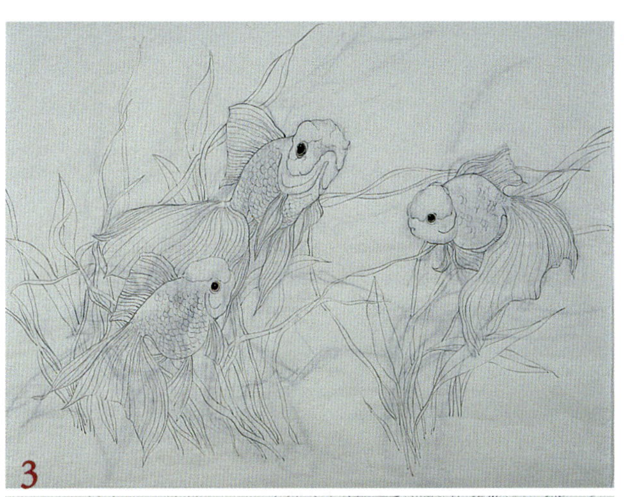

3

3 OUTLINE THE PLANTS

Use the same brush as in step 2 to outline the plants with light ink. Feel free to change the shapes of the plants. Paint the front leaves first. You do not have to paint continuous long strokes, but keep your brushstrokes smooth.

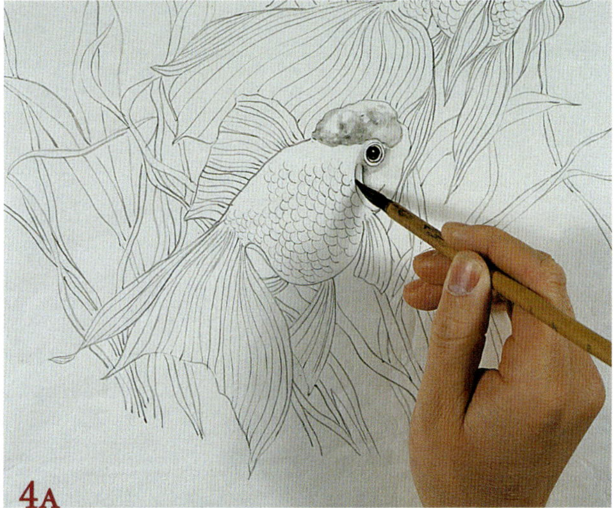

4A

4 A & B TONE THE BOTTOM LEFT FISH WITH INK

Use two medium brushes for toning. One is for inking and the other is for blending. Use the blending brush to lightly wet the fish. Next, use the inking brush to apply medium ink on the crown and around the eye. Leave some white on the crown. While the ink is wet, use the blending brush to blend it. Next, tone the other parts of the fish in the same way.

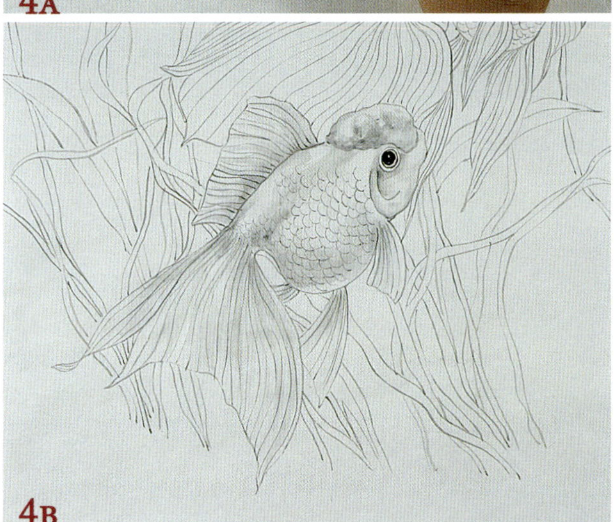

4B

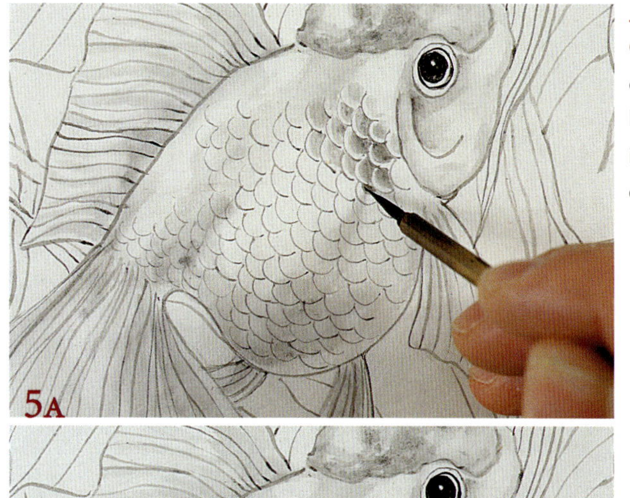

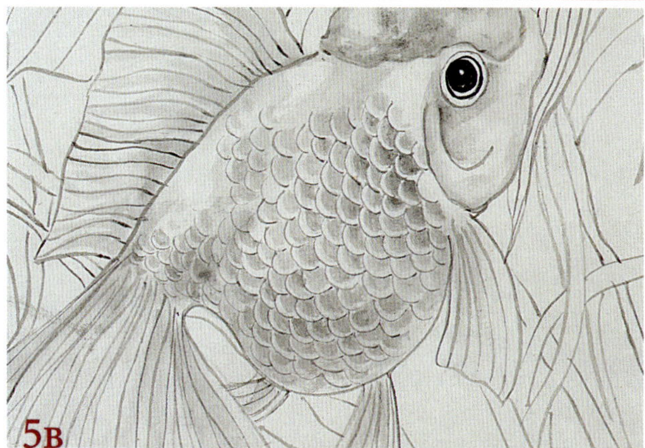

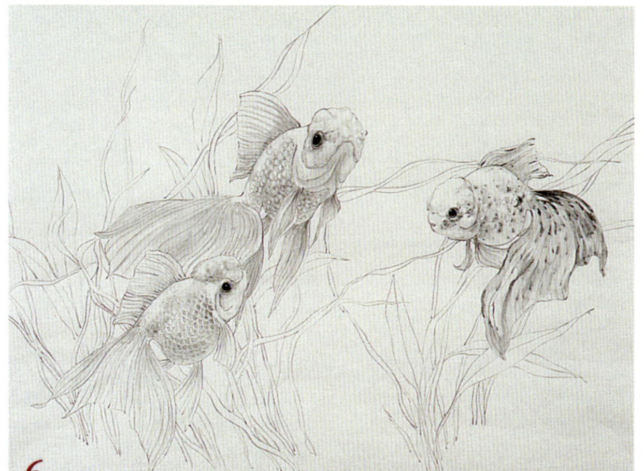

5 A & B **TONE THE SCALES**

Once the ink is dry, use two small brushes to tone the scales one by one. For each scale, use the inking brush to apply medium ink at the base. Immediately use the blending brush to blend and drag the ink into the edges and tip. Use lighter ink for the scales on the upper part of the body where it catches the light.

6 **TONE THE OTHER TWO FISH**

Even though these two fish are different from the one you just painted, use the same technique to tone them. For the circular scales on the upper left fish, leave white at the centre of each scale rather than at the edges.

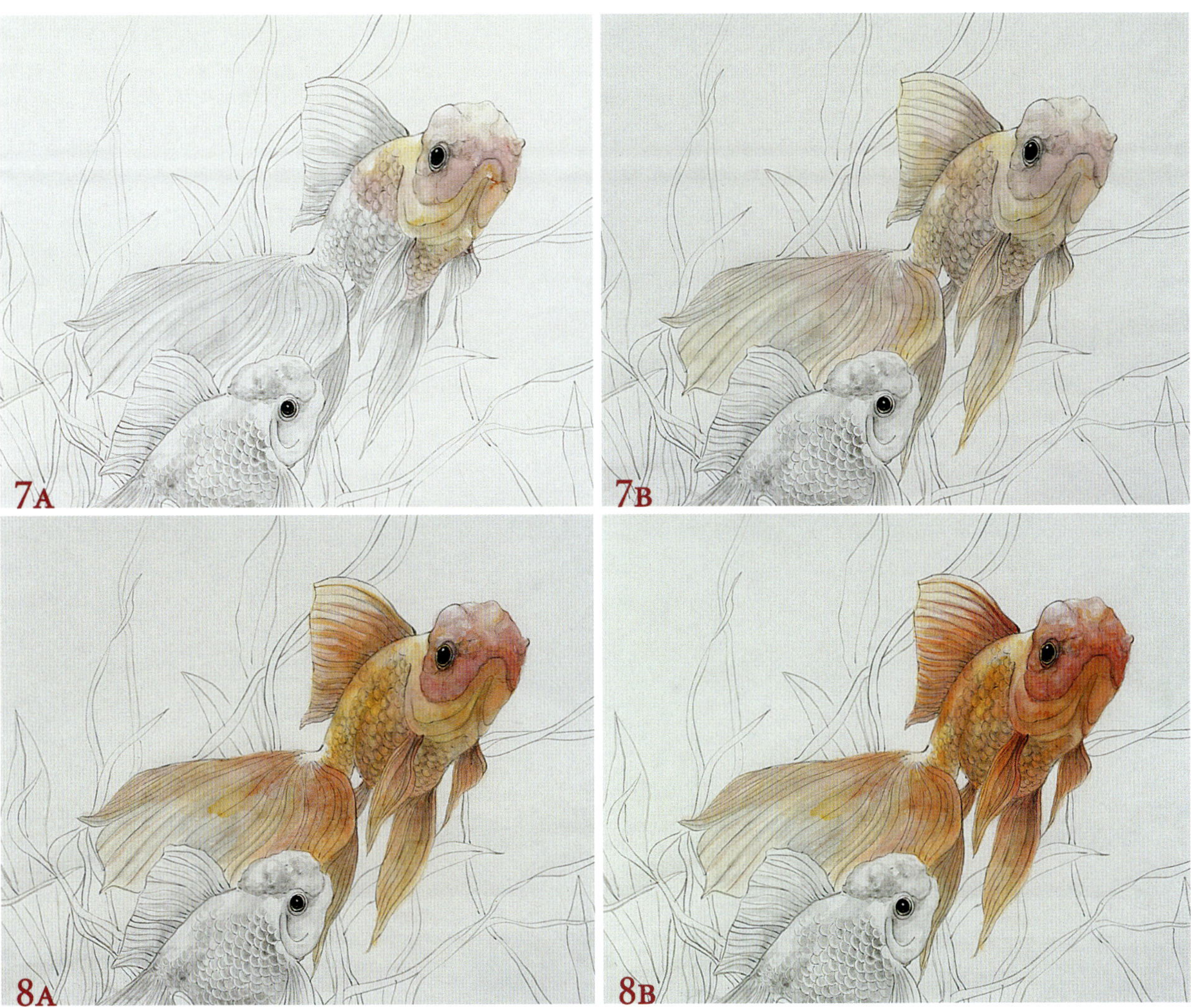

7 A & B APPLY COLOUR ON THE FISH AT UPPER LEFT

After the ink is dry, use a large brush to lightly wet the head and body. Use a medium brush to apply light yellow on the crown and medium yellow on the gill and back. Immediately use another medium brush to apply carmine on the bottom parts of the crown, mouth and body. Smoothly blend the colours. Paint the other parts of the fish in the same way.

8 A & B ADD MULTIPLE LAYERS OF COLOUR TO THE FISH

Wait for the colours to dry. Use the same brushes and colours to paint the fish a second time. Dry the colours and paint a third time. With each layer, apply more intense colours than used for the previous layer.

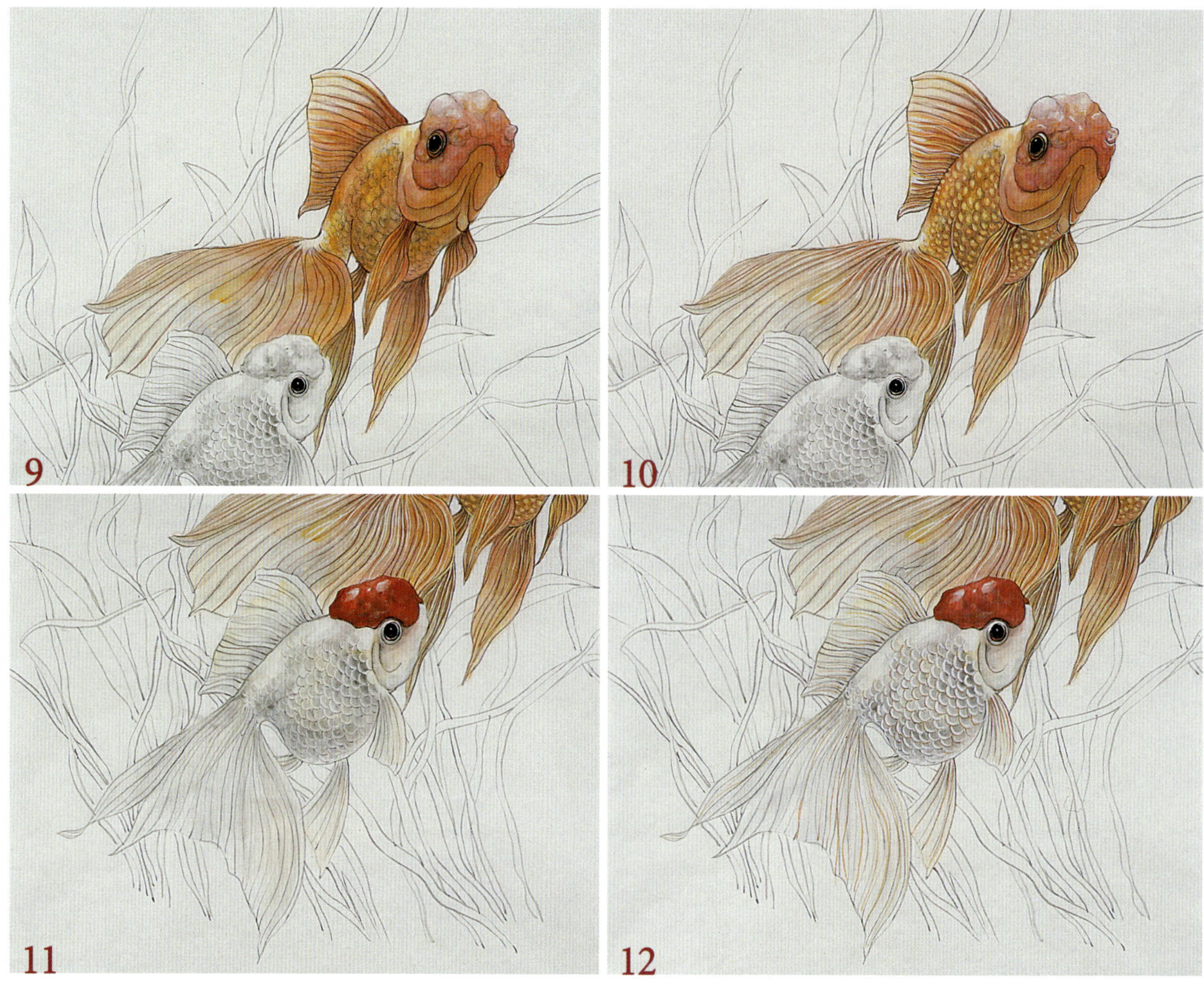

9 PAINT SECOND OUTLINE ON THE FISH

Use an extra-small brush to mix intense carmine and ink. Hold your brush straight to paint the second outlines over the first outlines.

10 ADD DETAILS

Use an extra-small brush to paint long strokes on the tail and fins with intense white and yellow. Use a medium brush to paint the spots on the scales with intense yellow. Highlight the crown and upper area of the eye with white.

11 COLOUR THE FISH AT BOTTOM LEFT

Use a large brush to lightly wet the fish. Apply light yellow. Next, apply very light carmine at the bottom of the body. Use a medium brush to paint the crown with intense carmine. Immediately add rouge to the lower portion. While the colours are wet, use another medium brush to blend the colours into the eye area. Add yellow around the eye and gill.

12 ADD DETAILS

Use an extra-small brush to mix carmine and yellow to paint the long strokes on the tail and fins. In addition, outline the scales. Next, use a small brush to highlight the scales with very intense white. Finally, paint the eyeball with carmine, yellow and ink.

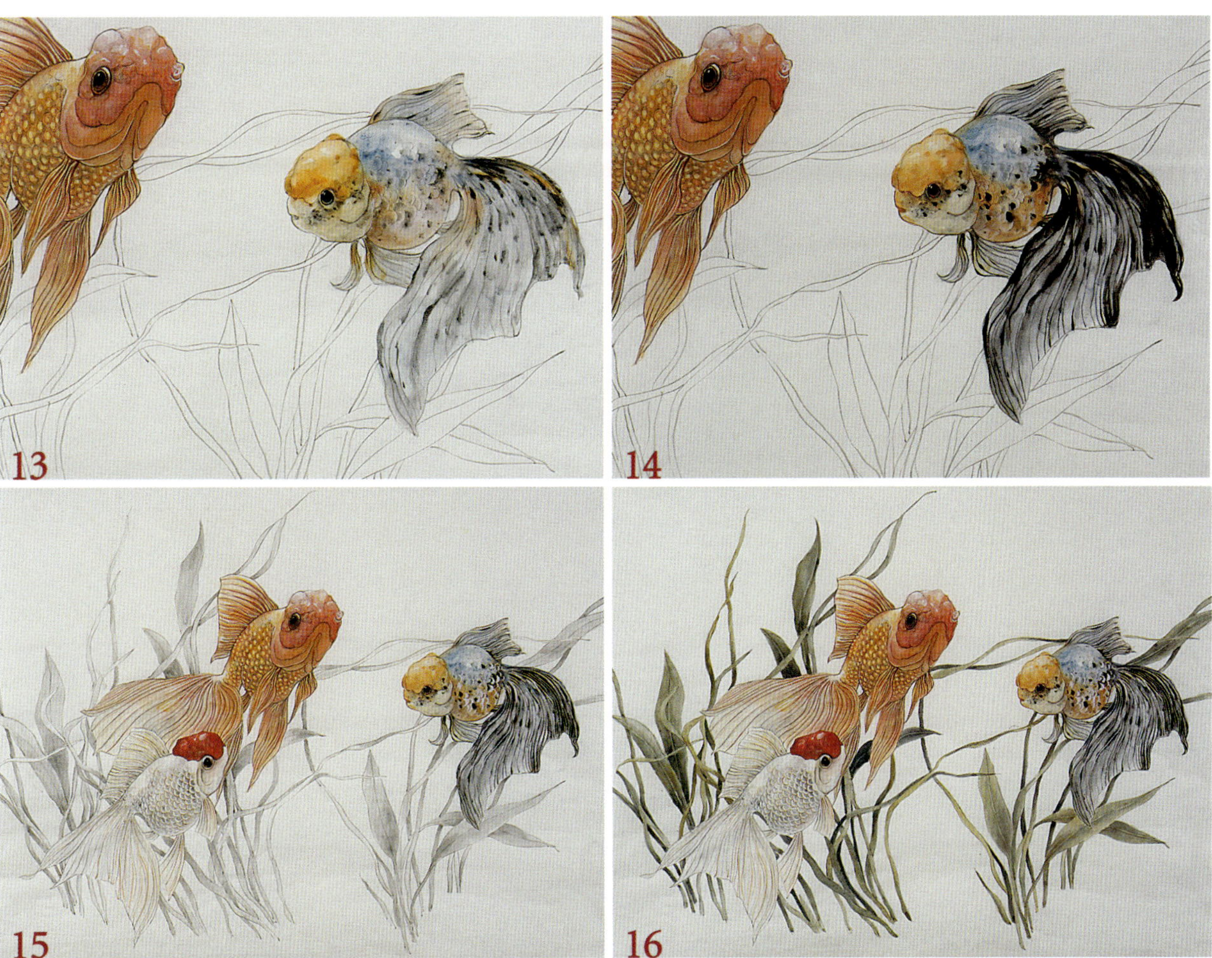

13 COLOUR THE FISH AT RIGHT

Lightly wet the fish. Use a medium brush to mix yellow and vermilion. Paint the crown, gill, mouth and lower portion of the body. Next, apply phthalocyanine blue on the upper portion of the body, the fins and the tail. Finally, apply yellow and vermilion to the top of the dorsal fin, the beginning of the pectoral fin and the upper part of the tail.

14 ADD INTENSE INK TO THE TAIL AND FINS

When the colours are halfway dry, use a medium brush to add intense ink on the tail and fins. In addition, paint some intense ink spots on the body and gill.

15 PAINT THE DETAILS OF THE FISH AND TONE THE PLANTS WITH INK

Use an extra-small brush to mix very intense white and a little light carmine. Paint the tiny and long strokes of the fins and tail. Also, use a small brush to highlight the scales with the same colours. Next, use two medium brushes to tone the leaves of the plants with ink one by one. Wet a leaf with one brush, then use the other brush to apply medium ink on the lower part. Immediately blend the ink with the wetting brush.

16 COLOUR THE PLANTS

Wait for the ink to dry. Use a medium brush to mix yellow and indigo to paint the leaves. After the colours dry, paint them again with the same brush and colours. Leave a centre line on each large leaf.

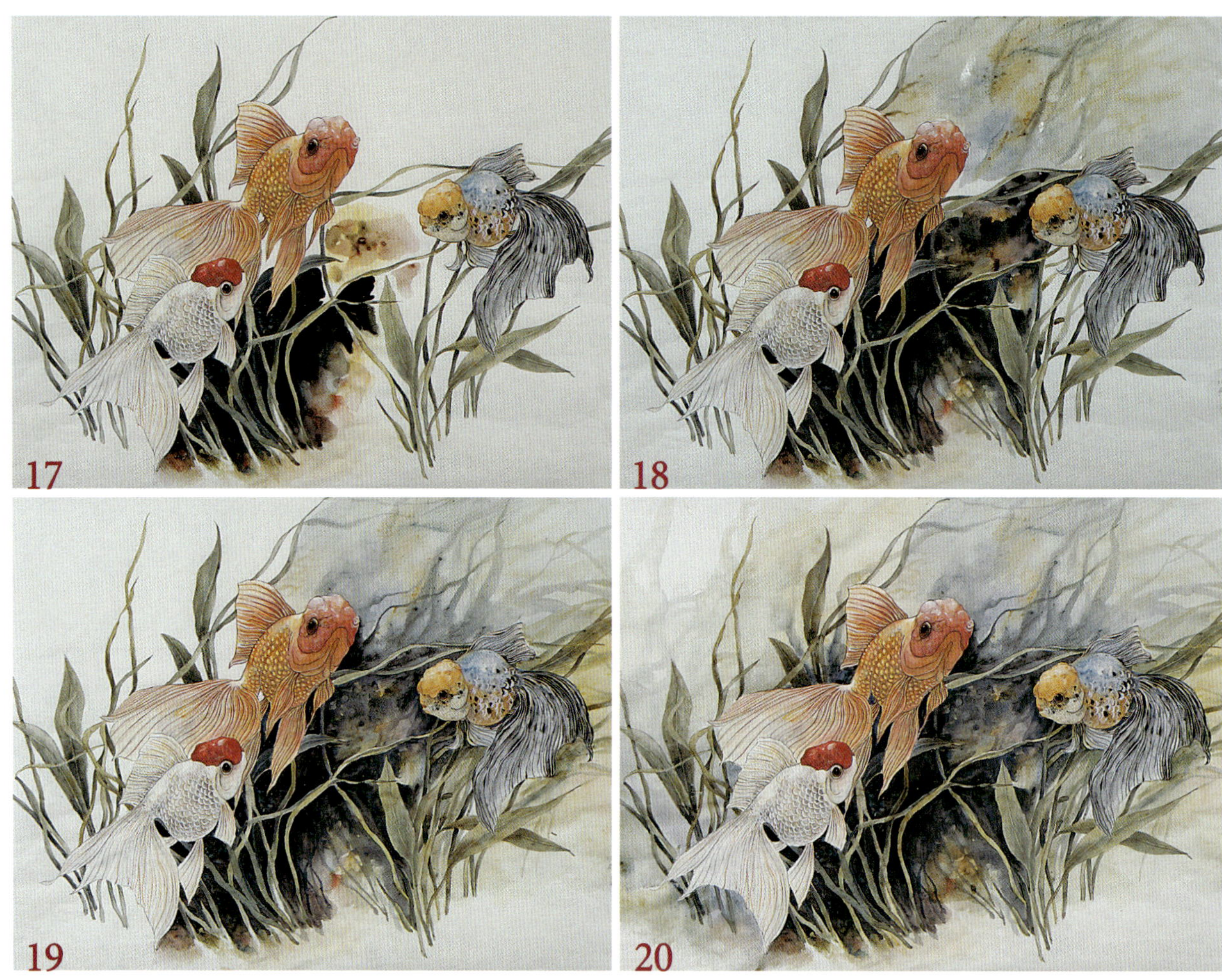

17 PAINT THE BACKGROUND

Use a large brush to mix yellow, carmine and a little indigo. Paint the area between the fish without touching the plants. While the colours are wet, use a small brush to add intense ink to define the edges of the fish and plants.

18 CONTINUE PAINTING THE BACKGROUND

Use a large brush to wet the upper right quarter of the background. Apply yellow, indigo and a little vermilion to it. While the colours are wet, paint the distant plants with light ink and indigo.

19 CONTINUE PAINTING THE BACKGROUND

Use the small brush to define the edge of the top fish with intense ink. Blend the ink into the other colours at right. Next, wet the background at the middle right. Apply yellow and a little vermilion to it. Then paint the distant plants with ink and yellow.

20 CONTINUE PAINTING THE BACKGROUND

Wet the left side of the background. Paint light yellow and indigo on it. Leave some white at the upper left corner.

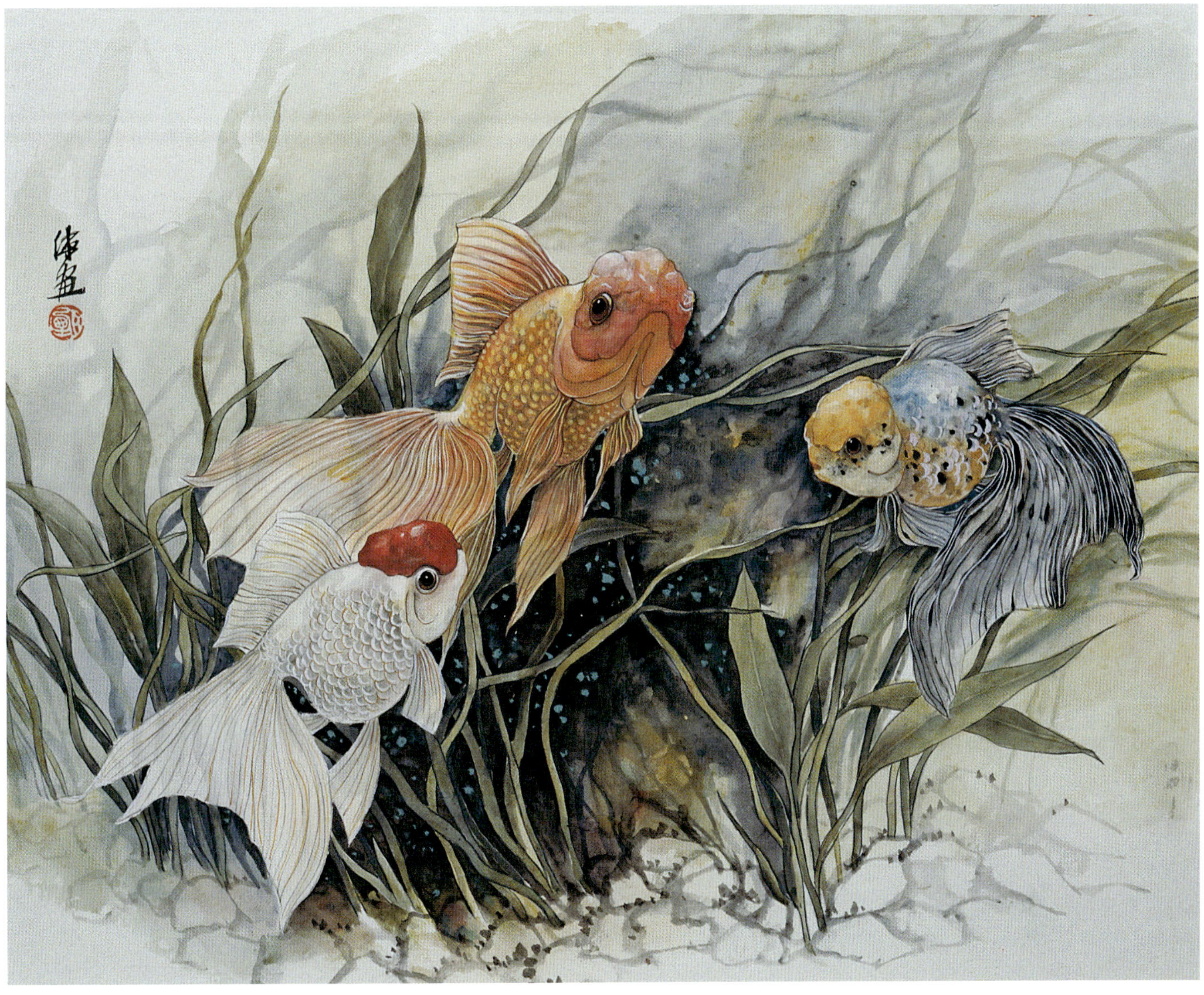

21 *PAINT THE ROCKS, SIGN AND SEAL YOUR PAINTING*

Use a medium brush and ink to outline the rocks. Fade out the distant rocks by using lighter ink. Mix intense blue and green to paint some spots on the intense colour area between the fish, a technique referred to as 'calling out the moss'. Finally, sign your name and stamp you chop on the upper left.

THREE GOLDFISH
38 x 48cm (15 x 19in)
Chinese ink and colours on mature Shuan paper
Detail style

PAINTING A LIONFISH IN HALF-DETAIL, HALF-SPONTANEOUS STYLE

Strong colour contrasts can create very interesting paintings. For instance, the rear fish has black stripes that cause the red fish in the front to stand out. The background for the red fish uses dark colours, while the background for the rear fish uses light colours.

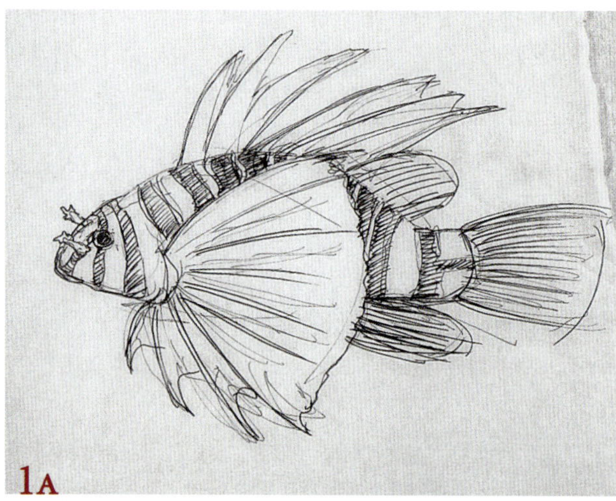

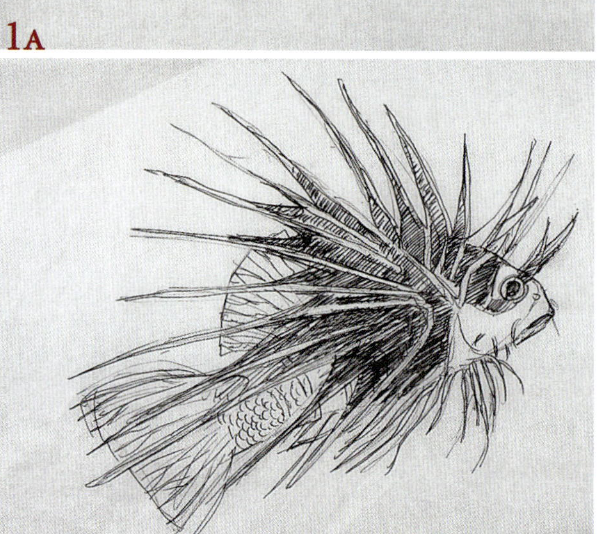

*1 A & B **SKETCH THE FISH ON TRACING PAPERS***

Sketch the fish separately on two sheets of 20 x 25cm (8 x 10in) tracing paper. First use a pencil to draw the outlines, then use an ink pen to draw over the pencil lines and add more details.

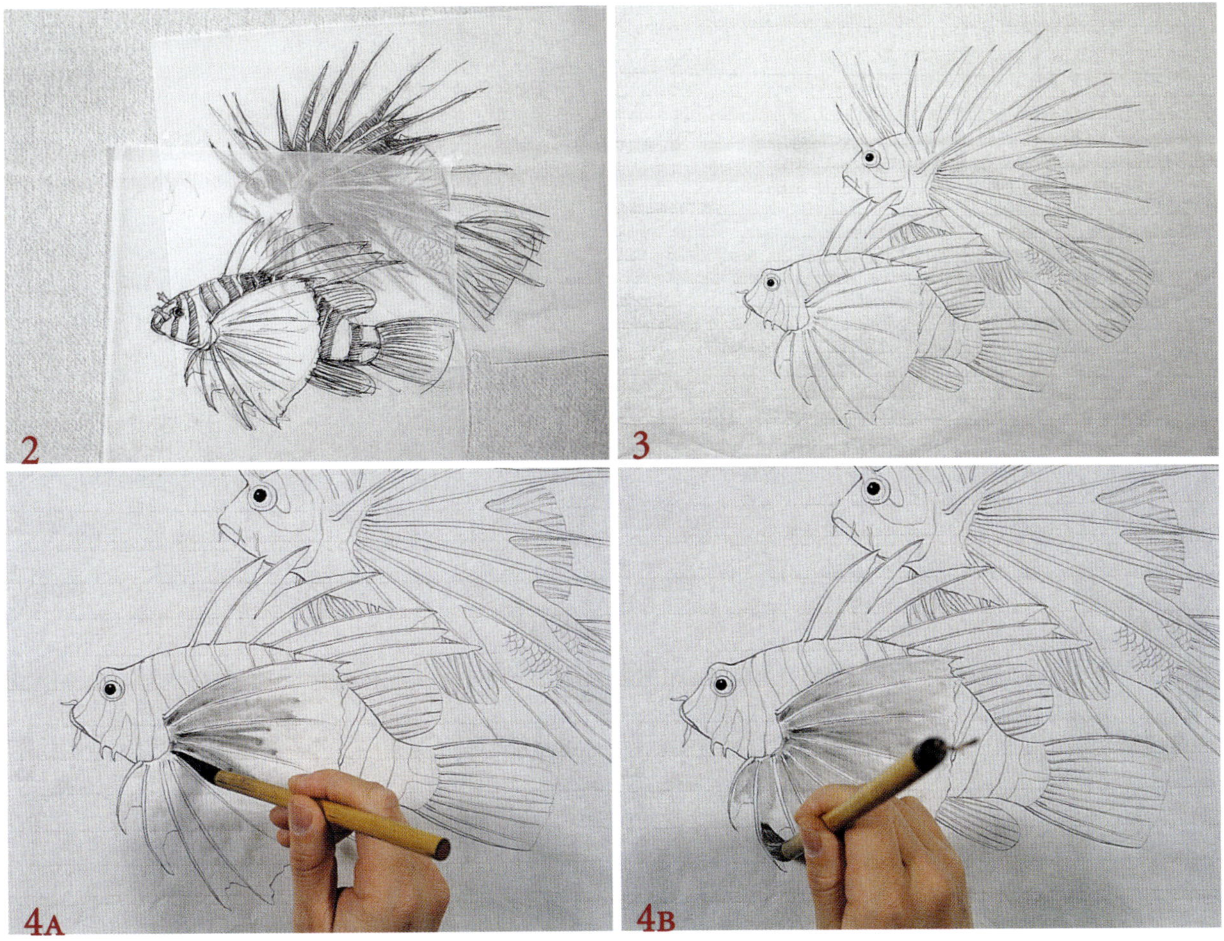

2 *Arrange the fish to create a good composition*

Arrange the sketches until you find a composition you like. In this composition, the back fish is flipped from its original position.

3 *Outline the fish with ink*

Overlay an 46 x 61cm (18 x 24in) piece of mature Shuan paper on the sketches. Use an extra-small brush to outline the fish. Hold the brush straight. Paint the eyes with intense ink. Paint the heads, edges of the fins and tails with medium ink. Use light ink to outline the other parts.

4 A & B *Tone the pectoral fin of the front fish*

Use two large brushes for toning. One is for inking and the other is for wetting and blending. Wet the fin without touching its bones. Next, apply medium ink at the beginning of the fin. Use the blending brush to drag and blend the ink to the tip of the fin. Leave the bones unpainted.

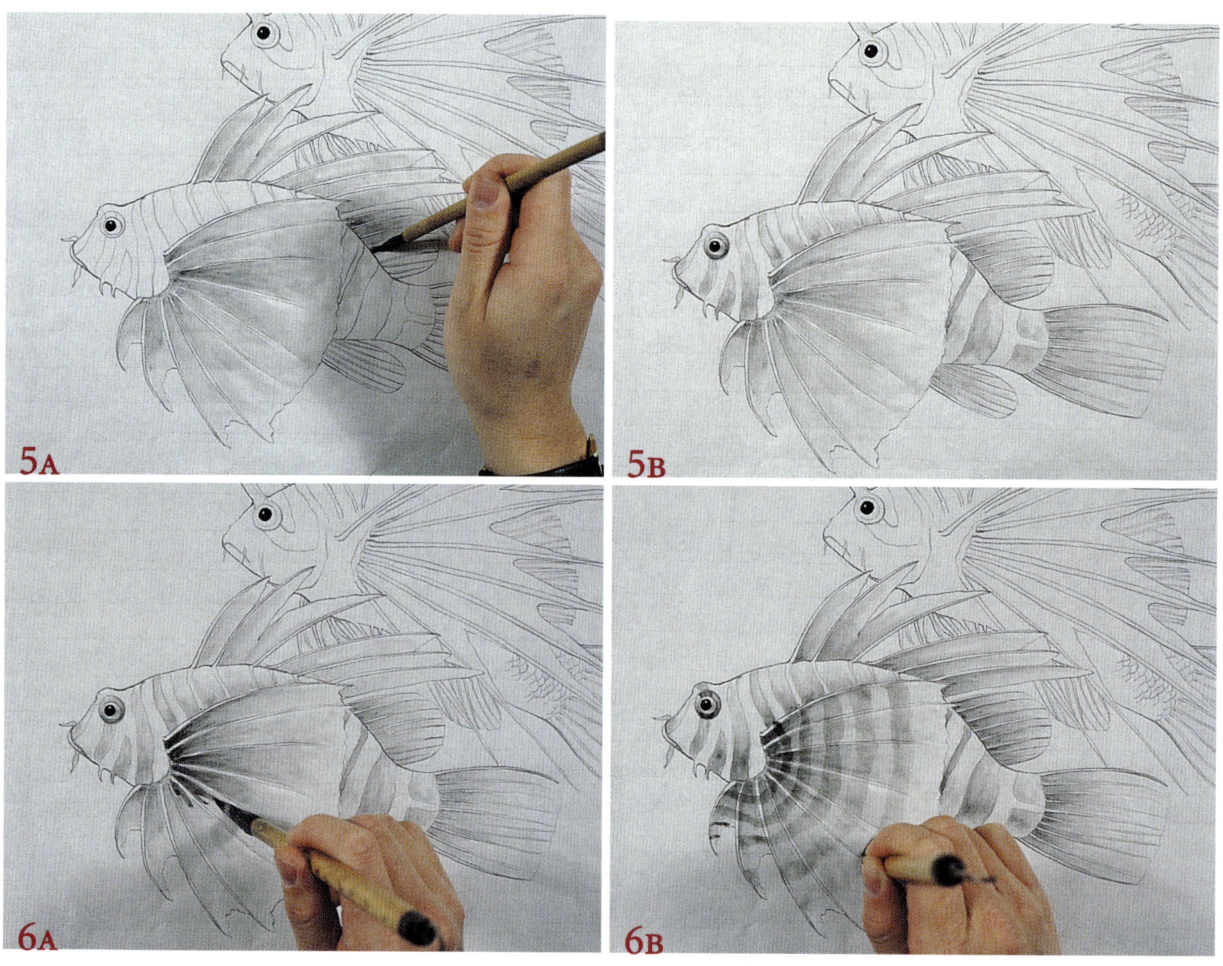

5 A & B TONE THE OTHER PARTS OF THE FISH

Tone the other parts of the fish in the same way. Use smaller brushes to paint the tiny areas. Leave white areas on top of the body.

6 A & B ADD A SECOND LAYER OF TONING TO THE PECTORAL FIN

After the ink is dry, use the same brushes but more intense ink to tone the pectoral fin in the same way. When the ink is almost dry, use the inking brush to paint the stripes. Use intense ink for the stripe at the beginning of the fin and lighter ink towards the tip.

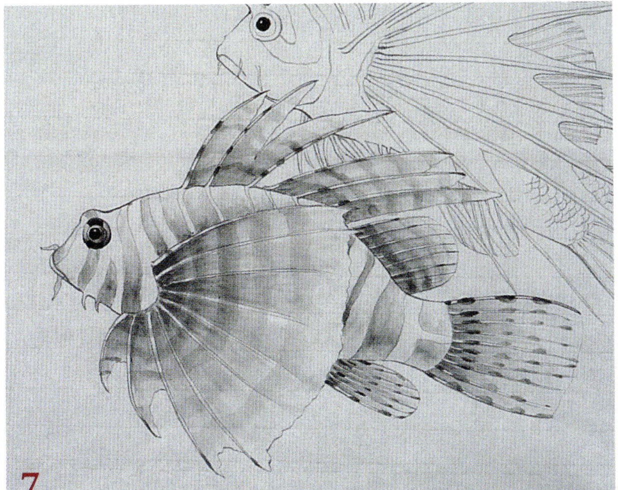

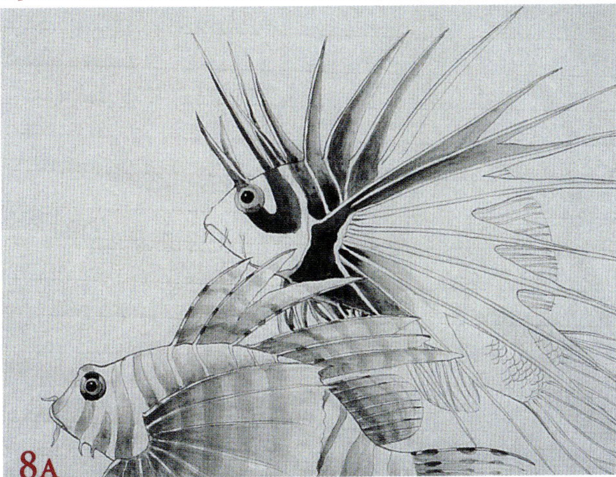

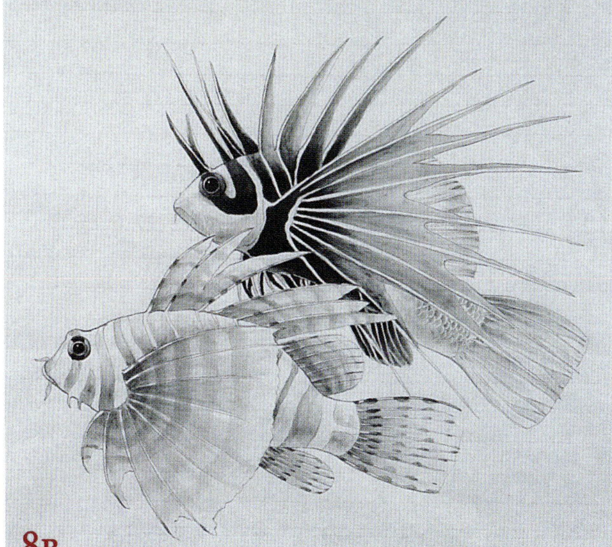

7 APPLY A SECOND LAYER OF TONING TO THE OTHER PARTS OF THE FISH

Tone the dorsal fin similar to the way you did the pectoral fin. Apply more intense ink to the eye, body and tail. Use a small brush to paint the small dark spots on the fins and tail.

8 A & B TONE THE BACK FISH

Tone the back fish in the same way as the first fish. Starting in the darkest areas, apply very intense ink on the ventral and anal fins. Also, tone the pectoral fin with more intense ink than used for the dorsal fin of the front fish.

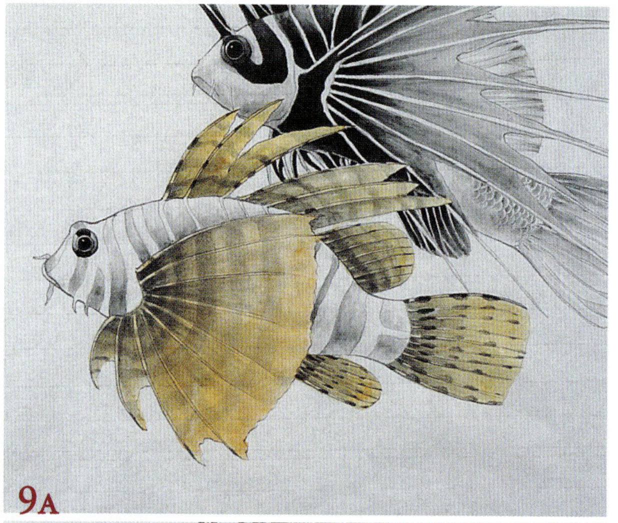

9 A & B ***APPLY THE FIRST LAYER OF COLOURING***
TO THE FRONT FISH

Use a large brush to wet the fish, then apply yellow and vermilion. Get more yellow to paint the body. Use a small brush to mix blue and indigo to paint the eye.

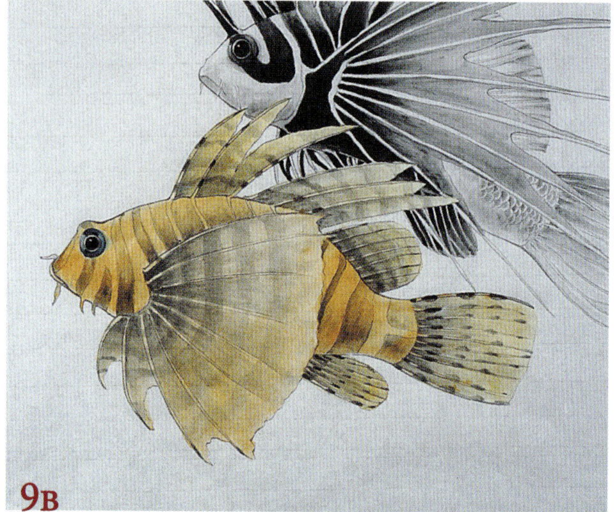

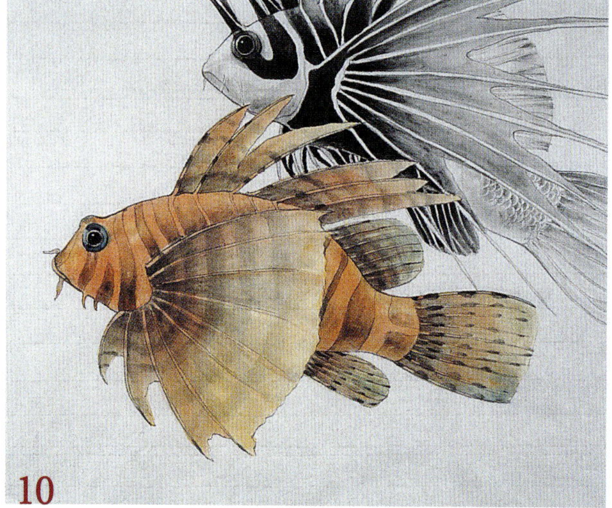

10 ***APPLY THE SECOND LAYER OF COLOURING***
TO THE FRONT FISH

After the first layer of colour is dry, lightly wet the fish again. Apply light rouge. Paint lighter colour on the tips of the fins and tail.

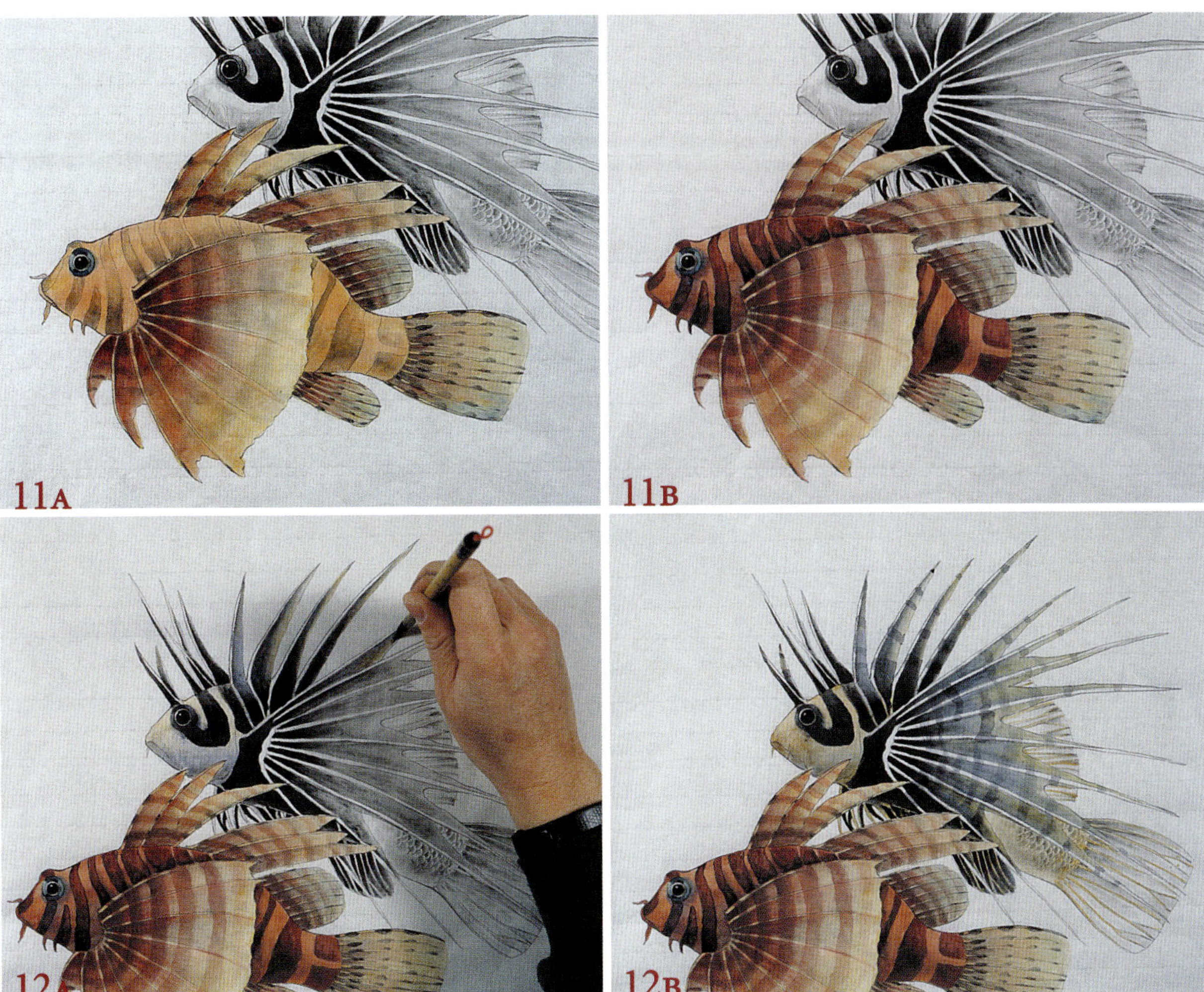

11A   *11B*   *12A*   *12B*

11 A & B ADD THE THIRD LAYER OF COLOURING TO THE FRONT FISH

Wait for the second layer of colours to dry. Lightly wet the fish again. Use a medium brush to mix rouge and ink to paint the lower portions of the dark stripes. Then blend the colours towards the upper portions. Use a large brush to paint the stripes on the fins with rouge, intense at the beginnings and light at the tips.

12 A & B COLOUR THE BACK FISH

Lightly wet the back fish. Use a medium brush to apply blue on the fins, tail and lower half of the head. Apply yellow on the upper portion of the head, the tips of fins and the body. After the colours are dry, lightly wet the fish again and apply the same colours a second time. Next, use a medium brush to paint the stripes on the fins with indigo and light ink.

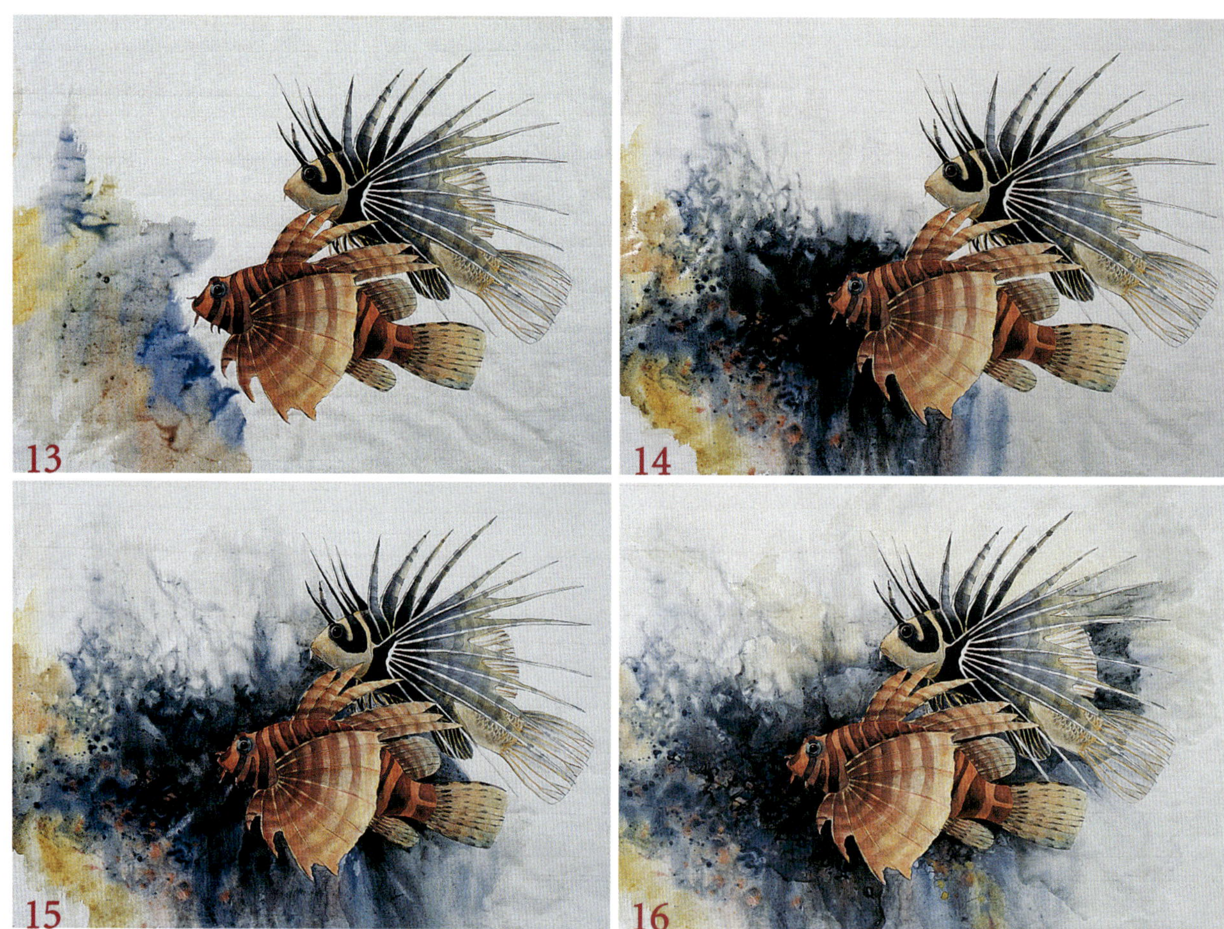

13 Paint the background at left

Use a large brush to wet the background, then paint the area with phthalocyanine blue, yellow and vermilion. Use another large brush to blend the colours.

14 Continue painting the background

Apply more intense yellow and phthalocyanine blue, then splatter cinnabar on the area. Use a medium brush to apply intense ink and carefully define the outlines of the front fish. Next, drag the colours to the upper left to create the illusion of plants and moving water.

15 Paint the centre part of the background

Wet the centre area. Apply phthalocyanine blue and cinnabar on the middle bottom and between the fish. Use a small brush and add intense ink to define the outlines of the fish.

16 Paint the background at right and define the rocks

Wet the background area at right, then apply ink and phthalocyanine blue on the right side of the rear fish. Apply light yellow at top right, next to the fish. Use a medium brush and ink to define the rocks.

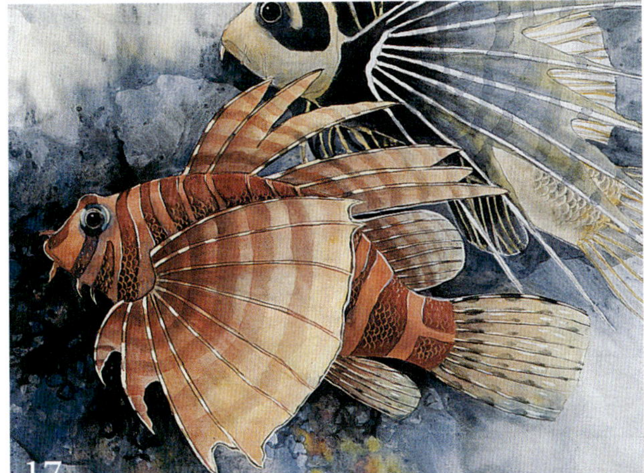

17 *ADD DETAILS AND HIGHLIGHT THE FISH*

Use an extra-small brush to mix very intense yellow and white. Highlight the bones on the fins and tails. In addition, paint the outlines on the head of the front fish. Next, mix cinnabar and white to paint the scales on the front fish. Then use very intense white to highlight the dorsal and pectoral fins of the rear fish.

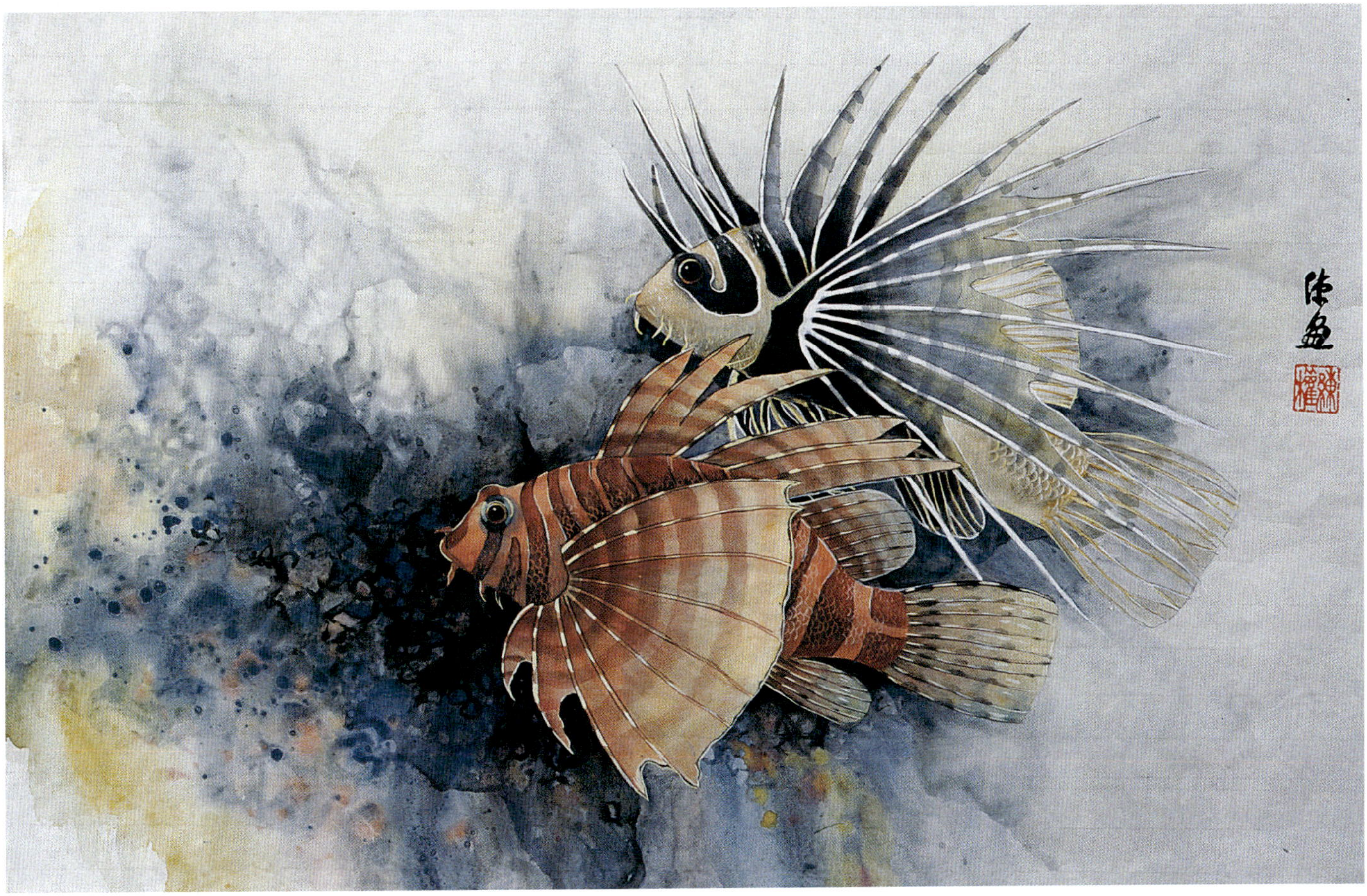

18 *ADD MORE DETAILS TO THE REAR FISH, SIGN AND SEAL YOUR PAINTING*

Use an extra-small brush to highlight the scales and upper eyeball with yellow and white. Also paint the texture of the gill and head. Next, paint the lower eyeball with vermilion and ink. Finally, sign your name and stamp your chop at middle right. This area needs objects to balance the motions of the fish.

LIONFISH
46 x 61cm (18 x 24in)
Chinese ink and colours on mature Shuan paper
Half-detail, half-spontaneous style

PAINTING BUTTERFLY FISH IN SPONTANEOUS STYLE

This is an ink-pouring type of painting. You will pour colours and ink on the raw Shuan paper. Then you will adjust the images according to the result you get from the pouring.

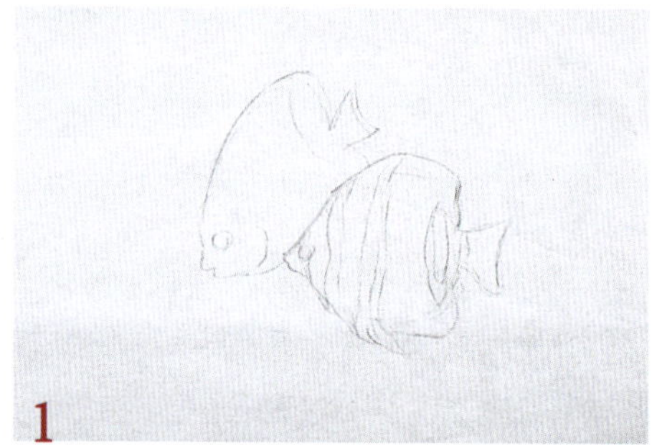

1 Sketch the fish and prepare the colours

Use a charcoal stick to sketch the main outlines of the fish on 41 x 58cm (16 x 23in) double-layer raw Shuan paper. Use the three small dishes you used for the watercolour painting in chapter four to prepare the colours. Squeeze about 12mm¹ (½in) of pigment from yellow, cinnabar and phthalocyanine blue tubes into the dishes, placing one colour per dish. Dilute each with about 6ml (¼ cup) of water.

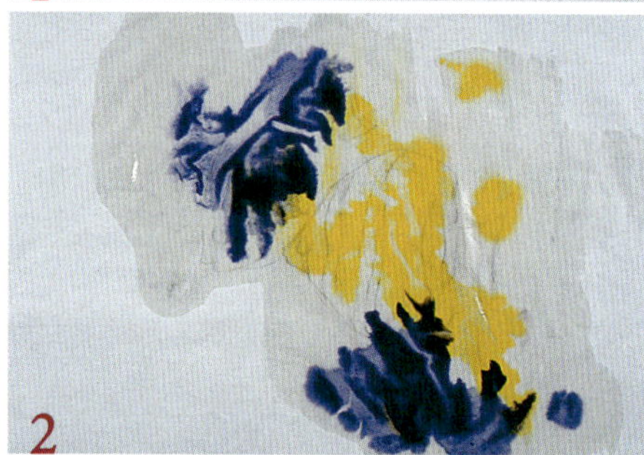

2 Pour the colours

Use a 10 to 13cm (4 to 5in) flat brush to wet the centre part of the painting where the two fish are located. Pour the yellow on the yellow fish area and the phthalocyanine blue on the bluish fish area.

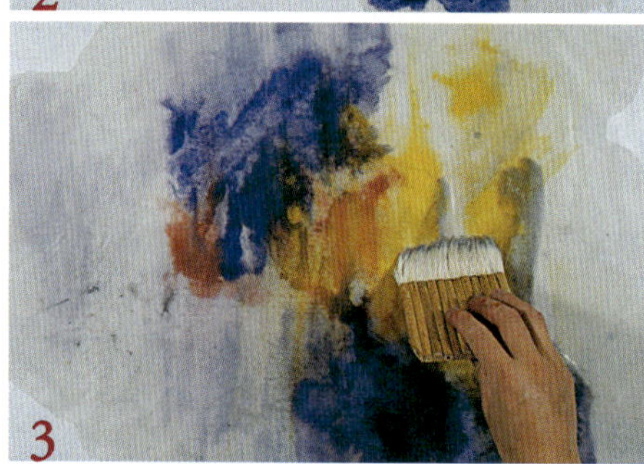

3 Direct the blending of the colours

Pour the cinnabar on the head area of the bluish fish and on the upper head and body areas of the yellow fish. Use a flat brush to drag the yellow towards the lower left. In addition, drag the phthalocyanine blue to the upper middle.

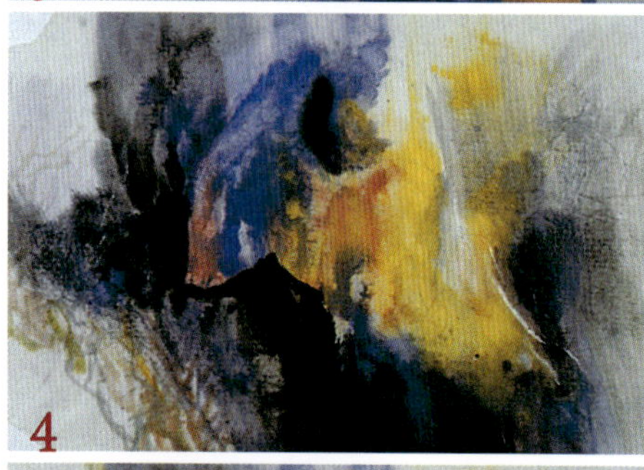

4 Apply ink on the background

Soak a large brush with intense ink and paint the area around the fish. Use a medium brush to define the outlines of the fish. Next, use a medium brush to paint the water plants at lower left with the colours and ink.

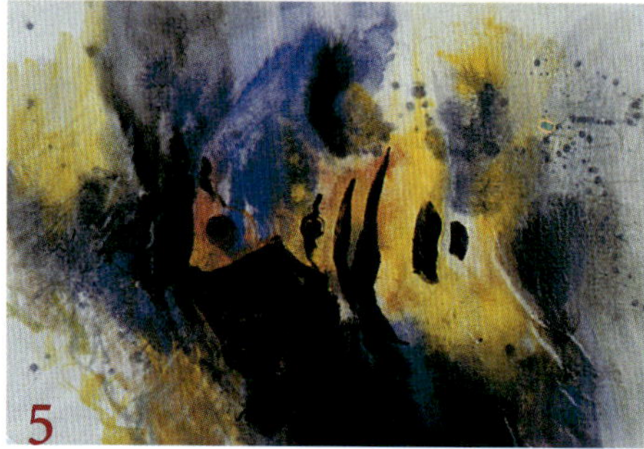

5 Continue painting the background and start painting the fish

Pour more yellow on the upper left. Use a large brush to mix light ink and phthalocyanine blue. Splatter the colours randomly on the background. Use a medium brush to paint the eyes and the black stripes on the fish with intense ink. On the bluish fish, paint yellow on the mouth, cinnabar on the head and rouge around the eye.

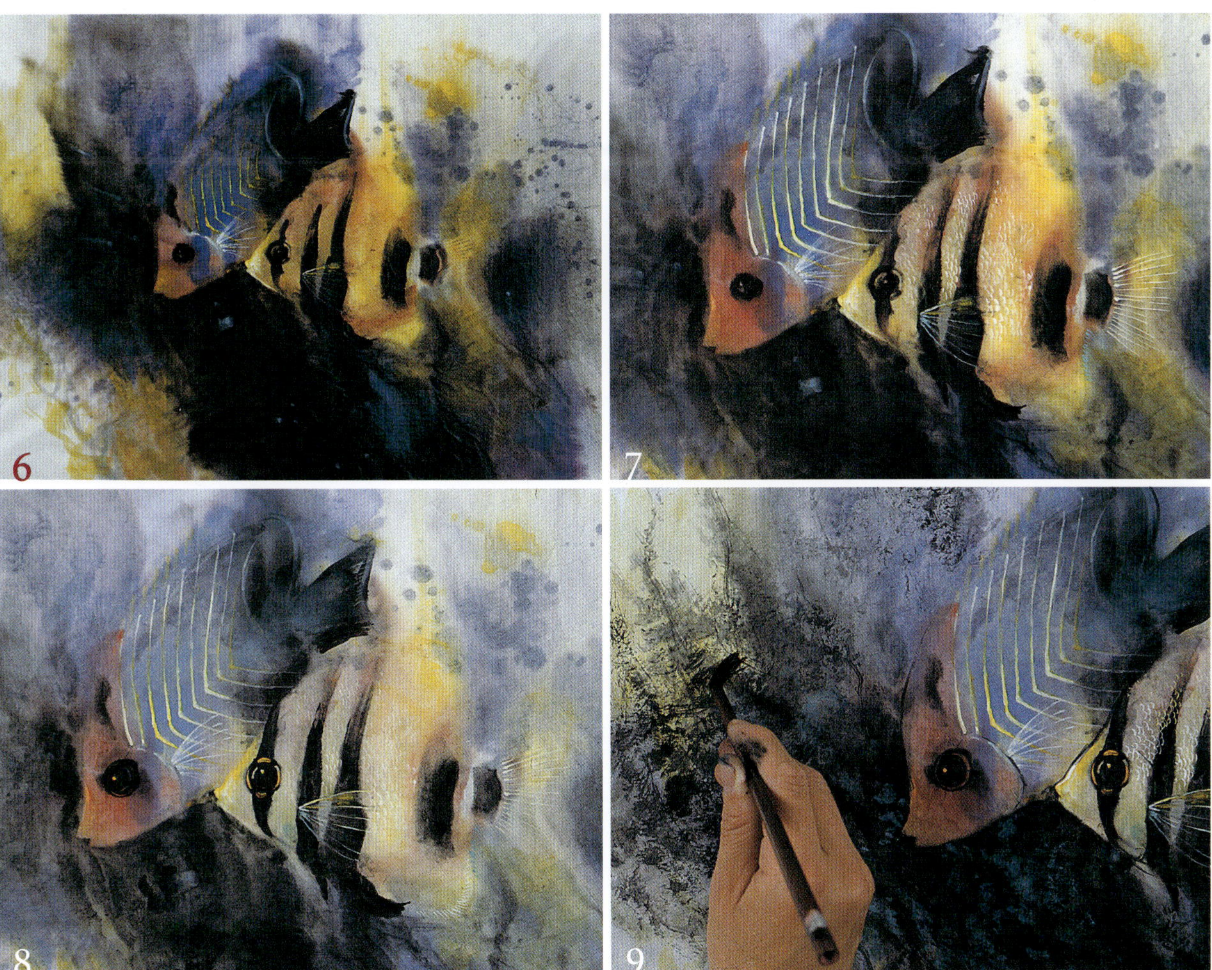

6 Continue painting the fish

Use a medium brush and intense white and yellow to paint the yellow fish's mouth and pectoral fin. On the bluish fish, use a small brush and very intense white to define the gill and pectoral fin. In addition, highlight the dorsal fin and the tail with very intense blue. Next, use a small brush to paint the stripes with very intense yellow and white.

7 Continue painting the fish

When the painting is halfway dry, some of the colours on the fish will have soaked into the paper. Apply more colours to the fish. On the yellow fish, use a small brush and very intense white and yellow to paint the scales and tail. On the bluish fish, paint the stripes again with intense white and yellow.

8 Paint the fish eyes

Use a small brush to mix intense yellow, cinnabar and a little white. Paint the highlights on the pupils and the outlines of the yellow fish's eyes. Apply a little intense cinnabar on the bottom of the eyeballs.

9 Paint the background again

When the painting is dry, the background colours around the mouths and heads will not be intense enough. Use a medium brush to paint more intense ink strokes on the background. Next, make the brush into a split tip to paint some dry brushstrokes to abstractly depict the water plants.

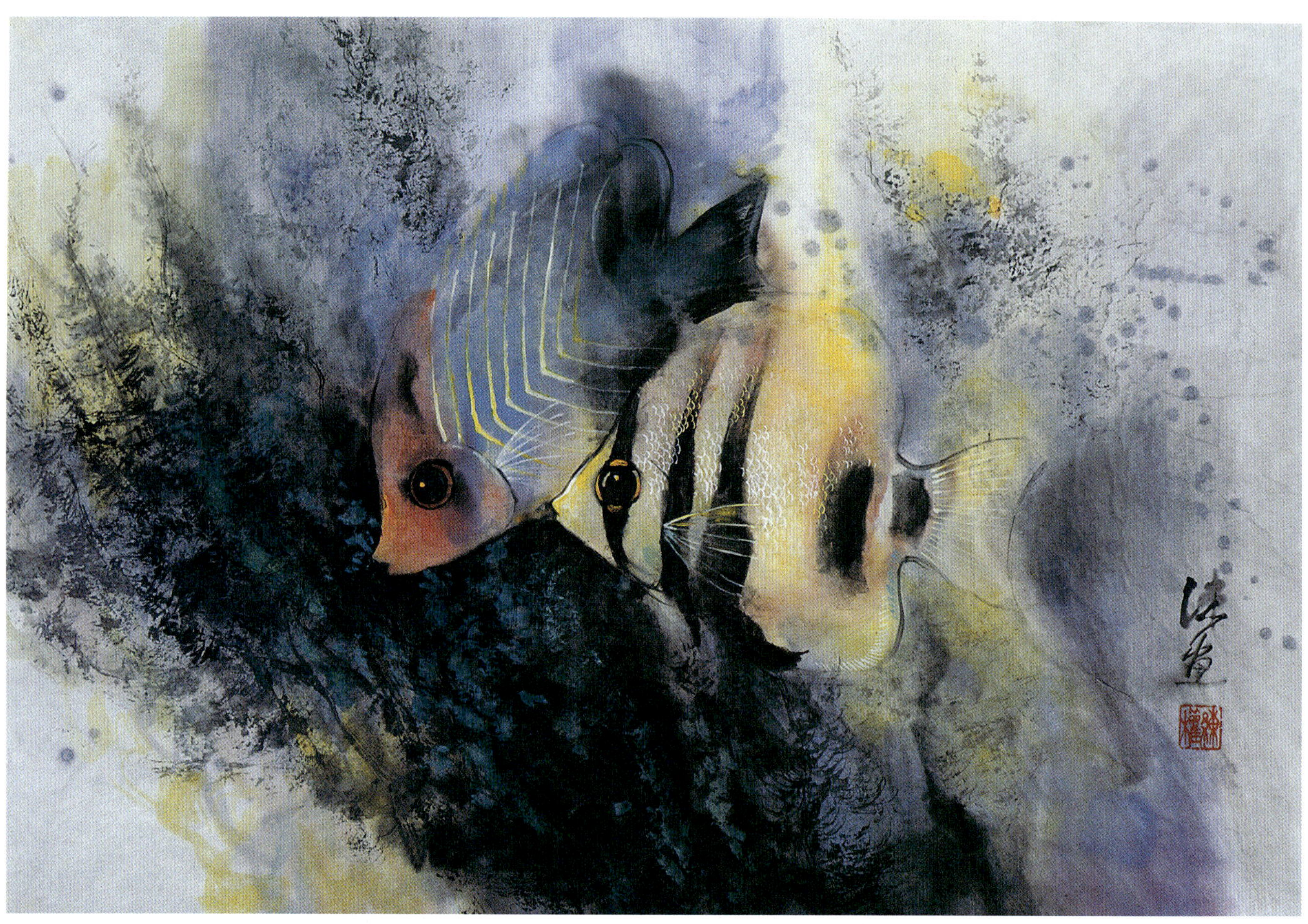

10 APPLY COLOURS ON THE BACKGROUND AGAIN, SIGN
AND SEAL YOUR PAINTING

Use a large brush to mix intense blue and indigo. Apply the colours to
the background. Use a small brush to outline the yellow fish with ink.
Finally, sign your name and stamp your chop on the lower right corner.

TWO BUTTERFLY FISH
41 x 58cm (16 x 23in)
Chinese ink and colours on double-layer raw Shuan paper
Spontaneous style

PAINTING ANGELFISH

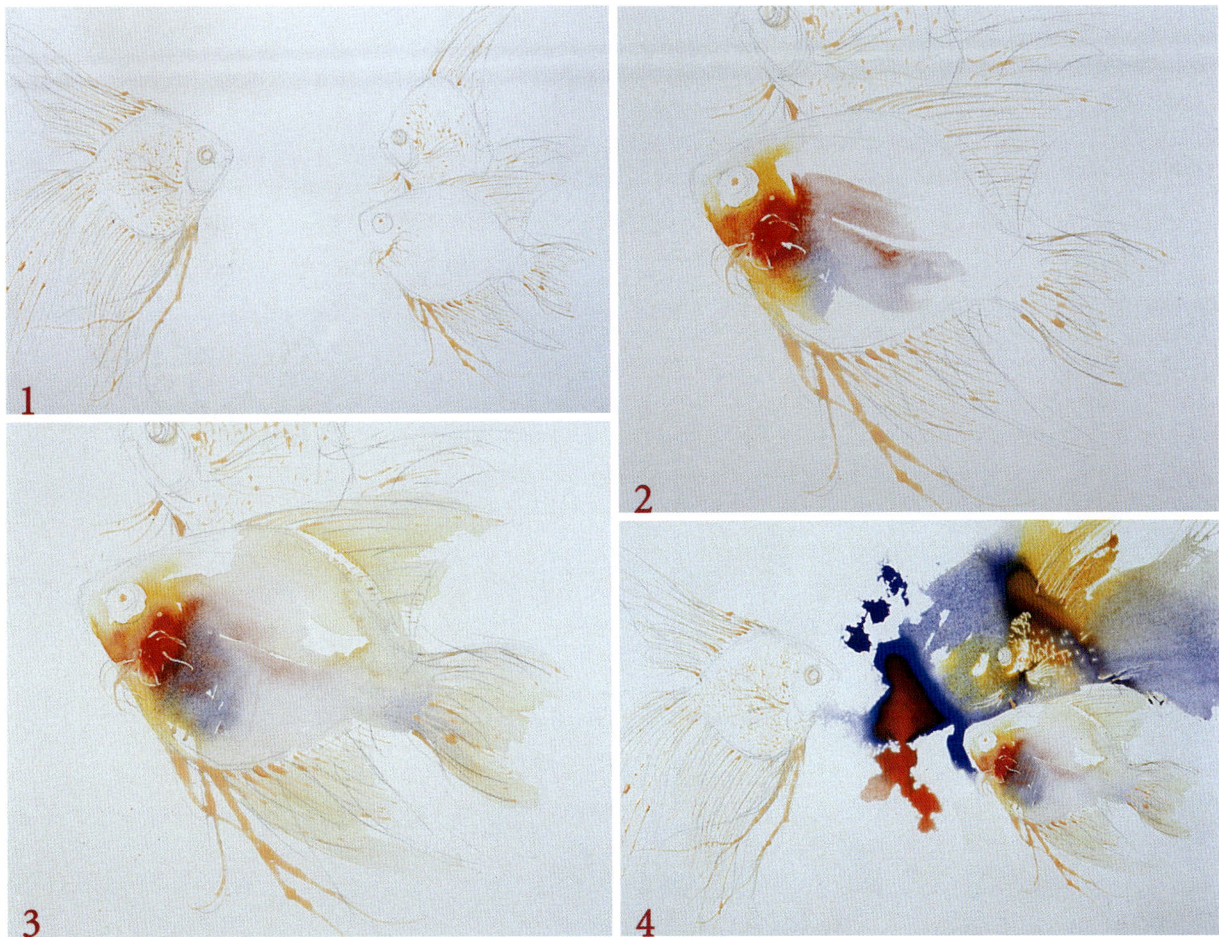

1 *Sketch the fish and apply the masking fluid*

Using a pencil, lightly sketch the fish on a 36 x 53cm (14 x 21in) 300gsm (140lb) cold-pressed watercolour paper. Apply masking fluid with a bamboo pen or an Incredible Nib. Try to use thin strokes on the fins and tails. Next, prepare the three colours as you did on page 87.

2 *Paint the white angelfish*

Dry the masking fluid with a hair dryer. Use a 19mm (¾in) flat brush to wet the head, gill and body. Next, use a No. 10 round brush to apply yellow around the eye and on the gill. While the colours are wet, apply very intense red on the gill and blue on the body. Let the colours blend into each other.

3 *Paint the body and fins*

Use a 19mm (¾in) flat brush to apply light yellow on the upper part of the body and light blue on the lower part. Leave a white line in the centre of the body to depict the spine. Paint the fins and tail with very light yellow.

4 *Pour the colours on the upper-right quarter of the painting*

Wet the area with a water sprayer without spraying the white fish. Pour yellow on the fish and blue and red around the fish. Blow the colours from the upper left towards the corner and let the colours blend into each other.

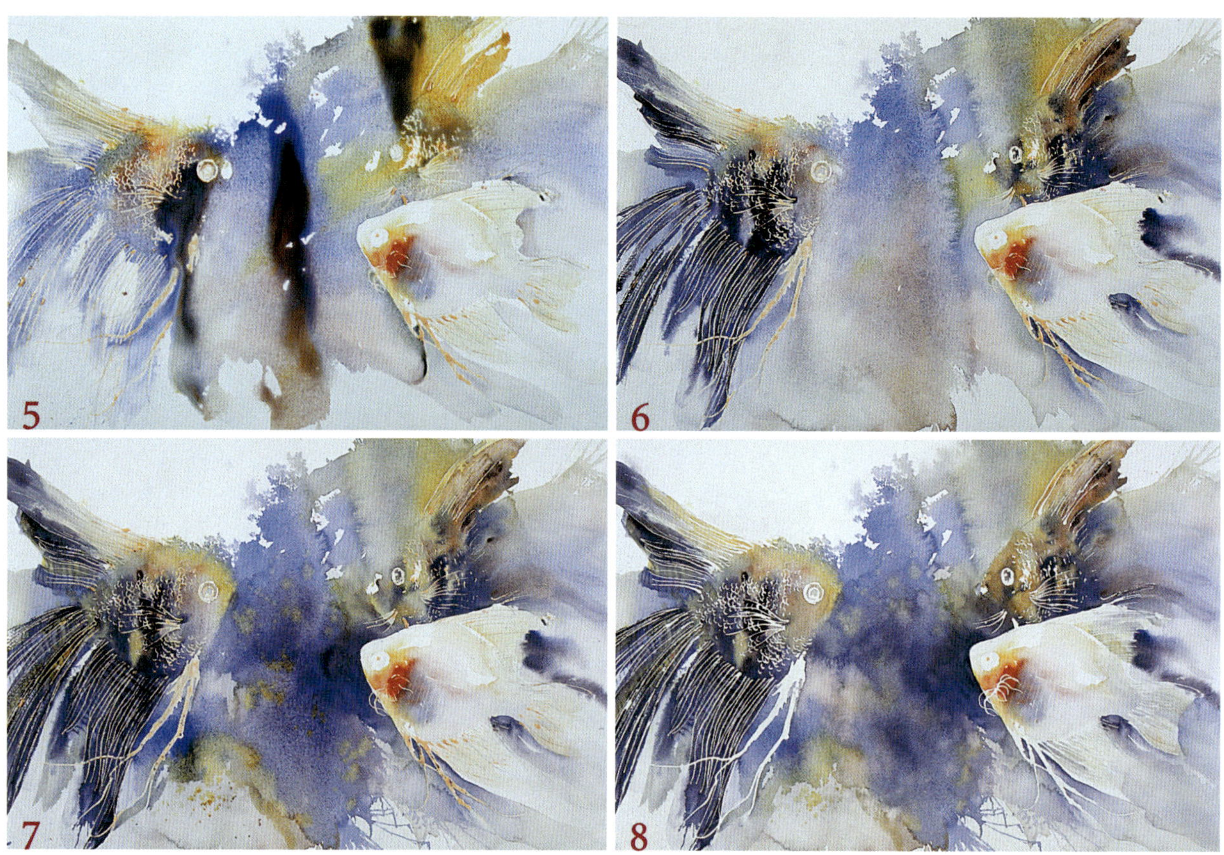

5 *Pour the colours on other areas of the painting*

Wet the remaining areas without wetting the white fish. Pour yellow on the dorsal fin and head of the left fish, red on the body and blue on the other fins and tail. Use a 25mm (1in) flat brush to drag the colours into the background against the white fish to define its tail and fins.

6 *Absorb the excess colours and paint the two yellowish fish*

Use paper towels to absorb the excess colours. Then use a 19mm (³⁄₄in) flat brush to mix very intense blue and a little red. Paint the black stripes and fins. Apply more red on the dorsal fin of the fish at upper right.

7 *Paint the background and the bones on the white fish*

While the colours on the background are wet, use a 19mm (³⁄₄in) flat brush to paint intense blue and red in the areas behind the white fish and the ventral fins of the fish at left. This will create depth as well as strong contrast for your painting. Next, splatter yellow and red on the background. Now the colours on the white fish should be almost dry. Use a No. 6 round brush to paint the bones next to the gill with clear water. The water will push away the colours and create lighter-coloured strokes.

8 *Dry the painting and lift the masking fluid*

Use a hair dryer to dry the painting, then lift the masking fluid with masking tape.

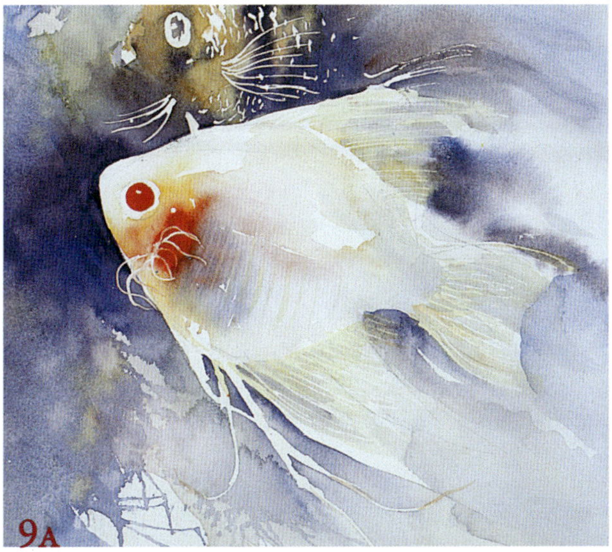

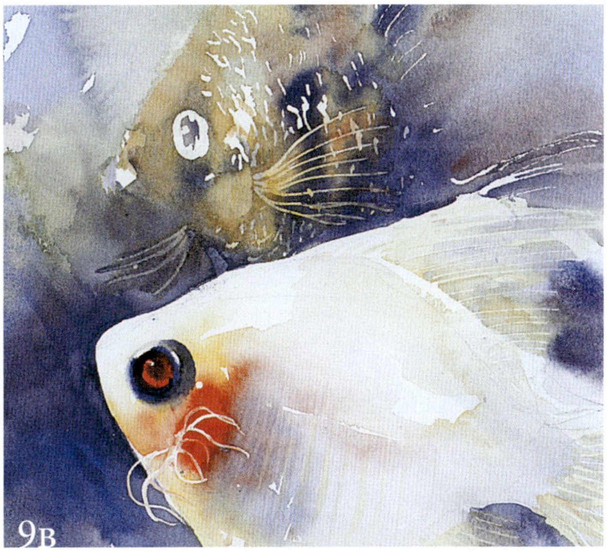

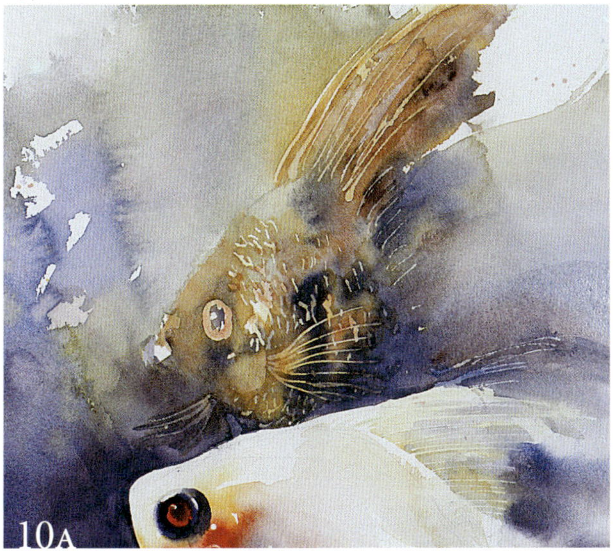

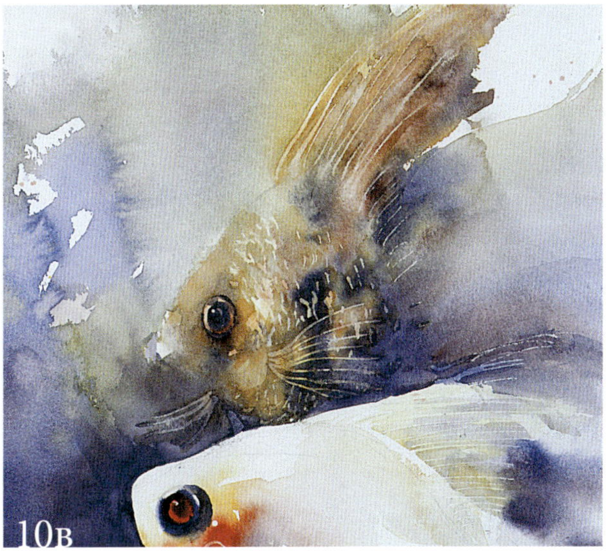

9 A & B *Paint the fins, tail and eye of the white fish*

Use a No. 6 round brush to paint light yellow on the white lines of the
dorsal, ventral and anal fins and the tail. On the pectoral fin, paint light
red. Next, use a No. 10 round brush to paint intense red on the eyeball.
Immediately use another No. 10 round brush to paint around the eyeball with blue. Then mix very intense blue and red to paint the pupil.
Leave a white spot on the pupil for highlights.

10 A & B *Paint the scales, fins, tail and eye of
the fish at upper right*

Use a No. 6 round brush to paint the white lines on the scales, fins
and tail with colours similar to their backgrounds. Next, mix yellow
and red into light orange to paint the eye. Then add a more intense
orange on the lower part of the eye. With very intense blue and red,
paint the pupil and the outline of the eye.

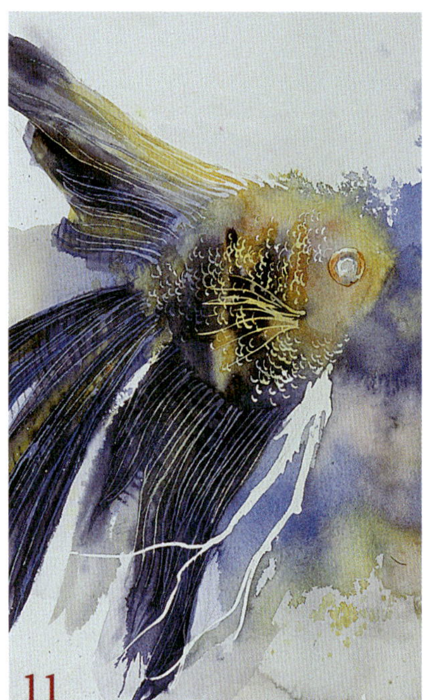

11 *PAINT THE FINS, TAIL AND EYE OF THE FISH AT LEFT*

Use a No. 6 round brush to paint the white lines of the scales, fins and tail with colours similar to their background. On the beginning of the ventral fin, use a wet paper towel to scrape out the colours so the connection between the fin and body is smooth. Next, paint the eye and define the head and mouth using light orange.

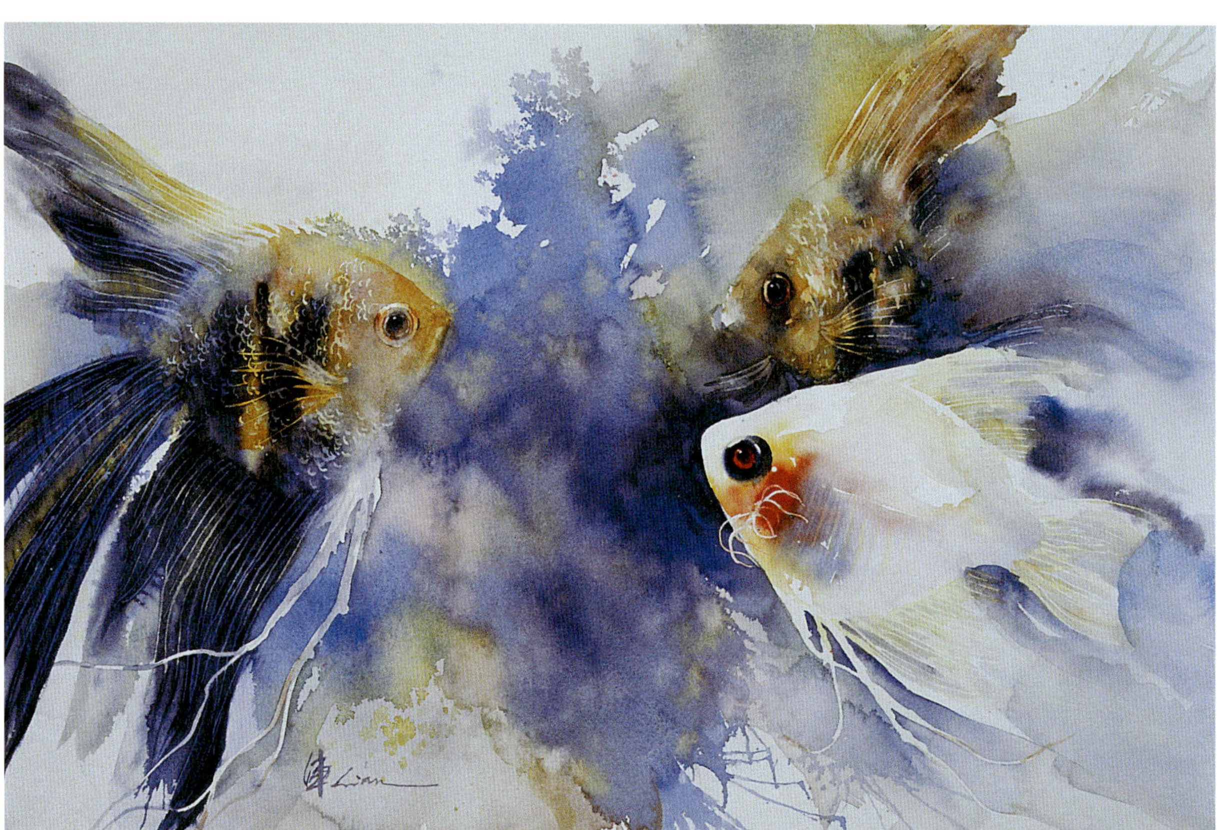

12 *FINISH THE EYE AND SIGN YOUR NAME*

Outline the eye of the fish at left with dark red, mixing red and blue.
Paint the pupil with very intense blue and red. Finally, sign your name
at bottom left next to the ventral fin of the fish at left.

THREE ANGELFISH
36 x 53cm (14 x 21in)
Watercolour on Arches 300gsm (140lb) cold-pressed watercolour paper
Colour pouring and blending

PAINTING KOI

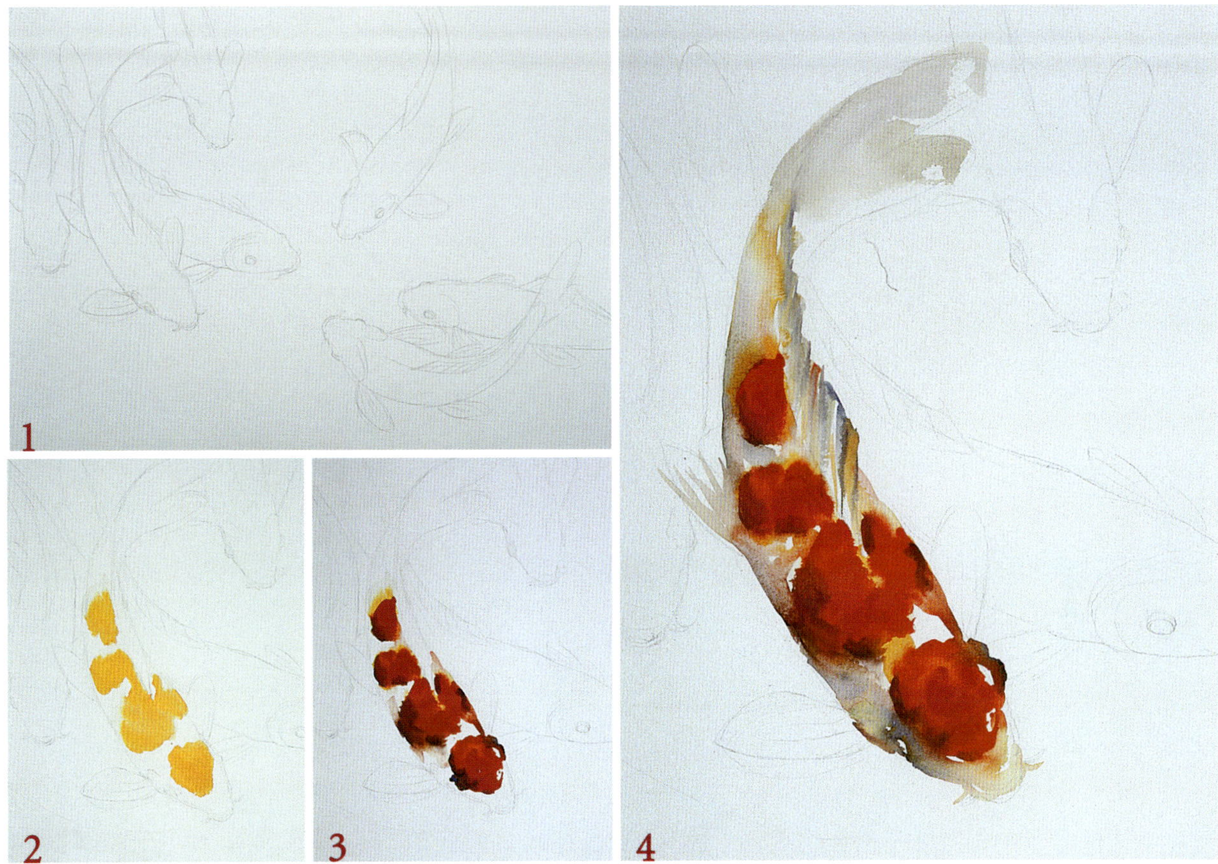

1 Sketch the fish and prepare the colours

Use a pencil to lightly sketch the fish on a 53 x 74cm (21 x 29in) 300gsm (140lb) cold-pressed watercolour paper. Prepare the three colours as you did on page 87, but use double the amounts of the pigments and water.

2 Paint the front fish at left

Use a 25mm (1in) flat brush to wet the intense red colour areas of the front fish's body. Apply intense yellow on the wet areas.

3 Paint intense red on the fish body

Use a 25mm (1in) flat brush to add very intense red to the yellow. Next, mix the red with a little blue to paint the lower portions of the red colours. This will depict the volume of the body.

4 Paint the body, mouth, fins and tail

While the colours are wet, use a wet 19mm (¾in) flat brush and a little light blue to paint the body. Let the colours blend. Use a No. 10 round brush to paint the mouth and barbels with light yellow and red. Next, mix light blue, red and a little yellow to paint the tail in three strokes. Use a wet 19mm (¾in) flat brush to drag the colours from the body to paint the ventral fin. Then mix medium blue and red to paint the dorsal fin.

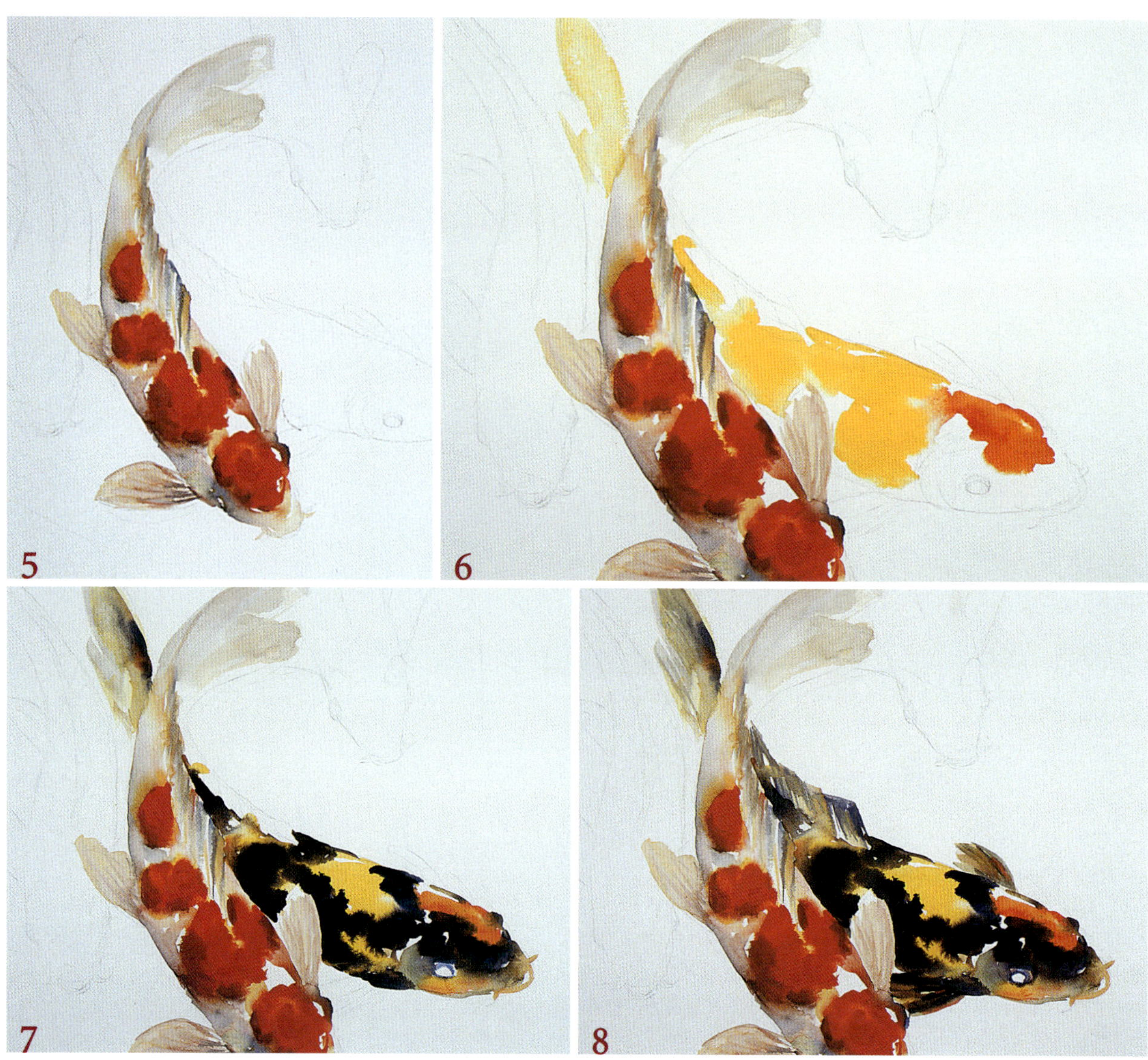

5 Continue painting the fins and tail

Use a 19mm (¾in) flat brush to apply yellow and red to the fins. When the colours are almost dry, add intense yellow and red strokes to the dorsal fin. Also paint light yellow on the tail.

6 Paint the yellow-black fish

Use a 25mm (1in) flat brush to wet the fish, randomly leaving small dry spots on the head and upper part of the body. Apply intense yellow to the head, body and tail. While the colour is wet, apply red on the head.

7 Paint the black pattern on the fish

Immediately use a 25mm (1in) flat brush and intense blue and red to paint the black patterns. Next, paint the mouth and gill with orange mixed from yellow and red. Let the black blend into the gill and mouth.

8 Paint the fins and outline the eye

Use a 19mm (¾in) flat brush and yellow to paint broad strokes for the fins. Then paint small strokes with blue and red to define the fins' textures. Also, paint a few small strokes on the tail to depict its bones. Next, use a No. 6 round brush to paint the outline of the eye with intense blue and red. Paint the upper area of the eye with red and a little yellow.

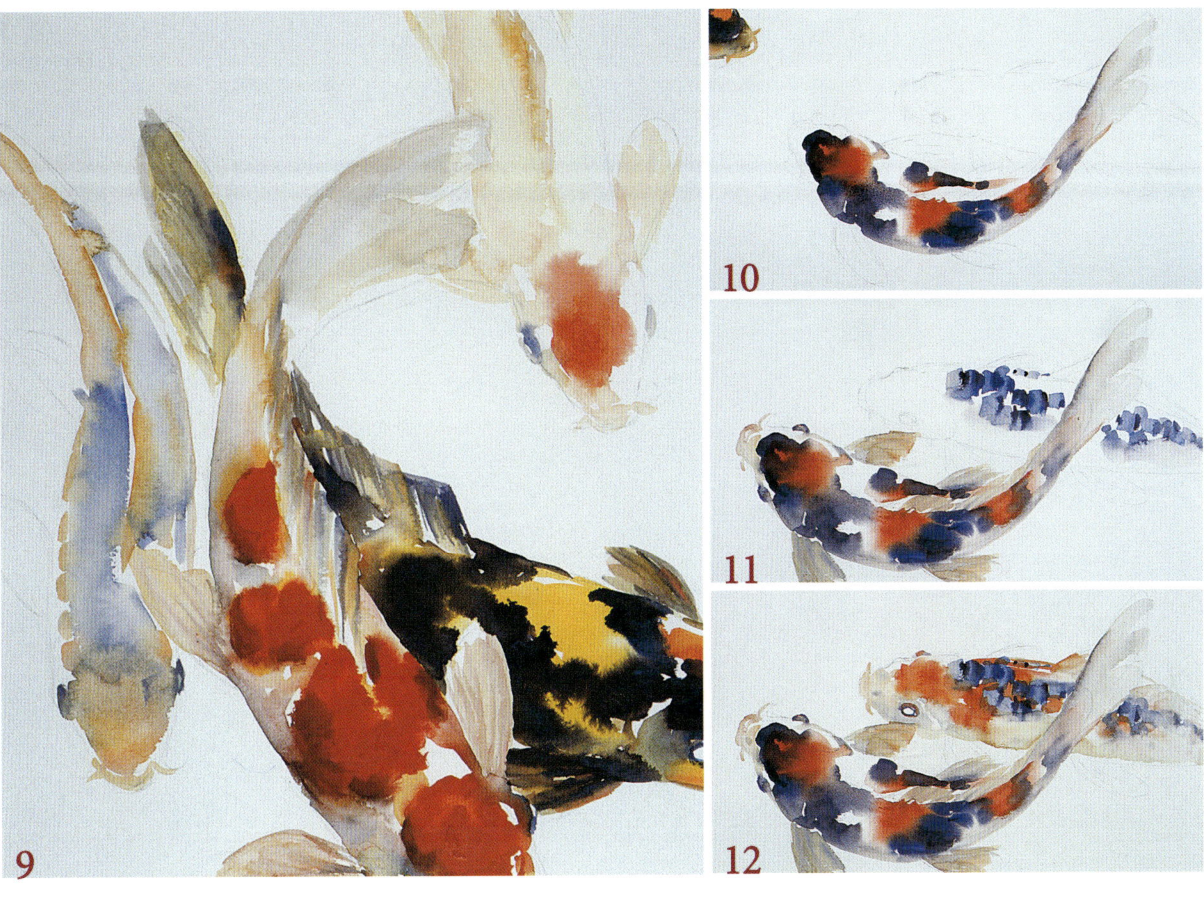

9 Paint the two distant fish

10

11

12

9 *Paint the two distant fish*

To paint the fish at right, use a 19mm (³⁄₄in) flat brush to wet it. Apply
medium red on its head. Mix light yellow and red to paint the mouth,
body and fins. Leave some white on the right side.

To paint the fish at left, wet it without touching its dorsal fin, then
use a 19mm (³⁄₄in) flat brush to paint the body with blue. Next, mix
yellow and red to paint its head, fins, tail and body outline. Finally, use
a No. 10 round brush to paint its eye with blue.

10 *Paint the fish at lower right*

Wet the fish, leaving dry areas on its dorsal fin, head and body. Use a
25mm (1in) flat brush to paint intense red on the head and body. Next,
paint intense blue on the head, gill and body. Use a wet 25mm (1in) flat
brush to drag the colours from the body to paint the tail.

11 *Paint the fins, mouth and eye and start*
painting the fish above

Use a 19mm (³⁄₄in) flat brush to paint the fins and mouth with light
yellow and red. Use a No. 10 round brush to paint the eye with blue.
To paint the fish above, use a 19mm (³⁄₄in) flat brush to paint some
blue strokes for its scales. Immediately apply intense blue and red on
the left side of the blue strokes to define the scales.

12 *Continue to paint the fish above*

Use a 19mm (³⁄₄in) flat brush to apply medium red to the head and
body. Paint the lower part of the body with light yellow. Next, drag the
colours from the body to paint the dorsal fin and gill. Paint the mouth
with light yellow and red.

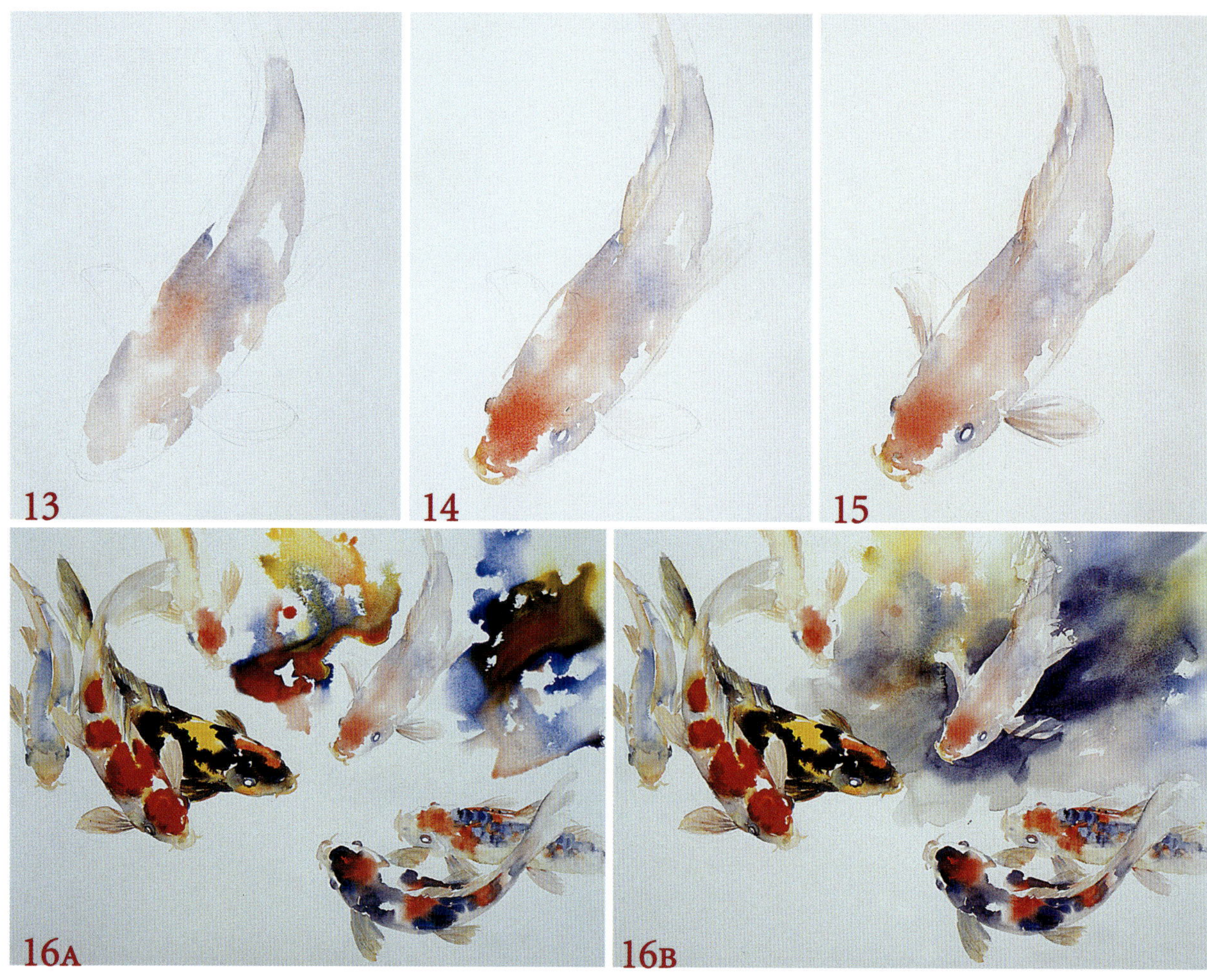

13 PAINT THE BODY OF THE FISH AT MIDDLE RIGHT

Use a 25mm (1in) flat brush to heavily wet the body, leaving a few dry
areas. Apply light red and blue to the body. Let the colours blend into
each other.

14 PAINT THE HEAD, MOUTH, FINS AND EYES

Use a 19mm (¾in) flat brush to paint the head with red. Use a No. 10
round brush to paint the mouth with a little yellow. Next, paint the dorsal fin with light yellow and blue. Then use a No. 10 round brush to
paint the eyes with blue.

15 PAINT OTHER FINS AND ADD MORE DETAILS

Use a moist 19mm (¾in) flat brush to drag the colours from the body
to paint the ventral fin. Next, paint the pectoral fins with light red and
blue. Use a No. 6 round brush and red to add the texture on the
dorsal fin. Apply one stroke with water from the dorsal fin towards the
head to create the top edge of the fish. Also, drip some water on the
body as bubbles.

16 A & B PAINT THE UPPER-RIGHT QUARTER OF
THE BACKGROUND

Paint the background when the colours on the fish are almost dry. Use
a 38mm (1½in) flat brush to wet the area without touching the fish.
Pour the colours. Use a 19mm (¾in) flat brush to guide the colours
towards the fish. Blow the colours towards the fish tail at upper centre. Use paper towels to absorb any excess liquid. Next, use the 19mm
(¾in) brush to mix intense blue and red to define the edge of the fish.

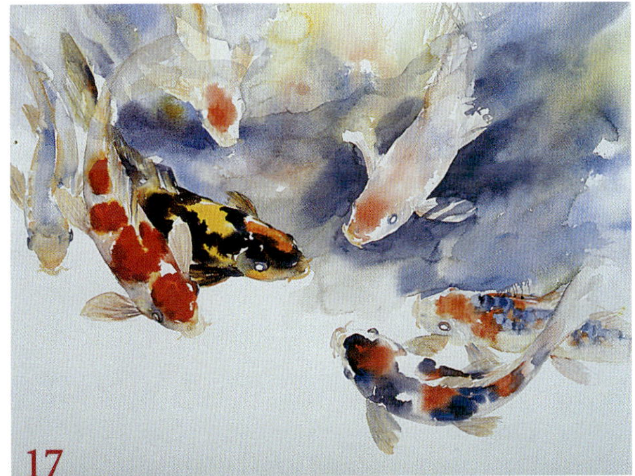

17 *PAINT THE UPPER-LEFT QUARTER OF THE BACKGROUND*

Wet the upper left background area without wetting the fish. Pour blue and a little red on it. Use a 19mm (¾in) flat brush to guide the colours so they do not flow into the fish. Next, mix intense blue and a little red to paint the water against the head of the distant fish at upper left. In addition, use light blue to paint a few strokes over the tail and body of the fish to depict the water.

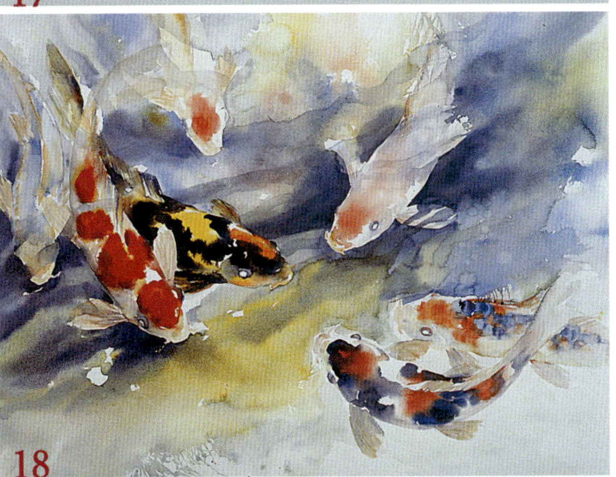

18 *PAINT THE LOWER-LEFT QUARTER AND MIDDLE AREA OF THE BACKGROUND*

Wet the lower-left and middle background areas without touching the fish. Pour yellow from the lower centre towards the lower left. Pour blue on the lower left. Blow the colours towards the lower middle area. Use a 19mm (¾in) flat brush to mix intense blue and red to paint the water against the heads of the red fish and the distant fish at left.

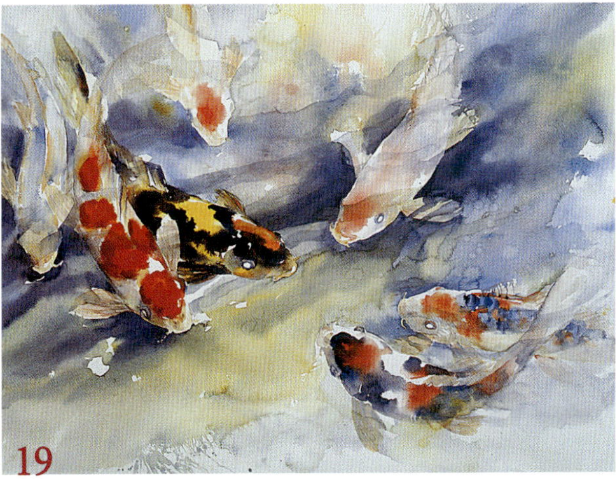

19 *PAINT THE LOWER-RIGHT QUARTER OF THE BACKGROUND*

Also wet the lower-right background area without touching the fish. Use a 19mm (¾in) flat brush to apply blue between the fish towards the lower right corner. Drag the colours into the two fish to paint a few strokes as water. Paint yellow on the body and ventral fin of the curled fish.

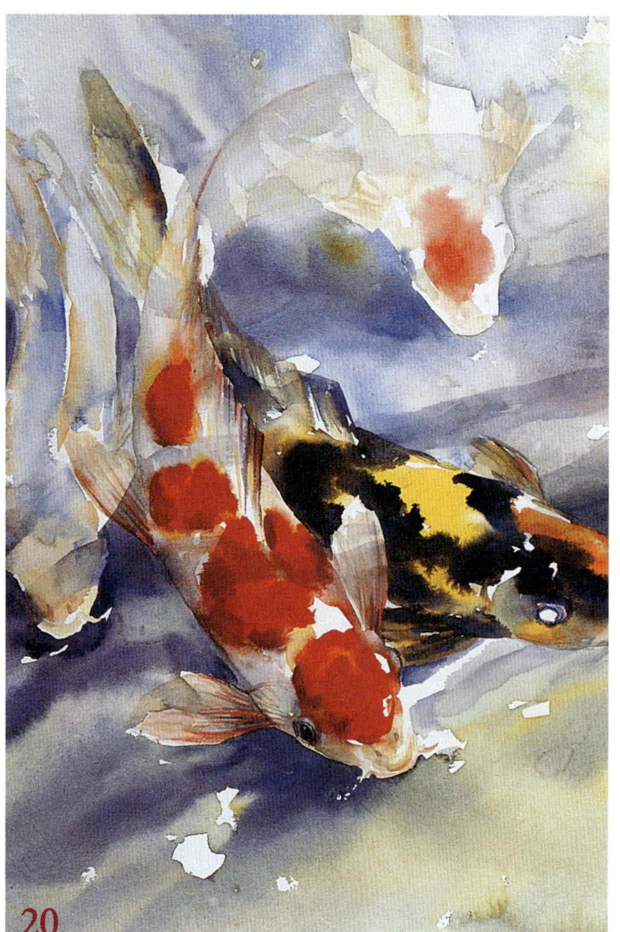

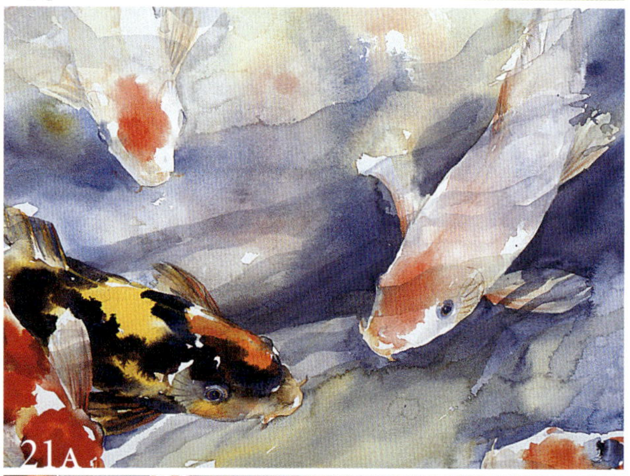

20 PAINT THE EYE AND ADD DETAILS ON THE RED FISH

Use a No. 6 round brush to mix blue and red into dark purple. Paint the outlines of the eye. Mix very intense blue and red into black to paint the pupil, leaving a white spot as the highlight. Next, paint intense red strokes on the pectoral and ventral fins. Also, paint the texture of the gill using light red and blue.

21 A & B PAINT THE EYES, GILLS AND FINS OF THE OTHER FISH

Use a No. 6 round brush to paint the eyes, gills and fins in a manner similar to that in the previous step, as shown in these two illustrations.

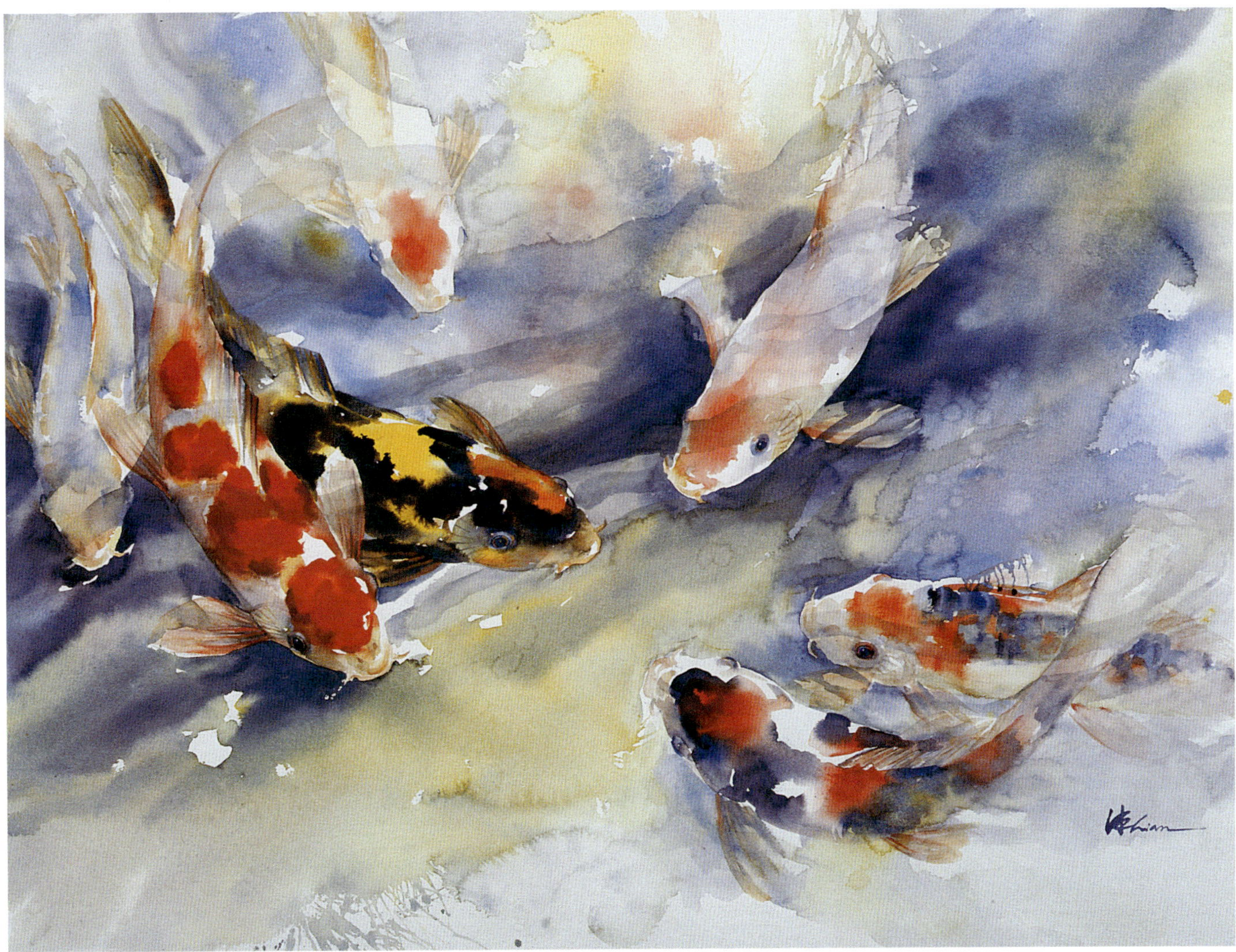

22 *Sign your name*

Sign your name on the lower right corner. This will balance the composition because there are more objects and action on the left side of

the painting.

KOI
53 x 74cm (21 x 29in)
Watercolour on Arches 300gsm (140lb) cold-pressed watercolour paper
Colour pouring and blending

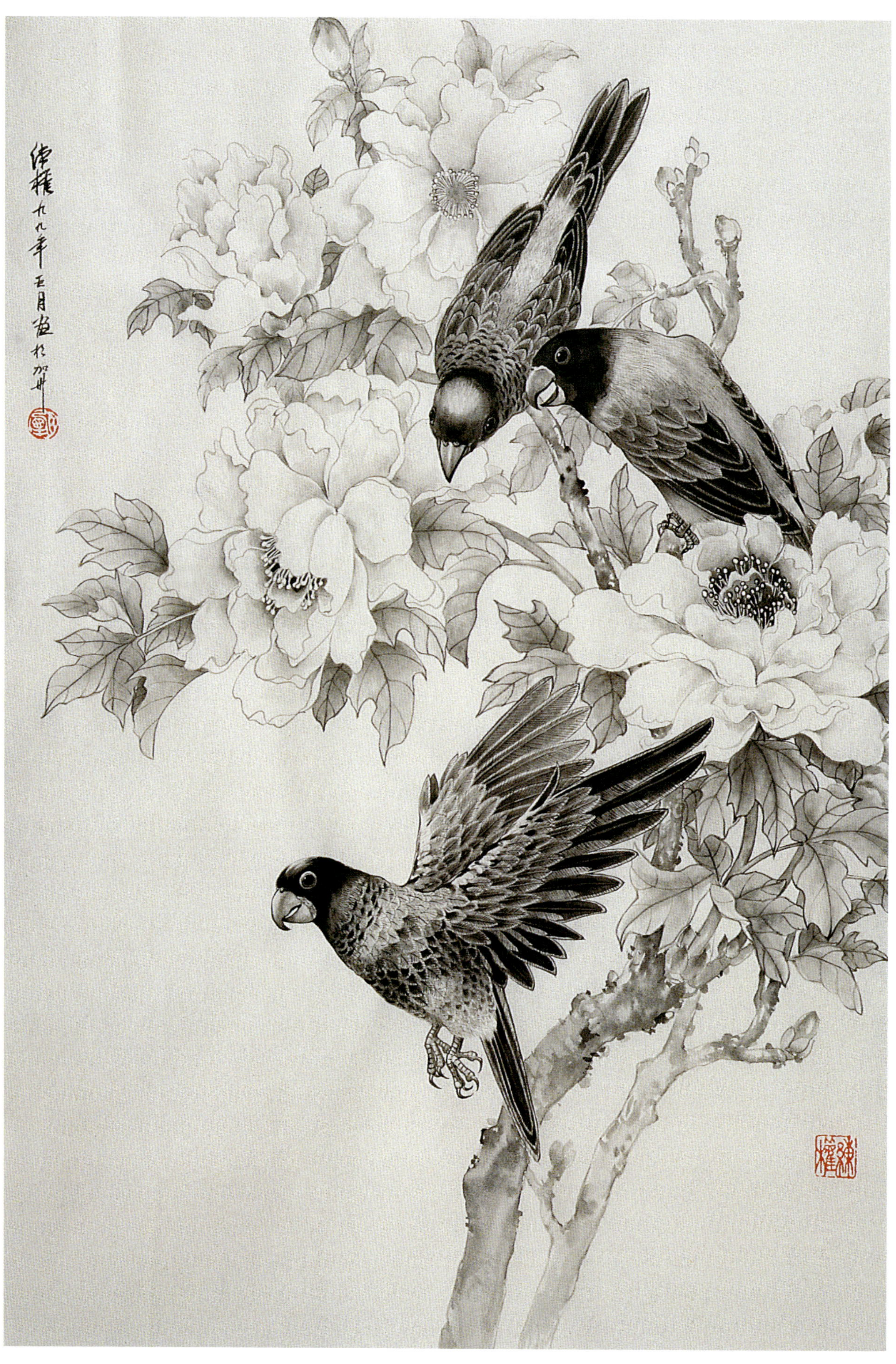

Chinese painting experience is of great benefit to me and my watercolours. It is not important to differentiate the two painting styles. Instead, learn and take advantage of Chinese painting, watercolour and other cultures' arts. Then create paintings that reflect the changing and progressing world.

My paintings focus on freedom and creation, and I will continue to work hard along that track. I am greatly rewarded if you found this book helpful to you and your artistic creations.

THREE PARROTS AND PEONY
61 x 43cm (24 x 17in)

MATERIALS

For Chinese painting demonstrations in this book
(also see pages 16-18):

Brushes: Extra-small, small, medium and large soft- and hard-fur 102mm (4in) or 127mm (5in) flats

Colours: Gamboge, vermilion, indigo, cinnabar, burnt sienna, phthalocyanine blue, white, carmine (Marie's Chinese painting colours)

Paper: Rice, Shuan (mature, double- and single-layer), tracing

Other: Ink, rouge, foamcore board, tape, ink pen, chop (optional), charcoal stick, china palette or small dishes for colours

For watercolour demonstrations in this book
(also see pages 58-59):

Brushes: Nos. 6, 8 and 10 round, 3 small brushes to mix paints, 19mm (¾in) flat, 25mm (1in) flat, 38mm (1½in) flat

Colours: Cadmium red deep (Winsor & Newton), cadmium yellow light and ultramarine blue (Utrecht)

Paper: Arches 300gsm (140lb) cold-pressed watercolour paper

Other: Grumbacher's Miskit masking fluid, 3M 3 or 4cm (1 or 1½in) masking tape, 91cm x 122cm (3 x 4ft) 3-ply plywood for working surface, soft-lead pencil, three small dishes for paint, hair dryer, Incredible Nib or bamboo pen, spray bottle, paper towels

RESOURCES

Atlantis Art Supplies
7-9 Plummer's Row
London E1 1EQ
Tel: 020 7377 8855

Chinese brushes and watercolours

Guangua Company
7 Newport Place
London WC2 H7JR

Chinese brushes, liquid inks and
rice paper

Inscribe Ltd
The Woolmer Industrial Estate
Bordon
Hampshire
GU35 9QE
Tel: 01420 471119

Wholesale suppliers of all Chinese
painting equipment; call for advice
on your nearest stockist

Zhen Studio
P.O. Box 1060
Pinole, CA 94564
Tel and Fax: (510) 724-3971
E-mail: lianzhen@yahoo.com
Web site: www.zhenstudio.com

Another option for locating the
materials listed above, including
Chinese paper, brushes, ink, ink
stones, colours, rouge and chops, is
to contact Lian Zhen.

INDEX